Putting Voters in their Place

Geography and Elections in Great Britain

Ron Johnston and Charles Pattie

OXFORD

UNIVERSITY PRESS

*This book has been printed digitally and produced in a standard specification
in order to ensure its continuing availability*

OXFORD
UNIVERSITY PRESS

Great Clarendon Street, Oxford OX2 6DP

Oxford University Press is a department of the University of Oxford.
It furthers the University's objective of excellence in research, scholarship,
and education by publishing worldwide in

Oxford New York

Auckland Cape Town Dar es Salaam Hong Kong Karachi
Kuala Lumpur Madrid Melbourne Mexico City Nairobi
New Delhi Shanghai Taipei Toronto
With offices in
Argentina Austria Brazil Chile Czech Republic France Greece
Guatemala Hungary Italy Japan South Korea Poland Portugal
Singapore Switzerland Thailand Turkey Ukraine Vietnam

Oxford is a registered trade mark of Oxford University Press
in the UK and in certain other countries

Published in the United States
by Oxford University Press Inc., New York

ISBN 978-0-19-926805-4

OXFORD GEOGRAPHICAL AND
ENVIRONMENTAL STUDIES

Editors: Gordon Clark, Andrew Goudie, and Ceri Peach

PUTTING VOTERS IN THEIR PLACE

EDITORS' PREFACE

Geography and environmental studies are two closely related and burgeoning fields of academic enquiry. Both have grown rapidly over the past few decades. At once catholic in its approach and yet strongly committed to a comprehensive understanding of the world, geography has focused upon the interaction between global and local phenomena. Environmental studies, on the other hand, have shared with the discipline of geography an engagement with different disciplines, addressing wide-ranging and significant environmental issues in the scientific community and the policy community. From the analysis of climate change and physical environmental processes to the cultural dislocations of postmodernism in human geography, these two fields of enquiry have been at the forefront of attempts to comprehend transformations taking place in the world, manifesting themselves as a variety of separate but interrelated spatial scales.

The *Oxford Geographical and Environmental Studies* series aims to reflect this diversity and engagement. Our goal is to publish the best original research in the two related fields, and, in doing so, to demonstrate the significance of geographical and environmental perspectives for understanding the contemporary world. As a consequence, our scope is deliberately international and ranges widely in terms of topics, approaches, and methodologies. Authors are welcome from all corners of the globe. We hope the series will help to redefine the frontiers of knowledge and build bridges within the fields of geography and environmental studies. We hope also that it will cement links with issues and approaches that have originated outside the strict confines of these disciplines. In doing so, our publications contribute to the frontiers of research and knowledge while representing the fruits of particular and diverse scholarly traditions.

Gordon L. Clark
Andrew Goudie
Ceri Peach

PREFACE

Most academic study of British voting behaviour is conducted by political scientists, although economists, sociologists, lawyers and psychologists have made important contributions—as indeed have a small number of geographers. The latter bring a particular perspective on the subject, one that involves much more than simply mapping election results. This has been generally recognized among the academic community of electoral specialists, with geographers playing significant roles in the deliberations of the Elections, Parties and Public Opinion Specialist Group of the Political Studies Association.

We have been part of that community since it was founded, a few years after we began our collaboration in studies of various aspects of electoral geography, mainly, though not exclusively, in the UK. Our perspective—basically, highlighting the importance of space and, especially, place in the understanding of voting and the operation of electoral systems—has become part of the contemporary discourse of UK electoral studies, rather than a separately identifiable sub-sub-discipline. In this book we synthesize that perspective by providing both an overview and an insight into the most recent research. It is not a textbook in the standard mould, therefore. The first three chapters provide the overview, making the case for the geographical perspective within British electoral studies and reviewing the relevant literature: not all of it by geographers, by any means—most students of elections incorporate some geography into their work, we stress it. The remaining five chapters illustrate the case for that perspective, reporting on recent research—some of it, notably, on the 2005 general election, previously unpublished—which illustrates in depth (rather than in summary) the insights that our approach brings. Four of those chapters focus on geography and voting; the last looks at the translation of votes into seats.

During our collaboration over the past 20 years a number of colleagues have joined us (including some with whom one of us worked before the collaboration began). Philip Cowley, David Cutts, David Denver, Danny Dorling, Ed Fieldhouse, Alan Hay, Kelvyn Jones, Iain McAllister, Colin Rallings, David Rossiter, Andrew Russell, Andrew Schumann, Pat Seyd, Peter Taylor, Michael Thrasher, Helena Tunstall, and Paul Whiteley have all contributed in various ways, not only to specific pieces of work but also to the development of our ideas, and we are grateful to them for their collaboration and companionship. Others, too, have contributed importantly, if indirectly, to our work—not least the various teams who have managed the British Election Studies programmes, without whose data much that we have done—and have reported here—could not have been undertaken: in particular, David Butler, Harold Clarke, Ivor Crewe, John Curtice, Geoff Evans,

Anthony Heath, Roger Jowell, David Sanders, and Marianne Stewart have done much to make our task feasible.

Finally, our thanks to Anne Ashby and her colleagues at Oxford University Press, and to Ann Kingdom, our superb copy-editor, not least for their patience in waiting for a book delayed by the exigencies of university administration; but they now have a book about the 2005 election instead of the 2001 election.

Ron Johnston
Charles Pattie

CONTENTS

LIST OF FIGURES

LIST OF TABLES

LIST OF ABBREVIATIONS

BES	British Election Study
BEPS	British Election Panel Study
CLP	Constituency Labour Party
ED	Enumeration District
ERM	European Exchange Rate Mechanism
PCA	principal components analysis
PEB	party election broadcast
SNP	Scottish National Party

1

Models of Voting

When electors enter the polling booth at UK general elections the ballot paper invites them to select an individual to be their Member of Parliament (MP), but most choose their preferred candidate not because of her or his qualities and characteristics but rather because of the political party he or she is standing for. Indeed, since ballot papers were revised in 1969 to allow candidates to include a small amount of information about themselves, most have used this opportunity to give the name of their party. This is because parties dominate UK general elections and most people's voting choice is determined by the party whose policies they wish to support and which they hope to see in government. The same is now also true at most local government elections (although this is a relatively recent development, especially in rural areas where 'independent' county and district councillors were for long the norm: see Johnson, 1972) and in those for seats in the Scottish Parliament and Welsh Assembly. Only in European Parliament elections and for the 'list seats' (a minority of the total) in the Scottish and Welsh legislatures are electors invited to vote just for a party. In Northern Ireland, the electoral system for all contests other than seats in the House of Commons invites voters to rank order candidates according to their preferences for them—but again, the main determinant of their choice is not the individuals' characteristics but rather the party they represent.

Parties dominate British politics therefore—as they do in all comparable countries, and have done in the UK for most of the past two centuries, especially at general elections, on which this book concentrates. Parties play three interrelated roles in national politics (as identified by a leading American political scientist, V. O. Key, 1964): in government, in the electorate, and as organizations. Their role in government is to provide parliamentary majorities—either separately or in coalition—which will enable their policy objectives to be implemented: the government has a guaranteed majority (unless some of its members defect), which allows it to enact its programme. Parties are the media by which not only the government but also the opposition are organized; for the former, in particular, they provide the stability without which an executive would find both legislation and administration extremely difficult.

A parliamentary party thus comprises a group of elected members committed to an agreed legislative programme set within an established political (ideological) framework—or, if they are in a minority, to opposing those parts of the government's programme they consider unacceptable. Outside the legislature, a party requires a similar, though much larger, collection of individuals who support its ideas and programmes and who can be relied upon to vote for its candidates at most—if not all—elections. Once again, therefore, the party provides stability, this time in support outside the legislature. The presence of parties also clarifies (and usually simplifies) the choice process for voters, who are invited to select one from a small number of groups offering competing ways of running the country. The presentation of these choices to the electorate is part of a continuing process of political education.

Spanning these two sets of activities in the legislature and among the electorate is the role of the political party as an organization. It recruits members from among the public to articulate and promote its interests through political campaigning, and from its members it selects candidates for various contests. Parties recruit and train political elites and activists; without them they could not mobilize support within the electorate and advance their supporters' interests in the legislative and administrative process. (For more detail on these three roles for political parties, see Dalton and Wattenberg, 2002; Seyd, 1998.)

Given these crucial roles for political parties, how do they achieve the required stability of support within the electorate that enables them to operate in the legislature? In most countries, this has been achieved by groups identifying major cleavages within society—fundamental divisions on basic political issues—around which they can build a core of support that individual members will adhere to and campaign for, and to which other voters will make commitments. Such cleavages may originate with a focus on a single issue that dominates political debate at a particular time, but in order to survive and thrive over long periods most develop ideologies (sets of key beliefs) that can be applied to changing situations. Thus a party becomes the organizing structure for a set of ideas about the role of government within society, drawing its support from those who identify with those ideas and are prepared to promote them by voting for representatives who will operate on those principles. In addition, in order to be viable, a party requires supporters who will contribute to it both financially and with their time.

What, then, are the sets of ideas that underpin such political structures? Within Western Europe, a seminal framework was provided by a theory of social cleavages (Lipset and Rokkan, 1967). There were two key moments in the history of those societies—the national revolution and the industrial revolution—each of which provided fertile ground for parties to be organized as the potential representatives of particular sets of political views. The *national revolutions* involved conflicts over the creation of the modern nation-state. Some led to cleavages between Church and state, between groups who accepted the arguments for a secular state apparatus separate from that of the dominant religion, on the one hand, and on the other those who saw a central role for religious principles and practices in state operations. Other conflicts stimulated a cleavage between those promoting a centralized, relatively homogeneous state apparatus—focused on the national capital—and opponents who argued for relative regional autonomy, usually based on ethnic differences. The first of these is termed the *church–state* cleavage; the other is generally known as the *core–periphery* cleavage.

The conflicts and cleavages associated with the *industrial revolution* focused on issues related to materialism. Again, two main cleavages were identified by Lipset and Rokkan (1967). The first involved different commercial interest groups within society, almost invariably contrasting agricultural interests, which wanted government policies that promoted farmers' concerns (such as protection from imports), with industrial interests, which wanted policies that supported and advanced manufacturing industry. These agriculture–industry interests were frequently mutually exclusive, leading to a *town–country cleavage* in political arguments and the formation of parties to represent and mobilize support on each side of the divide. The second cleavage was between employers and workers, between whom there was increased conflict over working conditions as industrialization spread. This *class cleavage* involved the formation of parties promoting the different interests of the two groups.

Not every cleavage was reflected in the emerging partisan structure of each Western European country, and some that did emerge later diminished in importance. Only one—the class cleavage—was virtually universal across those countries, especially as the franchise was expanded to incorporate an increasingly large proportion of the workers (the 'working class' or 'proletariat'; see Bartolini, 2000). This was certainly the case in Great Britain, where no strong, nationwide church–state cleavage ever developed (though it became strong in some cities, notably those with large Roman Catholic populations with Irish roots, such as Glasgow and Liverpool) and the town–country cleavage that dominated much of the nineteenth century was submerged in the twentieth by the class cleavage, with commentators identifying Britain as the paradigm case of the relative importance of that single divide within the electorate (e.g. Alford, 1964).

Until 1921 there was also a major core–periphery cleavage, with the conflict between Britain and Ireland reflected in the Irish National Party's electoral successes in the latter island. After self-rule (and then independence) was achieved for the majority of Ireland, however, that cleavage disappeared except in Northern Ireland, where the two sides of the divide coalesced around a religious split—between the Roman Catholic Church representing the periphery (and a wish to be part of the Irish Republic) and the Anglican and Presbyterian churches representing the core (defending the union with Great Britain). New core–periphery cleavages emerged from the 1970s on with the growing demands for Scottish and, to a lesser extent, Welsh devolution (if not independence), and also with the growth of parties (notably the Liberal party and its successors) that sought to mobilize cross-class support around a set of political ideas that were not addressed at particular class segments, although they did tend to win greater support among some groups (such as the educationally more qualified) than others.

Sociological Models

Arguments regarding the dominance of the class cleavage in Great Britain's electoral politics provide a sociological model of the voting process: electors are mobilized to support the party that promotes their 'class interests'. According to some American models of voting behaviour, the process of socialization with a particular set of class interests, associated with mobilization by the party representing those interests, leads individuals to identify with a particular party. They develop personal political ideologies (Scarbrough, 1984) associated with sets of political attitudes relevant to decision-making on contemporary issues and, following that, a partisan identification with a particular party. This process—part of the clarification and simplification role that parties play, which has already been identified—provides the framework for electoral decision-making. Having identified with a particular party that best represents their interests, individuals then normally vote for it—perhaps as a habitual series of acts without much further deliberation. Occasionally they may vote against the party they identify with because of particular issues related to one or more elections. And even more occasionally they may alter their identification as they become persuaded that another party can best represent their interests—perhaps because those interests have themselves changed. (On the American literature on party identification and 'normal voting' see Campbell et al., 1960.)

Given the assumed importance of the class cleavage in Great Britain, there should be differences between members of different classes in their political attitudes, their party identifications, and the parties they vote for. Class is a theoretical construct comprising a number of generalized fractions—upper, middle, and working, for example, as well as bourgeoisie and proletariat. Operationalizing these ideas into measurable constructs has generally deployed information on people's occupations. Much work in political sociology has classified these into such broad categories as 'white collar' and 'blue collar'; or 'professional', 'routine non-manual', and 'manual'—with the latter sometimes further divided into 'skilled', 'semi-skilled', and 'unskilled'. In the work of Heath and Goldthorpe, this was made more precise by using arguments regarding the labour contract, particularly as it affects autonomy in the workplace; these have recently been adopted by the country's Office of National Statistics for the classification of occupations (Rose and Pevalin,

2003). Categories such as salariat, routine non-manual, petty bourgeoisie, supervisors, and manual workers are now commonly used in electoral studies. Also used, however, are individuals' own perceptions of their positions in the class system, most of which are collapsed into a twofold categorization—middle class and working class.

To illustrate these relationships between class and voting, we use the data collected by the British Election Study (BES), a series of surveys of the British electorate initiated in the early 1960s and since then including a major survey of the British (i.e. excluding Northern Ireland) electorate immediately after each general election. (On these studies, see Scarbrough, 2000.) In most cases, we use data from the most recent (2005) study, but in some cases where this is not possible—because the relevant questions were not asked—we use data from a previous study.

Although survey analysts normally determine individuals' class positions by their labour market position, most people are socialized into class attitudes and positions as children or young adults, before they enter the labour market: for many, such socialization includes identification with a particular political party. This is illustrated in Table 1.1 with data taken from the 1997 BES. In the first block of this table, respondents were categorized according to their fathers' occupations, using the schema developed by Heath and Goldthorpe. Those who came from 'middle-class' backgrounds, whose fathers were in white-collar occupations (salariat, routine non-manual, and petty bourgeoisie), were much more likely than those in manual occupations to vote either Conservative or Liberal Democrat rather than

Table 1.1. Party voted for at the 1997 general election in Great Britain, by home background

Home background	Vote (%)			
	Conservative	Labour	Lib Dem	Did not vote
Father's social class				
Salariat	28.4	28.4	17.1	20.6
Routine non-manual	34.3	30.4	30.4	16.7
Petty bourgeoisie	28.4	28.4	17.3	20.7
Manual foremen	21.9	39.9	10.7	23.0
Working class	18.3	45.3	11.4	20.8
Other	21.3	34.7	13.9	24.8
Party father voted for				
Conservative	40.2	20.7	16.6	18.2
Labour	13.9	52.1	10.6	19.6
Liberal	27.1	27.1	25.6	10.9
Other	16.7	25.0	20.8	16.7
Did not vote	15.9	22.7	13.6	43.2
Don't know	20.4	32.3	12.4	30.0

Note: Figures may not sum to 100 because voting for other parties has been omitted.
Source: BES data files (1997).

Labour, whereas those from blue-collar households were much more likely to vote Labour. (Recall that the Labour party won the 1997 general election with a majority over the Conservatives of some 10 percentage points.) Thus, for example, somebody whose father was in the salariat (i.e. in a professional or managerial occupation) was 10 percentage points more likely to vote Conservative than somebody whose father had a working-class occupation. The second block shows how respondents voted in 1997 according to their recollection of how their fathers had voted (when the respondents were 14): again, there are clear differences, with those whose fathers were Labour supporters much more likely to vote Labour themselves than those from families where their fathers supported other parties.

Turning to voting by respondents' own occupational class position, Table 1.2 shows the pattern at the 2005 general election, when Labour won 36.2 per cent of the votes overall in Great Britain, the Conservatives 33.2 per cent, and the Liberal Democrats 22.6 per cent. The class divide is clear, with the Conservatives getting most support from white-collar groups (the salariat, the routine non-manual workers, and the petty bourgeoisie—employers in small businesses, self-employed workers, and farmers) other than personal service workers: those in the higher salariat and the petty bourgeoisie were four times more likely to vote Conservative than were semi-skilled and unskilled manual workers, who in turn were more likely either to vote Labour or to abstain (see Chapter 7). (Nearly 40 per cent of the electorate abstained at the 2005 election, but it is generally accepted that surveys almost invariably under-report the number of abstainers.) The Liberal Democrats, too, obtained more support from the higher salariat than from those in blue-collar jobs. For several decades, Labour's support among the working class was sustained through the activities of the trades unions, most of which campaigned actively for the party and provided it with substantial financial resources. With the decline of manufacturing industry, however, the size

Table 1.2. Party voted for at the 2005 general election in Great Britain, by occupational class position

Occupational class	Vote (%)			
	Conservative	Labour	Lib Dem	Did not vote
Higher salariat	34.2	23.7	21.8	14.4
Lower salariat	28.2	31.6	17.4	18.8
Routine non-manual	32.2	23.1	19.6	19.6
Personal service	17.8	25.2	13.3	40.7
Petty bourgeoisie	34.4	24.4	8.8	28.8
Foremen and technicians	10.2	26.4	14.2	41.6
Skilled manual	12.4	33.3	7.8	42.6
Semi-skilled and unskilled manual	7.6	37.9	12.3	36.9

Note: Figures may not sum to 100 because voting for other parties has been omitted.
Source: BES data files (2005).

and power of the unions has declined too—a process speeded up by legislation passed in the 1980s: many fewer people are now in unions, and more union members are in white-collar jobs (especially in the public sector). Nevertheless, in 2005, of those BES respondents who had ever been in a trades union, 38 per cent voted Labour and only 19 per cent voted Conservative; among those who had never been in a union, the respective percentages were 26 and 24.

Although academics have expended much effort in trying to identify the major class divisions within British society using indicators such as occupation (and also income), for many people class is a subjective concept—they identify with a particular class for a variety of reasons (including home background), which may be inconsistent with their current labour market position. Many surveys ask respondents which class they identify with, generally using just two options—middle class and working class. Those identifying with each in general have the characteristics associated with their chosen option: people in blue-collar occupations, with low incomes, and who are members of trades unions are more likely than others to identify with the working class, for example. But so are those from working-class backgrounds—whose fathers were in blue-collar occupations and who voted Labour—irrespective of their own situations.

These subjective class positions are usually strongly linked to party choice at an election: people vote for the party identified as promoting the interests of their chosen class. Table 1.3 indicates that this was so in 2005: more of those who identified with the middle class voted for the Conservatives than for any other single party; more of those who identified with the working class voted Labour; and there was less difference between the parties among those who said that they identified with no class. And since class identification is to some extent inter-generational, this is also reflected in party choice at elections: in 1997, those who identified with the working class were much more likely to vote Labour than Conservative (and vice versa for those who identified with the middle class), even when their personal characteristics are taken into account, including their home backgrounds (Johnston and Pattie, 2005).

Table 1.3. Party voted for at the 2005 general election in Great Britain, by subjective class position

Class (subjective)	Vote (%)			
	Conservative	Labour	Lib Dem	Did not vote
Middle class	32.5	24.1	18.4	20.6
Working class	18.0	32.5	14.6	29.0
No class	22.5	28.1	16.3	28.2

Note: Figures may not sum to 100 because voting for other parties has been omitted.
Source: BES data files (2005).

Although the class cleavage dominated British electoral politics for much of the twentieth century, other divisions within society are also related to patterns of party choice. For example, there are variations in party choice by age and, sometimes, by sex. In general, older people have been more likely to identify with and vote Conservative, in part because some of them were politically socialized during an era (especially before the Second World War) when the main alternative—Labour—was not a viable choice for many. Many older people also have interests—such as property ownership—which the Conservatives rather than Labour promote. In general, people tend to become more conservative with a small 'c' as they age. Alongside this, there are class differences in mortality rates— middle-class people tend to live longer—so that the older elements of the population are more likely to be Conservative supporters. This is shown clearly in Table 1.4: voters aged 65 and over were almost four times more likely to vote Conservative than their counterparts aged under 25. Most marked, however, were the differences between the age groups in their abstention rates, with well over half the youngest voters failing to turn out at the election, compared to just 13 per cent of those in the oldest group—an issue to which we return later (see Chapter 7). (At some elections there has been a difference between males and females in their party preferences, with males more likely to support Labour, but this was not marked in 2005.)

One variable with a strong relationship to voting is housing tenure. With the expansion of the welfare state, especially after the Labour governments of 1945–51, an increasing proportion of the population were in publicly pro- vided and publicly subsidized housing. This created what became known as a *consumption cleavage*—linked to, but separate from, the class cleavage— whereby a substantial proportion of the electorate was dependent on the state for major items of consumption, such as housing, and voted for the party associated with that provision—Labour. During the 1980s, however, a substantial proportion of those who rented their homes from local authorities (who were responsible for most of the state housing

Table 1.4. Party voted for at the 2005 general election in Great Britain, by age group

Age	Vote (%)			
	Conservative	Labour	Lib Dem	Did not vote
Under 25	9.5	17.4	13.8	56.1
25–39	13.7	28.0	16.7	37.0
40–54	23.6	32.5	16.3	23.2
55–64	34.3	25.3	18.4	15.0
65 and over	35.3	30.7	15.3	13.0

Note: Figures may not sum to 100 because voting for other parties has been omitted.
Source: BES data files (2005).

sector) were able to purchase their homes at preferential rates under the Conservatives' right-to-buy policy. This increased the size of the owner-occupier fraction: between 1981 and 2005 the percentage of households in state housing fell from about 27 to 14. The cleavage remained, however. Table 1.5 shows a very clear difference between owners (including those buying their homes with a mortgage) and renters in their likelihood of voting either Conservative or, to a lesser extent, Liberal Democrat—both of which performed much better among the former category. Labour, by contrast, gained more support from renters (especially renters in the public sector) than from those who owned their homes outright. In addition, renters—especially those in the private sector (many of whom are young and highly mobile)—were much more likely to abstain. Other elements of the consumption cleavage included public services such as health, education, and transport: those who depended on state provision were more inclined to support the party committed to such provision, whereas those who used private-market provision ('public' schools, 'private' health care, and their own cars) were more likely to support the party favouring market provision—the Conservatives. (On consumption cleavages generally, see Dunleavy, 1979; Dunleavy and Husbands, 1985.)

Other individual and group characteristics are also related to voting behaviour, suggesting that the sociological model is more complex than a class-dominated account alone would suggest. For example, adherents of different religions, especially those who are active participants, tend to support different parties to a greater or lesser extent, reflecting the links between their religious beliefs and the core components of different party ideologies (Kotler-Berkowitz, 2001). The Conservative party, for example, has long been seen as 'representing' the interests of the dominant Anglican group within British society, whereas dissenting Protestants and Roman Catholics were generally associated with the Labour and Liberal parties—both supported Irish home rule campaigns, for example. None of the parties now makes explicit appeals to particular religious groups and secularization

Table 1.5. Party voted for at the 2005 general election in Great Britain, by housing tenure

Housing tenure	Vote (%)			
	Conservative	Labour	Lib Dem	Did not vote
Owned outright	39.7	23.3	17.3	14.0
Buying with a mortgage	19.4	32.1	17.3	25.8
Rented from local authority	9.3	32.0	11.0	40.6
Other social rented	7.6	36.0	9.9	43.6
Private rented	8.9	20.1	17.2	52.5

Note: Figures may not sum to 100 because voting for other parties has been omitted.
Source: BES data files (2005).

is proceeding apace within British society (especially outside Northern Ireland, where religion is intimately associated with the cleavage between those wishing to retain the link with Great Britain and those promoting an all-Ireland political unit). Nevertheless, the former strong links are still reflected in voting patterns and some voters clearly get some of their cues on which party to support from their religious backgrounds and contact patterns. Table 1.6 indicates this, showing, for example, the Conservative party getting much more support than Labour among those stating their religion as Church of England, whereas Labour out-performs its main rival among Roman Catholics, Presbyterians, Non-Conformists and, especially, Muslims—though the Liberal Democrats also attracted considerable support from Muslims in 2005, largely as a consequence of their opposition to the Iraq War, which was supported by both Labour and the Conservatives. In general, Labour has attracted much more support than any other party from among Britain's minority ethnic groups—especially blacks from both Africa and the Caribbean, and South Asians. Most electoral surveys have few respondents from these groups, however: those which have focused on them specifically have found that members of Britain's ethnic minorities have traditionally favoured the Labour party with their votes, though with varying turnout levels (Fieldhouse and Purdam, 2002; Saggar, 2000; Sobolewska, 2005).

Education, too, has been associated with voting patterns, although differences have not been strong in recent years. Until the rapid expansion in the number of students remaining at school until age 18, and also the number attending higher education institutions, educational attainment was closely associated with occupational class, with the children of middle-class parents very much more likely to remain at school beyond the official leaving age (15 until 1969, 16 thereafter) to obtain qualifications such as A-levels, and then to attend universities. Table 1.7 shows voting in 2005 by two educational measures. Both show that the main beneficiary of people staying on at school and gaining post-16 qualifications (A-levels and degrees) has

Table 1.6. Party voted for at the 2005 general election in Great Britain, by religious adherence

Religion	Vote (%)			
	Conservative	Labour	Lib Dem	Did not vote
None	15.7	26.8	16.3	35.7
Church of England	34.5	27.3	13.9	20.2
Roman Catholic	23.9	32.6	16.7	24.6
Presbyterian	20.6	28.4	18.6	18.6
Nonconformist	23.9	33.1	18.0	13.7
Muslim	11.4	41.4	28.6	15.7

Note: Figures may not sum to 100 because voting for other parties has been omitted.
Source: BES data files (2005).

Table 1.7. Party voted for at the 2005 general election in Great Britain, by age at which finished full-time education and highest educational qualification

Education	Vote (%)			
	Conservative	Labour	Lib Dem	Did not vote
School-leaving age				
15 or younger	25.8	29.6	13.9	25.1
16	21.4	26.0	13.1	33.8
17	22.0	26.5	14.8	32.2
18	33.5	21.7	14.8	25.5
19 or older	27.6	29.1	21.2	17.4
Still in education	3.9	18.8	29.7	44.5
Highest educational qualification				
Postgraduate	20.2	34.4	25.2	16.6
First degree	22.2	28.6	28.1	15.0
Other tertiary	29.5	28.0	16.5	20.4
A-level	17.0	30.9	20.0	30.0
GCSE/O-level	25.4	24.9	11.0	33.3
Other school	14.1	23.0	19.9	39.9
Trade	30.4	36.6	14.3	12.5
Technical	38.2	15.1	10.5	30.9
None	21.8	31.7	10.8	30.1

Note: Figures may not sum to 100 because voting for other parties has been omitted.
Source: BES data files (2005).

been the Liberal Democrat party, which—especially since the creation of the Social Democratic Party in 1981 (Crewe and King, 1995) and its later merger with the then Liberal party—has attracted much more support from those who have undertaken tertiary education than from other groups.

Sociological models have underpinned much of the work on British voting behaviour since the 1950s. Class has dominated in the discussions, but has not predominated. A number of indicators of people's social positions have been related to their partisan choice. More recently, however, these relationships have become weaker—though they have not disappeared, as demonstrated here. Other influences have increased in importance, as outlined below.

Responsive Voter Models

The sociological models emphasize stability in voting behaviour: individuals are socialized into supporting a particular set of beliefs and a political party, and then habitually vote for that party at elections. Some clearly do. But others do not—otherwise all election results would be virtually foregone conclusions. Some change their minds over time, perhaps as their circumstances change through social mobility and movement between classes (either upwards or downwards), and through alterations in their material

Models of Voting

situations. Others never become fully committed to a particular set of beliefs
and an associated party. Over time, this level of commitment or attachment
to a particular party—usually referred to as *party identification*—has declined
quite substantially. Respondents to electoral surveys are usually asked if they
identify with a party and, if so, how strongly, in three categories—very strong,
fairly strong, and not very strong. Table 1.8 gives data from four BES surveys
over four decades and shows a major change in the percentage of respondents
who identified very strongly with any party—from 42 per cent in 1970 to less
than one-quarter of that just 35 years (and nine general elections) later. Voters
have become much less committed to the parties over this period.

One assumed consequence of this decline in the strength of party identification is that people may be more prepared to shift their vote from one party to
another (or in and out of abstention) between elections. These are the so-called
'floating voters', whose support parties campaign for at each election.
Although parties can rely to a considerable extent on their core support (unless
it has been alienated for some reason), they need a substantial proportion of
the votes held by the remainder of the electorate if they are to succeed at any
one contest. The size of this floating-voter population varies across elections,
and the trends also vary according to party popularity. Table 1.9 gives the
flow-of-the-vote matrix for the 2001–5 inter-election period, according to
respondents to the 2005 BES, who were asked how they voted at each of
the elections. Each party retained the support of a majority of its 2001 voters,
the Conservatives more so than Labour. Nevertheless, the volume of change
was much greater than the net outcome indicated. Some 22.4 per cent
of respondents reported voting Conservative in 2001, for example, and 23.5
per cent in 2005: to sustain their vote share in 2005, therefore, the Conservatives had to win over a substantial number of converts from the other parties
and from abstentions in order to compensate for the losses they incurred.

Table 1.10 shows how the respondents who were much less committed to a
party (according to the party identification measure) were much more likely
to change their vote between the two elections (although, because this is not a
panel study it may be that those who changed their vote also changed their
party identification; we don't know what the strength of their identification
was in 2001). Among Conservative voters, for example, 90 per cent of the

Table 1.8. Strength of party identification at various elections,
1970–2005 (percentages)

Party identification	1970	1979	1992	2005
Very strong	42.1	21.4	17.1	9.8
Fairly strong	36.3	46.2	44.6	41.2
Not very strong	11.2	23.6	32.2	38.1
No party identification	10.4	8.3	6.1	10.9

Source: BES data files (1970, 1979, 1992, and 2005).

Table 1.9. The inter-election flow of the vote, 2001–5

Party voted for, 2001	Party voted for, 2005 (%)			
	Conservative	Labour	Lib Dem	Did not vote
Conservative	74.5	4.4	7.4	11.6
Labour	7.3	61.7	12.8	14.8
Liberal Democrat	9.6	9.9	66.0	10.9
Did not vote	11.2	18.6	8.4	59.1

Note: Figures may not sum to 100 because voting for other parties has been omitted.
Source: BES data files (2005).

very strong identifiers remained loyal to the party between the two contests, compared to 78 per cent of the fairly strong identifiers, 69 per cent of the not very strong identifiers, and just 30 per cent of those with no party identification. The same was true for Labour and, in large part, for the Liberal Democrats—among whom there were few very strong identifiers. Continued abstention was also much more likely to be the case, the weaker the respondents' party identification.

How do these 'floating' or 'relatively uncommitted' voters determine which party to support at any one election? An increasing body of electoral literature over recent decades has argued that their decisions are made

Table 1.10. The inter-election flow of the vote, 2001–5, by strength of party identification in 2005

Party voted for, 2001	Party voted for, 2005 (%)			
	Conservative	Labour	Lib Dem	Did not vote
Very strong party identification				
Conservative	90.4	4.3	1.1	4.3
Labour	2.2	87.4	2.2	4.4
Liberal Democrat	7.1	14.3	71.4	0.0
Did not vote	18.5	59.3	0.0	14.8
Fairly strong party identification				
Conservative	77.6	3.1	8.1	10.0
Labour	3.6	69.3	10.2	14.0
Liberal Democrat	7.8	5.5	74.2	10.2
Did not vote	15.6	25.6	7.5	46.2
Not very strong party identification				
Conservative	68.6	5.2	9.4	14.1
Labour	11.5	47.7	16.7	20.1
Liberal Democrat	13.0	13.8	57.2	11.6
Did not vote	11.1	17.3	11.1	59.4
No party identification				
Conservative	30.5	5.1	18.6	35.6
Labour	16.4	27.3	29.0	24.5
Liberal Democrat	15.6	6.7	60.0	17.8
Did not vote	5.0	9.9	5.0	77.9

Note: Figures may not sum to 100 because voting for other parties has been omitted.
Source: BES data files (2005).

according to their evaluations of the incumbent government's performance on salient issues, and their confidence in its plans for the future, as against those of the opposition parties. Alongside this, they will also judge the parties' credibility as future governments (including their leaders' prime ministerial potential). For a party currently in power, that judgement will reflect evaluations of the recent past as well as expectations for the near future; for those in opposition, it will reflect their plans and personnel (especially the relative merits of the party leaders), as well as recollections of past performance when in power (if at all).

Most applications of these responsive voter models in the British context focus on economic policy by relating partisan choice to measures of economic success (or otherwise). Although a number of earlier studies had made some reference to the link between economic evaluations and government popularity—most of them showing a relationship between the latter and such aggregate variables as interest rates and the rate of inflation (e.g. Hibbs and Vasilatos, 1981)—a major contribution to this debate came with a pioneering paper by Sanders, Ward, and Marsh (1987). Conventional wisdom in the mid-1980s associated the Conservative government's re-election in 1983 (after a period when it had fared particularly badly in the opinion polls) with the country's success in the 1982 Falklands War and Margaret Thatcher's 'strong leadership', which was seen as largely responsible for bringing that about. Sanders, Ward, and Marsh (1987) argued, however, that contemporaneous with the end of the war was a very substantial upsurge in economic optimism among the British electorate, and it was this rather than the much more ephemeral 'Falklands factor' that generated the 1983 victory. They later revised their conclusions somewhat, though still pressing the economic voting explanation (Sanders, Ward, and Marsh, 1992). Their general argument with regard to the importance of perceptions of the economic situation—past, present, and future—rapidly became part of the conventional wisdom on British voting patterns (Sanders, 2003) and has been used to create successful predictive models (Sanders, 1996, 1999, 2004), despite some arguments to the contrary. Evans (1999a), for example, has contended that these economic variables are much less significant than Sanders and others have suggested what is termed an 'endogeneity effect': people who voted a party into power are much more likely to say its economic policies were successful than those who voted against it (see also Johnston et al., 2005a.; Pattie, Johnston, and Sanders, 1999).

To gauge people's evaluations of the economic situation, many surveys use two types of question. One asks for evaluations of the state of the economy nationally—so-called *sociotropic questions*—whereas the other inquires about the individual's own (or their household's) financial situation—*egocentric questions*. Such questions may be either retrospective or prospective, with the former asking about recent economic changes and the latter about expectations for the near future. Both have some problems. Asking questions about expectations in surveys conducted soon after an election has been held is unlikely to be very illuminating: people who voted for the party elected into power are more likely to be optimistic than those who voted against it, so their financial evaluations are likely to reflect that choice. With the retrospective evaluations, people who voted for a party at the previous election (in part at least because they supported its economic policies) are more likely to think that the economy has performed well under its governance than those who voted for an opposition party (or abstained), so that their economic evaluations reflect their partisan choice rather than vice versa.

Despite these difficulties in testing the ideas derived from responsive voter theories, many recent studies have indicated close links between partisan choice and both sociotropic and egocentric economic evaluations. The 2005 BES did so also, with the respondents being asked their economic evaluations in a pre-election survey, and then how they voted in a post-election follow-up. Table 1.11 shows voting by retrospective evaluations, indicating that as people reported more positive feelings about the national economic situation (the sociotropic evaluations), their level of support for Labour increased more than fourfold—while that for the Conservatives decreased nearly ninefold. The same patterns, though less extreme, were also recorded according to the egocentric evaluations: Labour got more votes among the economically satisfied; their main opponent gained more among the dissatisfied. Similar patterns are shown for prospective evaluations (Table 1.12), although few people thought the national situation was going to get a lot better and the majority of them abstained.

Retrospective voter models are based on the use of credit–blame mechanisms in electoral decision-making. These argue, for example, that if individuals

Table 1.11. Party voted for at the 2005 general election according to retrospective economic evaluations

Economic evaluation	Vote (%)			
	Conservative	Labour	Lib Dem	Did not vote
Sociotropic				
Got a lot worse	43.0	11.7	9.8	25.8
Got a little worse	30.5	20.0	16.1	28.3
Stayed about the same	18.7	32.6	18.1	26.1
Got a little better	14.9	40.4	15.3	25.6
Got a lot better	4.8	50.0	7.1	31.0
Egocentric				
Got a lot worse	24.3	18.5	10.7	43.6
Got a little worse	35.6	19.5	13.7	26.5
Stayed about the same	20.9	29.7	18.9	24.8
Got a little better	14.8	40.3	15.7	24.3
Got a lot better	13.0	29.3	19.5	33.3

Note: Figures may not sum to 100 because voting for other parties has been omitted.
Source: BES data files (2005).

Table 1.12. Party voted for at the 2005 general election according to prospective economic expectations

Economic expectation	Vote (%)			
	Conservative	Labour	Lib Dem	Did not vote
Sociotropic				
Get a lot worse	31.9	14.1	13.3	34.8
Get a little worse	33.3	16.6	18.5	24.6
Stay about the same	22.0	30.8	17.2	26.1
Get a little better	13.5	39.8	11.8	30.1
Get a lot better	6.3	25.0	9.4	56.3
Egocentric				
Get a lot worse	30.0	17.5	8.3	39.2
Get a little worse	31.5	17.2	17.1	28.5
Stay about the same	24.8	29.6	17.3	23.2
Get a little better	11.8	37.8	15.7	30.3
Get a lot better	17.1	19.5	13.4	47.6

Note: Figures may not sum to 100 because voting for other parties has been omitted.
Source: BES data files (2005).

think the national economy has been performing badly then they will vote against the incumbent government. This assumes, however, that they will blame the government for that poor performance. If they do not—and governments always seek to deflect the blame for poor performance elsewhere (onto global economic conditions over which they have no control, for example) while claiming the credit for good performances—then there is no reason why their voting calculus should take the economic situation into account. That this is indeed the case is demonstrated in Table 1.13, which shows voting in 2005 by how well respondents thought the government had handled the economy. There is a sixfold difference in Labour's support across those five categories: fully 60 per cent of those who thought the Labour government had handled the economy very well voted for it, as against just under 10 per cent who thought it had done very badly.

Table 1.14 approaches this in a different way, looking at how people voted not only according to their retrospective sociotropic evaluations but also

Table 1.13. Party voted for at the 2005 general election according to views on how well the government has handled the economy

Government handled economy	Vote (%)			
	Conservative	Labour	Lib Dem	Did not vote
Very well	6.0	60.4	14.8	13.8
Fairly well	20.8	32.3	18.6	24.6
Neither well nor badly	25.1	19.7	15.7	33.3
Fairly badly	39.4	10.3	12.1	32.2
Very badly	43.3	9.6	8.7	28.8

Note: Figures may not sum to 100 because voting for other parties has been omitted.
Source: BES data files (2005).

their responses to a question on how much they thought government policies affected the economy (omitting the small number who gave the answer 'not at all'). The difference in the support given to the two main parties is much greater, the greater the perceived impact of government policies. Among those who thought that policies had a great deal of impact, there was a fivefold difference in support for the Conservatives and Labour among those who thought things had got a lot worse and a sixfold difference among those who thought they had got a lot better. Among those who thought policies affect the economy a fair amount, there was only a fourfold difference among those who thought things had got a lot worse, whereas among those who thought policies did not have much impact the comparable ratio was less then threefold. (Few said things had got a lot better.) Thus the government was punished most by those who thought things had got worse because of its policies, and got its greatest rewards from those who thought those policies had made things a great deal better.

As already noted, economic evaluations may be very important in voter decision-making, but not to the exclusion of all other issues and policy arenas. For example, the quality of public services has become a major issue in British general elections, and many voters have been influenced in

Table 1.14. Party voted for at the 2005 general election according to retrospective sociotropic evaluations and beliefs in the degree to which government policies affect the economy

Sociotropic evaluation	Vote (%)			
	Conservative	Labour	Lib Dem	Did not vote
Believe policies affect the economy a great deal				
Got a lot worse	51.9	9.9	14.8	14.8
Got a little worse	34.0	18.4	19.9	22.7
Stayed about the same	18.4	38.5	18.0	22.2
Got a little better	14.3	53.9	11.0	16.9
Got a lot better	9.1	59.1	13.6	18.2
Believe policies affect the economy a fair amount				
Got a lot worse	50.7	12.3	6.8	19.2
Got a little worse	31.0	20.1	13.3	30.0
Stayed about the same	20.1	32.8	19.9	22.9
Got a little better	16.2	37.3	17.2	25.0
Got a lot better	0.0	50.0	0.0	50.0
Believe policies affect the economy not very much				
Got a lot worse	28.6	11.1	11.1	36.5
Got a little worse	26.1	18.5	18.5	33.7
Stayed about the same	19.0	27.5	14.2	32.7
Got a little better	9.4	20.3	21.9	45.3
Got a lot better	0.0	0.0	0.0	50.0

Note: Figures may not sum to 100 because voting for other parties has been omitted.
Source: BES data files (2005).

their choices by government performance and opposition policies on these as well as economic policy areas. And in the 2005 election, there were also concerns about the Iraq War, about terrorism, and about control over immigration and asylum-seekers. Table 1.15 shows the percentage voting Labour in 2005 according to the BES respondents' evaluations in the pre-campaign survey of the government's performance on such issues. On each, it gained a larger share of the respondents' votes among those saying that it had performed either 'very well' or 'fairly well' than it did among those replying 'very badly' or 'fairly badly. Whether these particular issues were important in determining the outcome depended on how salient they were with the electors, however. For example, when asked to identify the single most important issue facing the country at the time, 18 per cent said asylum-seekers and 15 per cent the National Health Service, with Iraq being identified by 7 per cent and terrorism by 5.5 per cent; only 3.5 per cent said the state of the economy, 2.0 per cent taxation, and 1.9 per cent unemployment.

Finally, for many voters the characteristics of the parties and of their leaders are crucial in determining how they vote. In 2005, the Prime Minister's standing with the electorate was considered crucial. BES respondents were asked to place Tony Blair on a number of 11-point scales according to how much they liked him, thought him competent, and considered him both responsive and trustworthy; they were also asked to rank how well they liked the Labour party on the same scale. Table 1.16 shows major differences in the percentages voting Labour at that election according to their opinions of Tony Blair: in particular, the greatest range in party support was linked to how much they trusted him, with 77 per cent of those who had a great deal of trust voting Labour, compared to just 6 per cent of those who had no trust in him.

Table 1.15. Percentage of BES respondents voting Labour at the 2005 general election according to their evaluation of how well the government had handled certain policy areas

| Policy area | Evaluation | | | | |
	Very well	Fairly well	Neither well nor badly	Fairly badly	Very badly
Crime	25.0	46.0	27.5	19.7	17.0
Education	61.4	36.9	28.6	18.7	11.7
Asylum-seekers	30.4	53.6	37.3	30.8	17.3
Health system	56.3	39.4	27.6	21.7	13.1
Terrorism	48.4	33.1	24.9	19.8	18.7
Economy	60.4	32.3	19.7	10.3	9.6
Railways	40.0	35.2	30.6	28.3	18.4
Iraq	40.6	42.5	30.0	28.8	18.6
Taxation	58.7	46.6	29.6	15.3	10.8
Pensions	60.9	40.1	28.8	26.1	16.7

Source: BES data files (2005).

Table 1.16. Percentage of BES respondents voting Labour at the 2005 general election according to their views about Tony Blair and the Labour party

Score	Like	Competence	Responsive	Trustworthy	Party
0	4.3	4.6	7.4	6.0	1.0
1	4.2	3.5	4.5	6.6	6.2
2	8.4	11.7	6.3	7.5	6.9
3	13.2	3.5	8.6	15.3	10.6
4	18.7	15.2	20.7	21.4	11.6
5	23.6	21.7	25.6	30.3	20.3
6	39.3	25.1	37.4	42.0	30.7
7	42.8	36.2	46.6	49.1	52.3
8	53.0	40.3	57.3	55.4	61.0
9	63.0	58.5	45.5	69.6	78.1
10	68.8	62.9	68.6	77.1	77.8

Source: BES data files (2005).

The sociological and responsive voter models are not entirely independent of each other: to some extent, as suggested by the economic voter models, people in different social locations evaluate political trends and personalities in different ways. But the responsive voter models do extend our appreciation of how and why (and, as we demonstrate in this book, where) people vote as they do.

From 'Normal' to Responsive Voters

'Traditional' approaches to British electoral behaviour argued that sociological factors dominated party choice decisions, with the responsive voter factors important only for that portion of the electorate who were not firmly committed to one of the political parties and were therefore open to persuasion either before or during the election campaigns. Over recent decades, however, this position has come under considerable attack. A decreasing proportion of voters now identify with and habitually vote for one party, and more are making their decisions on the basis of contemporary conditions and their evaluations of the relative merits of the political parties—their policies, their credibility as governments, the quality of their leaders, and so forth. There has been what is widely termed a process of *partisan dealignment*, with fewer people identifying with a party, and fewer of those who do identifying strongly with it—with the implication that they will almost certainly vote for its candidates at forthcoming elections. (The classic work on dealignment in Britain was Crewe, Särlvik, and Alt, 1977; see also Crewe, 1986; Franklin, 1985.) There is continuing debate on the extent of this dealignment, however: Sanders (1998) claimed that class voting is dead, for example, whereas Goldthorpe (1999) argued that until 1992 there had been what others—(Heath, Jowell, and Curtice, 1987; see also Crewe, 1986)—had termed 'trendless fluctuation', with the 1997 pattern (on which Sanders based his argument) being nothing more than another zigzag in that continuing pattern. Nevertheless, employing two widely deployed indices of class voting developed by Alford (1964)—the absolute and relative indices of class voting—Sanders (1998) showed a very clear decline over the period 1964–97 (see also Denver, 2003, 70). This work has been updated in Figure 1.1 to include the 2001 and 2005 elections. In 2005, both indices were little more than one-third of their 1964 values, indicating that even if class differences remain, they are much less marked now than they were four decades earlier.[1]

The reason for this apparent disagreement is illustrated by the data in Table 1.17, which shows voting by social class at the first and the most recent elections for which BES data are available. (Definitions of social class have varied over the 40 years and it is difficult to get exactly comparable figures: these provide a very broad-brush picture.) The difference between the two dates are substantial—remembering that in 1964 Labour won 44.1 per cent of the votes cast and the Conservatives 43.3 per cent, compared to 36.2 and 33.2 per cent, respectively in 2005. The first difference is the substantial growth in the Liberal Democrat (Liberal in 1964) vote: the party gets significantly more of its support from the 'middle classes'. The second is the decline in class

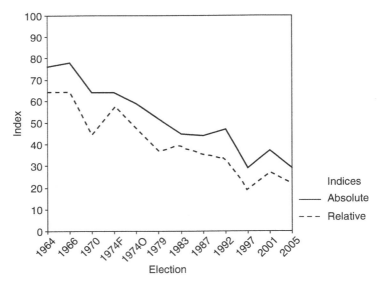

Fig. 1.1. Absolute and relative indices of class voting in Britain, 1964–2005

[1] For these purposes, the relative index has been multiplied by 10. The absolute index is the sum of the differences between non-manual and manual workers in their percentages voting Conservative and Labour; the relative index is the ratio of Conservative to Labour votes among non-manual workers divided by the similar ratio for manual workers.

Table 1.17. Voting by socio-economic class, 1964 and 2005

| | Vote (%) | | | | | |
| | 1964 | | | 2005 | | |
Class	Lab	Con	Lib Dem	Lab	Con	Lib Dem
Managerial/professional	17	70	13	30	31	31
Other non-manual	25	57	18	39	33	21
Skilled manual	62	29	9	49	28	13
Other manual	69	25	6	60	13	13

Notes: In this and subsequent tables the following abbreviations are used: Lab = Labour; Con = Conservative; Lib Dem = Liberal Democrat. Figures may not sum to 100 because voting for other parties has been omitted.
Source: BES data files (1964 and 2005).

polarization: if we compare the 'most Conservative' class with the 'most Labour' class in 1964, we see that each gave around 70 per cent of its votes to the relevant party; in 2005 the 'most Labour' class gave only 60 per cent of its support to that party, whereas the comparable figure for the 'most Conservative' was only 33 per cent. The class differences in support for the Conservatives and Labour have been substantially muted. Nevertheless, a significant class divide remains—although it is smaller than it was in the 1960s. In 1964, the 'class difference' in support for Labour (i.e. that between the 'most Labour' and the 'least Labour' class) was 52 percentage points, dropping to 30 points in 2005; for the Conservatives, the respective figures were 45 and 18. (If Conservative and Liberal Democrat support is combined, the relevant figures are 52 and 36.) The result, as Denver (2003, 70) has shown, is a decline in the intensity of the class cleavage. Nevertheless, class differences in voting remain, and they are much more pronounced in support for Labour.

Several reasons are suggested for this trend. The first is the relative redundancy of the ideological basis of the political parties. For much of the twentieth century, the Conservatives promoted the interests of the 'middle classes' whereas Labour sustained those of the 'working class' in a bi-polar simplification of the political situation. By the end of the century, however, economic change had narrowed, if not removed, that cleavage: many fewer manual workers are now employed in large factories where they are represented and mobilized by trades unions linked to the Labour party, for example, and many more are employed in small workplaces (an increasing proportion in the burgeoning service industries), where unions are at best weak and in many cases non-existent.

These changes in the economic structure were accentuated in the 1980s with the rapid decline of manufacturing industry under Thatcherism, with which was also associated a major reduction in trades union powers and welfare state cut-backs—there was no further building of public-sector housing and tenants of existing properties were encouraged to purchase them on favourable terms. In such circumstances, parties of the left and right—Labour and Conservative, respectively—became less relevant.[2] More important was 'good government' by whatever party, and long-term ideological commitments were increasingly discarded as parties sought to present themselves simply as the best able to manage the government and public services. This was clearly illustrated by the transformation of the Labour party after its 1979, 1983, and 1987 defeats by the Conservatives under Margaret Thatcher, with the final outcome—'New Labour' led by Tony Blair from 1994 on—adopting many of the policy stances of its major opponent but presenting itself as better able to govern in the same mould, though with a stronger sense of 'social justice'. After comprehensive defeats in 1997 and 2001, the Conservative party, too, shed some of its traditional positions, joining Labour and the Liberal Democrats as one of three largely 'centrist' parties competing on pragmatic rather than principled positions. This is clearly illustrated by analysing the contents of party manifestos (on which see Budge, 1999). For much of the period since 1945, Bara and Budge (2001, 28) showed a relative wide left–right gap between Labour and the Conservatives, with the Liberal Democrats (and their predecessors) occupying the 'centre ground'. That gap was particularly wide between 1974 and 1992, but closed rapidly over the next two elections, mainly as a result of a massive shift by Labour into the centre: indeed, at the 1997 and 2001 elections the Liberal Democrats were slightly to the left of Labour, making the latter the 'party of the centre'.

Alongside these economic changes has been a range of linked social changes. The class division of society has become much less clear cut, given alterations in the labour market, while mobility has enabled an increasing number of people to change their social and material situations very considerably. As Franklin (1985) has shown, by the 1980s many fewer people than in the 1950s and 1960s had most (let alone all) of the characteristics associated with a stereotype working-class individual (a Labour-voting father with a working-class occupation; a working-class occupation oneself; membership of a trades union; living in public housing), which thus eroded much of Labour's traditional support base. At the same time, the working class, as traditionally defined, has declined both relatively and absolutely: British society is now dominated by service industries and middle-class lifestyles. To survive in that changed milieu, the Labour party had to extend its appeal. If it remained a predominantly working-class party, it could no longer hope to gain majority support and so form governments (Crewe, 1986). Class continued to underpin the difference between the two main parties, but it no longer dominated. To be successful—as it was in 1997 and 2001, and less so in 2005—the Labour party had to win substantial support among white-collar workers; at its nadir in the 1980s, not only did it garner relatively little support from this group (many of whom turned to the

---

[2] See also the discussion of the affluent worker studies in Chapter 5.

Liberals and the SDP if they did not support Thatcherism) but at the same time the Conservatives were able to win substantial numbers of votes from among skilled manual workers.

Recent trends in party support in Britain therefore reflect not so much a continuation of the dominant class cleavage as its modification in the light of contemporary political and economic circumstances. Thus in their analyses of trends in the social basis of support for the parties from 1964 to 1997 (i.e. using all of the BES data sets except that for 2001), Heath, Jowell, and Curtice (2001) concluded that over that period the Conservatives were consistently seen as the party of the right wing and the middle classes, with this continuity in their image being paralleled by continuity in the social bases of their support. Labour, on the other hand, had moved from being a party of the left and the working class to a more centrist position: it had become a 'catch-all' party (New Labour), no longer reliant only on certain sections of the electorate for support. Even then, they noted, 'the usual pattern of support continued—it was simply muted' (p. 142) by Labour's success at winning votes from classes where it usually gained relatively little support. For Heath, Jowell, and Curtice, the class basis for political support remains the foundation of the British experience, with the particular political circumstances of the 1997 election (and the pattern continued in 2001 and 2005) being the collapse in Conservative support across the class spectrum. Political changes may modify the sociological underpinning of voting in certain circumstances, but the underlying class pattern remains—with the result being 'trendless fluctuation' (see above, p. 20).

Tactical voting

One particular aspect of voting that has characterized British general elections since the 1980s has been tactical voting. From the 1940s until the 1970s, the Conservative and Labour parties predominated, capturing a very large percentage of all of the votes cast, and virtually all of the seats—in 1966, for example, the Conservatives and Labour together obtained 90.2 per cent of the votes cast and won 98 per cent of the seats in Great Britain. The two 1974 general elections signalled the end of this hegemony, however, at least as far as vote-winning was concerned. The combined Conservative–Labour vote was reduced considerably (to 76 per cent) by the combined electoral successes of the Liberals (as they then were), the Scottish National Party (SNP), and Plaid Cymru. Since then, the Conservative–Labour joint share of the votes has averaged 75 per cent, falling to its lowest level (69.4) in 2005. They have received an incommensurate share in the number of MPs, however, only falling below 95 per cent at the 1997, 2001, and 2005 elections, for reasons discussed in our analysis in Chapter 8.

The success of these 'third parties' (often termed 'minor parties') has provided electors with a wider choice: the Liberal Democrats now contest virtually every seat in Great Britain at all elections and the SNP and Plaid Cymru similarly contest all constituencies in Scotland and Wales, respectively. English voters, therefore, have the choice between three parties, and their Scottish and Welsh counterparts have four candidates from parties that all have a Westminster presence—for whom support may no longer be perceived as no more than a 'wasted, protest vote'. Because of a lack of resources with which to conduct campaigns and thereby to make inroads into the Conservative–Labour hegemony across the country as a whole, however, most have concentrated their efforts in a few relatively favourable milieus, where they have replaced one of the 'big two' as the leading contender to replace the incumbent Labour or Conservative MP. For the Liberal Democrats, for example, these were mainly suburban and rural constituencies in southern England, in some of which they received their initial boost through success at a by-election; they tended to replace Labour as the main challenger to the Conservatives in such places. In the 1990s they began to make inroads into some of Labour's urban 'heartlands', however, such as Sheffield.

This 'third-party advance' has created the conditions for tactical voting (known as strategic voting in North America). In a constituency where party *A* wins 45 per cent of the vote at an election, party *B* gets 38 per cent, and *C* 17 per cent, *B* is much better placed to win the seat at the next election than is *C*. In another constituency, however, *A* may again win 45 per cent at the first election, but *B* gets only 18 per cent and *C* gets 37 per cent: in this case, *C* is the best-placed to overturn *A*'s victory next time. To promote its campaign in the second constituency, *C* may campaign on the platform that it is the only party able to defeat *A*, and it will seek to persuade as many of *B*'s supporters as possible to vote for it next time: if it could win over two-thirds of them, then it would have 49 per cent of the votes to *A*'s 45 per cent. Party *B* would conduct a similar campaign in the first constituency.

Tactical voting thus involves switching support from the party one prefers to one's second-choice party, on the grounds that this will enable the defeat of a third party, which is the desired outcome. Thus if both Labour and Liberal Democrat voters want to see Conservative MPs defeated, the best tactics (strategies) are for Labour supporters to vote Liberal Democrat in constituencies where the latter are best-placed to unseat a Conservative incumbent and for Liberal Democrats to switch their support to Labour candidates in constituencies where the latter are most likely to win. Various estimating procedures have identified substantial proportions of voters acting in this way since the 1980s, in many cases responding to party campaigns urging them to do so. (Although central party organizations—notably Labour's—have resisted pressures to campaign overtly for such tactical voting, there is little doubt that local parties have done so in many constituencies.)

How many voters have been convinced that their preferred party has no chance of victory locally, and that they should instead vote tactically for their second choice, depends on the nature of the contest in their constituency and the intensity of the party campaigns promoting this option. Curtice and Steed (2002, 318) argued that this occurred on an 'unprecedented scale' in 1997, claiming that voters apparently found 'it easier to switch their support between the two main opposition parties than ever before' (Curtice and Steed, 1997, 313). Evans, Curtice, and Norris (1998) estimated that approximately 10 per cent of those who voted in 1997 did so tactically, one percentage point more than in 1992. In 2001 it was somewhat less, undertaken on this occasion to protect Labour and Liberal Democrat incumbents against possible Conservative advances, especially the former (see Denver, 2001). Estimates of tactical voting at earlier contests vary quite considerably. Niemi, Whitten, and Franklin (1992), for example, estimated from survey data that some 17 per cent of those who voted at the 1987 general election did so at least partly for tactical reasons—that is, tactical voting was part of the reason that they gave (or was imputed from the answers they gave) for their voting choice—although Evans and Heath (1993) re-analysed the data and suggested that the figure was 10 per cent. Johnston and Pattie (1991; see also Galbraith and Rae, 1989) estimated that, in Conservative-held seats alone, where anti-government tactical voting would be concentrated, the volume of tactical voting was approximately 6 per cent of all voters in 1983 and 8 per cent in 1987.

Not only did tactical voting help Labour to win its 1997 landslide, when many of its own supporters voted Liberal Democrat in order to oust a Conservative incumbent and many Liberal Democrats similarly voted Labour where that party's candidate was best placed to defeat the Conservative candidate, but its second landslide in 2001 owed much to similar tactical voting—this time in order to prevent a Conservative candidate removing the Labour or Liberal Democrat incumbent. At that latter election, Fisher and Curtice (2005; see also Fisher, 2004) reported that tactical voting involved about 9 per cent of those who participated in the election. And the same percentage reported voting tactically in 2005, when there was a slight 'unwind' in the degree of tactical voting involving supporters of Labour being prepared to vote for Liberal Democrat candidates compared to 2001, but not vice versa; in addition, there was an increase in the number of Conservative supporters prepared to vote Liberal Democrat for tactical reasons.

Tactical voting is very much a geographical issue at British elections, varying considerably in its direction and intensity from place to place according to the situation in individual constituencies. There are many where there is little call for it, because either one party has the support of a large majority and no amount of tactical voting is likely to unseat it and/or the third party has too weak a foundation to provide sufficient 'second-choice' voters to assist the second-placed party in defeating the incumbent. We discuss this in more detail in Chapter 6 on local campaigning.

To Vote or Not to Vote

Both the sociological and the retrospective voting models discussed above focus very largely on the choice between political parties at elections. Some people—a steadily increasing proportion of the total according to recent trends—don't vote, however. The trend in turnout over British general elections since 1950, shown in Figure 7.1, indicates this. At the first two contests shown, as many as 82 per cent of the UK's registered electorate turned out to vote; in 2001 only 59.3 did so, and in 2005, 61.3 per cent.

Why has turnout declined? One of the paradoxes of voting identified by some theorists is that most votes have no impact on the outcome of an election. In a mass polity (Britain had some 43 million registered electors in 1945) where two parties predominate, unless the contest is extremely close most people know before the election takes place that however they vote it will not influence the final outcome. (This is particularly the case with the British first-past-the-post electoral system, as we discuss further in Chapter 7.) The benefits to be derived from voting are in no way commensurate with the costs, so the rational individual will abstain, according to a well-known theory which has been much deployed in recent decades (Downs, 1957; see also Franklin, 2004; Wattenberg, 2002). The chances of any individual's vote making a difference to the election result, in her/his constituency let alone nationally, are so remote that actually going to the polling booth can be seen as little more than a waste of time.

Against this, it is argued that some may realize—perhaps not until one election result has been against their interests—that if too many people take that position, then their party will lose, so they vote just to make sure that doesn't happen (see Dunleavy, 1991). At the same time, at least some of them are convinced that voting is an important civic duty, part of one's obligations as a member of a democratic society. So they turn out to vote to fulfil that obligation, especially if they think that the difference between the main contestants is significant and it is important (to them, and perhaps to the country as a whole) who wins. They may be less likely to do so if they are alienated from the political system, however, perhaps feeling that they have no impact on political decision-making whatever they say or do, or that the decision-makers are never likely to act for their benefit.

A further argument against Downs's theory of the rational voter abstaining is that it treats individuals as atomized members of society rather than, as is the case with many, as members of interest groups with shared political and other goals. According to such arguments, the rational calculation that people undertake is not 'Will my vote make a difference to the overall result?' but rather 'Will my vote make a difference to my group's interests prevailing?' (on which see Franklin, 2004). In the latter case, it may well be that electors can be convinced that their party's chances of victory in the local constituency will be enhanced if they, and others like them, turn out to vote—and that if they don't they will be 'letting the side down'. In such situations, strong local campaigning by a party may be crucial to achieving the needed conviction, which is why Wattenberg (2002) argues that the decline in party activism mobilizing voters is a major cause of recent turnout decline in the USA.

If turnout has fallen, therefore, is it because more people are politically alienated, more think that the result is a foregone conclusion, more think there is little difference between the parties, more aren't contacted by parties and convinced of the value of a vote locally, or what? The probable answer is 'yes' to all of these—at certain times, and in certain places. Turnout was almost certainly lower in 1997 than in 1992, for example, because a substantial Labour victory was expected. But the same was true again four years later; was this the sole reason for the largest drop in turnout in recent history (from 72 to 59 per cent), or was there greater alienation from, distrust of, and lack of confidence in the political process as well? Crewe (2002, 225–6) has divided non-voters in 2001 into four types:

1. *Apathetic abstainers*—those without any knowledge of or interest in politics, who abstain accordingly;
2. *Alienated abstainers*—those who abstain because they have no confidence that politicians and governments are addressing their concerns;
3. *Indifferent abstainers*—those who fail to vote because they are indifferent to the election outcome and which party wins;
4. *Instrumental abstainers*—those who fail to vote because it would make no difference to the outcome.

All of these abstain deliberately as a result of a clear decision not to go to the polls (or to avail themselves of the proxy and postal voting alternatives). In addition, however, there are those who abstain because they are unable to get to the polling station on election day. Under the UK electoral system up to and including the 2005 contest, electors were required to vote at a designated polling booth, usually that closest to their home, apart from those who had applied for a postal or proxy vote. (This was made much easier by legislation introduced before the 2001 election. Between 1997 and 2001 the number of postal votes returned doubled, to 1.4 million—5.3 per cent of all votes cast: Butler and Kavanagh, 2002, 211.) Electoral rolls were only compiled annually, however, so many of those who had moved were unable (or unwilling because of the effort) to return to their former home area to vote.[3] Others are precluded from doing so, either through some form of incapacity or by being away from home on election day. Set against the deliberate (or voluntary) abstainers identified by Crewe (2002), therefore,

[3] Electoral rolls were compiled in October of each year, coming into force the following February, so that an election held in January would use a roll compiled 15 months earlier. A rolling register process was introduced in 2001, allowing people to register at any time before an election is called, but its impact is as yet unknown.

there are also the unintentional (or involuntary) abstainers, who would have voted if they could have done so.

Several recent British Election Studies have asked respondents who abstained why they didn't vote; Table 1.18 shows the pattern of responses at the 1987, 1992, and 1997 contests. In general, involuntary abstainers outnumbered voluntary abstainers: more failed to turn out because of circumstances that they claimed were beyond their control than did so as an explicit choice. The 2001 and 2005 BES did not ask the question in the same form, but the data produced (Table 1.19: discussed in detail in Johnston and Pattie, 2003b) suggest that the two types were approximately of equal size in 2001, although there are reasons to suggest that at least some of those who claimed an involuntary cause for their abstention (i.e. they would have voted if circumstances had not prevented them) were in fact deliberate abstainers—probably either 'indifferent' or 'instrumental' according to Crewe's (2002) categories, rather than 'apathetic' or 'alienated' (see Johnston and Pattie, 1997c, 2001c). In 2005, when the response categories were slightly different, voluntary abstainers substantially outnumbered the involuntary.

If non-voters are categorized as involuntary or voluntary according to their response to the 'Why didn't you vote?' question, then some clear differences emerge between the two types, as well as between abstainers and those who voted. The 2001 BES asked respondents the likelihood of them participating politically in a number of ways, on an 11-point scale ranging from 0 (very unlikely) to 10 (very likely). Table 1.20 shows not only that

Table 1.18. The reasons given for not voting at the 1987, 1992, and 1997 general elections (percentage of all BES respondents reporting that they did not vote)

Reason	1987	1992	1997
Voluntary non-voters			
Not bothered/interested	17	17	13
Deliberately abstained	6	10	5
Vote would not affect outcome	8	7	4
Undecided between parties	6	7	8
Never vote	4	3	2
Religious reasons	2	3	1
TOTAL	43	47	33
Involuntary non-voters			
Away on election day	26	22	16
Sickness prevented me	10	17	5
Other commitments/no time	7	8	14
Work prevented me	6	7	8
Poll card/polling station problem	2	4	11
Had moved	8	3	6
TOTAL	59	61	60
Other reasons/no reasons	6	4	14

Note: Respondents were allowed to give up to three reasons for not voting.
Source: BES data files (1987, 1992, and 1997).

Table 1.19. The reasons given for not voting at the 2001 and 2005 general elections (percentage of all BES respondents reporting that they did not vote)

Reason	2001	2005
Voluntary non-voters		
Not interested	19	23
Obvious who would win	14	13
Party changed	4	4
All parties the same	—	12
Can't trust politicians	—	19
No real democracy	6	—
TOTAL	43	71
Involuntary non-voters		
Circumstances prevented	42	33

Note: Respondents were allowed to give up to three reasons for not voting.
Source: BES data files (2001 and 2005).

those who voted in 2001 were more likely to vote at future elections than non-voters, but also that involuntary non-voters were more likely to vote than their voluntary (i.e. deliberate abstainer) counterparts. Overall, involuntary non-voters were more like voters than like voluntary non-voters.

Understanding turnout involves unravelling a complex series of reasons why some people vote and others abstain at any particular election. As shown in some of the earlier tables in this chapter (and discussed further in Chapter 7), there are some socio-economic correlates of abstention. Working-class people are more likely to report non-voting than the middle class, for example (Tables 1.2, 1.3); people who own their own homes are more likely to vote than are renters (Table 1.5); more-educated people are more

Table 1.20. Political knowledge and activity by voters and non-voters in 2001 (mean value for each group on a scale of 0–10)

		Mean likelihood of activity	
		Non-voters	
Activity	Voters	Involuntary	Voluntary
Voting in next European election	7.0	5.4	2.8
Voting in next local election	8.9	7.5	3.7
Working in a group on political problem	3.6	3.5	2.6
Participating in a protest	2.7	3.0	2.5
Being active in voluntary organization	4.7	4.9	3.9
Giving money to political party	1.3	0.9	0.4
Trying to convince others how to vote	1.8	1.4	0.7
Working in an election campaign	1.3	1.1	0.5
Discussing politics with family or friends	5.4	4.5	2.7
Joining a boycott	5.5	4.4	3.3

Source: BES data files (2001).

likely to turn out than the lesser educated, for example, perhaps because they have a greater sense of civic duty and/or awareness of the potential value of their vote to their party's interests in their local constituency (Table 1.7); and, most noteworthy of all, older people are much less likely to abstain than the younger generation (Table 1.4). What is clearly important in the British electoral system, however, is that turning out to sustain one's party's cause is much more likely to be efficacious in some constituencies than others. Furthermore, the political parties are, not surprisingly, well aware of this, and target their vote-mobilization resources accordingly. We should therefore expect to find a clear geography to both turnout patterns at any one election and also the turnout decline that began in the 1990s.

The Contemporary Pattern of Voting

Given the arguments above regarding changing influences on British voting behaviour, with the relative decline of the cleavage model and the growth of responsive voting, what then is the pattern of voting? Which of the various factors identified above accounts for whether or not people abstain (or report that they do[4]), for example, and which of the factors account for the patterns of party choice? In this section, we report on analyses of the 2005 BES data.

In this, and in many of the other statistical analyses reported in this book, we use the technique of binary logistic regression. Our goal is to use these models to illuminate the basic patterns and so we pay little attention to many of the statistical details. In binary logistic models, the dependent variable is a simple yes/no classification, and the goal is to predict which individual responded 'yes', and which 'no', using a set of independent variables. Many of those variables may be classifications—such as socio-economic class—and the regression model compares the likelihood of people in one category in a classification answering 'yes' relative to somebody in another category. That likelihood is shown by the exponent of the regression coefficient, which is the only statistic shown in the tables. Only statistically significant exponents are shown—that is, those in which we are very confident (with only a 5 per cent chance of being in error) that the relationship we have found is 'real' and not the result of statistical chance.

Table 1.21 illustrates the use of this procedure in the analysis of whether people abstained (the 'yes' answer) at the 2005 election, as shown by the BES data. Seven socio-demographic variables are deployed in the first model,

---

[4] Checks on reported voting at previous elections suggest that there is a deal of mis-reporting: in 2001, for example, of 1821 individuals interviewed in the BES for whom a check could be made, 88 (some 5 per cent) said that they had voted but did not; a further five said they had not voted, but did. Results of those checks were not available for the 2005 BES when these analyses were undertaken.

Table 1.21. Binary logistic regression model of abstention, 2005

Independent variables	Model I	Model II
Socio-economic class (comparator = higher salariat)		
Lower salariat	1.48	—
Routine non-manual	—	
Personal service	2.49	1.89
Petty bourgeoisie	1.82	—
Foremen and supervisors	2.96	2.36
Skilled manual	2.54	2.41
Semi-skilled/unskilled manual	2.20	1.67
No information	1.50	—
Belong to a social class (comparator = middle)		
Working	—	—
None	—	—
Age finished education (comparator = 15 or under)		
16	0.74	0.75
17	—	—
18	0.54	0.67
19 or over	0.37	0.49
Still in education	0.57	1.25
No information	—	—
Housing tenure (comparator = own outright)		
Buying	—	—
Social rented	2.56	2.07
Other rented	3.28	2.92
Religion (comparator = none)		
Church of England	—	—
Roman Catholic	—	—
Presbyterian	—	—
Nonconformist	0.44	—
Muslim	0.28	0.40
Other	—	—
Age group (comparator = under 25)		
25–39	0.73	0.77
40–54	0.42	0.49
55–64	0.23	0.34
65 and over	0.19	0.38
Strength of party identification (comparator = very strong)		
Fairly strong	1.44	—
Not very strong	2.41	1.48
None	5.57	2.90
No information	—	—
Not to vote is a serious neglect of duty (comparator = strongly agree)		
Agree		2.15
Neither agree nor disagree		4.99
Disagree		6.30
Strongly disagree		12.66
No response		—
I feel very guilty if I do not vote (comparator = strongly agree)		
Agree		2.46
Neither agree nor disagree		2.81
Disagree		5.67
Strongly disagree		11.33
No response		—

Table 1.21. Continued

Independent variables	Model I	Model II
R^2	0.24	0.42
% correctly classified		
Total	76.6	81.2
Abstainers	34.3	54.9
Non-abstainers	93.4	91.5

Note: Only significant exponents are shown. Exponents <1.0 indicate a smaller likelihood of abstaining than is the case with the comparator group.

selected from among those already analysed above: socio-economic class, whether individuals said that they belonged to a class, the age at which respondents completed their education (which is strongly correlated with their reported qualifications, hence we don't use that variable as well), housing tenure, religion, age group, and strength of party identification.

The exponents for the first model show that members of all socio-economic classes, other than those in routine non-manual occupations, were more likely to abstain than those in the higher salariat: indeed, those in the three working-class occupational groups were more than twice as likely to abstain (exponents of 2.96, 2.54, and 2.20, respectively) than those in the higher salariat (holding constant all other variables, as is always the case in such models). Similarly, people who rented their homes were more likely to abstain than were owners. The longer people stayed in education, the less likely they were to abstain; however, the likelihood of those still in education abstaining was 0.57 of that for those who left school at the age of 15 or younger (exponents less than 1.0 indicate a smaller likelihood of abstaining than is the case with the comparator group). Older people were very much less likely to abstain than their younger counterparts—an exponent of 0.19 indicates that people aged under 25 were five times more likely to abstain than those aged over 64. Abstention was also much more likely among those with weak or no party identification: those who identified with no party were 5.57 times more likely to abstain than those who very strongly identified with a party.

Measures of goodness-of-fit tell us how good the models are at predicting the outcome on the dependent variable. We use two measures here—a pseudo R^2 measure (the Nagelkerke R^2), which can be compared to the multiple correlation coefficient deployed in standard regressions, and the percentage of the responses correctly classified. (The binary logistic model gives a probability for each respondent being in the yes/no categories; a correct classification here is one in which the probability of a response being in the category it was recorded in is 0.5 or greater.) The results at the foot of the first column for Model I in Table 1.21 show a small R^2 and only just over one-third of the abstainers correctly classified: the model was much better at predicting who *didn't* abstain (93 per cent of those were correctly identified) than predicting those who did.

As discussed above, many people abstain because they see little point in voting and don't consider it their civic duty to do so. To add this alienation from politics to the analysis, Model II adds the responses to two attitudinal items, in which respondents were asked whether they agreed or disagreed with statements that 'Not to vote is a serious neglect of duty' and 'I feel very guilty if I do not vote'. The second column in Table 1.21 shows that the addition of these two further independent variables substantially increased the model goodness-of-fit: some 55 per cent of the abstainers were correctly identified by Model II. The exponents show very large differences: those who strongly disagreed with the civic duty question were 12.66 times more likely to abstain than those who strongly agreed, and the comparable ratio for the guilt variables was 11.33. Abstention in part varies according to one's position in society, but much more according to one's attitudes to the democratic process.

Three further binary logistic models were fitted to tease out which sorts of people voted for which of the three parties (looking only at those who voted and excluding the abstainers). Three models were fitted. The first included six of the seven variables employed in the abstention analyses (omitting the party identification question). The second added responses to three questions asking how well the government had handled the health system, the economy, and education. Finally, Model III added six variables representing respondents' views of the three main party leaders and of the parties themselves: these involved respondents placing the individuals/parties on an 11-point scale from 0 (strongly dislike) to 10 (strongly like).

The results for Labour are in Table 1.22. The statistically significant exponents for Model I indicate the continued class cleavage, with respondents in the three working-class categories 2.2–3.6 times more likely than those in the middle class to vote Labour (the lack of significant exponents for most of the others indicate that they were no more likely to vote Labour than members of the comparator group, the higher salariat). Similarly, those who identified with the working class were almost twice as likely to vote Labour as those who identified with the middle class—even when their occupational class had been taken into account—and those in tenures other than outright ownership of their homes were also much more likely to vote Labour than their comparator group. Older people were less likely to vote Labour than their younger counterparts.

Model I successfully identified 44 per cent of all Labour voters, and indicated the continued salience of the class cleavage in the sociological voting model. When the three responsive voting variables are added in Model II, however, somewhat surprisingly the ability to separate out Labour

Table 1.22. Binary logistic regression model of Labour voting, 2005

Independent variables	Model I	Model II	Model III
Socio-economic class (comparator = higher salariat)			
Lower salariat	1.77	2.02	1.78
Routine non-manual	—	—	—
Personal service	—	—	—
Petty bourgeoisie	—	—	—
Foremen and supervisors	2.63	—	—
Skilled manual	2.22	1.88	—
Semi-skilled/unskilled manual	3.65	2.88	2.41
No information	1.43	1.66	—
Belong to a social class (comparator = middle)			
Working	1.95	1.51	1.45
None	—	—	—
Age finished education (comparator = 15 or under)			
16	—	—	—
17	—	—	—
18	—	—	—
19 or over	—	—	—
Still in education	0.41	—	—
No information	—	—	—
Housing tenure (comparator = own outright)			
Buying	1.97	1.53	—
Social rented	2.86	1.85	—
Other rented	1.57	1.18	—
Religion (comparator = none)			
Church of England	0.74	—	—
Roman Catholic	—	—	—
Presbyterian	—	—	—
Nonconformist	—	—	1.74
Muslim	—	—	—
Other	—	—	—
Age group (comparator = under 25)			
25–39	—	—	—
40–54	0.60	—	—
55–64	0.46	—	—
65 and over	0.49	—	—
How well the government has handled the health service (comparator = very well)			
Fairly well		—	—
Neither well nor badly		—	—
Fairly badly		0.60	—
Very badly		0.38	0.58
No information		—	—
How well the government has handled the economy (comparator = very well)			
Fairly well		0.37	0.47
Neither well nor badly		0.24	0.42
Fairly badly		0.14	0.27
Very badly		0.18	—
No information		—	—
How well the government has handled education (comparator = very well)			
Fairly well		0.55	—
Neither well nor badly		0.45	—
Fairly badly		0.28	0.41

Independent variables	Model I	Model II	Model III
Very badly		0.22	0.38
No information		—	—
Feelings about Tony Blair			1.11
Feelings about Michael Howard			—
Feelings about Charles Kennedy			—
Feelings about Labour party			1.18
Feelings about Conservative party			0.85
Feelings about Liberal Democrat party			—
R^2	0.14	0.23	0.33
% correctly classified			
Total	64.4	73.4	78.1
Labour	44.4	35.9	51.5
Non-Labour	79.0	90.9	90.5

Note: Only significant exponents are shown. Exponents <1.0 indicate a smaller likelihood of abstaining than is the case with the comparator group.

voters falls by nearly 10 percentage points, although 91 per cent of non-Labour voters are successfully identified. Those who thought that the government had handled the economy very well were over five times more likely to vote Labour than those who thought its record was either bad or very bad (exponents of 0.14 and 0.28), and there were similar differences in voting intentions according to opinions on Labour's record on education and, to a lesser extent, the health service.

Finally, Model III not only produces a better fit than Models I and II but also shows the predominance of just two variables—respondents' feelings about Tony Blair and the Labour party. For every one-point increase in their liking for the Prime Minister, the likelihood of respondents voting Labour increased by 11 per cent (an exponent of 1.11), with a comparable figure of 18 per cent in the case of their liking for his party. Furthermore, most of the other variables are not significant in Model III compared to Models I and II, with the exception of those relating to the government's handling of the economy. This indicates that liking for Blair and Labour were themselves more common among the working class than among the middle class, and also that the same relationship held with regard to views on how well the economy had been handled. Blair and Labour's popularity was in part class-based, and in part based on respondents' economic evaluations—but it was those feelings that dominated the outcome.

Not surprisingly, the models for Conservative voting in Table 1.23 are to a considerable extent the reverse of those for Labour, with one major difference—the class/housing tenure cleavage remains even in Model III, although the age difference disappears. Conservative voters were drawn disproportionately not only from among the middle classes, but also from those who thought that the Labour government had handled the economy badly, and disliked both Mr Blair and his party. (For every one-point increase in

Table 1.23. Binary logistic regression model of Conservative voting, 2005

Independent variables	Model I	Model II	Model III
Socio-economic class (comparator = higher salariat)			
Lower salariat	—	0.64	—
Routine non-manual	—	—	—
Personal service	—	—	—
Petty bourgeoisie	1.65	—	—
Foremen and supervisors	0.34	0.26	0.27
Skilled manual	0.66	0.32	0.34
Semi-skilled/unskilled manual	0.29	0.24	0.28
No information	—	0.62	0.68
Belong to a social class (comparator = middle)			
Working	0.60	0.69	0.61
None	—	—	—
Age finished education (comparator = 15 or under)			
16	—	—	—
17	—	—	—
18	—	—	—
19 or over	—	—	—
Still in education	—	0.32	0.20
No information	—	—	—
Housing tenure (comparator = own outright)			
Buying	0.54	0.56	0.63
Social rented	0.29	0.22	0.23
Other rented	0.49	0.41	0.43
Religion (comparator = none)			
Church of England	1.81	2.07	2.19
Roman Catholic	—	1.60	1.98
Presbyterian	—	—	—
Nonconformist	—	—	—
Muslim	—	—	—
Other	—	—	—
Age group (comparator = under 25)			
25–39	—	—	—
40–54	1.60	—	—
55–64	2.15	1.65	—
65 and over	2.25	1.88	—
How well the government has handled the health service (comparator = very well)			
Fairly well		—	—
Neither well nor badly		2.78	—
Fairly badly		3.51	—
Very badly		3.14	—
No information		—	—
How well the government has handled the economy (comparator = very well)			
Fairly well		3.42	2.81
Neither well nor badly		5.03	3.07
Fairly badly		9.21	4.86
Very badly		17.15	9.09
No information		6.89	6.92

Independent variables	Model I	Model II	Model III
How well the government has handled education (comparator = very well)			
Fairly well		—	—
Neither well nor badly		4.78	—
Fairly badly		5.18	—
Very badly		4.73	—
No information		—	—
Feelings about Tony Blair			0.77
Feelings about Michael Howard			—
Feelings about Charles Kennedy			—
Feelings about Labour party			0.94
Feelings about Conservative party			1.08
Feelings about Liberal Democrat party			0.96
R^2	0.16	0.31	0.43
% correctly classified			
Total	69.9	78.6	82.9
Conservative	29.3	40.0	55.9
Non-Conservative	90.5	92.4	92.5

Note: Only significant exponents are shown. Exponents <1.0 indicate a smaller likelihood of abstaining than is the case with the comparator group.

Blair's popularity, the likelihood of a Conservative vote fell by 23 per cent—an exponent of 0.77.) People who liked the Conservative party were more likely to vote for it but, very interestingly, there was no significant relationship between voting Conservative and feelings about their leader, Michael Howard: it seems that Blair could deliver votes for his party but Howard couldn't for his.

Finally, the models of Liberal Democrat voting in Table 1.24 indicate, as expected, that the sociological model very largely fails, although working-class respondents were less likely to vote for the party than were their middle-class counterparts. Nor did the responsive voting models provide much in the way of significant results, with one clear exception: the Liberal Democrats were much more likely to get votes among those who thought that the government had handled the education system badly. It was also more likely to get support from those still in education (many of whom abstained, of course: see Table 1.21) than from any other group. Education was a clear vote-winner (the party had campaigned strongly against the introduction of top-up fees for university students, having successfully resisted them in Scotland where it was part of the coalition government). It also performed better among those who felt negatively about Tony Blair—but not those who felt positively about the Liberal Democrat's own leader Charles Kennedy. Finally, and interestingly, Models II and III show a strong age effect: once views on education are taken into account (on which clearly young voters have strong opinions), older people are more likely to vote for the Liberal Democrats (rather than for the other main parties) than are their younger counterparts.

Table 1.24. Binary logistic regression model of Liberal Democrat voting, 2005

Independent variables	Model I	Model II	Model III
Socio-economic class (comparator = higher salariat)			
Lower salariat	—	—	—
Routine non-manual	—	—	—
Personal service	—	—	—
Petty bourgeoisie	0.43	0.37	0.42
Foremen and supervisors	—	—	—
Skilled manual	—	0.43	0.44
Semi-skilled/unskilled manual	—	0.60	0.59
No information	—	—	—
Belong to a social class (comparator = middle)			
Working	—	—	—
None	—	—	—
Age finished education (comparator = 15 or under)			
16	—	—	—
17	—	—	—
18	—	—	—
19 or over	—	—	—
Still in education	3.14	5.59	5.22
No information	—	—	—
Housing tenure (comparator = own outright)			
Buying	—	—	—
Social rented	—	—	—
Other rented	—	—	—
Religion (comparator = none)			
Church of England	0.71	0.76	—
Roman Catholic	—	—	—
Presbyterian	—	—	—
Nonconformist	—	—	—
Muslim	—	—	—
Other	—	—	—
Age group (comparator = under 25)			
25–39	—	2.62	2.47
40–54	—	2.58	2.30
55–64	—	2.94	2.61
65 and over	—	2.56	2.26
How well the government has handled the health service (comparator = very well)			
Fairly well		—	—
Neither well nor badly		—	—
Fairly badly		—	—
Very badly		—	—
No information		—	—
How well the government has handled the economy (comparator = very well)			
Fairly well		—	—
Neither well nor badly		—	—
Fairly badly		—	—
Very badly		—	—
No information		—	—

Independent variables	Model I	Model II	Model III
How well the government has handled education (comparator = very well)			
Fairly well		2.54	2.39
Neither well nor badly		2.95	2.68
Fairly badly		4.13	3.53
Very badly		3.59	3.01
No information		—	—
Feelings about Tony Blair			0.91
Feelings about Michael Howard			—
Feelings about Charles Kennedy			—
Feelings about Labour party			—
Feelings about Conservative party			0.95
Feelings about Liberal Democrat party			1.01
R^2	0.07	0.08	0.10
% correctly classified			
Total	76.1	81.7	81.6
Liberal Democrat	4.4	2.7	3.1
Non-Liberal Democrat	98.7	99.4	99.2

Note: Only significant exponents are shown. Exponents <1.0 indicate a smaller likelihood of abstaining than is the case with the comparator group.

Conclusions

A great deal has been written about electoral behaviour in the UK since the mid-1960s, and an increasing volume of data has been analysed to test ideas regarding which people vote for what party (or don't vote at all), and why. This chapter has presented a very brief overview of that literature, stressing its main arguments and illustrating its major conclusions.

The general argument developed in the remainder of this book is that much of the literature either ignores or downplays one significant aspect of the voting decision—where it takes place. The goal is not to replace the standard models by geographical theories, but rather to ensure that geographical (or spatial, place-based) considerations are central to debates and analyses regarding voting in the UK: the intention is not disciplinary imperialism but rather inter-disciplinary commonality.

2

Bringing Geography In

The core of this book's argument is that incorporating geography—as a synonym for 'place' not as an academic discipline—to the generally used models is central to understanding British voting patterns. Most voting behaviour models are based on a *compositional* approach, arguing that electors' choice of party or candidate is predominantly influenced by either their position within society or their personal evaluations of the contemporary political-economic situation: the sociological and responsive voter models discussed in the previous chapter exemplify this approach. Our argument here stresses a *contextual* approach,[1] according to which people making voting decisions are influenced by elements of the milieux within which their daily lives are engaged. Some of those influences may not be directly linked to the intimate geography of their lives, such as the newspapers they choose to read and the radio and TV channels they tune in to, which are national in their coverage. But many are: the people they talk to about political issues, the organizations that they join which have political purposes, their responses to changes in the local economy—these and many more are place-based, so that where they live (their personal geographies) can have a strong impact, may even be the major influence, on their political and electoral choices.

The contextual approach is not presented as an alternative to the compositional one, however. The two are complementary, interacting in a great variety of ways. Thus, for example, we may argue that people occupying particular positions within society are likely to choose one party over another (working-class people preferring Labour, for example), but that tendency is stronger in some places than others because of the impact of local milieux on the development of class consciousness and its relationship to political ideologies. In this way, geography becomes part of the core models—sociological and responsive voter—that are the basis of most analyses of voting patterns.

The incorporation of geography within the basic models avoids treating it as what Agnew (1990, 18) terms 'epiphenomenal', whereby geographical variations in voting decisions are seen as the 'outcome of "deeper" national or global economic or political processes', which have not been directly

---

[1] On the compositional and contextual approaches, see Thrift's (1983) pioneering essay.

addressed in the choice of variables for any analytical model. According to such arguments, in a fully specified model, with all the influential processes recognized, geographical variations as independent influences on voting outcomes would disappear (see, for example, McAllister and Studlar, 1992). Such a position, Agnew argues, 'denies the pervasive geographical constitution of social processes...[and that] the geographical is intrinsic rather than epiphenomenal to explanation'. Thus:

> The key claim on behalf of geographical social theory is that national social categories are neither empirically appropriate nor theoretically coherent as causes of voting behaviour. National categories cannot cause individual voting decisions. Causality can only be discovered as specific social mechanisms that translate social structure into individual acts and vice versa. (Agnew, 1990, 18)

Agnew (1987) first developed this argument in his *Place and Politics*—part of a wider attempt to counter what he perceived as the 'devaluation' of place in contemporary social science (Agnew and Duncan, 1989). It has underpinned his intellectual project for some two decades, characterized as a case against disengaging 'space from any constitutive role in politics' (Agnew, 1996a, 144).

In responding to Agnew's (1996a, 144) argument that 'context counts in electoral geography' (but has largely been ignored, because of the dominant concern 'with mapping distributions which are then "explained" by non-spatial factors': p. 129), King (1996, 159) contended that 'political geographers should not be so concerned with demonstrating that context matters'. This was based on three arguments: 'in fact, context rarely counts'; 'the most productive practical goal...should be to show that it does not count'; and much previous work on context has been misleading. King's first claim very much parallels that of McAllister and Studlar (1992): there is considerable spatial variation in voting behaviour 'but after we control for what we have learned about voters, there isn't much left for *contextual effects*' (King, 1996, 160: his emphasis). Hence his argument that the most productive research path would be to seek to show that context counts for little: if context really matters, then critical experiments designed to show otherwise, but which fail, would really make the geographical case convincing (on which see also Green and Gerber, 2004). Agnew's (1996b, 165) immediate response was that

> King's alternative [to contextual analyses] is ontological (and methodological) individualism. Geography [according to King] is about how individuals are spread around and divided into aggregates. It is a monument to our ignorance in that the dispersion and aggregation limit the possibilities of making straightforward inferences about the choices and acts of individuals. However, once we find out what drives individual choices across enough individuals we will no longer need to worry about it. Explanation and generalization about individuals are the same. But my point is that we can never satisfactorily explain what drives individual choices and

action unless we situate the individuals in the social-geographical contexts of their lives.... In other words, the causes of the political beliefs and actions of individuals are organized geosociologically.

As such, he refutes the argument that the neighbourhood effect is 'a deviation from a national standard that defines "normal" voting behavior' (p. 167). On this interpretation, it seems, geographies of voting are built from the 'bottom-up'. They result from a myriad local processes, albeit linked—more strongly in some places than others, perhaps—to processes operating at other places and scales, rather than from a national (or more general) pattern from which there are some local deviations. Because many of those processes have been active for a long time, they have been aggregated into national patterns—such as the class cleavage. Agnew's argument, however, is that appreciating such aggregation is crucial. What we observe nationally (as set out in the tables in Chapter 1) is the sum of a large number of interacting local processes. Because of that interaction, similar places tend to have similar outcomes—voting patterns in this case. But it is the aggregation that matters. Voting patterns by class are not imposed on places by some nationally invariant process: rather they are the summation of a myriad interacting local processes, the interactions perhaps becoming increasingly important with current levels of spatial mobility and the pervasiveness of national media, but still building on locally produced social contexts.

Most of Agnew's empirical work has been undertaken in Italy, where his argument gains a great deal of support from the considerable evidence that 'the identities, values and preferences that inspire particular kinds of political action ... are embedded in the places or geographical contexts where people live their lives' (Agnew, 2002, 3). His exploration of those contexts is set within a reworking of his original theoretical position, and a claim that the arguments regarding locational specificity (i.e. against the case that 'any place within the boundaries of a specific country may well be more or less substitutable for any other place in terms of the main attributes of its politics': p. 13)[2] are more widely questioned than was the case when he wrote his first book on this issue (Agnew, 1987). For Agnew, a place has three separate but interrelated aspects: it is a locale in which most people's everyday lives are situated; it is a location linked, through various networks, to a wide range of other locales; and it is a site with which people identify—a sense of place is part of many people's personal identity. His case regarding the crucial role of these three in the creation of political attitudes, and thence of geographies of voting behaviour, is as follows (Agnew, 2002):

• Locales—the micro-geography of life—provide the settings for much inter-personal social interaction; they are the arena for political socialization.

---

[2] On this issue of locational substitutability in the UK, see Bogdanor's (1983) claim that there were no spatial variations in voting in the UK, Johnston's (1986a) riposte, and the subsequent debate (Bogdanor, 1986; Johnston 1986b).

- Those locales are embedded within a wider social division of labour, and part of their character is derived from their position within such wider socio-economic structuring.

- Communications networks link the locales together, mediating flows of information between people and places.

- All locales are embedded within national territories, and their political representatives to national institutions are important in both representing local concerns and interpreting wider trends to the local population.

- The general tensions within capitalist societies—between classes, sexes, ethnic groups, etc.—are mediated within the locales, influencing 'the relative weight and various meanings attached to social divisions...and hence the appeal of different ideologies, [which] are not the same everywhere'.

- Political movements use geography in their search for electoral and other support, using claims relating to locales, regions, and so forth to mobilize this support.

Thus what Agnew calls a 'place perspective' is based on a theoretical argument regarding the importance of places, at various scales, in the creation of personal political identities and the mobilization of support for political parties (on which see also Franklin, 2004).

Agnew's argument underpins the basic theme of the present book, though we contend that the linking together of locales in national political networks has developed much more, and over a much longer timespan, in the UK than in Italy. This does not mean that British politics have essentially been 'nationalized', with some remnant local 'deviations' only, but rather that an appreciation of the general in UK politics must be based on an appreciation of the crucial role of places as crucibles for political socialization and electoral mobilization.

Context and Scale

If the argument regarding geography and contextual affects is to be accepted, we need to provide not only empirical evidence of the strength of the case regarding geographical variations in voting behaviour but also, and more importantly, theoretical arguments to underpin such findings. Without the latter, it is always possible to present any observed geographies of voting as epiphenomenal. Two related questions are raised in this context: how do these geographical variations come about, and at what spatial scales do the relevant processes operate?

A number of spatial contexts at a variety of scales is identified in Figure 2.1, some or all of which may be influential for the voting and related political decisions taken by individual members there. The most immediate (or local)

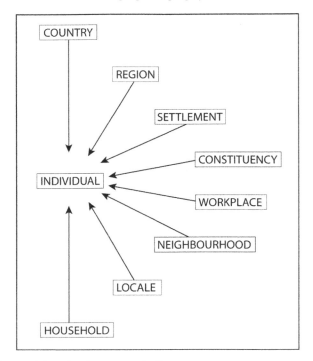

Fig. 2.1. The spatial scale of contextual effects

scale for most voters is the *household*, comprising the people with whom he/she has the greatest amount of informal social contact, and with whom discussions of political issues, including which party to vote for at a forthcoming election, are likely to take place. Households are located within *neighbourhoods*, small areas of only a few hundred people with whom residents may be in frequent, in some cases daily, contact—with that contact potentially including discussions about political and related issues. Such neighbourhoods are sometimes termed 'locales', a technical term (introduced by Giddens, 1984) used by some social scientists for 'interaction settings'.

Small neighbourhoods—maybe just a cul-de-sac or a couple of street blocks—are set within wider areas, which we term *home areas*. These are groups of adjacent neighbourhoods, which may form larger social and/or political units—such as the wards used in the organization of both local government and political parties, church and school catchment areas, and so forth. In turn these are components of *places*: separate, spatially bounded settlements in which physical, social, and perhaps political identities are intertwined. They are the places that many people identify with when asked where they come from, and can range from a small village to a large city. Some of those places form separate *constituencies*, the districts that send MPs to the House of Commons (each currently (2006) contains an average of some 70,000 voters in England and 6,000 in Scotland and Wales); others (the smaller ones) are part of a constituency; and many—the large cities and conurbations—are divided into several constituencies. Although these units are ephemeral, with the constituency map being regularly revised to ensure that their electorates are of similar size, as far as is practicable (Rossiter, Johnston, and Pattie, 1999a), many voters identify with them, in that they provide their national political representation; they are also major units within which political parties are organized and develop their election strategies.

Places are located within *regions*, larger-scale relatively homogeneous areas, many of which have long histories as separately defined units within a country, and with which many of their residents have a sense of identity— as with Yorkshire, for example.[3] That sense of identity, and an associated wish to act in the interests of their region, may influence how people vote. Finally, in the UK context, regions are nested within *countries*—England, Northern Ireland, Scotland, and Wales. Many identify with their country (either of origin or of residence) and their voting decisions may reflect their consideration of national interests, especially where parties campaign to represent those interests.

These six separate, nested (though sometimes overlapping) scales are not the only spatially defined contexts that are relevant to political decision-making. As well as in their homes and neighbourhoods, for example, many people have considerable amounts of social and occasionally politically relevant interaction at their workplace, both informally, through contacts with fellow workers during leisure time, and more formally, through workplace-based organizations such as trades unions. There are also the geographical units created to enhance political organization, notably local government units. These range in scale from the parish and town council through local and district councils to regional governments—such as the Greater London Assembly—plus the legislatures established in the late 1990s for Scotland, Wales, and Northern Ireland, and proposed in the early twenty-first century for some of the English regions.

All these spatial contexts are geographically defined containers (some with more precisely defined and apparent boundaries than others) which may be relevant to the voter's choice: they are contexts into which voters are put (or put themselves, when they choose where to live) and within which social and other processes may prove influential in their decision-making. But for what reasons? And are those reasons scale-specific: do some social processes underpinning voting choice operate at particular spatial scales only? In the remainder of this chapter we look at the main sets of processes that have been identified, and the scales at which they operate. The following chapter then reviews some of the evidence consistent with those arguments before moving on to more detailed evaluations of the processes involved.

---

[3] For an early work on regions as areas with common political trajectories, see Pelling (1967).

Bringing Context In

People, according to the argument being developed here, are influenced by mechanisms operating in at least some of their spatial contexts when they make voting decisions. But how do those influences operate? A number of separate—though sometimes linked—processes have been suggested. Some, as Burbank (1995) classifies them, involve interpersonal interaction and influence, whereas others involve 'perceptual influence in which people learn from their own observations' (p. 169). Books and Prysby (1991), for example, identified four different ways in which local context is linked to voting choice: observation of local conditions, contact with neighbours and others in local social networks, information flows through local media, and the mobilization and campaigning strategies of political parties and other interested actors. The processes by which each of these operates differ, but all carry the same message—how we think politically, and how we vote, can be influenced by our local context, by the material circumstances we observe there, and by the people, organizations, and institutions with whom we interact.

Not all processes—whether based in a neighbourhood or some other locale—influence behaviour in the same way. For example, Jencks and Mayer (1990; see also Duncan and Raudenbush, 2001) identified five ways in which contextual effects might operate:

1. epidemics, whereby the influences of peers are spread through the milieux;
2. collective socialization, in which neighbourhood role models are important to residents' socialization;
3. institutional effects, such as the role of interaction within neighbourhood forums (e.g. schools);
4. competition models, in which residents compete for scarce resources;
5. relative deprivation models, in which individuals evaluate their positions relative to their perceived interpretations of their neighbours' positions.

The first three of these should produce contextual-enhancement effects, whereby particular behaviour patterns in a neighbourhood are promoted; the fourth and, in some cases, the fifth may have the opposite effect, with some residents actively opposing the pervasive influences. For the present discussion, we identify three separate sets of processes.

Social Interaction and the Neighbourhood Effect

The 'neighbourhood effect' is a commonly employed phrase covering processes that involve social interaction, usually (but not necessarily) in locales—the immediate environs of the individual voter's home; it is occasionally extended to cover other settings for interaction, such as workplaces. The processes underlying its operation involve interpersonal interaction—in effect, 'conversion by conversation' so that, as Miller (1977, 65) put it, 'people who talk together vote together'.

The origins of the neighbourhood-effect model lie in the work of two political scientists—a Swede and an American. Tingsten (1937), for example, found that working-class support for the Swedish socialist party increased the more working class the precinct in which the class members lived. Key (1949) mapped voting for candidates in non-partisan elections across the southern states of the USA (such as intra-party primary contests), showing that many individuals gained much greater support in areas close to their home than elsewhere in the relevant constituency. This has been termed a 'friends-and-neighbours effect', on the assumption that at least some people vote for local candidates on the basis of local knowledge, perhaps acquaintanceship. A considerable volume of American work building on this foundation was brought to geographers' attention through essays by Kevin Cox (1969a, 1969b) and David Reynolds (1969a, 1969b), in which they presented a theoretical basis for the role of social contexts in the creation of neighbourhood effects.

Cox's (1969a) model of the voting decision utilized the concept of a social network, comprising individuals (nodes on the network) among whom there is informal and/or formal contact. The links between the nodes act as channels along which politically relevant information flows, so that the stronger the links between two individuals, the more substantial the flow of information is likely to be. If individuals' political views are influenced by such information, then the nature of the material flowing into a node should have an impact on voting decisions. Individuals can play three roles in the network: as information receivers, as information processors, and as information senders. Some receive more information than others, depending on the extent of their networks and the strength of their links; some process information more than others—they evaluate its meaning with reference to decisions yet to be made, such as how to vote at an upcoming election; and some send out more information (processed or not) than others. As a consequence, some members of a network may be more influential than others, in both the transmission and modification of information.

The importance of information flows through networks is that they may carry clues regarding political action that will help people make up their minds about political issues, including how to vote. The more information that flows through a network, the more clues people receive and the greater the probability that their voting decisions will reflect that input. Much information received may be redundant because it repeats material already taken into account. Some of it may be new, however. It may reinforce information already held and processed, leading to a hardening of positions and voting preferences; or it may counter what the individual already believes, stimulating a reconsideration of her/his position on issues or candidates and even resulting in a change of voting intention.

Different members of one's social network may have more impact than others. Granovetter (1973), for example, suggested that weak ties, involving links between casual acquaintances, may convey more influential information than stronger ones, involving close friends. The latter are usually very similar to each other in their backgrounds, attitudes, and political orientations—hence their close links—and so contacts among such people are likely to mutually reinforce their positions. Contacts with more casual acquaintances, on the other hand, may expose people to different views and lead them to reconsider their own views. Huckfeldt and Sprague (1995, 188) summarized Granovetter's argument as:

> So long as all ties are strong ties, society will be highly segmented into families, cliques and friendship groups characterized by introverted information patterns. The strength of weak ties is that they further the diffusion process by tying these groups together... weak ties might be influential in creating a political community—in creating a political opinion that is genuinely more than the aggregation of opinions held among component individuals and socially cohesive sub-units.

This suggests a two-step process of information flow and attitude conversion. The weak ties bring new information into a cohesive (perhaps locally concentrated) network and may then be effectively distributed through that network, especially if the 'entry-point' is one of the network's 'opinion leaders'. It was because of this, they claim (p. 288), that 'casual acquaintances are no less influential than intimates'.

Social networks as the channels for distributing politically charged information will stimulate neighbourhood effects—people in a particular area voting in the same way—if those networks are spatially biased. For the effect to be produced there has to be a geographical distance bias to the networks: people who live close together are more likely to be members of the same social network than those who live further apart. Many social networks are indeed to some extent spatially biased, with individuals having some, if not all, of their close friends and casual acquaintances living nearby. However, as Przeworski (1974), Weatherford (1982), and others have argued, such local networks are almost never closed systems—the individual members have contacts outside the neighbourhood area, however it is defined—and interaction within an area is rarely random: people are more likely to interact with those having similar attitudes to themselves, for example. Studying neighbourhood effects thus involves recognizing that most local networks comprise individuals who also have friends and acquaintances living outside their immediate locales and home areas. These 'distant links' can introduce information to a local area from other locales, which in turn is then diffused through that part of the network that is relatively spatially compressed. Each network is interacting with many others, and the flow of information within a neighbourhood is thus always likely to be subject to outside as well as internal influences.[4]

---

[4] As long ago as the 1960s, Webber (1964) identified the existence of 'communities without propinquity' as communications media made contact with (relatively) distant others much easier and removed the tight constraints of distance on interaction that had characterized earlier eras.

Many people who live in relatively close proximity in a neighbourhood are likely to come from similar backgrounds and, accordingly, have similar political stances. Because of the sorting processes that produce separate types of residential area within the mosaic of most towns and cities, similar people tend to live together and so vote together, a process that may then be accentuated because people choose to interact with those similar to themselves (Sprague, 1982). But such segregation is rarely complete—save in extreme circumstances, as with *apartheid* and other discriminatory practices—so that all neighbourhoods have a degree of social mix, and not all people with similar social backgrounds and characteristics share the same political views. This social mix is crucial to the neighbourhood effect as conceptualized by Cox and others. Most neighbourhoods are dominated by people of similar socio-economic and demographic backgrounds who share political attitudes. Their contacts with others like themselves largely reinforce their own views, producing neighbourhood solidarity in political attitudes that is reflected in common voting choices. Those in a minority within a neighbourhood and its local social networks may find themselves exposed to views different from those usually associated with their positions in society (the compositional effects discussed above), especially if they are members of social networks dominated by people of the majority persuasion locally. As a consequence, the information and political cues they receive may convince them to vote with the majority, perhaps changing their previous choice. They are thus converted by the predominant set of political attitudes in their neighbourhood. However, members of the majority group are much less likely to be influenced by the relatively small amount of information disseminated by members of the minority to move in the latter direction.

The neighbourhood effect thus involves members of the local majority having their views reinforced and strengthening their commitment to the party most associated with their compositional position within society, whereas members of minority groups living there may be convinced by arguments that they should switch their allegiance to the party supported by the majority. Socio-spatial polarization of the electorate is the expected outcome: in any neighbourhood with active local social networks, support for the majority's preferred party should be greater than predicted from knowledge of the area's socio-economic composition alone.

Not everybody participates to the same extent in local social networks, of course, so the flow of information within a neighbourhood may not accurately reflect its social composition. If the flow is biased towards certain opinions and preferences, that will be reflected in the neighbourhood-effect

Nevertheless, despite the technologies that have evolved since his essay predicting the 'death of community'—and Putnam's (2000) later analyses suggesting that this has come about in the USA—local interaction continues to be a substantial element in many people's daily lives.

outcome. Similarly, some people are more resistant to persuasion than others, and few choose their friends and acquaintances at random from among their neighbours: many select people like themselves, even if they are in the minority locally, and so partially insulate themselves from aspects of the variety of information circulating locally. The neighbourhood effect will almost certainly not generate a total polarization of voting behaviour, therefore, whereby everybody living in an area, whatever their background, eventually votes for the same party.

Furthermore, people move between neighbourhoods, with some being 'incomers' the majority might try to convert; a major change in a neighbourhood's composition may ultimately mean that the majority is now in the minority and the processes are reversed! Some in-movers may differ from the majority of their new neighbours in compositional terms, but that may be why they moved there: they aspire to be among such people, and part of their assumption of that identity is the decision to vote with the majority. For them, the neighbourhood does not influence their partisan choice, but their partisan choice (among other things) influences where they choose to live. Few have complete freedom over where to live (indeed some, such as those reliant on locally provided state housing, have virtually no choice at all), but self-selection can produce the equivalent of a neighbourhood effect (or contribute to it) independent of the processes discussed here (Cox, 1970b).[5]

Finally, as already noted, relatively few people live out their lives in spatially circumscribed local neighbourhoods only. Most have social networks that extend beyond such confines—involving kin and acquaintances among whom there may be flows of politically relevant information, even though direct (especially face-to-face) contacts may be less frequent than those with their neighbours. Furthermore, many are members of not one but a number of separate networks with virtually no overlap, such as home, locale, and workplace. They may also be members of formal organizations that circulate politically relevant information and in some cases mobilize support for particular candidates and parties. As nodes within local social networks, such individuals act as inter-network intermediaries, importing information and cues from outside their local area, and in turn sending information out onto other networks. This interpellation of networks further influences the operation of the neighbourhood effect (as discussed in Savage, 1997).

The concept of the neighbourhood effect was being developed by British analysts of voting behaviour at the same time that Cox and others were developing their arguments in American electoral geography. In their pioneering

---

[5] This is the endogeneity problem widely discussed by econometricians and others seeking to identify causal influences for contexts: for a review of that literature see Duncan, Magnuson, and Ludwig (2004).

major study of the British electorate, Butler and Stokes (1969) included sections in their chapter entitled 'Variations of alignment' (i.e. deviations from the 'national pattern') on 'National uniformity and regional variations' and 'The influence of a local political environment'. On the former, they suggested that 'once a partisan tendency becomes dominant in a local area processes of opinion formation will draw additional support to the party that is dominant' (p. 182), an argument that was sustained by their analyses of more local-scale variations at the constituency level (see below, p. 73). Although they treat these as deviants from the norm, rather than—as Agnew (1990) has argued—the norm from which general (national) patterns might be built, nevertheless they provide strong evidence that, in the British context, in some cases similar people living in different places tend to vote differently—place matters.

This work was taken up by Miller (1977, 1978), who argued that neighbourhood effects (he termed them 'environmental effects') are 'simply a special case of the general effect of social contact' (Miller, 1977, 48). Developing arguments from American political scientists (Berelson, Lazarsfeld, and McPhee, 1954), he argued that 'contact is a condition for consensus' which, save for the operation of mitigating pressures, means that 'contact produces consensus'. Contact theory works as follows (Miller, 1977, 48):

social contacts are structured by family, choice of friends, social characteristics and locality. If party appeals to group interest or group attitudes evoke any differential political responses, the patterns of contact between individuals will tend to increase the political consensus within high-contact groups.

He identified six types of effect:

1. individual-level social effects, resulting from appeals to different interest groups (i.e. compositional effects);
2. socially structured effects, produced by contacts within and between groups which amplify the individual effects;
3. area-wide deviations from general patterns stimulated by appeals from parties to voters in particular places (these are discussed in more detail below);
4. environmental social effects stimulated through social contacts that are areally structured;
5. inter-generational effects, resulting from contacts within families;
6. individual persistence created by self-selected contacts (such as friends).

Only the fourth necessarily involves a neighbourhood effect (i.e. it is generated through contacts within local areas) but other forms of contact (types 2, 5, and 6 in his list) may also involve locally structured contacts and generate neighbourhood-like patterns of voting.

These arguments were subjected to a scathing critique by Dunleavy (1979, 413):

Theoretically, inter-personal influence models have never explained which causal mechanisms affect political alignment, given that voting by secret ballot is hardly in the public realm (unlike other aspects of lifestyle), and that political alignment is not apparently involved in any extensive way in the social life of the locality (unlike the workplace). Empirically, these models have never been effectively connected with any evidence of the extensive community social interaction that is essential if they are to have plausibility. We cannot simply assume that political alignment brushes off on people by rubbing shoulders in the street, as exponents of 'contagion models' invariably seem to imply. The status of such explanations, then, is highly suspect, since effects on political alignment which are interpretable in a large number of different ways are ascribed to particular causal mechanisms which are themselves unsatisfactory theoretically and unproven empirically.

In response, Harrop (1980, 389) stressed Butler and Stokes's empirical evidence that 'manual workers in the most solidly working-class constituencies are almost half as likely again to identify with the Labour party as manual workers in the most middle-class constituencies', claiming that 'it is surely undeniable that a social influence model of some kind is needed to explain' this. Dunleavy (1980) disagreed, although his cause was partially countered by an earlier micro-study of three streets in Manchester: Fitton (1973, 471) concluded from his study of social networks that 'in so far as change took place it was predominantly in the direction of the street sub-group to which the individual changer was attached'. Not all took part in local networks, and not all were open to persuasion—but of those who did and were, some shifted to go along with the majority view. (Fitton's work is discussed in more detail in Chapter 4; see also Eagles, 1990; Eagles and Erfle, 1988.)

Others offered similar arguments to Dunleavy's, however. Prescott (1972, 87), for example, claimed that:

My own experience in talking to individuals about the way they voted in particular elections, is that many did not know exactly why they voted as they did. Certainly in rationalizing their decision, no one ever explained their votes in terms of the flow of information or the political complexion of the area in which they live.

This view largely prevailed—if for no other reason than, as discussed in the next chapter, there was no substantial empirical evidence with which to sustain the neighbourhood-effect hypothesis, and few more detailed surveys to complement Fitton's. Nevertheless, other empirical studies strongly suggested that 'the neighbourhood effect will not go away' (Johnston, 1983a) and the 'contagion-through-contact' hypothesis continued to attract attention. Andersen and Heath (2002), for example, presented the case for the role of contextual effects—described by Huckfeldt and Sprague (1995, 11) as 'any effect on individual behavior that arises due to social interaction within an environment'—and deployed Miller's argument regarding its operation (Andersen and Heath, 2002, 126):

If Mr *A* and Mr *B* have similar social characteristics but Mr *A* lives in an area where the middle class forms twice as large a fraction of the local population as in the area where Mr *B* lives, then Mr *A* is likely to have more middle-class contacts than Mr *B* even if he is unlikely to have twice as many. Thus Mr *A*'s contact group will be biased towards the middle class compared with Mr *B*'s contact group. (Miller, 1978, 265)

As a consequence Mr *A* will be much more likely than Mr *B* to vote Conservative.

The result of contact-inspired voting decisions would—as Cox (1969b) also argued—generate patterns of voting consistent with the neighbourhood effect, which might be differential across space according to variations in the extent and nature of social contact:

we would expect to find tendencies towards class voting to be reinforced among voters who regularly associate with others from the same social class. On the other hand, we would expect to find the tendency towards class voting to be undermined among voters who frequently interact with people from other social classes since the interaction will tend to move them towards agreement with the other social classes. Simply put, the more that people interact with members of other social classes, the weaker we expect class voting to be. (Andersen and Heath, 2002, 126)

One potential reason why these effects vary from area to area might be the relative strength of local social interaction, so it could be that:

The influence of contextual social class will differ in the case of middle-class and working-class individuals. It is plausible that locally based communities may be strongest for the working class. Professional and managerial careers typically involve greater geographical mobility and lead to the development of looser-knit and geographically wider-ranging social networks than do manual careers. Such looser networks may well be less effective in developing strong community sanctions in favour of a particular party, even if the network is composed of people from the same social class. If working-class people are indeed involved in denser social networks, then this might tend to magnify the role of social environment on their voting behaviour, while the looser networks of the middle class might tend to permit a more individualistic pattern of voting behaviour. (Andersen and Heath, 2002, 126)

The neighbourhood effect could be much more a feature of working-class than middle-class milieux, therefore, creating stronger contextual influences among those living in the former than in the latter. Nevertheless, in noting that people with similar attitudes but different class backgrounds tended to vote according to the latter rather than the former—'members of the salariat [i.e. the professional middle class] who had exactly the same left-wing policy preferences as members of the working class were nevertheless less likely to vote Labour'—Heath, Jowell, and Curtice (2001, 165) suggest that this may be the result of a neighbourhood effect. 'Individuals in the salariat tend to conform to the voting behaviour of those around them' as a result of intra-class social interaction and communication (on which they cite Akerlof, 1997).

Little of the literature on contextual effects pays much attention to the nature of the politically relevant discussion that takes place: it is assumed that it is about which party is best placed to rule the country, who is the best candidate for prime minister, and so forth. Such general discussions undoubtedly take place and can influence voting behaviour. But the discussion may be much more locally specific: which candidate is most likely to represent the interests of local residents well; which party is best able to tackle issues relevant to the local economy or to the state of local public services, and so on. In this way, contextual effects are involved in debates that can be linked to responsive voter models: people respond to local conditions—with their attitudes to those conditions mediated by their local contacts—in making their voting decisions. Indeed, it may well be that this is a major stimulus to neighbourhood effects: rather than responding to cues and debates about relatively 'abstract' aspects of the voting decision, individuals act on the basis of their beliefs, moulded in places, regarding important material features of their everyday lives.

Parties Representing Places

The neighbourhood effect, in its several forms, is a model based on contacts among individuals who are not acting formally as representatives of an interested party. This is a very partial view of political milieux, which contain many other actors working both alone and within collectives. The most important of these, by far, are political parties, which are continually seeking support from members of the electorate by mobilizing such support in the places where they live.

Parties win support through two separate but linked processes. The first operates over the long term, aiming to get individuals to identify with them and provide them with consistent—if not guaranteed—backing at elections. People may provide other resources too, such as money and time to be used in electoral and other campaigns. Parties want people to be politically socialized in such a way that they identify closely with them. This socialization is strongly aided by contact processes, notably in the home for those approaching electoral decision-making for the first time: a party will want young people—through their parents, other kin, and acquaintances (perhaps at school)—to identify it as the one that will best represent their interests. This may be presented as a compositional effect, but will almost certainly be strongly bolstered by local contacts producing contextual effects: people from the working class, for example, may be convinced by their family and neighbours that Labour is the party they should identify with and vote for, because it is most likely to act in their interests, including their local interests. The second process is mobilization, a short-term goal focused on individual electoral contests: the aim is to get people to turn out and vote for the party with which they identify. Again, this could be largely a compositional issue—'We need your vote in order to win power and represent you'—but, as we argue below, much of it is place-based.

Parties in Places I: The Geography of Socialization and Support

Where does a contextual effect appear within these socialization models? For some people, identification with a party might be a relatively abstract issue, as they have no contact with the party other than voting for it; they decide at some stage in their life that it is the best one for them to support, and do so thereafter. (Franklin (2004) suggests that individuals' decisions on whether to vote at the first two or three elections after they are enfranchised may well become the basis of their habitual behaviour—'the past leaves a "footprint" in subsequent elections' (p. 43).) Others may need to be persuaded (and re-persuaded), and so need to be provided with evidence regarding the party's goals and commitment. This calls in many cases for party–voter contact, so party representatives have to be visible in the area and actively involved in its social networks. Party members are needed to mobilize support, to win their neighbours' commitment to their cause in the long term, and to convince them of the value of voting for it in the short term. Thus the more activists a party has in an area, relative to its opponents, the better able it should be to win commitment and support and create strong electoral foundations there (as argued in Seyd and Whiteley, 1992, and Whiteley, Seyd, and Richardson, 1994).

Place-based activity and commitment can create party strongholds at a variety of scales, and also the corollary—party deserts, where the lack of a viable organization sustained by activists means it has little or no support in an area. An excellent example of the former is provided by Wales, which Cox (1970a) divided into two parts:

- *Traditional Wales*—rural areas with strong Welsh-language and non-conformist religious roots and a tradition of opposition to English, Anglican landlords;
- *Modern Wales*—the coalfield and industrial areas which had been extensively Anglicized and incorporated into the British class system.

In the former, radical politics were largely expressed through the Liberal party, which had long represented 'Welsh' interests there (as exemplified by the politics of David Lloyd George); in the latter, the radical concerns of the working class were mobilized, as they were in most other parts of Great Britain, by the Labour party. One part of Wales thus became part of a national voting pattern (exhibiting the class cleavage mobilized by the Conservative and Labour parties), whereas the other retained its particular expression of the local (class and religious) cleavage, mobilized by the Conservative and Liberal parties.

Agnew has also shown how regional variations in support for political parties emerge from spatially varying geographies of political socialization and mobilization. An essay on the geography of Scottish nationalism, for example (Agnew, 1987), showed how spatial variations in both local conditions and external economic relationships created the situations that particular political parties could capitalize upon—such as the Crofter's Party in the late nineteenth century and the Scottish National Party (SNP) in the 1960s and 1970s. This meant that 'a number of distinctive sets of places in Scotland' (p. 141) provided the settings within which local concerns were the catalysts for particular party developments, whereas elsewhere—notably in the Strathclyde region—class-based politics prevailed and the Labour party prospered accordingly. These geographies are illustrated by vignettes of several places, such as Peterhead, a fishing town where economic change created the conditions mobilized by the SNP in 1974. Similar vignettes of American places provided comparable evidence that 'place survives in the United States both in providing the fundamental setting for political behavior and in the form of distinctive political expression' (Agnew, 1987, 189).

Whereas Cox's work on Wales showed the impact of a strong party presence locally, Waller's (1983) on the Dukeries coalfield in north Nottinghamshire illustrated the creation of a 'party desert', where one party was notable by its absence. The Dukeries coalfield was opened up in the 1920s in a rich agricultural area dominated by the large estates of a few titled landowners—hence its name. The companies that managed the mines employed different methods to those in adjacent fields—notably South Yorkshire—where there were large cohesive workforces with very strong union representation. The Dukeries face-workers were split up into small independent gangs ('butties'), which competed with each other: the more coal that each small group dug out, the more it was paid—in contrast to the situation in other coalfields, where a standard wage was paid across the entire workforce. The Dukeries miners were more individualistic than their contemporaries elsewhere as a consequence of the local pay structure, and less likely to support militant unions fighting for collective agreements and rights. The relative weakness of the unions was apparent in the lack of support given to both the miners' and the general strike in the mid-1920s: Dukeries miners were less inclined to strike for benefits for other miners than their colleagues elsewhere. This pattern of attitudes continued not only until the coalfields were nationalized in the 1940s but for another 40 years beyond: Dukeries miners did not strike during the 1984–5 dispute between the National Union of Mineworkers (NUM) and the then National Coal Board. The continuation of work there (led by a breakaway union from the NUM), in one of the country's most productive fields, was an important element in the defeat of the strike nationally, since coal supplies to the power stations were sustained (Johnston and Griffiths, 1991; see also Martin, Sunley, and Wills, 1993).

The nature of the working environment in the Dukeries and the relative weakness of trades unions there meant that the Labour party had a poor base on which to mobilize votes locally—as shown by its performance during the

1930s and 1940s at both general and local government elections there. This weak electoral base was exacerbated by other factors. Most of the miners lived in relatively well-appointed but isolated pit villages, where access to housing was governed by the coal companies: those who were dismissed lost not only their jobs but also their homes. Loyalty to the company was thus considerable. Other controls—over who could operate shops, for example—further ensured worker loyalty. Most importantly of all, the coal companies (and thus their aristocratic owners) forbade the formation of Labour party branches in the villages. The party of the working class thus had no access to its potential members, and so Labour continued to perform relatively badly there—even in the 1960s and 1970s. (In 1970, for example, Labour won Newark with a margin of only 2.4 percentage points over the Conservatives.) Prevented from establishing a strong local organization, the Dukeries was for some 50 years a virtual 'Labour party desert' (Jones, Johnston, and Pattie, 1992).

Differential patterns of party support reflecting the geography of party organization can be found at spatial scales smaller than that of a whole region, as in Wales, or an entire coalfield, as in the Dukeries. Some places become associated with a particular political party because of the intensity of its activists' work on the party's behalf. For example, when members of the Labour party followed the example of the 'Gang of Four' leaders and split off to form the Social Democratic Party (SDP) in the early 1980s (Crewe and King, 1995), larger proportions did so in some places than others. Where those individuals remained active they were able to establish electoral bases in local government—as in Colchester—which formed the foundations for later success in general elections in the 1990s, after the SDP had merged with the Liberals to form the Liberal Democrat party (see Russell and Fieldhouse, 2005). The Liberals were also able to build local bases of support as a result of by-election successes, even in areas where they had little history of strength but benefited from protest votes against an unpopular incumbent government. In the Isle of Ely, for example, the Liberal party had not fought the 1970 general election, but won a by-election there in 1973: the newly elected MP, Clement Freud, retained the seat at the next four general elections, but lost it in 1987 to the Conservatives. (On by-elections generally, see Cook and Ramsden, 1997; Norris, 1990.) More generally, Upton's (1991) analyses suggest that where by-elections involve a change of party holding the seat, the by-election result is four times as important as the result of the previous general election in predicting the result at the next general election, whereas in those with no change of incumbency, the two variables are of equal importance (holding constant national average changes between the two elections across all constituencies).

Parties in Places II: The Geography of Sectional Interests

Although the presence of activists may be a necessary condition for mobilizing support for a party in an area—over and above any compositional effects operating at a national scale—it may be far from sufficient. As well as knowing about the party, many voters may want evidence that it will promote their particular interests—either clearly stated indications that it will fight for certain causes or past-performance records that it has done so. In other words, a party will probably perform better in an area if it is attuned to the majority of its residents' most important and immediate concerns and can validly claim that it has succeeded in promoting their causes.

Evidence of links between parties' claims and the nature of the electorate within which they make them goes well back into the nineteenth century, with the clear electoral division of the country into those parts favouring free trade, where the Liberal party dominated, and those favouring protection— where the Conservative party promoted their interests. (For a discussion of these and other variations, see the concluding chapter in Pelling, 1967.) That urban–rural cleavage lingered long after the formative issue retreated from the public consciousness, although the party promoting each side changed: from the mid-twentieth century on, Labour became the party of the indus-trial regions and the large cities while the Conservatives promoted country-side interests—along with those of suburban dwellers. To some extent, this policy was akin to that of pork-barrelling in the USA, whereby parties and their representatives seek continued support from their constituents by promoting legislation that will favour them. This is less likely to happen at a local scale in the UK, where parties are much more centralized, but there are clear examples of its occurrence, as when Labour promised to build the Humber Bridge in order to win a crucial by-election in Hull in 1966—and, having won, did so. At the 2001 general election, voters in Kidderminster ousted their incumbent MP (himself a Labour health minister), replacing him by an independent whose main campaign pledge was to fight to retain a range of services in the town's local hospital.

Although parties dominate British general elections, and most voters make their decision on which candidate to vote for in their home constituency based on which party they prefer to form the next government, that decision can nevertheless be influenced by the parties' activities, and especially their candidates' activities, in their constituency. One of the strongest arguments made for retaining the first-past-the-post electoral system in the UK is the clear link between MPs and their constituencies: while acting as a trustee for the constituency electorate in Parliament on issues of national concern, the MP also acts as a representative for individuals and groups on issues concerning them and the constituency more generally. Thus 'constituency service' is a major activity undertaken by all MPs, though more so by some than others (Cain, Ferejohn, and Fiorina, 1987; Wood and Norton, 1992). That service may be rewarded at subsequent elections (as illustrated above by the Isle of Ely by-election).

There is evidence that many new MPs get a bonus when they first stand for re-election, suggesting that the local electorate is rewarding them for their service, especially those who spend considerable time in their constituencies promoting their own and their party's chances in the run-up to an election (Johnston et al., 2002b). Butler and Kavanagh (1988, 266) suggested that at the 1987 general election the personal vote for Conservative MPs elected for the first time in 1983 averaged some 2 per cent of their total; Curtice and Steed (1980) found the same effect for Labour MPs standing in the 1979 election who had first won their seats in 1974. But this is not a permanent effect, it seems: in 1983, Curtice and Steed (1984, 346) found that, on average, candidates for the SDP who had previously been Labour MPs for the same constituencies gained an increase in the vote share for the Alliance that was 8.2 percentage points higher than the national increase; four years later, however, those personal votes 'proved to be an ephemeral asset' (Curtice and Steed, 1988, 335), with only one of the 'defectors' bucking the tide by securing an increase in his vote share compared to 1983. The general pattern continued, especially for the Liberal Democrats, for whom constituency success at a general election is frequently built on winning in the relevant local authorities and is followed by much 'constituency service': at the 2001 general election, 'the Liberal Democrat vote fell on average by 4.9 per cent in those seats where the incumbent Liberal Democrat MP was not defending the seat . . . [but] the party's vote rose on average by 6.3 per cent in those seats which the party captured for the first time in 1997 and where the incumbent MP was restanding' (Curtice and Steed, 2002, 319).[6]

This promotion of sectional interests links more to the model of the responsive voter rather than the sociological models identified in Chapter 1. Responsive voter models involve individuals reacting to their perceptions of the incumbent government's performance, especially with regard to economic policy. Their perceptions of its potential performance, based on its past record and compared to that of its rivals, over the next parliamentary term may strongly influence their voting decision. In general, it is argued, people will vote for the return of a government that has overseen relative prosperity—both for the country as a whole and/or for their own household financial situation.

Why should economic voting be geographically based? In all but the very smallest advanced capitalist societies, economic prosperity is rarely evenly distributed across the national territory: there is a geography of uneven development. In times of relative hardship, some areas suffer more than others, reflecting the distribution of industries and other activities suffering most from the economic conditions. (In the run-up to the 2004 US presidential election, for example, much attention was given to the decline in the number of jobs in manufacturing industry, and in a series of weekly articles

---

[6] In some cases, incumbent MPs may be rewarded or punished by the electorate on the basis of their performance on certain issues: see Pattie et al. (1994), also Cowley (2002, 2005) and Cowley and Stuart (2005).

on the 'swing states', *The Economist* identified the number of jobs lost in each.) Periods of growth, too, almost invariably see rising prosperity concentrated in some areas relative to others. Even if all areas are growing, some grow faster than others, generating spatial variation at a variety of scales in how people feel about the economy and their own financial situations. Voters living in areas of relative prosperity and growth should be more likely to feel that the incumbent government is performing well, and deserves re-election, than those living in areas experiencing relative poverty and decline. These patterns of uneven development, comprising areas of relative prosperity alongside those of relative poverty, are generally long lived: in the UK, for example, analyses of unemployment trends (Pattie and Johnston, 1990) suggest that regions that become depressed first when a downturn commences are also the last to emerge from it.

If the geography of uneven development is a stimulus for differential voting patterns, these could well be accentuated if governing parties claim responsibility for prosperity and their opponents allocate blame to them for decline. Such claims may be both sectional and localized. If a government argues that it has been promoting the interests of sections of society that are concentrated in certain places—the fishing industry, for example—it may well get support there as a consequence. Such claims will be localized in their impact; they may also be localized in their making—a party that claims to promote the fishing industry may not do so widely, if only to avoid alienating other sectional interests that may feel support for that industry is at the expense of their own.

Although economic issues—national, local, and personal—dominate the application of most responsive voter models, and much election campaigning ('It's the economy, stupid!'), others may affect some groups of voters, in some places, at some times. As illustrated above by the election of the Kidderminster MP (at the 2001 UK general election) committed to a single issue only (retaining services at a local hospital), public service provision and performance is a major concern of many voters (Johnston and Pattie, 2001a), and it is possible to mobilize that concern in particular places because of perceived policy failings (or even successes!) there. But pork-barrel politics, whereby candidates (especially incumbents seeking re-election) promote their cause on the basis of what they have done, or will do, for the constituency, are not as developed in the UK as in some countries because of the centralized nature of British parties and Parliament. Particular issues, such as the closure of a local school or hospital, might be of sufficient concern to some people to influence how they vote, but it is rare for enough people to make their decision on such a local basis for it to influence the electoral outcome in their constituency.

Parties Seeking Electoral Success

Finally, local variations in voting patterns may emerge because of differential patterns of campaigning by parties and other interest groups. Outside countries where there is compulsory voting, one of the major tasks for political parties at election time is to mobilize support and ensure that voters—especially those who support them (or those that the parties believe will do so)—either turn out and vote on election day or, if it is feasible, apply for a postal or proxy ballot.

In some electoral systems, it is in a party's interest to mobilize voters throughout the relevant territory, but in most—certainly in the UK—it is more important to ensure higher turnout of one's potential supporters in some places than others. The British electoral system is based on single-member constituency contests: the UK is divided into separate constituencies (646 in 2005), each returning one MP to the House of Commons. The candidate/party with the most votes in each constituency is the winner there, even if he/she gets less than a majority of all of the votes cast, let alone of all the potential votes (given that some voters abstain, an increasing problem discussed in Chapter 7). In such a system there is less pressure on parties to mobilize support to the same extent in every constituency—especially if they lack the necessary resources (of money and workers) to mount a full campaign everywhere. It is logical for them to focus on those constituencies where they have the greatest chance of either winning or not losing, and use the techniques best able to produce the desired outcome (Green and Gerber, 2004).

Each party has a differential appeal across the electorate, with certain groups more likely than others to provide it with support: a party that appeals to workers in manufacturing industries will have a larger potential base in some towns than others, for example, and certainly more than in the countryside. In some constituencies, its potential supporters will form a large majority of the electorate; it should be able to count on victory there without a great deal of activity aimed at winning over voters and making sure that they turn out on election day. In other constituencies, however, its potential supporters, according to the social composition of the local electorate, might be so small relative to the total that the party has no chance of victory. And then there is a third category of constituencies, where the situation is such that (at least) two parties believe that they have a chance of victory. They should focus their efforts on mounting election campaigns that will both win over the floating voter and ensure that the committed supporter does not abstain, perhaps backing these short-term campaigns with strategies aimed at building substantial local organizations that can mobilize the electorate, which might include winning power in local government in order to illustrate their ability to govern.

There should be a geography of campaigning and canvassing in the British electoral scene, therefore, with parties varying in the extent to which they try to win in the various constituencies. (Cox (1969a) called this aspect of the geography of voting the 'forced-field' effect.) Party vote-seeking is thus another likely component of the contextual model, with activity focused on particular places on a particular scale—the constituency, although there may be a geography to intra-constituency activity as well—with parties concentrating efforts on those areas within the territory where voters are most likely to favour them.

All such vote-seeking requires resources with which to conduct campaigns—both human resources (particularly party members who are prepared to work voluntarily to advance the cause by, for example, distributing literature and canvassing voters on their doorsteps and/or by telephone) and financial resources (to pay for advertising and the other costs of a campaign). Both sets of resources are usually in short supply, relative to what a party might like in order to run a viable campaign. And so they have to be rationed spatially, allocated to those places—both constituencies and areas within constituencies—where the potential returns in terms of votes and seats won are likely to be greatest. To the extent that campaigns are efficacious—and there is strong evidence to this effect (Denver and Hands, 1997b; Denver, Hands, and McAllister, 2004)—then the geography of campaigning will be reflected in the geography of election outcomes.

Conclusions

Like all other forms of behaviour, decision-making about voting is a learned activity. Most of that learning occurs in places, at various scales. In some of them, its location may be largely immaterial to the decision-making—as with watching a television party political broadcast. But in most, the nature of the place is very important, since the learning involves interaction with others who are there. In some situations, that interaction is directly related to the behaviour, as with discussions within a family regarding the relative merits of different candidates at an upcoming election. In others, it is indirect: learning about one's position in society and how to promote interests associated with that position may involve long-term processes of observation and discussion, perhaps occasionally punctuated by important local events that have a significant influence on positions and attitudes.

Those place-bound learning processes take place in a range of different contexts and through a variety of mechanisms at a number of spatial scales. They come together as voting patterns: differences in the nature and degree of support for different political parties and campaigns across places that cannot be reduced to the characteristics of the individuals alone. Political attitudes and their consequences, political behaviour, reflect the contexts within which they are learned. In the next chapter, we review work on voting in the UK that illustrates the resulting geographies of voting, before turning to more detailed analyses of the major social processes involved in their production.

3

The Geography of Voting: Regions, Places, and Neighbourhoods

The previous chapter outlined a number of reasons why there should be a geography of voting patterns in the United Kingdom—over and above those that simply reflect compositional effects. Integral to those compositional effects, we argued, are contextual effects which result from three sets of processes: people interacting with others in social networks, people interacting with their material environments, and political parties interacting with people. All of those interactions are locationally specific: they take place in places. The result should be a geography of voting that reflects spatial variations in the nature and intensity of the interactions. In this chapter, we review the empirical evidence currently available that is consistent with that expected geography, before turning in the next four chapters to detailed explorations of the processes involved.

Given that, as shown in Chapter 1, some social groups (especially the so-called middle class) have been more inclined to support the Conservatives than any other party over more than a century, whereas others (notably the so-called working class) have been more likely to give their support to Labour, a geography of party support is certain, since those two social groups are not evenly distributed across the country. If that were the only reason for a geography of voting there would be little to analyse. The arguments discussed in Chapter 2 suggested very strongly that it is not the only reason, however: there are a number of processes operating at a variety of spatial scales and modifying the map of party support that would emerge if no contextual effects were present—perhaps substantially so. Some places may be more pro-Conservative than expected according to their social composition, for example, and some less so. The task for geographical analysts of voting patterns is to uncover those modifications and suggest why they have occurred.

The Problem of Data

Data availability is a major difficulty facing analysts of the geography of British voting behaviour at anything smaller than the constituency scale.

The UK, much more than many other countries, suffers from a relative paucity of material with which to analyse spatial variations in party support. This partly reflects late-nineteenth-century changes in the electoral system, which were designed to ensure the secrecy of the ballot and make it impossible to identify how a particular individual had voted. (Interestingly, this condition of secrecy does not extend to whether or not individuals did vote at an election: records of turnout—though not of which party voted for—are available for public scrutiny for a year after any general election.) No general election voting data are released for areas smaller than individual constituencies, for example, (of which there were 646 at the 2005 general election), and this is the only scale at which voting patterns can be analysed using officially produced data.

Until the 1970s there was a further constraint on analysing these data. To examine whether patterns of voting across constituencies are consistent with hypotheses regarding support for the various parties from different sections within society, it is necessary to know not only how many votes were cast for each party in each constituency but also the social composition of its population. Data on the socio-economic and demographic composition of different areas within the country are collected in the national censuses—held decennially in every year ending in 1 since 1801 (i.e. 1801, 1811, 1821, etc.) except in 1941 because of the war, and with an additional (sample) census in 1966. Until 1971 these data were not collated by parliamentary constituency, however, so it was not possible to relate voting patterns to socio-economic data in the only set of areas for which the former were available.[1] Because census data were available for local government areas, within which most constituencies were nested,[2] pseudo-constituencies could be created (Miller, Raab, and Britto, 1974) and analysed (Miller, 1977, 1978), although some of them (notably in the largest cities) involved combining several parliamentary constituencies to create large (almost certainly heterogeneous) units with 200,000 or more voters, with consequent loss of detail in major centres of population.

The only alternative data on voting patterns are obtained by polling. Ever since opinion polls were started in the UK by the British Institute of Public Opinion (an arm of the Gallup organization) in 1937 (Moon, 1999), data have been available for national samples of the population which allow conclusions to be drawn about sources of support for political parties. (At one of the first general elections for which such surveys were conducted—in

---

[1] Socio-economic data were collated by wards, and in most cases (certainly after 1944) very few wards were divided between constituencies, but without computers the task of aggregating these data to the constituency scale would have been very time consuming, and was not done.

[2] The Boundary Commissions, which are responsible for defining constituencies, are required—as far as practicable—not to split local government areas (counties and county districts) between constituencies, and not to have constituencies that cross their boundaries. On their success at meeting this guideline, see Rossiter, Johnston, and Pattie (1999a).

1945—Gallup predicted a Labour victory, which was disbelieved by the pundits and other commentators!) These surveys have rarely allowed analyses of geographical variations, however, because the samples were too small to enable fine-grained spatial analyses to be carried out, even at the constituency scale.

The middle decades of the twentieth century saw a number of major American voting studies based on surveys conducted in particular places (as in the classic works by Berelson, Lazarsfeld, and McPhee, 1954; Campbell et al., 1960; Katz and Lazarsfeld, 1955). Only a small number of similar surveys was conducted in the UK, however, reflecting the small social science community then and the absence of resources to fund such large-scale research endeavours. One of the few undertaken, based on an American exemplar (Lazarsfeld, Berelson, and Gaudet, 1944), involved a sample of 1022 randomly elected voters in the Greenwich constituency in 1949–50, from which 914 individuals were surveyed, most of them at least twice and about half of them on three occasions. The full results of this survey were presented in Benney, Gray, and Pear (1956). They included a chapter entitled 'The social geography of voting', which was very much a misnomer, since its content was all about the sociology of voting, with no reference at all to geography—that is, to variations in voting behaviour within the Greenwich constituency. Indeed, their only discussion of contextual effects related to intra-household voting patterns: they argued that women, especially married women, were much more socially isolated than men because few of them worked (in 1950, remember) and were much less likely than men to go to other locales—notably pubs—where political issues were discussed. Thus 'women talk politics less often than men and when they do, it is mainly with their families. The most usual partners in male political discussion were workmates, and they reported talking with friends as often as with family members' (pp. 108–9).

A second survey, also based at the London School of Economics, covered two constituencies—Greenwich and Hertford. Its main focus was on social stratification, but information was collected on voting at both the 1945 and 1950 general elections. Similar surveys were also conducted in a small number of other places—two in Bristol (Milne and Mackenzie, 1954, 1958) and one each in Glossop (Birch, 1959) and Newcastle-under-Lyme (Bealey, Blondel, and McCann, 1965). There was also the special study of Sheffield by Hampton (1970). But the limited resources available did not allow any wider study of the electorate.

To the extent that they investigated spatial variations in voting patterns, these studies produced results entirely consistent with the neighbourhood effect and other hypotheses. For example, using the Greenwich survey data, Benney and Geiss (1950) showed high levels of homogeneity within households: around 70 per cent of respondents said that all members of their household were likely to vote the same way in 1950. Similarly, when asked about the voting propensities of both their three best friends and their three closest co-workers, the respondents were more likely to vote for the same party as their closest friend and co-worker when both of those two agreed: if both voted Conservative, 82 per cent of the respondents also intended to, whereas if only the friend voted Conservative, the figure fell to 68 per cent. Extending this, when comparing voting in both Greenwich (which returned a Labour MP in 1950) and Hertford (which returned a Conservative), Martin (1952) found that members of each socio-economic class were more likely to vote Labour in the former than in the latter, clearly suggestive of a neighbourhood effect at the constituency scale. Similarly, Bealey, Blondel, and McCann (1965) found that Conservative voting was higher in all classes in middle-class wards than in working-class wards, and also that people who voted Conservative were more likely to identify themselves as members of the working rather than the middle class if they lived in predominantly working-class wards than if they lived in middle-class areas. They were unable to uncover any clear processes linking the observed 'influence of the environment on voting behaviour' (p. 185), but suggested that there was more pressure to conform politically in wards that were dominated by a single class than in those with a greater social mix.

In two studies of the Bristol Northeast constituency, Milne and Mackenzie found evidence of contextual effects involving 'friends and neighbours', although these were not geographically located. At the 1950 general election, for example, they found that 'personal contacts, especially family ones, were ... an important factor in helping floaters [i.e. those who were undecided before the campaign started] to make their final decision' (Milne and Mackenzie, 1954, 124). At the 1955 contest, they found that where respondents' families' political preferences differed from those of the respondents' friends, the respondents were more likely to be unstable in their voting behaviour (i.e. made their decisions late). There were also differences between the two types of contact in the nature of their influence: 'The elector's family exerted its influence mainly in the weeks just before the election, while the influence of friends and workmates made itself felt over a longer period' (Milne and Mackenzie, 1958, 92), and within families they noted that 'a particularly high proportion of Labour waverers were wives who had been re-converted by their husbands' (p. 162).

A wider range of sampling areas was used in a later study by Jessop (1974), designed to test the hypothesis of deferential voting, which he defines as a 'non-class-conscious' vote in which an individual's choice reflects deference to a local social and political elite. Five constituencies were selected: an established working-class urban community, a mixed residential area, a solidly middle-class suburb, a rural agricultural area, and a north-eastern mining constituency (the first three were all in north-east London). Two main types of deference were identified: ascriptive (i.e. to the 'high-born or wealthy': p. 34) and meritocratic (i.e. to those who earn respect), with

12 per cent of the respondents being clearly ascriptive in their responses. Among the middle class, 68 per cent of those who were ascriptive voted Conservative in 1966, compared to 32 per cent of those who were merito-cratic (the Labour party won the election); among the working class, 40 per cent of those displaying ascriptive deference voted Conservative, as against just 16 per cent of the meritocratic. Those who were ascriptive were concen-trated into certain of the constituencies—the middle class, the mixed, and the rural—and were also more likely to have traditional attitudes, especially in the rural areas: 52 per cent of the rural constituency middle-class respondents were traditionalists, for example (compared to 41, 36, 32, and 30 in the other four constituencies), as were 45 per cent of the working class (the others had 34, 27, 25, and 21 per cent). Traditional ascriptive-deferential non-Labour voters were thus most likely to be found in the rural area, where working-class Conservatism was most likely to be found (an argument extended by Newby, 1977).

A slightly different study was the first in Britain to investigate the impact of the parties' campaigning strategies on turnout and the electoral outcome in a single constituency—Baron's Court, in the London Borough of Hammer-smith, at the 1964 general election. Two North American political scientists (Holt and Turner, 1968) studied many aspects of the campaign, including the extent and efficiency of each party's canvassing (identifying individuals who were likely to support them) and then its effectiveness at translating those 'pledges of support' into actual votes by mobilizing its declared supporters on election day. They found that Labour—who won the seat—had more pledges than the Conservatives but had to undertake more effort to ensure that their supporters turned out on election day. Working-class voters (i.e. the core of Labour's support) were less likely to turn out 'without prodding' than were middle-class voters, and were also more likely to vote after the working day had ended, so much of Labour's task was concentrated in the last hour. (Since then, however, the time when the polling stations close has been extended from 6 p.m. to 10 p.m.) Each party was most effective at turning out pledged supporters in those parts of the constituency where it was strongest and had concentrated its campaigning: Labour turned out 85 per cent of its pledges in the strong Labour areas, for example, against 79 per cent in the strong Tory areas; the Conservatives successfully translated 85 per cent of their pledges into votes in the strong Tory areas but only 69 per cent in the strong Labour areas (p. 235).

Although such localized surveys allowed the testing of hypotheses regard-ing voting behaviour in particular places (a recent detailed example is Cutts, 2006a), they provided a weak foundation for more general statements about the British electorate. It was another decade before this became possible. In the USA, major academic surveys of the electorate after each national election began in 1948, using nationally taken samples, providing material for detailed statements about electoral behaviour there, although with little attention to geographical variations. This approach was introduced to the UK in the 1960s by David Butler and Donald Stokes, a British and an American political scientist, respectively (the latter closely associated with the earlier US developments). They undertook three surveys in the first phase of their work, in 1963 and then after the 1964 and 1966 general elections; each involved questionnaires administered to just over 2000 individuals selected according to a geographically stratified, clustered random-sampling procedure.

The pioneering work of Butler and Stokes was followed by the establishment of the British Election Study (BES), funded by the Social Science Research Council and its successor. Run by a series of teams based successively at the University of Essex, the University of Oxford, and then again at Essex, its major component has been a large post-election survey of several thousand electors designed to test hypotheses regarding the sources of party support. These surveys became the mainstay of British election studies over the last third of the twentieth century and their data have been the major source of our understanding of voting patterns there—including the geography of voting. BES data have been used in most of the research reported here.

Whereas constituency-level data provide a relatively coarse-grained picture of geographical variations in voting patterns, individual-level survey data can result in the exact opposite—too fine-grained an approach. Surveys such as the BES focus almost exclusively on individual voters and do not place them in their spatial contexts. From the beginning of those surveys, information on the respondents' home constituencies and regions have been added to the data, from which some conclusions could be drawn regarding variations at those scales, but only relatively recently have more data been added to the survey files to allow analyses at a range of finer-grained spatial scales. The main available sources of data—constituency election results alongside census data and national representative surveys with few respondents in any one place—have therefore considerably restricted studies on the geography of voting in the UK and hence tests of the arguments outlined in the previous chapter. Nevertheless, in the absence of anything better, these have provided most of the available insights into the interaction of the compositional and contextual models, as identified below.

The Aggregate Pattern: Variations by Constituency

One of the earliest uses of constituency data to explore voting patterns in Britain was Cox's analysis of London's 69 constituencies (1968, 1969c) at the 1950 and 1951 general elections (the 69 were those contained within the area served by the Metropolitan Police). He hypothesized that the Conservative party should get its strongest support in suburban areas, where there should also be higher turnout. Support for the Conservatives should be greater than anticipated there on the basis of socio-economic characteristics of the population alone because 'the suburban context exercises a conversion effect' (Cox, 1969c, 350)—voters who move there are more likely to vote Conservative than similar people living in the city centre, either through contacts with their neighbours or because those who are more pro-Conservative in their attitudes are more likely to move to the suburbs.[3] London's suburbs, he suggested, would comprise milieux in which pro-Conservative neighbourhood effects dominated.

To test these hypotheses, Cox assembled 20 variables from the 1951 census data for each of the constituencies,[4] to which he added the distance from the centre of each constituency to London's central business district. These variables were reduced, using principal components factor analysis, to four composite factors:

1. This placed the constituencies on a scale reflecting their residents' 'social rank', as indicated by their occupations, social class, and educational attainment.
2. This arranged constituencies on a city–suburban dimension, with high-density areas having large percentages of households in shared accommodation at one extreme, and low-density, rapidly growing constituencies on London's edge at the other.
3. This scaled constituencies according to their ratio of out- to in-commuters—another dimension of suburbanization.
4. This contrasted constituencies according to their age structure.

Analyses showed that Conservative support increased not only with a constituency's social rank and age structure (areas with older people and with more white-collar residents had more Conservative voters) but also with its location: suburban areas were more pro-Conservative than their inner-city counterparts, even with variations in social rank and the other factors held constant. Turnout was also higher in suburban areas and those with large numbers of out-commuters. Overall, Cox (1969c, 368) concluded that 'suburbanism exercises effects on both party preference and participation independent of other social contexts'. More recently, Walks (2005) has shown similar pro-Conservative voting patterns in suburbia across the whole of Great Britain over the period from 1950 to 2001 (paralleling similar findings in Canada: Walks, 2004a, 2004b).

Although indicative of neighbourhood and other effects, Cox's analyses were no more than that—as he himself recognized. Noting that they were 'based on aggregate data . . . whereas most previous work [in the USA] has been based on sample survey data for individuals', he accepted that, as a

---

[3] A later (American) study tested this migration hypothesis directly (Cox, 1970b).
[4] This was feasible because each constituency comprised a number of wards within a single metropolitan borough.

consequence, 'there are a great many intervening variables that have been omitted owing to lack of data: although one can see that suburbanism affects party preference independent of other contextual factors, one is still left in a quandary as to how this effect occurs' (Cox, 1969c, 364). (Walks, 2005, did find a 'suburban effect' when analysing BES data for the 2001 election.) Cox's work is therefore typical of a whole genre that potentially commits the 'ecological fallacy'—of making conclusions about individual behaviour from data referring only to population aggregates. (Just because areas with more old people have more Conservative voters doesn't necessarily mean that old people are more likely to vote Conservative—though it may do; on attempts to circumvent this problem, see King, 1997.) Nevertheless, in the absence of other data it at least gives supporting circumstantial evidence that apparently similar people vote differently in different types of area.

Earlier work (Roberts and Rumage, 1965) used data for 157 separate towns in the UK to examine spatial variations in support for Labour at the 1951 general election. This found that, among other relationships, such support varied negatively with the sex ratio: the more males in a constituency, the higher the Labour vote. It also varied positively with the proportion of the workforce employed in 'manufacture, mining and agriculture' (p. 176): the more people employed in those occupations, the greater the Labour vote. Their final model included seven statistically significant variables. It substantially under-predicted the Labour vote in towns in South Wales and, to a lesser extent, most of the other coalfields, however, but over-predicted it in the Lancashire cotton textile region and in most of the south coast resorts. This suggested that factors peculiar to those groups of places influenced voting patterns as well as the generic patterns linked to each constituency's socio-demographic structure. Both compositional and contextual processes appeared to be in operation.

Once census data became available for all parliamentary constituencies it was possible to extend Cox's approach, as illustrated by Barnett (1973) and Rasmussen (1973). It was relatively easy to correlate voting patterns with a range of variables taken from the census with little underlying theory to aid either the selection of data or the interpretation of the results. Thus the outcome may be little more than statements of general relationships—people in rural areas were more likely to vote Conservative; residents of mining constituencies were more likely to vote Labour—without any appreciation of whether the extent of the differences between constituencies reflected anything more than differences in their social composition. And some of the relationships were difficult to relate to any underlying theory—either compositional or contextual—save in the most indirect way: Rasmussen (1973), for example, reported positive relationships between the size of the Labour vote in urban constituencies and the percentage of households with exclusive use of both a WC and a bath!

More sophisticated analyses are feasible with such data. Crewe, for example, tested hypotheses associated with the 'affluent worker' or embourgeoisement thesis (Goldthorpe et al., 1968), that members of the working class employed in 'boom' industries (such as car manufacture in the 1960s and 1970s), and thereby relatively affluent (with higher rates of home- and car-ownership than typical of the class as a whole), would be more likely to support the Conservatives than their working-class counterparts in other industries. To do this, Crewe (1973) identified three separate groups of constituencies: with concentrations of affluent workers (living in owner-occupied—almost certainly mortgaged—homes), traditional workers, and affluent tenants, respectively. He found that, as expected, those in the first and third groups not only had higher percentages of Conservative voters than predicted from an analysis of all constituencies combined using class composition as the independent variables, but also that they had experienced greater swings towards the Conservatives over recent elections than had been the case elsewhere. This clearly suggested that affluent workers (especially those who were buying their homes) were less likely than other members of the working class to vote Labour, but provided no evidence whether their concentration in particular constituencies exaggerated this trend, thereby giving direct support for the contextual-effects argument. Johnston's (1981b) analysis of the 1974 election result—using the technique developed by Crewe and Payne (1976, see below)—similarly found that more-affluent workers (as indexed by their car-ownership levels) were much more likely to vote Conservative than were less-affluent workers, thus again validating the embourgeoisement thesis within the limits allowed by aggregate data.

Detailed analysis of constituency-level results using census data alongside the voting returns has characterized a series of reports since the 1970s by Curtice and Steed in the Nuffield election study volumes. Spatial analysis was also a feature of their work on trends over the period 1955–79, which focused on changes by region and constituency type (Curtice and Steed, 1982). Aggregating constituencies into two types—by region and an urban–rural scale—they showed that a 'pattern of change that started shortly after 1955 has proved remarkably consistent, with the North and urban areas moving cumulatively towards Labour and the South and rural areas cumulatively towards the Conservatives' (p. 258). Several arguments were assembled to account for this opening-up of north–south and urban–rural divides:

- changes in the class composition of the different areas as a consequence of economic shifts;
- selective migration, particularly of those with pro-Conservative leanings, to areas in the south and to the less urban constituencies (see below);
- the differential behaviour of voters in the same social group according to where they live;
- spatial variations in the local strength of the political parties, and hence their ability to mobilize support.

The relative strength of these potential influences was not assessed, however.

More sophisticated statistical analysis of constituency results and associated census data—following Cox's example[5]—was a major advance in British electoral study in the 1970s, underpinned by theoretical arguments regarding the likely cause of observed variations. A study by Crewe and Payne (1971) characterized this approach. They regressed Labour voting at the 1970 general election against three measures taken from the 1966 census constituency tables: the percentage of manual workers in the constituency, the percentage employed in agriculture, and the percentage of the workforce classified as professional or managerial. They argued that if class is the major determinant of British voting behaviour, then these variables should be very good predictors of the pattern of Labour support—and found that they accounted for 74 per cent of the variation. If there were constituencies where the Labour vote was substantially either under- or over-estimated, however, this would indicate areas where the class thesis broke down, to some extent at least. This was certainly the case in several constituencies: in Rhondda, for example, Labour gained 32.9 more percentage points of the votes cast than the national trend suggested, whereas in Cornwall North it won 35.3 percentage points less.

Focusing on the two sets of 50 constituencies where the Labour vote was most under- or over-estimated, Crewe and Payne found that they fell into several clear groups. The constituencies where Labour performed much better than expected included mining areas in South Wales, Scotland, and South Yorkshire; mining and heavy manufacturing areas in the north-east of England; London's East End (especially the dockland areas); and very homogeneous working-class constituencies, including many with very large percentages of households in local-authority-rented homes. Those where Labour performed less well than expected included many agricultural areas (where it has long been argued that members of the working class are more likely to vote Conservative than their urban working-class counterparts, because of their deferential attitudes to landowners and farmers with whom they are in daily contact: Jessop, 1974; Newby, 1977), as well as a block of constituencies in the West Midlands (some of which Labour lost in racist campaigns: Deakin, 1965; Foot, 1969), plus constituencies with higher than average proportions of Commonwealth immigrants, members of the armed forces, and electors aged over 65. Labour also performed relatively poorly in seats where either the Liberals or the Scottish/Welsh nationalists pushed its candidate into third place.

---

[5] Cox's pioneering work was not referred to by most of the political scientists involved, however—even though other chapters in the book that included two essays by Cox were referred to by Miller (1977) and Clive Payne graduated as a geographer before undertaking graduate work in statistics. Butler and Stokes (1969) did refer to Cox (1969a), however.

The implications of Crewe and Payne's findings, and those of most of the other analyses of aggregate data at the constituency scale, were that although compositional accounts received strong support—a constituency's social structure provided a good predictor of its voting pattern—there was considerable residual variation that could not be accounted for. Particular types of places had either larger or smaller proportions of their electors voting for one of the two major parties than their social structure suggested, providing strong circumstantial evidence that similar people voted differently in different places.

Combining Constituency and Survey Data

Use of constituency (or aggregate, or ecological) data alone in analyses of election results can, at best, only provide circumstantial evidence of why people voted the way that they did. They can do little more than suggest whether hypotheses regarding contextual effects are valid. Further evidence calls for a focus on individual voters, placed in their local contexts, and this requires the use of individual survey data to which other data—on constituency characteristics, for example—can be linked.

Such a strategy characterized part of the pioneering work on British electoral behaviour—Butler and Stokes's first British Election Studies conducted with reference to the elections in 1964, 1966, and 1970 (with retrospective data on the 1960 election as well). In their first book—published prior to the 1970 election—they noted that 'the tendency of local areas to become homogeneous in their political opinions has attracted the attention of many observers and been described in many ways' (Butler and Stokes, 1969, 182). They provided evidence for this by contrasting two stereotypical community types—mining settlements and seaside resorts. Their sampled respondents living in those two types differed very significantly: in the mining areas, for example, only 14 per cent identified with the middle class, compared with 43 per cent in the resorts. Furthermore, in the mining seats, of those who identified with the middle class 64 per cent voted Conservative, whereas in the resorts 93 per cent of those who identified with that class voted for the Conservatives; and among those identifying with the working class, only 48 per cent in the resorts voted Labour, compared to fully 91 per cent in the mining communities. Being a (self-ascribed) member of a particular social class apparently meant different things, in terms of which party to support, in different places.

In a further analysis, Butler and Stokes amalgamated data from 120,000 interviews conducted by National Opinion Polls in 184 constituencies over the period 1963–6. These gave an average of some 600 responses per constituency and allowed them to calculate the proportion of members of each class who would have voted for the relevant party (Conservatives for the middle class, Labour for the working class) if an election had been held at the time of the interview. These proportions were plotted against the proportion of the constituency population that was working class or middle class, respectively. This showed very clearly that the larger the constituency proportion that was middle class (working class), the larger the proportion of the members of that class there who voted Conservative (Labour). Having observed these relationships, Butler and Stokes (1969, 184) noted that:

Several processes could have helped to exaggerate a partisan tendency...Some writers have argued that a local electorate will perceive and conform to local political norms. Others have suggested that this tendency reflects the pervasive influence of informal contacts on the shop floor, in the public house and other face to face groups in the elector's world. These processes will draw those who hold a minority opinion towards the view that is dominant in their local milieu, exaggerating the strength of a leading party and altering the pattern of party support by class.

They also noted that other influences—such as membership of a trades union—could be as important as class itself.

Elsewhere in the book (though combined with the above material in the second edition: Butler and Stokes, 1974), they looked at patterns of change in voting between elections and their links to the local milieux. This began with the observation that there tended to be a very uniform pattern of swing between elections across all constituencies: if the overall pattern between two elections was for Labour's percentage of the vote won by the two main parties to increase by two points (e.g. from 49 to 51), for example, whereas the Conservative share fell by the same amount, this shift—a swing of two percentage points—tended to be the same everywhere. However, if the Conservatives lost one in ten of their votes overall, and this was the same everywhere, it would not produce a uniform swing: a loss of 10 per cent where they won 75 per cent at the first election would produce a drop of 7.5 points (from 75 to 67.5), whereas in a constituency where they won only 25 per cent at the first contest it would fall by only 2.5 points (from 25 to 22.5). If there were a uniform swing, they would have lost less than one in ten in the first constituency and more in the other (this was first noted by Berrington, 1965).

What brings this about? According to Butler and Stokes, in a constituency where the Conservatives have 75 per cent of the votes, there is much more pressure in the local milieu for electors to remain with the majority view than there is in one where they have only 25 per cent. (This, of course, is the classic neighbourhood effect based on interaction in local social networks, as discussed in Chapter 2.) In seats with a large Conservative majority, therefore, local pressures are likely to see less movement away from the party than in those where the party is much weaker. Labour is likely to pick up more votes from the Conservatives where it is strong and less where the Conservatives are strong. The pressures work in different directions in different constituencies, with the overall result being the uniformity of swing: thus, 'when such influences are summed . . . [they are likely] . . . to have benefited the dominant party in a more homogeneous area' (Butler and Stokes, 1974, 144). They go on to observe, 'the voter's social ambience need not of course lie in his constituency', so that some people—especially those who work outside their local area—may be more open to influence from their immediate milieux than others. To test for this, they looked at different voters according to whether they were nationally or locally oriented in their major sources of information.

Electors differ in their sources of information about politics. Most people feel they get their information mainly from television and the national press and are therefore primarily exposed to political stimuli that are broadly similar in all parts of the country. But some apparently get their information mainly from personal conversation and are therefore exposed to political stimuli that depend more on their local social milieu. Some, of course, receive their information in both of these ways. (Butler and Stokes, 1974, 147)

And their findings were consistent with this argument: 'In both the strong Labour and strong Conservative areas we find a tendency towards even greater solidarity with the local majority' (pp. 147–8). People who talk about politics locally tend to move with the local pattern of opinion; those who interact with politics through national media tend to move with the national trends.

Ecological Estimates of Individual Behaviour

Following Butler and Stokes's lead in combining survey and constituency data, Crewe and Payne's (1976) re-analysis of the 1970 general election result expanded their original model (Crewe and Payne, 1971). They incorporated two further variables to represent whether the constituency was an agricultural or a mining area, plus a number of others relating to the 1966 result there (basically how easily it was won by one of the two main parties). The new model accounted for almost 90 per cent of the variation in Labour voting. As well as variables representing the constituency's social composition (percentages of manual, agricultural, and mining workers), and the strength of both the major and minor parties at the 1966 contest, they also included interaction variables, looking at the impact of the percentage of manual workers in different types of seat according to the 1966 outcome. The latter identified a 'possibility that when Labour voters are in a small minority they are *less* loyal than Conservatives in the same situation' (Crewe and Payne, 1976, 67; their emphasis). Crewe and Payne also identified the main residuals—the constituencies in which their estimates of the Labour vote were substantially different from the actual outcome. Compared to their first model, these were much less extreme—the largest over-estimate was 13.4 percentage points and the largest under-estimate 20.8 points (whereas the largest deviations reported in their 1971 paper—see above—had been 32.9 and 35.3 percentage points.) Incorporating further information about the nature of the constituency and its recent electoral history made estimation of the outcome much more accurate (indicating that whether the constituency was mining or agricultural in nature were important indicators of Labour's performance there).

Crewe and Payne then used the model to estimate the proportion of manual workers who voted Labour in each constituency, grouping them into different types of seat (very safe Labour seats, marginal seats, etc.), and compared their estimates with Butler and Stokes's survey figures for each type, producing very close fits overall. For example, they estimated that 80 per cent of manual workers and 39 per cent of non-manual workers voted Labour in very safe Labour seats (where Labour won over 70 per cent of the votes cast); Butler and Stokes's estimates from survey data gave figures of 82 and 38 per cent, respectively. Table 3.1 shows both their ecological estimates and Butler and Stokes's survey estimates in four types of seat according to the total Labour vote, claiming (in a good example of litotes) that the comparisons are 'encouraging', producing 'tolerably close fits' (p. 77). The agreement is very close indeed, suggesting that sophisticated use of ecological methods could produce very similar results to survey-based studies. Further, these results also indicated clear spatial variations that were very consistent with notions of contextual effects: for example, 'the proportion of manual workers voting Labour rather than Conservative is almost twice as high in "very Labour seats" (80–82 per cent) as in "fairly Conservative seats" (44 per cent)' (p. 79). Their suggested explanation for this was that:

A process of political self-selection may be part of the explanation: strong Labour areas may be politically and socially uncongenial to workers voting Conservative, who therefore leave (or refuse to move in), whereas non-manual Labour voters may be peculiarly prone to find such areas attractive and therefore to stay put (or move in). It is also possible that the occupational composition of both manual workers and non-manual workers in strong Labour areas is skewed towards relatively low-status occupations, thereby producing an unusually high Labour vote. But community influence is probably the strongest factor. In this respect, it is interesting that the

Table 3.1. Ecological and survey estimates of Labour voting by socio-economic class according to Labour's overall percentage of the constituency vote

Labour vote 1970 (%)	Ecological estimates (%)		Survey estimates (%)	
	Manual	Non-manual	Manual	Non-manual
>75	80	39	82	38
55–75	67	33	68	38
45–54	56	29	58	26
25–44	44	24	43	26

Source: Crewe and Payne (1976, 78).

difference between the proportion of manual workers and non-manual workers voting Labour ranged from 41 percentage points in 'very Labour' seats to 20 percentage points in 'fairly Conservative seats'. This can be attributed to the particularly wide variation in the proportion of manual workers voting Labour across different types of constituency—a fact that reinforces our earlier suggestion that the partisanship of manual workers is more open to the influence of the locality than is that of non-manual workers. (Crewe and Payne, 1976, 79–80)

Like others, they suggest that the neighbourhood effect is stronger for working-class than middle-class individuals.

Miller (1977) also combined aggregate and survey data to test his argument regarding neighbourhood effects, but whereas for Crewe and Payne the possibility of a neighbourhood effect was a by-product of their analyses, for Miller it was the central focus. He maintained that such effects are generated by the relative importance of two 'core' class fractions in a constituency—the 'controllers' (managers), who were the Conservative party's strongest supporters, and the 'anti-controllers' (the working class), who were Labour's strongest supporters. The larger the proportion of the electorate in a constituency who were 'controllers' then the larger the number of members of each class who would vote Conservative, according to his argument, whereas the larger the proportion who were 'anti-controllers', the larger the number of members of each class who would vote Labour.

To test whether taking account of the constituency context produced different results, and thereby provided circumstantial evidence of his hypothesized neighbourhood effects, Miller analysed both survey and constituency data for 1966. Using BES survey data, and looking only at those who voted either Labour or Conservative, he found that 73.4 per cent of middle-class members (those in non-manual occupations) voted Conservative, as against 30 per cent of those in manual occupations. Thus in a hypothetical constituency where everybody was in manual occupations, the Conservatives would get 30 per cent of the votes, whereas in another which was entirely middle class in its composition they would get 73.4 per cent. When he used constituency data to regress percentage middle class against percentage of the votes going to the Conservatives, however, he found that in a constituency that was entirely working class the Conservatives would get just 16 per cent of the votes, whereas in one that was entirely middle class it would get over 100 per cent (Miller, 1977, 42). Of course, there are no constituencies with these extreme class compositions: the actual range was from 15 to 55.

Like Butler and Stokes, therefore, Miller found that the more middle class the constituency, the more votes the Conservative party garnered relative to the class composition, implying that members of both classes were more likely to support it in such areas. Figure 3.1 shows the two relationships—that derived by estimating the constituency vote from the survey data and that derived from the constituency-level ecological analysis. The latter slope is much steeper than the former, clearly implying that Conservative support

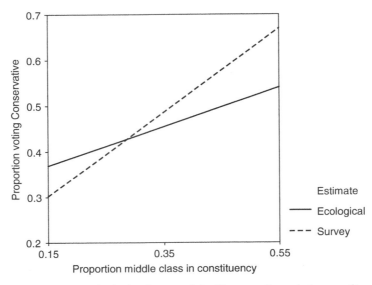

Fig. 3.1. Survey and ecological estimates of the Conservative vote by constituency, 1966, according to the proportion of the constituency who are middle class
Source: Derived from data in Miller (1977).

increased more rapidly than expected, the more middle class the constituency. Indeed Miller (1978, 273) suggested that the contextual element was more important than the individual—with individual class position accounting for some 34 per cent of the variation in Conservative voting and constituency context over 52 per cent. He then estimated the proportion of middle- and working-class voters who supported the Conservative party in 1966 according to the constituency middle-class proportion, indicating that the tendency for both groups to vote Conservative increased the more middle class the constituency (Figure 3.2).

Predicting Local Patterns from Aggregate Data

An alternative approach to those used by Butler and Stokes, Crewe and Payne, and Miller deployed a mathematical procedure to estimate voting by each class in each constituency. If the national pattern of voting by occupational class, according to a survey, applied equally in every constituency, and class was the dominant determinant of voting, it should be possible to predict support for each party in each constituency with considerable accuracy. (This is the same as the hypothetical 'average' constituency deployed in Miller's argument.) Using this procedure in analyses of the 1979, 1983, and 1987 elections, Johnston, Pattie, and Allsopp (1988) found that this was not the

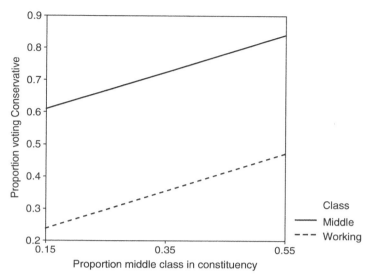

Fig. 3.2. Ecological estimates of the Conservative vote by constituency, 1966, according to the proportion of the constituency who are middle class
Source: Derived form data in Miller (1977, 47).

case, however. Survey data from the 1983 BES showed that the white-collar classes gave most of their support to the Conservatives, whereas the blue-collar classes were more likely either to vote Labour or to abstain (although the skilled manual workers gave almost as many votes to the Conservatives as to Labour at that contest). Deploying census data on the class composition of each constituency, they then used those survey data to predict the pattern of voting in each constituency. Expressing the actual percentage for each party as a percentage of the predicted value produced a great deal of 'error' across the 633 constituencies. For the Conservative party, the actual percentage was between 125 and 150 in 50 constituencies (i.e. the actual Conservative vote was between 25 and 50 per cent larger than predicted), whereas in a further 150 constituencies the actual Conservative vote was only 75–100 per cent of the predicted; it was only 50–75 per cent in another 100, and in a further 50 or so it was less than 50 (i.e. the actual Conservative vote was less than half of the value predicted from knowledge of its class composition). For Labour, the variation was even greater: the actual value was within 25 per cent of the predicted (i.e. between 75 and 125) in only just over 200 of the constituencies.

Knowledge of a constituency's class composition and how members of each class voted nationally according to survey data was thus a poor predictor of the outcome in most constituencies. Indeed, if it were a very good predictor, the Conservative party would have won all but one of the 633 constituencies at the 1983 general election, instead of the 397 it actually won, while Labour would have claimed victory in just one; it actually won 209. If the pattern of voting in each constituency cannot be accurately predicted from its class composition alone—as demonstrated in the 1983 study as well as Miller's earlier work—then clearly the patterns of voting by members of the various classes must have been different across the constituencies. How different? In the early 1980s, a method was developed that provided the maximum-likelihood (i.e. mathematically the best, given the available information) estimates of voting by class in each constituency, given available census data on its class composition, the number of votes for each party there, and survey estimates of the number of votes given by members of each class to each party in the country as a whole.[6]

In their successful analysis of the 1970 results, Crewe and Payne (1976) not only used data on constituency class composition and type but also information on the result of the previous election—on the grounds that relatively few people change their minds between elections, so that performance at one should be a good predictor of performance at the next. Knowledge of the national pattern of the flow of the vote and the result at the first election of a pair should therefore allow the outcome in each constituency at the second election to be predicted. Between 1979 and 1983 the flow of the vote nationally, derived from the 1983 BES, showed that most people remained loyal to the party they had supported in 1979 (Table 3.2), but there was also considerable inter-party shifting, especially from those who voted Liberal in 1979.[7] But was that pattern repeated everywhere? The predicted 1983 results in each constituency using the 1979 result and the flow-of-the-vote matrix produced better outcomes than the exercise using class alone: nevertheless, the wrong

Table 3.2. The inter-election flow of the vote, 1979–83 (percentage of those who voted for a party in 1979)

Vote 1979	Vote 1983				
	Conservative	Labour	Alliance	Nationalist	Did not vote
Conservative	72.6	3.2	9.7	0.4	14.1
Labour	5.1	63.8	17.6	0.4	13.0
Liberal	11.9	8.2	67.1	0.2	12.6
Nationalist	5.4	10.4	25.3	47.2	11.7
Did not vote	15.2	9.2	10.5	0.3	65.1

Source: BES data files (1983); Johnston, Pattie and Allsopp (1988, 116).

[6] The initial papers on this were Johnston and Hay (1982, 1983), and early applications included Johnston (1983b, 1985). Recent work has evaluated the estimates' accuracy (Johnston and Pattie, 2000, 2001d, 2003a, 2003c). Such estimates also compare well with those produced by an alternative method King, 1997 of solving the ecological inference problem (Johnston, Gschwend, and Pattie, 2005).

[7] The Alliance was created in 1981, the Liberal party and the SDP (see p. 57) agreeing to fight the election together and not to put candidates against each other in any constituency.

outcome was predicted in 60 of the 633 constituencies. Again, there must have been differences across the constituencies in the degree to which voters who supported a party at the first election of a pair did so again at the second. The entropy-maximizing procedure was thus used to estimate not only the geography of voting by class but also the geography of the flow of the vote.

This estimation procedure (entropy-maximizing) adapted a method previously used in transportation studies to estimate traffic flows (Johnston and Hay, 1982, 1983). These estimates have been used to show that, for example, differences across constituencies in the performance of the various parties are not consistent with a hypothesis that people in the same class tend to vote the same way everywhere: to get the observed results at every election since 1964 similar people must have voted differently in different places (Johnston, 1983b). Similarly, other studies have shown that applying the national flow-of-the-vote matrix between two elections to the result in every constituency at the first election will not reproduce the result of the second in the pair: similar people changed their minds in different ways in different places (Johnston and Pattie, 1987, 2000; Johnston, Pattie, and Allsopp, 1988).

To exemplify the differences across constituencies in voting by members of a given occupational class as indicated by application of the entropy-maximizing method, we return to the example of the 1983 general election. Among the professional and managerial classes, for example, on average 37 per cent voted for the Conservative party, as against 14 per cent for Labour and 24 per cent for the Alliance; the remaining 26 per cent either abstained or voted for another party. But the percentage of that class voting Conservative varied across the constituencies from 7 to 55 and the inter-quartile range (i.e. containing the central half of the 633 constituencies) was from 30 to 45 per cent, with a median of 40. The variation was even greater in some other cases: among the semi-skilled and unskilled manual classes, for example, the Labour vote ranged from just 3 to 58 per cent, with an inter-quartile range of 15–37 and a median of 27, and abstentions ranged from 21 to 77 per cent. Similarly with variations in the flow of the vote across the constituencies between the 1979 and 1983 elections: of those who voted Conservative in 1979, on average 67 per cent in each constituency did so again in 1983, but the figure varied from 31 to 79. Although the inter-quartile range of 64–71 suggested that in many places the percentage remaining loyal was very similar, there were clearly some places where the Conservatives retained much more support than usual, and others where there was considerable 'leakage'. Much of this was to the newly created Alliance: it averaged just 10 percentage points across all constituencies but varied between 4 and 30 points, with an inter-quartile range of 8.6–10.9 indicating that there was a similar pattern in many places but a considerable number which deviated from that very substantially.

The variations shown here for the 1983 election and the 1979–83 inter-electoral period are typical of those for other elections and periods. They indicate that there was a marked geography to electoral behaviour in Great Britain throughout the post-Second-World-War period. But are those variations consistent with the arguments developed in Chapter 2 regarding the causes of such geographies?

A North–South Divide in Voting Patterns in the 1980s?

The estimates just described have been used to test for the existence of a growing regional divide in Great Britain from the 1970s on (as identified by Curtice and Steed, 1982: see above, p. 71). Entropy-maximizing estimated voting patterns by class and estimated flows of the vote in each constituency were used to demonstrate a widening gap in the geography of voting— basically, a wider north–south divide. Analyses of those estimates not only showed patterns of voting entirely consistent with those identified by Miller (1977) and discussed above (p. 77), but also significant spatial variations over and above those patterns. Members of each class were more likely to vote Labour in northern than southern regions, for example, and in urban and industrial constituencies than in suburban, small-town, and rural areas. With the flow of the vote, Conservative loyalty between elections was greater in the southern than the northern regions, with the reverse for Labour loyalty. And complementing these loyalty patterns, switching from Conservative to Labour was greater in the north than the south, with more people switching in the opposite direction in the southern than the northern regions.

These findings are not only entirely consistent with Miller's arguments and tests of his neighbourhood effect model at the constituency scale, therefore; they are also correlated with the country's changing economic geography. In the areas of relative economic prosperity—the south, where the service sector was booming—the (Conservative) government was apparently being rewarded with a greater proportion of votes from all classes; in the areas of relative depression—the north—it was seemingly being punished for this outcome of its policies by a relative decline in support, again across all classes. Undoubtedly, several processes were interlinked: people were aware of decline in the north simply through observation and media coverage; that issue was discussed within social networks and its political origins determined; and the opposition parties campaigned on the grounds—among others—that the government was not delivering prosperity there and so creating an increasingly divided society (on which see Hudson and Williams, 1989). Between 1979 and 1987 the northern and southern regions grew further apart in their voting behaviour (Johnston and Pattie, 1989c).

Although the evidence for a widening inter-regional gap was very strong (irrespective of the regional classification deployed: Johnston, Pattie, and Russell, 1993; Jones, Gould, and Watt, 1998), this case was challenged by McAllister and Studlar (1992). They did not dispute that regional variations in support for the main parties had increased during the 1979–87 period, but instead argued that rather than interpret this as a 'territorial polarization of voters either for or against particular parties . . . dependent on local material conditions manifesting themselves in differential economic expectations and local political cultures' (p. 169), the growing divide could be 'largely the result of increasing socioeconomic differences between the regions'. In which case, 'regional voting is caused by certain individuals with certain social characteristics being concentrated in certain geographical areas through a combination of vertical and horizontal social mobility; it is not a territorial division, merely a functional division that reflects differing patterns of social composition in the regions' (p. 170).

To sustain their argument, they used survey data from the BES and deployed a wide range of variables representing individual voter characteristics (father's occupation, parents' voting records, and respondent's age, gender, race, educational achievement, occupational class, employment status, family income, housing tenure, trades union membership, identification with the middle class, political attitudes, views of the party leaders, and retrospective economic evaluations) to predict the likelihood of them voting Conservative at the 1979, 1983, and 1987 general elections. They argued that if all these influences are taken into account and regional variations remained significant, this would indicate spatial variations in voting that could not be accounted for without incorporating the regional context. They expected to find no significant regional variations, however, and in general this is what their analyses showed. They claimed to have tested the 'relatively simple proposition that regional deviations are due to clustering of countrywide variations in social structure', concluding that 'we could find little territorial effect per se generated by living in a particular region . . . Only in Wales was there a significant regional vote in all three elections, and in the North of England and Scotland in two of the three' (p. 191).

Given that McAllister and Studlar (1992) divided Great Britain into just six regions (South, London, Midlands, North, Wales, and Scotland) and that their method of analysis involved comparing voting in each of the others with the situation in the South, these findings are perhaps not as bleak for the regional hypothesis as they suggest—especially as the election with no significant differences between the South and the North of England and Scotland was 1979; in other words, there was a significant north–south divide in 1983 and 1987. However, more important in responding to their critique is the argument that many of the variables that they ascribe to individual characteristics are themselves probably contextually stimulated—such as political attitudes, class identification, and economic evaluations: they were probably learned 'in place', as Agnew (1990) argued. By treating the regional division as a residual category, McAllister and Studlar deny the possibility that similar people may be more likely to identify with the middle class in some regions than others and more likely to develop certain political attitudes in some places than others; similarly, respondents' economic perceptions may well reflect their local experience rather than a more abstract 'national economic situation'. As we have argued here, geography is intimately involved in many aspects of the voting decision; it is not just an add-on at the end of an analysis.

The validity of this argument was illustrated in an analysis of regional differences in party support in the first five years of a panel study of a large number of respondents (the British Household Panel Study, considered in more detail below). Holding constant a wide range of variables consistent with those deployed by McAllister and Studlar (age, sex, occupation, housing tenure, employment sector, educational qualifications, personal and household income, trades union membership, attitudes on a range of family, social and political issues, and personal financial situation, both retrospective and prospective), substantial (and statistically significant) inter-regional differences were found in the respondents' propensity to vote for each of the country's three main parties in each year between 1991 and 1995, inclusive. (The question asked was 'If there were a general election today, which party would you vote for?': Johnston and Pattie, 1998b.)

Table 3.3 shows the exponents associated with the differences in the propensity to vote Conservative rather than Labour; the contrast is between each of the named regions and the Outer Southeast (i.e. the Home Counties). Where these are significant, they indicate the probability of an individual in

Table 3.3. The probability of voting Conservative rather than Labour, by region (compared with the Outer Southeast), 1991–5

Region	1991	1992	1993	1994	1995
Inner London	0.39	0.34	0.35	0.31	0.55
Outer London	—	—	—	0.66	—
Southwest	—	—	—	—	0.74
East Anglia	—	—	—	—	—
East Midlands	0.73	0.71	0.59	0.75	—
West Midlands Conurbation	0.60	0.51	0.65	0.66	—
Rest of West Midlands	0.57	0.48	0.53	0.57	0.69
Greater Manchester	0.38	0.32	0.34	0.47	0.48
Merseyside	0.39	0.26	0.38	0.39	0.50
Rest of Northwest	0.70	0.59	0.56	0.69	—
South Yorkshire	0.34	0.30	0.33	0.48	0.45
West Yorkshire	0.31	0.32	0.36	0.39	0.49
Rest of Yorkshire/Humber	—	0.57	0.54	0.61	—
Tyne and Wear	0.35	0.23	0.18	0.19	0.25
Rest of North	0.50	0.34	0.39	0.34	0.43
Industrial South Wales	0.22	0.14	0.19	0.17	0.31
Rural Wales	0.38	0.49	0.29	0.35	0.41
Strathclyde	0.39	0.28	0.34	0.51	0.46
East Central Scotland	0.47	0.21	0.32	0.31	0.42
Rural Scotland	—	0.49	0.58	—	—

Note: Only statistically significant exponents are shown.

the named region voting Conservative rather than Labour. Thus, for example, individuals living in Inner London (holding all individual characteristics constant) were only 0.39 times as likely to vote Conservative in 1991 as their contemporaries in the Outer Southeast. There is a clear north–south divide. All the significant exponents are less than 1.0, indicating a lower propensity to vote Conservative in most regions relative to the situation in the Home Counties. With a few single-year exceptions, voters in every region save four (Outer London, East Anglia, Southwest, and Rural Scotland) were significantly less likely to vote Conservative than those in the Outer Southeast in each of the five years. (In addition, other analyses not recorded here showed that voters in a majority of regions were less likely to vote Liberal Democrat in most northern regions and more likely to vote Labour than they were in the Home Counties comparator.) The regional divide was still marked at the beginning of the 1990s, therefore. But it appeared to be declining in its intensity: in 9 of the 12 regions for which there was a significant exponent in every year, that for 1995 was larger than that for 1991, indicating a smaller difference in the propensity to vote Conservative rather than Labour at the latter date.

Other evidence confirming the existence of a widening north–south divide in the 1980s was provided by Field (1997), and McMahon et al. (1982) suggested that this widening gap may have been produced in part by migration, whereby people moving from northern to southern regions were more likely to change their voting preference from Labour to Conservative than vice versa (on the impact of migration on turnout, see Denver and Halfacree, 1992). Other analysts have also found regional variations in a range of voting-related behaviours using an increasingly sophisticated suite of analytical techniques. Fieldhouse (1995), for example, looked at the geography of political attitudes over the period 1964–87, using BES data; depending on the detail available (there were only five attitudinal variables common for the period 1964–87, but 13 for the shorter period 1974–87), he found separate sets of attitudes related to economic ownership and the role of the state, government spending, racial issues, and law and order. He tested whether individuals varied in their scores on these dimensions according to their occupational class, their region, and their constituency type. There were significant differences among the classes on all the dimensions at all elections, and also significant differences by region and constituency type on most of them at most elections. With regard to region, he found that (holding class constant) the north–south divide became wider over the period (whether 1964–87 or 1974–87), especially on issues relating to economic ownership, the role of the state, and government spending. Members of the various socio-economic classes differed in their attitudes according to their regional location, and these differences increased during the 1980s: as he concludes, 'there was a widening geographical cleavage in attitudes towards economic issues over the period 1964–87' (p. 22).

This work was extended by Russell (1997), using opinion poll data over the 19-month period leading up to the 1992 general election. As expected, he found that middle-class people were more likely to intend voting Conservative than their working-class contemporaries, as were economic optimists rather than pessimists, people living in affluent rather than depressed areas, and people living in southern rather than northern regions. He also found interaction effects among some of the pairs of variables, indicating that, in certain groups, the combination of two or more of the characteristics accentuated the likelihood of voting Conservative (or not). For example, economic optimists were 4.26 times more likely to intend voting Conservatives than were pessimists, and those living in depressed areas only 0.84 times as likely as those in affluent areas. In addition, optimists in depressed areas were 2.86 times more likely to intend voting Conservative than pessimists in affluent areas, but were only 0.67 times as likely as optimists in affluent areas, and 3.42 times more likely than pessimists in depressed areas. Being optimistic or pessimistic influenced vote intention differentially in different areas. Thus Russell concluded that:

the Celtic regions, the north and depressed areas were associated with a reluctance to express support for the Conservative government, while economic optimists were typically pro-Conservative in their reported vote intentions. However, when these factors coincided the most likely outcome was that the regional characteristics would overcome individual economic evaluations in predicting how an individual would behave. (Russell, 1997, 107)

Johnston et al. (2000b) found a similar pattern, suggesting that there were altruistic voters who, whatever their personal situation, were more likely to support the government party if those living around them were prospering than if they were not.

The Closing Divide? 1992 Onwards

The regional variable is thought to play several roles in the voting decision calculus. First, it reflects long-standing variations in political culture, demonstrating the differential success of the various parties at mobilizing local electorates at key periods. These are long-established patterns that should be identified in all analyses since they are parts of a local political culture that are not reducible to other variables. Secondly, there are inter-regional variations which are the summation of smaller-scale differences—between neighbourhoods and places, for example—which should also be identified in any analysis that is unable to investigate those finer-grained differences. Finally, there are variations that reflect inter-regional differences in economic prosperity. These will be widest when those differences are greatest. In the UK, the 1980s was a period of such major inter-regional differences, but from then on they declined somewhat: as a consequence, as suggested above, inter-regional differences in voting patterns should also have been reduced since then.

Curtice and Park (1999, 127) showed that this was indeed so: 'between 1987 and 1997 about a quarter of the gap that opened up over the previous 30 years between the north of England and the south of England was reversed, and over a third of the same gap between the south of England and Scotland'. Economic trends could account for only part of that change, however, and they suggested that Labour's economic strategy aimed at more affluent workers and others in the southern regions was just as important. By 1997, Labour had changed its image in the south—it was as likely to be seen as 'moderate', 'good for all classes', and 'capable of strong government' there as in its traditional heartlands of the north, Scotland, and Wales. Only a decade earlier it had not been viewed favourably in the south. Regional variations remained in whether people voted Labour or Conservative—at a coarse scale only (they divided their sample into just five regions—South of England, Midlands, North of England, Scotland and Wales)—but they were less pronounced in 1997 than in 1987, largely because of the changed perceptions of Labour. Curtice and Park (1999, 145) concluded that:

the main reason why Britain's electoral geography changed in 1997 was because voters' perceptions of the parties had altered. The new pattern did not arise because the motivations that bring voters to the ballot box have changed. The future of Britain's electoral geography would therefore appear to rest in the parties' hands.

Party strategies aimed at particular types of people in particular types of places can change the country's electoral geography if they are successful—and therefore the voting patterns of similar people in different places are different.[8]

Region remains a significant component of British voting patterns, therefore, but not as substantially so as in the 1980s, as shown by analyses of voting and turnout at the 1992, 1997, 2001, and 2005 elections (Johnston, Pattie, and Rossiter, 2005). Variations across constituencies were compared by both region (with Great Britain divided into 11 regions) and constituency type (with constituencies classified into 20 types according to their socio-economic and demographic characteristics). The latter accounted for a much larger proportion of the variation than did regional location. For the three parties the regional effect accounted for 12–16 per cent of the Conservative vote share, 4–6 per cent of Labour's, and 7–10 of the Liberal Democrats', compared to 54–59, 61–67, and 16–33 per cent, respectively for constituency type. The geography of voting at the constituency scale at those four elections was much more a function of the type of place than its regional location.

---

[8] The importance of party strategy is a major theme of a larger study of the 'rise of New Labour'—although regional variations get only a brief mention therein (Heath, Jowell, and Curtice, 2001, 129).

Moving Away from the Two Main Parties

Most of the analyses of the geography of voting at British general elections have focused on the two largest political parties during the second half of the twentieth century—Labour and the Conservatives. This is largely unsurprising, since for a considerable part of that time these two dominated the electoral scene, winning on average 92.2 per cent of the votes at the general elections between 1950 and 1970, and virtually all of the seats (an average of 98.7 per cent). From 1974 onwards, however, there was a substantial revival in support not only for the Liberals—notably in the areas where they had been strong in the 1920s (when the party was in rapid decline), suggesting continuity of support in areas where they had been deeply embedded in the local political ethos (see the maps in McAllister, Fieldhouse, and Russell, 2000, 422)—but also for the Scottish National Party and/or Plaid Cymru. By the 1980s, the Liberals were contesting virtually every constituency—having fielded candidates in only 109 at the party's nadir in 1951—and the other two were doing the same in Scotland and Wales, respectively.

To establish or re-establish itself as an electoral force, a party has to build up sufficient strength in places to be able to win seats, and therefore show that a vote for it is not necessarily 'wasted'. This means that it needs to be visible, and if possible credible. The Liberals did this from the 1970s on by identifying places where they could mobilize support for candidates for local government office through active programmes of community politics; where they were successful in this geographically targeted strategy they then had the foundation on which to build general election campaigns and also to demonstrate their credibility to people in neighbouring authorities. Dorling, Rallings, and Thrasher (1998) showed the effectiveness of this strategy: Liberal (and later Liberal Democrat) support tended to spread out wavelike over successive elections from wards where the party was successful into their neighbours. The outcome of this process—which two sets of authors liken to the spread of a disease (Dorling, Rallings, and Thrasher talk of the epidemiology of the vote and McAllister, Fieldhouse, and Russell, 2000, use the metaphor of yellow fever in their title)—was the creation of what McAllister, Fieldhouse, and Russell call the party's 'emerging heartlands', which were to be found in southwest England and Wessex, in rural Scotland and Wales, and in London's outer suburban ring. In those emerging heartlands, the Liberal Democrats held 55 per cent of the seats on the local government councils in 1997, won 62 per cent of the contested seats between 1994 and 1997, and gained 43 per cent of the votes cast at the 1997 general election: by contrast, the three percentages for the remainder of the country were 18, 17, and 14, respectively.

To illustrate the importance of these locally focused strategies—which were substantially assisted in a few places by by-election successes (the Liberal Democrats won 14 of these between 1983 and 1997)—McAllister,

Fieldhouse, and Russell (2000) developed models of both Liberal Democrat performance (the percentage of the vote gained) and its success (whether or not a seat was won) by constituency in 1997 using aggregate data. They found some support for hypotheses based on arguments that the Liberal Democrats were more successful in mobilizing certain types of voters (those who were older, who had both degrees and cars, and who lived in areas where agriculture was an important industry). In general, the Liberal Democrats had few 'natural supporters' (Fieldhouse and Russell, 2001), however, and their support was greater, and electoral success most likely, in constituencies where the party had a majority on the local council, where it had won a by-election since 1983, and where it campaigned most intensively in 1997. (They were also excellent at defending the seats they had won at previous contests, with their incumbents continually mobilizing support 'back home': Russell and Fieldhouse, 2005.) The importance of the latter variables indicate how crucial local campaigning is to the Liberal Democrats, but this creates a problem for them: in some constituencies the main opposition is the Conservative party whereas in others it is Labour, so that policies and strategies that appeal in one might not in the other, leading Russell, Fieldhouse, and McAllister (2002, 72) to conclude that the Liberal Democrats must 'tailor their electoral strategy according to which party they are competing against'.

The crucial geographical element to the Liberal Democrats' electoral strategy has been emphasized in a number of recent studies. Russell and Fieldhouse (2005), for example, have stressed the importance of grassroots campaigning in the party's post-1970 resurgence, on the belief that 'local credibility begets national credibility' (p. 38) for a party with no experience of government for over half a century. This has involved strong local election and by-election performances as platforms on which to build general election campaigns, especially important since the party had few 'natural supporters' (though see Johnston and Pattie, 1988) and few strong identifiers. More recently, strong performances—both in and out of coalition government—in the Scottish Parliament and Welsh Assembly have been further platforms on which to build credible general election campaigns.

The latter have presented the party with certain difficulties, however, because of its limited resources. Campaigns concentrated on key (i.e. winnable) seats have won parliamentary representation but have left many areas of the country with only a weak foundation on which to build for the future. The party's strategy has to combine focused campaigning for winning seats with more widespread attempts to lay the foundations for further expansion of support; the first can result in an increase in the ratio of seats to votes, but will not provide the basis for increasing that ratio in the future (Fieldhouse and Cutts, 2005). At the same time, particular policy positions might allow the party to win substantial numbers of votes in certain constituencies, thereby broadening the platform. This was the case in 2005, for example, when opposition to the war in Iraq allowed the party to win over some traditional

Labour supporters, including many Muslims (although this was apparently not sufficient to deliver any constituency victories), and the stance against university 'top-up fees' was the basis for several victories in constituencies with large numbers of students and workers in education (Fieldhouse and Cutts, 2005; Russell, 2005).

Russell and Fieldhouse's (2005, 214) conclusion that 'enhanced local campaigning in target seats' has been the successful basis of the Liberal Democrats' strategy to build incrementally from its areas of strength is confirmed by Cutts's analyses at both local government and general elections. In Bath and North-East Somerset in 1999, the Conservative party's performance at the ward level was much more accurately predicted by variables indexing the ward population characteristics than was the Liberal Democrats' (with regression analyses accounting for 71 and 38 per cent of the variation in their vote shares, respectively: Cutts, 2006c). When variables representing the amounts spent by the parties and their targeting strategies were added to the equations, the percentages accounted for changed to 92 and 91, respectively: the Conservatives' performance built on the party's established social base whereas the Liberal Democrats' strongly reflected geographical variations in the intensity of their ward-level campaigning (see also Cutts, 2006a). Similar findings were reported for analyses of the 2001 general election results (Cutts, 2006b): the Liberal Democrat vote share increased significantly against both Conservative and Labour where it campaigned intensively, as indexed by both its targeting strategy and its spending.

Far from being a trivial exercise, the role of the local party in socialising then mobilising the identified Liberal Democrat vote remains a potent weapon in the party's armoury and could have made the crucial difference in close contests. (Cutts, 2006b, in press)

Constituency-specific campaigning makes a greater contribution to Liberal Democrat electoral success than it does for either the Conservatives or Labour.

Moving Down a Scale—or Two

The implication of the work reviewed in the previous sections is that almost all analyses of Britain's electoral geography have—largely because of data constraints—been conducted at either the regional or the constituency scale. Since the average constituency in England has some 70,000 voters (in Scotland and Wales the figure is around 10,000 less), this means that the neighbourhood effect as generally conceived has not been addressed. Analyses have been too coarse-grained to tackle such localized potential contextual effects and their causes, and the reliance on national surveys has not given access to local variations in voting behaviour.

With one exception, this remained the case until the mid-1990s. In an earlier study, however, Harrop, Heath, and Openshaw (1992) analysed variations in voting behaviour at the ward scale using the 1987 BES. Wards are administrative areas into which all local authorities are divided, and for which census data are published. Locating all the BES respondents in their home wards thus allowed a closer approximation of their local (neighbourhood) context than provided by constituency (let alone regional) location. All wards had been classified according to their socio-economic composition, and each BES respondent was placed into one from a ten-group categorization; these groups varied in their support for each of the two main parties by ratios of approximately 3.5:1. In addition, similar types of people voted differently in different ward types. Among homeowners, for example, 70 per cent of the salariat living in 'select suburbs' voted Conservative compared to only 45 per cent of those living in wards identified as 'poor council property with high unemployment'; the respective figures for working-class homeowners were 48 and 25. There were also regional variations: people living in the latter type of wards in southern Britain were more likely to vote Conservative (30 per cent of them) than their counterparts in northern Britain (where only 12 per cent did). Patterns of vote-changing varied too: of those who voted Conservative in 1983 and who lived in a pro-Conservative type of ward, 87 per cent voted Conservative again in 1987, whereas of those who lived in pro-Labour wards only 77 per cent remained loyal to their 1983 choice four years later. (The reverse was true of 1983 Labour voters: 84 per cent of those living in pro-Labour wards voted Labour again in 1987 compared to 76 per cent of pro-Conservative-ward residents.)

Statistical analyses of these data showed substantial inter-ward differences in voting both Conservative and Labour, holding constant individual characteristics such as father's class, respondent's class, housing tenure, income, employment status, union membership, and educational qualifications—and region. Whatever their backgrounds, individual characteristics, and regional location, people were more likely to vote for each party in some types of ward than others. That tendency to vote with the local area was stronger for Labour than for the Conservatives, suggesting—as did Crewe and Payne (1976: see above, p. 76)—that the neighbourhood effect operates more strongly in working-class than in middle-class districts.

Harrop, Heath, and Openshaw (1992) sought reasons for these inter-ward variations by examining five separate potential mechanisms. The first was the 'classic' neighbourhood effect of 'conversion through conversation'. The BES had asked about the people respondents discussed politics with, and they found slight evidence that people who discussed politics together tended to vote in the same way—especially if they were members of the same family and household. In particular, they were more likely to change their party choice between 1983 and 1987 to come into line with their discussants' preferences. This neighbourhood effect remained in place even when father's political preference was taken into account, as an indicator of within-family socialization. There was also slight evidence that part of the observed neighbourhood effect could be accounted for by whether the respondent was canvassed by the party he/she voted for, plus a small amount of evidence that people who moved from pro-Labour to pro-Conservative wards (i.e. the upwardly mobile) switched their vote accordingly. Most of these relationships were weak, but the overall conclusion was that a neighbourhood effect could be found that was independent of the BES respondents' individual characteristics. Indeed, in line with Miller's (1977, 1978) earlier findings, 'neighbourhood proved to be as good a predictor of voting among respondents . . . as individual class or tenure' (Harrop, Heath, and Openshaw, 1992, 118): political talk within the household, but not the neighbourhood, provided a partial (statistical) explanation for this and 'the mobile minority migrate to politically congenial neighbourhoods'. Curtice (1995, 207) reached similar conclusions in a separate analysis of the 1987 BES: 'While political talk may well influence voting behaviour, it does not appear to be a significant mechanism for the existence of the neighbourhood effect.' We return to this in Chapter 4.

Bespoke Neighbourhoods

Despite its success, the experiment of locating BES (and other survey) respondents in their home wards was not repeated for future elections, and further analysis of small-scale spatial variations was not considered again until after the 1997 general election. (Although see Fisher's (2000) innovative use of multi-level modelling of 1983 BES data, which identified no regional north–south divide in voting Conservative once individual-level variables were held constant, but did find evidence of more local, ward-level influences on voting.) Respondents to that survey were located in a series of specifically designed 'bespoke neighbourhoods' for two reasons: first, wards vary considerably in size, from average populations of a little over 1000 in rural areas to nearly 20,000 in some large cities, so that the nature of the local context being identified can vary considerably across the sample; and, secondly, in the absence of any information on the scale of the neighbourhood effect it seemed desirable to look at a range of sizes, uniform across all respondents.

The bespoke neighbourhoods were defined by locating all respondents to the 1997 BES within their home enumeration districts (EDs) —small areas used for census administration, containing on average 450 persons. Neighbourhoods were built on that base by adding further EDs until a threshold population had been reached—with the next nearest ED to the base district being added in turn. In this way bespoke neighbourhoods could be built around each respondent's home with a range of sizes—from the nearest 500 persons to the nearest 10,000. A range of census data was obtained for each respondent's bespoke neighbourhood, which allowed the area's characteristics to be defined, and these were used as contextual variables in analyses of voting at the 1997 election.

In several analyses of these 1997 BES data, the bespoke neighbourhoods were arranged along a 'neighbourhood status' scale, a composite measure reflecting variations in car-ownership, unemployment, homeownership, and household structure. Dividing the neighbourhoods into five equal-size groups allowed the percentage of members of each socio-economic class voting Labour and Conservative in different types of neighbourhood to be calculated (McAllister et al., 2001). Table 3.4 shows the ratio of Labour to Conservative votes in each of three classes (the salariat—professional and managerial workers; routine non-manual—i.e. lower-status white-collar; and working class—semi-skilled and unskilled workers) according to the position of their bespoke neighbourhood on the status scale, using neighbourhoods at six different sizes (the nearest ED to the respondent's home; and the EDs with the nearest 500, 1000, 2500, 5000, and 10,000 people to that point). If Labour and Conservative got the same number of votes, the ratio would be 1.00: a ratio exceeding 1.0 indicates more Labour than Conservative votes, with a ratio below 1.0 showing the converse. Three patterns, from which there are very few exceptions, stand out:

1. In each set of bespoke neighbourhoods, the ratio is higher for the routine non-manual respondents than for the salariat, and higher still for the working class, whatever the status of the bespoke neighbourhood. At the nearest-ED scale, for example, in the highest-status neighbourhoods there were more Conservative than Labour voters in the first two classes (ratios of 0.58 and 0.67, respectively), but more Labour than Conservative voters among the working class (1.74).
2. Within each class, the lower the status of the bespoke neighbourhood, the larger the number of Labour relative to Conservative voters. Among the salariat at the nearest-ED scale, for example, there were more Conservative voters than Labour in the highest-status areas (a ratio of 0.58) but more Labour than Conservative voters in the lowest-status areas (a ratio of 3.67).
3. In general, the difference in the ratios between the lowest- and the highest-status neighbourhoods is greater for the working class than for the salariat. For example, in the bespoke neighbourhoods involving the nearest 10,000 people to each BES respondent's home, the ratio between the Labour:Conservative ratio for the highest- and lowest-status neighbourhoods for the salariat is 5.3 (2.88/0.54), whereas for the working class it is 6.5 (5.67/0.87). The implication is—as suggested by others—that the neighbourhood effect has a greater impact on the working class than on the salariat.

The neighbourhood effect appears to operate to some extent at all the spatial scales. Indeed, its intensity varies differentially for the two 'extreme' classes.

Table 3.4. Labour:Conservative vote ratios by socio-economic class and neighbourhood status, 1997

Neighbourhood status	Nearest ED			Nearest 500			Nearest 1000			Nearest 2500			Nearest 5000			Nearest 10000		
	S	RNM	WC	S	RNM	WC	S	RNM	WC	S	RNM	WC	S	RNM	WC	S	RNM	WC
1 (High)	0.58	0.67	1.74	0.59	0.67	1.60	0.62	0.63	1.23	0.73	0.65	0.80	0.58	0.68	0.80	0.54	0.83	0.97
2	0.74	1.19	1.90	0.74	1.27	1.85	0.77	1.40	2.18	0.55	1.48	3.07	0.76	0.97	3.69	0.66	0.61	2.56
3	1.76	1.50	3.75	1.54	1.57	4.18	1.37	1.57	4.45	1.21	1.30	5.33	1.00	1.15	3.07	1.11	1.07	3.64
4	1.69	1.83	4.55	2.33	1.56	4.27	2.37	2.21	4.73	2.10	1.68	4.64	3.00	2.47	6.50	3.13	2.78	5.67
5 (Low)	3.67	3.00	5.55	3.54	3.00	5.67	2.63	2.53	5.56	3.14	3.21	5.10	3.13	3.36	5.78	2.88	2.87	5.66

Key: S = salariat; RNM = routine non-manual; WC = working class.

With the salariat, for example, the ratio between the Labour:Conservative ratio in the highest- and lowest-status neighbourhoods is 6.3 (3.67/0.58) at the nearest-ED scale, but only 5.3 (2.88/0.54) at that of the nearest 10,000 people; for the working class, the two figures are 3.2 and 6.5, respectively. The implication is that neighbourhood processes have their greatest impact on the salariat at the smaller scales, whereas for the working class their greatest impact is at the largest scale.

Comparing the scales is somewhat difficult, however, because all the areas involved at a smaller scale are part of the larger scales too: to a considerable extent, the neighbourhoods at the nearest-1000-people scale, for example, are comprised of those at the nearest 500. Separating out their various effects is possible, however, by looking at small areas within larger ones, as illustrated by Tables 3.5 and 3.6. Instead of looking at all BES respondents, Table 3.5 includes only the highest- and lowest-status constituencies (i.e. about 100 in each group since the analyses excluded Scotland) and looks at the bespoke neighbourhoods defined as the nearest 5000 and nearest 10,000 people to the respondent's home, respectively. In some cases, the number of respondents is too small to calculate a valid ratio (i.e. there are less than 10 respondents in the routine non-manual class in the lowest-status nearest-5000-people bespoke neighbourhoods within the highest-status constituencies). Because of this, the pattern of ratios is less clear cut than in the analysis of the entire sample in Table 3.4, but the overall trends are clear. Even with the characteristics of the constituency held constant, patterns of voting consistent with

Table 3.5. Labour:Conservative vote ratios by socio-economic class and neighbourhood status, 1997: nested neighbourhoods (nearest 5000 and nearest 10,000)

Neighbourhood status	Nearest 5000			Nearest 10,000		
	S	RNM	WC	S	RNM	WC
Smaller areas within high-status constituencies						
1 (High)	0.53	0.64	0.56	0.55	0.78	0.77
2	0.68	0.90	2.87	0.50	0.62	2.71
3	0.97	0.87	2.25	0.94	0.78	2.65
4	2.00	1.83	6.88	3.54	2.63	5.30
5 (Low)	2.05	—	4.85	2.54	—	6.89
Smaller areas within low-status constituencies						
1 (High)	0.67	1.00	1.55	0.46	1.29	1.22
2	1.00	1.42	6.52	9.95	0.88	2.40
3	1.15	1.15	3.89	1.62	1.17	6.35
4	3.73	3.07	6.29	2.81	2.87	6.56
5 (Low)	3.26	2.92	6.25	2.88	2.72	5.86

— = Number of respondents too small to calculate a valid ratio.
Key: S = salariat; RNM = routine non-manual; WC = working class.

Table 3.6. Labour:Conservative vote ratios by socio-economic class and neighbourhood status, 1997: nested neighbourhoods (nearest 500 and nearest 1000)

	Nearest 500			Nearest 1000		
Neighbourhood status	S	RNM	WC	S	RNM	WC
Smaller areas within high-status nearest 10,000 people bespoke neighbourhoods						
1 (High)	0.56	0.60	1.48	0.59	0.59	1.10
2	0.68	1.22	1.58	0.60	1.16	2.45
3	1.23	0.95	3.62	1.19	1.32	3.56
4	0.73	1.15	3.46	0.83	1.09	3.17
5 (Low)	—	—	5.26	—	—	3.76
Smaller areas within low-status nearest 10,000 people bespoke neighbourhoods						
1 (High)	0.72	0.91	9.50	0.71	0.54	5.02
2	0.92	1.15	2.81	0.88	2.11	3.68
3	2.13	2.50	4.26	2.00	1.65	4.81
4	3.59	1.65	4.19	4.90	2.69	4.43
5 (Low)	3.70	2.94	5.71	2.75	2.50	5.39

—— = Number of respondents too small to calculate a valid ratio.
Key: S = salariat; RNM = routine non-manual; WC = working class.

the neighbourhood effect remain; the lower the status of the neighbourhood, the larger the number of Labour relative to Conservative votes within each social class.

Table 3.6 carries this forward. It takes the bespoke neighbourhoods defined according to the nearest 10,000 people, splits these into five equal-sized groups according to their status, and then looks at just the highest-status and the lowest-status fifths. Again, the trends in the ratios are consistent with the neighbourhood effect: the lower the status of the smaller areas (nearest 500 and 1000 people, respectively) within those bespoke neighbourhood types, the greater the support for Labour relative to the Conservatives, especially among the working class.

In other words, neighbourhood effects appear to operate at a variety of scales nesting within each other. With any social class, the lower the status of the constituency they are living in, the greater the likelihood that respondents vote Labour rather than Conservative. And then, within high-status constituencies, the lower the status of the large bespoke neighbourhoods, the greater the probability of voting Labour. Furthermore, the lower the status of the small bespoke neighbourhoods nested within high-status, large bespoke neighbourhoods, the greater the probability of a Labour vote. Members of the working class, for example, are more likely to vote Labour the lower the status of their constituency; within that constituency, they are even more likely to vote Labour the lower the status of their home area; and within their home area, they are even more likely to vote Labour the lower the status of their immediate locale (i.e. the smallest areas around their homes).

Statistical analyses confirmed these findings, holding constant not only the respondent's class but also father's class, household income, self-assessed class, housing tenure, union membership, and whether he/she lived in an urban or a rural area: the neighbourhood effect operates at a variety of spatial scales (Johnston et al., 2000c).[9]

A further study using these bespoke neighbourhood data for England and Wales in 1997 extended the response to McAllister and Studlar's (1992) critique by incorporating further variables. For example, do people identify with the social class closest to their 'objective' situation (i.e. their occupation) wherever they live, or do they vary according to their local context? The answer was clear-cut: holding constant many individual respondent characteristics, there was a greater probability of a person identifying with the working class the greater the level of socio-economic disadvantage in the neighbourhood he/she lived in. And then, holding constant whether or not they identified with the working class, the greater their neighbourhood's disadvantage, the greater the probability that they would vote Labour and the lower the probability that they would vote Conservative. This is illustrated for stereotypical working- and middle-class respondents defined as follows (Johnston and Pattie, 2005, 194):

The stereotypical middle class individual whose father was in the salariat and voted Conservative, and who themselves are in the salariat, live in owner-occupied homes, are not members of a trades union, have a degree, have household incomes in excess of £41k, and are aged 25–44.

The stereotypical working class individual whose father was in the working class and voted Labour, and who themselves are in the working class, live in social housing, are members of a trades union, have no educational qualifications, have household incomes less than £12k, and are aged 25–44.

The probability of a middle-class individual voting Labour varied from 0.1 if living in the highest-status areas to 0.18 if living in the lowest status. For the stereotypical working-class individual, that range was much greater in absolute but not relative terms, from 0.5 to 0.64.

The bespoke neighbourhood approach has been extended using the British Household Panel Study (BHPS), which is conducted annually and collects data on partisan preferences and, in the relevant years, how respondents voted in general elections. For these, the neighbourhood data (which have also been used in studies of social exclusion: Buck, 2001) have been collated not only for the nearest n persons to each respondent's home (where $n = 500$, 1000, 1500, 2000, 2500, 5000, 7500, and 10,000) but also to all persons living within m metres of the respondent's home (where $m = 250$, 500, 750, 1000, 1500, and 2000). Together, these allow for a wide variety of analyses exploring the spatial scale of the neighbourhood effect.

---

[9] Similar findings have been reported when looking at the voting of people with different housing tenures (Johnston et al., 2001a) and economic evaluations (Johnston et al., 2000b).

Those explorations have all produced very strong evidence consistent with neighbourhood effects, at a variety of scales, when a range of individual voter characteristics has been taken into account. For example, in analyses of the probability of a respondent voting either Labour or Conservative and Labour or Liberal Democrat at the 1992 and 1997 general elections, there was a strong and highly significant neighbourhood effect at each of the four distances analysed (250, 500, 1000 and 2000 metres): the greater the neighbourhood socio-economic disadvantage (a composite measure reflecting differences in housing tenure, unemployment, car ownership, family structure, and occupational composition), the greater the probability that an individual respondent voted Labour rather than for one of the other two parties (Johnston et al., 2005d). (Other work has shown that the neighbourhood polarization was greater in the early and late 1990s than it was in the middle of the decade, when Labour won a landslide electoral victory: Johnston et al., 2004).

These neighbourhood variations were independent of significant regional differences. The extent of such differences—excluding the impact of the bespoke neighbourhoods—is shown in Table 3.7. The exponents—which are shown only where the ratio on the designated region differs statistically from that for Scotland (the baseline for all comparisons as being the most pro-Labour region)—are the ratios of an expected vote for the first-named party in the column over the second. Thus in 1992, for example, among those

Table 3.7. The probability of voting Labour rather than either Conservative or Liberal Democrat at the 1992 and 1997 general elections, by region[a]

Region	Conservative:Labour		Lib Dem:Labour	
	1992	1997	1992	1997
Inner London	—	—	—	—
Outer London	2.51	2.05	1.74	2.41
Rest of Southeast	3.50	3.05	3.70	3.91
Southwest	3.34	2.90	4.41	5.26
East Anglia	2.54	2.77	3.56	4.97
East Midlands	2.41	2.17	1.30	1.85
West Midlands Conurbation	1.77	2.39	—	—
Rest of West Midlands	—	1.86	1.52	1.76
Greater Manchester	—	—	—	—
Merseyside	—	—	—	—
Rest of Northwest	2.31	1.77	1.54	—
South Yorkshire	—	—	—	2.29
West Yorkshire	—	—	—	—
Rest of Yorkshire/Humber	—	1.80	2.72	1.89
Tyne and Wear	—	—	—	—
Rest of North	2.33	—	—	—
Wales	—	—	—	—
Scotland	—	—	—	—

[a] Each region is compared with Scotland and both individual characteristics and neighbourhood effects are held constant.

Note: Only statistically significant exponents are shown.

individuals who voted either Conservative or Labour, the ratio of voting Conservative rather than Labour for Outer London in 1992 was 2.51: a similar person (i.e. holding constant individual and neighbourhood characteristics) was 2.5 times more likely to vote Conservative in London than in Scotland in 1992. The overall pattern—for both the Conservative:Labour and Liberal Democrat:Labour comparisons at both elections—was a very clear north–south divide, despite the closure of the gap noted by Curtice and Park (1999). In regions in southern England (including the Midlands) similar people were much more likely to vote either Conservative or Liberal Democrat than Labour than they were in Scotland, but with few exceptions (mainly in the relatively rural areas outside the main industrial conurbations) there were no differences between the northern regions and Scotland. Similar people living in similar neighbourhoods voted differently in northern than in southern Britain.

Variations according to the characteristics of the bespoke neighbourhoods are nested within these regional variations: there are *both* regional differences *and* neighbourhood effects. Their extent is illustrated by looking at the propensity of four different types of 'stereotypical' individuals to vote Labour or Conservative in different regions and at different neighbourhood contexts at the 250-metre scale. The four types are:

- *Type 1: working class.* A male aged 45, with no qualifications and a semi-skilled/unskilled last occupation, living in a local authority rented home and with no cars available to the household, whose net income is £5797 (one standard deviation below the average). His current financial situation is 'alright' and he anticipates no change in that.

- *Type 2: middle class.* A male aged 45, with a first degree and a higher service last occupation, living in a mortgaged home with two cars available to the household, whose net income is £26,985 (one standard deviation above the average). His current financial situation is 'alright' and he anticipates no change in that.

- *Type 3: prosperous employer.* A male aged 45, with A-level qualifications, who is a small proprietor with employees, living in a home that is owned outright with three or more cars available to the household, whose net income is £37,579 (two standard deviations above the average). His current financial situation is 'comfortable' and he anticipates that it will 'get better'.

- *Type 4: poor working class.* A male aged 45, with no qualifications and a semi-skilled/unskilled last occupation, living in a local authority rented home with no cars available to the household, whose net income is £5,797 (one standard deviation below the average). His current financial situation is 'very difficult' and he expects it to 'get worse'.

Table 3.8 shows the probability of members of each of these 'ideal types' voting either Conservative rather than Labour (the first four columns) or Liberal Democrat rather than Labour (the second four columns), by region, in 1992—with the significant differences from the Scottish situation shown in bold. Again, there is a clear north–south divide, after any neighbourhood effect is partialled out. For all four types the probability of voting for one of the other two parties rather than Labour is significantly greater in the southern regions than in Scotland. In Outer London, for example, the probability of a prosperous employer (type 3) voting Conservative rather than Labour was 0.94 (i.e. he would almost certainly vote Conservative) compared to 0.51 in Scotland. Similarly, the probability of the same person preferring the Liberal Democrats to Labour was 0.56 in Outer London but only 0.27 in Scotland.

Turning to the neighbourhood effects, Figures 3.3 and 3.4 show trends in the probability of voting Conservative rather than Labour for each of the four 'ideal typical' voters according to the position of their 250-metre bespoke neighbourhoods on a socio-economic disadvantage scale (similar to that used in the earlier example). Two regions have been selected to represent the north–south divide—the Outer Southeast (i.e. the Home Counties) and the West Yorkshire conurbation (i.e. Leeds, Bradford, Huddersfield, Halifax and Wakefield). In each region, the two middle-class types (2 and 3) are much more likely to vote Conservative than are the two working-class types (1 and 4), with the class divide extremely wide (the probability of a type-1 or type-4 voter preferring the Conservatives rather than Labour is about half that of a type-2 or type-3 voter in both regions). In addition, and

Table 3.8. The probabilities of voting Conservative or Liberal Democrat rather than Labour by region, at the 1992 general election, by four 'ideal typical' voters

Region	Conservative:Labour voter type				LibDem:Labour voter type			
	1	2	3	4	1	2	3	4
Inner London	0.22	0.63	0.91	0.08	0.15	0.61	0.47	0.12
Outer London	**0.30**	**0.72**	**0.94**	**0.12**	**0.20**	**0.69**	**0.56**	**0.17**
Rest of Southeast	**0.34**	**0.76**	**0.95**	**0.14**	**0.27**	**0.78**	**0.66**	**0.24**
Southwest	**0.33**	**0.75**	**0.95**	**0.13**	**0.30**	**0.80**	**0.69**	**0.26**
East Anglia	**0.31**	**0.73**	**0.94**	**0.12**	**0.21**	**0.77**	**0.66**	**0.23**
East Midlands	**0.28**	**0.71**	**0.93**	**0.11**	**0.12**	**0.57**	**0.43**	**0.10**
West Midlands Conurbation	**0.34**	**0.76**	**0.95**	**0.14**	0.13	0.57	0.43	0.11
Rest of West Midlands	**0.22**	**0.64**	**0.91**	**0.08**	**0.15**	**0.61**	**0.47**	**0.12**
Greater Manchester	0.17	0.55	0.88	0.06	0.08	0.45	0.32	0.07
Merseyside	0.14	0.49	0.85	0.05	0.09	0.47	0.33	0.07
Rest of Northwest	**0.28**	**0.70**	**0.93**	**0.11**	**0.16**	**0.63**	**0.49**	**0.13**
South Yorkshire	0.16	0.54	0.87	0.06	0.10	0.50	0.36	0.08
West Yorkshire	0.17	0.55	0.88	0.06	0.09	0.47	0.34	0.07
Rest of Yorkshire/Humber	**0.27**	**0.69**	**0.93**	**0.10**	**0.15**	**0.62**	**0.48**	**0.13**
Tyne and Wear	0.16	0.54	0.87	0.06	0.05	0.34	0.22	0.04
Rest of North	0.16	0.53	0.87	0.06	0.07	0.42	0.29	0.06
Wales	0.12	0.46	0.83	0.04	0.09	0.49	0.35	0.08
Scotland	0.15	0.51	0.86	0.05	0.07	0.40	0.27	0.05

Note: For definitions of voter types, see text. Significant differences from the situation in Scotland are shown in bold.

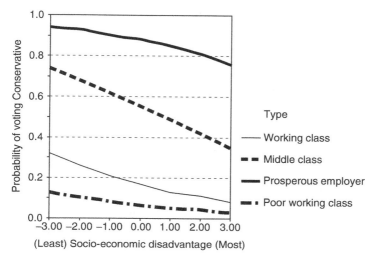

Fig. 3.3. The probability of voting Conservative rather than Labour by the four selected 'voter types' across the bespoke neighbourhood socio-economic disadvantage scale in the West Yorkshire region

Source: Johnston et al. (2005d, 510).

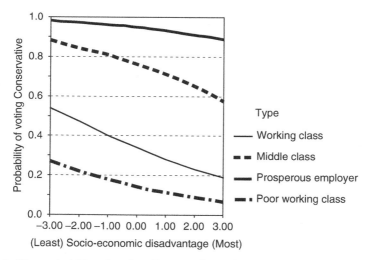

Fig. 3.4. The probability of voting Conservative rather than Labour by the four selected 'voter types' across the bespoke neighbourhood socio-economic disadvantage scale in the Rest of the Southeast region

Source: Johnston et al. (2005d, 511).

importantly with regard to the neighbourhood effect thesis, the more disadvantaged the respondent's local neighbourhood, the lower the probability of him voting Conservative. The slope is generally steeper for the middle-class than the working-class types, especially in West Yorkshire, where the probability of a prosperous employer (type 3) voting Conservative in the least-disadvantaged neighbourhoods was 0.73, compared to just half that in the most-disadvantaged. (Very similar patterns are shown for the probability of voting Liberal Democrat rather than Labour: Johnston et al., 2005c.)

Further analyses of these data show—as with the work on the 1997 BES—that neighbourhood effects operate independently at two separate scales. For both contrasts—Labour with Conservative and with Liberal Democrat—there are significant relationships between the voting probability and neighbourhood socio-economic disadvantage at both the 250-metre and the 2000-metre scale. The more disadvantaged the general area in which a respondent lived—at the 2000-metre scale—the greater the probability of a Labour vote. In addition, the more disadvantaged the local area—at the 250-metre scale—within that wider area, the greater still the probability of a Labour vote. If one's immediate neighbourhood is disadvantaged this will accentuate the likelihood of voting Labour associated with a similar level of disadvantage at a wider scale. If the general area in which one lives is disadvantaged, one is more likely to vote Labour than either Conservative or Liberal Democrat; if the immediately local area is similarly disadvantaged, one is even more likely to do so.

The patterns of voting shown by these bespoke neighbourhood studies are entirely consistent with neighbourhood effect hypotheses but provide little insight into the processes involved in their production. Further analyses are suggestive of such effects resulting from both local economic evaluations and social interaction, however. For example, in work using the 1997 BES data, voting for the incumbent (Conservative) government varied according to respondents' views on the state of the economy nationally and the level of unemployment locally (Johnston et al., 2000a). Table 3.9 shows that the percentage voting Conservative was greater among those who thought that the general standard of living had improved because of government policies (the first block) than if they thought it had either stayed the same or fallen (the other two blocks). Within each block, however, there is a very clear downward trend in Conservative voting according to the local level of unemployment, at every scale: in the smallest bespoke neighbourhoods, for example, 59 per cent of those who thought that the government's policies had produced an improvement in general living standards voted Conservative in areas with the lowest unemployment, compared to 34 per cent in those with the highest. Respondents were more likely to vote for the government to be returned to power if they thought its policies had been successful and if the local level of unemployment provided tangible evidence of this.

Similar patterns of Conservative voting in 1997 were observed when looking at egocentric rather than sociotropic voting. Those whose own standard of

Table 3.9. Percentage of respondents voting Conservative in 1997 by retrospective sociotropic economic evaluations, level of unemployment locally, and neighbourhood size

Unemployment (%)	Neighbourhood size[a]					
	n500	n1000	n2500	n5000	n10,000	PC
General standard of living increased because of government policies						
0.0–5.9	59	58	62	56	56	60
6.0–8.9	52	49	49	58	57	55
9.0–11.9	49	52	41	40	43	47
12.0–14.9	43	50	40	38	39	46
>15.0	34	32	34	36	38	30
General standard of living stayed the same because of government policies						
0.0–5.9	39	41	46	48	48	41
6.0–8.9	33	31	31	34	35	34
9.0–11.9	21	23	18	15	15	25
12.0–14.9	9	11	13	17	8	9
>15.0	11	11	7	11	9	10
General standard of living fell because of government policies						
0.0–5.9	9	12	13	14	13	18
6.0–8.9	8	6	6	7	8	6
9.0–11.9	4	5	4	3	2	3
12.0–14.9	2	0	3	2	3	3
>15.0	1	2	2	3	3	3

[a] n500 = nearest 500 persons; n1000 = nearest 1000 persons; n2500 = nearest 2500 persons; n5000 = nearest 5000 persons; n10,000 = nearest 10,000 persons; PC = parliamentary constituency.

Source: Johnston et al. (2000a, 136).

living had improved, and who attributed this to government policies, were more likely to vote for the Conservatives to be re-elected, but such support for the incumbent government was higher among residents of areas with low rather than high unemployment. (For example, in the *n*2500 bespoke neighbourhoods, 64 per cent of those whose living standards had improved voted Conservative in areas with the lowest unemployment compared to 30 per cent of those living in areas of high unemployment.) This suggested the presence of what were termed altruistic voters: although their own situations were good, those of many of their neighbours were not, and so they voted against the government that was delivering their own prosperity (Johnston et al., 2000b).

Whereas these two studies of the 1997 BES data indicated strong retrospective voting patterns according to neighbourhood context, those of the BHPS data (also looking at the 1997 general election) have identified patterns consistent with the intensity of respondents' neighbourhood social interaction. BHPS respondents were asked a series of eight attitudinal questions

Table 3.10. Percentage of respondents voting Labour at the 1997 general election by neighbourhood socio-economic disadvantage (in quintiles), for those in the highest and lowest quartiles of neighbourhood social capital

Neighbourhood social capital	Neighbourhood social disadvantage (quintile)				
	1st	2nd	3rd	4th	5th
Highest quartile					
Service class	27	61	58	72	72
Other non-manual	28	49	40	59	71
Manual	45	53	69	75	85
Lowest quartile					
Service class	44	53	43	65	62
Other non-manual	34	34	46	67	63
Manual	57	67	65	70	81

to identify the extent of their local community involvement, such as 'I feel that I belong to this neighbourhood', 'I regularly stop and talk to people in my neighbourhood', and 'If I needed advice about something I could go to someone in my neighbourhood.' This allowed them to be arranged on what was termed a 'neighbourhood social capital' scale, after the innovative work on social capital (Putnam, 2000). The bespoke neighbourhoods (in this case, the areas were the nearest 250 metres to each respondent's home) were divided into quintiles according to their scores on a neighbourhood disadvantage scale and the respondents were divided into quartiles according to their score on the social capital scale. Table 3.10 shows the percentages voting Labour in each category. Those in manual occupations were more likely to vote Labour than those in either of the non-manual groups but, in addition, in all three classes Labour voting increased the more disadvantaged the neighbourhood—from 27 to 72 per cent among members of the salariat in the first block (Johnston et al., 2005c). There was also much greater variation across the five neighbourhood types among those with high than those with low neighbourhood social capital. In the first group, for example, the difference in the percentage voting Labour between the least and most disadvantaged neighbourhoods was 45, 43, and 40 percentage points, respectively for the three occupational class groups; among those with low social capital, on the other hand, the respective differences were 18, 29 and 24 percentage points. People who interacted more with their neighbours were more likely to vote in the same way as their neighbours did, according to the characteristics of the neighbourhood that they shared.

Conclusions

This chapter has reviewed an increasingly large literature on spatial patterns of voting at British general elections. The overall conclusion to be drawn from that material is that geography clearly is important to understanding how people vote. Similar people, defined on a range of characteristics, living in different sorts of places tend to support different parties—at a range of spatial scales, from the very local to the regional. Those patterns are all consistent with several of the arguments introduced in Chapter 2 regarding the processes underpinning such geographies. Regional variations in voting are consistent with theories of economic voting (the government is more popular in more prosperous areas), for example, and are greater when the regional divide in economic well-being is widest. Neighbourhood variations show people tending to vote with the majority in their local area, especially if they interact with their neighbours. And constituencies where parties campaign most intensively tend to be those where they perform best.

Although all these findings are consistent with the assumed underlying processes, there is a general absence of material on how those processes operate. Exploring them is the purpose of the next four chapters, in which we both review previous work and present new analyses of data designed to show that 'people who talk together, vote together', that people respond to local economic circumstances in deciding how to vote, that they also respond to parties' local campaigns, and that they are more likely to turn out at a general election in places where they think that their votes will count. In these ways we move from descriptions of the geography of voting to analyses of the geography of voting.

4

Talking Together and Voting Together

In the preceding chapters, we discussed the neighbourhood effect in some detail. Voters do seem to pay attention to local cues when deciding how—and even whether—to vote. However, the exact nature of those cues remains to be examined. Thus far, we have shown aggregate patterns that are consistent with geographical influences. Voters in the same sorts of places tend to vote in the same sorts of ways. But how does context influence voters? In pre-reform nineteenth-century elections, the answer could be crude and simple—coercion. Where votes were cast in public, in full view of other voters, there was a risk that individual voters would vote against their true views in order to comply with local majority (or locally socially powerful) opinion. In some cases, too, direct vote buying was possible: support a successful candidate and he could provide one with goods and services. Hence, geographical variations in voting could have resulted from direct social or economic pressure.

But the introduction of the secret ballot to Britain in 1872 changed that. It was no longer possible for candidates to force compliance. Voters can now, if they wish, dissemble to their fellows, claiming to support a party other than their true preference for the sake of a quiet life, knowing that, once in the privacy of the polling booth, they can vote their sincere preferences. If my friends are convinced Conservatives while I am not, I may feel pressure to agree with them in public. But they may not know I vote Labour. That can be my secret. Why, therefore, should voters be subject to the pressures of their local environments? It is very unlikely that voters 'catch' the locally dominant view by rubbing shoulders in the street (Dunleavy, 1979). We need, therefore, to demonstrate not only end-results that are compatible with contextual effects, but also the mechanisms by which contextual effects operate. It is that task to which we turn in this and subsequent chapters. We begin in this chapter by considering whether people's voting decisions are in part a function of the contexts in which they live. In particular, are they influenced by the opinions of those they talk to?

Talking Together and Voting Together?

This question formed the core of a pioneering study of electoral behaviour in the USA—Lazarsfeld, Berelson, and Gaudet's (1944) analysis of the impact of socialization processes on vote choice. For them, voters were influenced by the opinions of their friends and relations. Considerable social and attitudinal cohesion developed through these tightly-knit groupings, each member agreeing with the others. Voters came to share the views of those they lived with, worked with, and talked to. Social interaction helped create political agreement.

The social networks approach was an early influence on electoral geography, through Cox's (1969a) seminal work on information flows and the neighbourhood effect (see Chapter 2). However, Lazarsfeld, Berelson, and Gaudet's detailed community studies were not widely repeated. Most subsequent work has adopted one of two different traditions. Perhaps the most influential tradition draws on the Michigan studies of the American electorate (Campbell, Guerin, and Miller, 1954; Campbell et al., 1960), which were based on national surveys of voters. The approach formed the basis for most subsequent national election studies in the USA and overseas (including the UK). But since each survey respondent is very unlikely to know other respondents, analysing the effects of social networks on the vote is, therefore, very difficult. The results, while nationally representative, are not representative of processes within any particular locality. Rather than being seen as members of active communities, in touch with their fellow voters, the Michigan-derived national samples treat respondents as isolated individuals, making their decisions largely alone (Agnew, 1987, 1996a; Zuckerman, 2005). Clearly, this is a simplification, albeit a powerful one. We know from our own daily experiences that we interact regularly with family members, friends, and others. We talk to people, we gauge their views, and we sometimes rethink our own opinions in the light of what we see and hear around us. As Lazarsfeld, Berelson, and Gaudet (1944) demonstrated over half a century ago, individuals' political decisions are taken not in isolation but in context.

The constituency-level analyses discussed in Chapters 2 and 3 provide an alternative to the methodological individualism of post-Michigan national election. Such work has demonstrated aggregate patterns consistent with a neighbourhood effect (e.g. Butler and Stokes, 1969; Johnston, Pattie, and Allsop, 1988; McAllister et al., 2001; Miller, 1977). Whatever their own personal social class, voters living in areas dominated by one class were more likely to vote for that dominant class's party than would be expected from national trends. But aggregate patterns alone cannot demonstrate the existence of the neighbourhood effect, far less uncover the processes involved. There are two problems.

The first is the problem of equifinality: different processes might result in the same outcome. If I live in an area where (say) the Conservatives are the most successful party, I am more likely randomly to encounter Conservative voters living there than I am to encounter voters of any other particular party. I might therefore begin to take on the mindset of a Conservative voter.

Replicated across many local voters, this might result in a neighbourhood effect whereby individuals adopt the locally dominant view through their interactions with other members of the community within which they live, producing a better than expected Conservative performance in areas where the party is already strong. But this is not the only mechanism by which such an outcome might be created. Returning again to my Conservative-supporting area, I might find, if I am not a Conservative voter, that, far from being persuaded to vote Conservative, I am, rather, discouraged from voting at all locally since my party has no chance of winning. Once again, the outcome would be a better than expected Conservative performance in areas where the party was already strong. Or a third possibility may be that Conservative supporters choose to live in the same areas as each other for reasons that have nothing to do with electoral choice—for instance, the quality of local housing or local schools. Again, this could produce a larger than expected vote for the Conservatives in such areas, but with no necessity for neighbourhood interaction. At least three very different processes might result in an identical outcome, but we cannot resolve which really operates just from a study of that outcome.

A second, and equally problematic, difficulty is the ecological fallacy (King, 1997; Robinson, 1950): an aggregate relationship does not mean that an equivalent relationship also applies at the level of the individual voter. For instance, we might encounter higher than average support for far right and anti-immigrant parties in areas with high concentrations of ethnic minority populations. But that does not mean members of those ethnic minorities vote for the far right; rather, some of their white neighbours do.

Neither conventional national election samples nor aggregate data are sufficient to understand whether social networks influence voting, therefore. Other methods are required.

Measuring the Conversation Effect Directly

In the following pages, we measure the effects of social interaction and conversation directly. Most of us have relatively wide-ranging circles of acquaintances, family, friends, work colleagues, neighbours, casual and occasional contacts, and so on. Our acquaintance circles are maintained and lubricated by talk. Whether we gossip about mutual friends, discuss the fortunes of our favourite sports teams, bemoan the weather, or talk about other things, each conversation involves the exchange of information, sometimes serious and sometimes trivial. And politics does feature frequently in our conversations. In the remainder of this chapter we report on detailed analyses of data about political discussions that were collected as part of the 1992 BES. Subsequent surveys have not repeated these questions, so we rely primarily on those data.[1] But we have no reason to believe the situation will have changed since then.

How frequent are political conversations? Over two-thirds (69 per cent) of respondents to the 1992 BES said they did regularly discuss important matters with others. Clearly, there is a lot of conversation going on. Just under two-thirds (65 per cent) of respondents said they talked about politics to others at least occasionally. Similarly, in 2005, 78 per cent of BES respondents said they discussed politics with someone else at least sometimes and only 22 per cent seldom or never discussed politics; 29 per cent said they discussed politics frequently. The frequency of political conversation has remained relatively constant in Britain and the USA since the 1950s (Bennett, Flickinger, and Rhine, 2000). That said, the BES is likely to underestimate levels of political discussion, as much political conversation is occasional, and some conversations have political content even without those involved realizing it (as, for instance, when parents discuss the schooling of their children).

Levels of political discussion in the UK are average for well-established democracies and were similar to levels in the USA, Austria, and France, in all of which 65–71 per cent of respondents to the 1990 World Values Survey reported discussing politics with others either occasionally or frequently (Anderson and Paskeviciute, 2005). This was better than a group of mainly south European democracies (Belgium, Ireland, Italy, Portugal, and Spain), where only 49–60 per cent reported even occasional political discussions. But UK discussion rates were lower than in Canada, Denmark, Germany, the Netherlands, Norway, and Sweden, where 75–88 per cent of respondents reported occasional or frequent discussions. The major factor underlying cross-national variations in levels of political discussion among voters is the heterogeneity of the national political environment: the more diverse political opinion is in a country, the more political discussion takes place, other things being equal (Anderson and Paskeviciute, 2005).

Do people have a sense of which parties their conversation partners support? The 1992 BES asked voters to name the three individuals they talked to most about politics and to say which party they thought those individuals supported. These data showed that 37 per cent of individuals could not name the party supported by any of their discussion partners (or said they had no regular conversation partner). A further 22 per cent reported only Conservative supporters among their conversation partners, 14 per cent named only Labour supporters, and 4 per cent named only Liberal Democrats. But 23 per cent of all respondents talked to partisans of several different parties: for instance, around 12 per cent talked to both

---

[1] The 2005 BES also asked about political conversations. But the questions used were far less detailed than those employed in 1992 and, crucially for what follows, only tell us whether people thought their discussants supported the same party as they did themselves.

Conservative and Labour supporters. For some individuals, most of those they talked to regularly supported the same political party; but others received conflicting messages from their discussion partners.

If anything, these survey results may underestimate political disagreement. The BES conversation questions depend upon survey respondents' own evaluations of their discussion partners' partisanship. This raises a problem. A well-known phenomenon in social psychology is the tendency of individuals to reduce cognitive dissonance by mis-perceiving the views of others. Most people do not like conflict, and can persuade themselves that their friends and families agree with them. Insofar as this occurs within the BES data, therefore, individuals' estimates of their discussion partners' views will tend to be biased away from the actual views of discussants and towards the views of respondents. Hence the risk of underestimating how often people talk to others with different political views.

Huckfeldt and Sprague's (1987, 1988, 1995) innovative study of the 1984 US presidential election in South Bend, Indiana gives us some idea of the extent to which this might be a problem. Unusually, they interviewed not only a sample of local voters, but also the individuals their initial respondents said they talked to about politics. Whereas the BES only has evidence from one side of each discussion partnership, therefore, Huckfeldt and Sprague give us information from both, making it possible to check the accuracy of respondents' perceptions of their discussants' views. The results are telling (Table 4.1). Respondents were generally good at recognizing the partisanship of discussants who agreed with them: just over 90 per cent of Reagan supporters who talked to Reagan-supporting discussants got their conversation partners' views right, as did 92 per cent of Mondale supporters who talked to other Mondale supporters. But where respondents and discussion partners disagreed, respondents were less likely to perceive their conversation partners' views correctly. Only just over half of Mondale voters who talked to Reaganites realized they were doing so, while two-thirds of Reagan supporters who talked to Mondale voters got their partner's views right. Interestingly, non-voters faced with partisan discussants were generally quite successful in gauging their views: 79 per cent of those who talked to Reaganites correctly named their discussants' partisanship, as did 82 per cent of those talking to Mondale voters.

Table 4.1. Percentage of respondents correctly perceiving discussant's voting behaviour, South Bend, IN

	Discussant		
Main respondent	Non–voter	Reagan	Mondale
Non-voter	22	79	82
Reagan	40	91	66
Mondale	33	55	92

Source: Huckfeldt and Sprague (1995, 131).

The accuracy of individuals' perceptions of their discussion partners' views was higher where they agreed with each other than where they did not, therefore. But note that in every case a majority of respondents who talked to a partisan discussant got that person's views right (see also Huckfeldt, Sprague, and Levine, 2000). Overall, just over three-quarters (77 per cent) of respondents correctly specified their discussants' views. Where they found this hardest to do was when the discussant was a non-voter, with no clear partisan loyalty. Huckfeldt and Sprague's data suggest, therefore, that cognitive dissonance does distort individuals' perceptions of their conversation partners' views. But the data also suggest that most people talking to a party supporter will correctly evaluate that person's opinions. And where their evaluation is wrong, they will tend to assume their discussion partners agree with them. In so far as cognitive dissonance is a factor, therefore, it will tend to lead to relatively conservative (with a small 'c') estimates of the conversation-conversion effect.

Who Talks Politics?

Political discussion is relatively frequent, therefore, and most of those who do talk politics accurately perceive the opinions of their friends and colleagues. But there is variability in the number of people individuals have political discussions with. Around 35 per cent of 1992 BES respondents said they never talked politics with anyone. Meanwhile, 10 per cent said they talked politics at least occasionally to one other person, 26 per cent talked to two others, and 29 per cent reported political conversations with three or more individuals. Among those who did talk politics with at least one of their discussants, the frequency of these discussions varied too. Some, presumably very politically motivated individuals (around 12 per cent of all who said they discussed politics), claimed that politics came up in conversation on every occasion when they talked to at least one of their named discussants. Just under three-quarters of all those who named at least one political discussant said that politics was, at most, an occasional conversational topic. Only 16 per cent of those who claimed to discuss politics said it was, at most, a topic that only seldom came up in their conversations.

But who talks politics, and who does not? Kwak et al. (2005) conceptualize political conversation as a form of political participation. Most forms of political participation are influenced by the socio-economic resources available to individuals (including income, education, and time): the resource-rich are more likely to participate than the resource-poor (see Chapter 7; see also Parry, Moyser, and Day, 1992; Pattie, Seyd, and Whiteley, 2004; Verba, Schlozman, and Brady, 1995). In addition, participation is influenced by cognitive engagement, the extent to which individuals are interested in, or invest value in, an issue: greater interest, not surprisingly, engenders greater participation (Dalton, 2002; Pattie, Seyd and Whiteley, 2004, 138–40). And civic voluntarism models show that those who feel efficacious ('Can I make a difference?'), those who are mobilized ('Was I asked to take part?'), and those who are partisan are more likely to participate in politics than are those who are not (Pattie, Seyd, and Whiteley, 2004, 144–7; Verba, Schlozman, and Brady, 1995).

   If political conversation is indeed just another form of political participation, then we might reasonably assume that the extent to which people talk politics to their fellows will be structured by these factors. If this is the case, political conversation merely reinforces pre-existing inequalities in participation: those who are already inclined to be politically active also talk a lot about it. Alternatively, if political conversation is not related to these factors, then talk may prove a vehicle for redressing and countering some of these participation inequalities. Bennett, Flickinger, and Rhine (2000) provide evidence to support the former interpretation. They report higher rates of political conversation in both Britain and the USA in the 1950s and 1990s among the wealthy than among the poor, among those interested in politics than among those who are not interested, and among the more highly educated than among those with less formal education.

How Many People Do They Talk To?

We can get some appreciation of the impact of these factors on political conversation by analysing their relationship with the number of political discussants named by respondents to the 1992 BES survey, using regression analysis (Table 4.2), with number of political discussants as the dependent variable. Model I looks at the influence of socio-economic factors on discussion. As the independent variables in this model are categorical, we define dummy variables for all bar one category of each variable. For instance, social class is measured on the five-point Heath–Goldthorpe scale, so dummy variables are created for four of the groups: the middle-class salariat, routine non-manual workers, the petty bourgeoisie, and manual foremen and supervisors. Each dummy variable is coded 1 if the respondent is in the appropriate class, and 0 otherwise. The remaining category, manual workers and those with no job, serves as a reference group. The coefficients for the other dummy variables tell us how many more or fewer political discussants individuals in those categories have than do members of the reference group. Hence for class, each of the coefficients in the regression model tell us how much members of that class differ from members of the working class and from those with no jobs. Positive coefficients indicate more discussion partners, and negative fewer. Similar procedures are followed for our other socio-economic variables: education (for which the comparison group is those with no formal educational qualifications), age (where we take those aged over 65 as the reference group), and gender (men serve as the reference group here).

Table 4.2. Who talks politics, and how widely? OLS regression models of number of political discussants

Independent variables	Model I	Model II	Model III
Age (comparison group = aged 65+)			
18–24	0.32	0.40	0.34
25–34	0.43	0.49	0.42
35–44	0.40	0.44	0.32
45–54	0.40	0.40	0.30
55–59	0.22	0.22	—
60–64	0.24	0.26	—
Gender (comparison = male)			
Female	—	—	0.21
Class (comparison = working class or no job)			
Salariat	0.55	0.44	0.33
Routine non-manual	0.34	0.28	0.23
Petty bourgeoisie	0.29	0.20	—
Foremen and supervisors	—	—	—
Education (comparison group = no qualifications)			
Degree	0.87	0.71	0.38
Post-school	0.55	0.43	0.29
School	0.55	0.45	0.33
Strength of partisan identification (comparison group = no party ID)			
Very strong		0.29	—
Fairly strong		0.27	—
Not very strong		—	—
Cared who won the election (comparison = did not care very much)			
Cared a good deal		0.46	0.35
Personal efficacy scale		0.08	0.07
Political knowledge score			0.21
Political confidence scale			−0.07
Attitude uncertainty scale			−0.04
Social tolerance scale			−0.07
Allow anti-government meetings			−0.07
Constant	0.51	−0.40	0.91
R^2	0.16	0.21	0.25
N	2393	2393	2393

Note: Only significant coefficients are shown.
Source: BES data files (1992).

Model I confirms that the incidence of political discussion is significantly related to social status. Compared to members of the working class (who have the smallest political discussion networks), members of the middle-class salariat have the most extensive networks, followed by members of the routine non-manual class, and then by the petty bourgeoisie. Manual foremen and supervisors, however, were no different from other manual workers (and those with no job) in their number of political discussants. Formal education, too, has an impact: degree-holders named most political discussants and those with no formal educational qualifications the fewest.

Thus far, the pattern of political discussion revealed by these analyses follows the same patterns we would expect from studies of other forms of political participation. The resource-rich participate more than the resource-poor. To this extent, biases in who talks politics reinforce other participation biases. However, this is not true in all cases. Gender differences exist in some forms of political participation. For instance, women are more likely than men to take part in some forms of participation, such as voting, making donations to organizations, and engaging in ethical consumption practices, and are less likely to take part in others, such as demonstrations (Pattie, Seyd, and Whiteley, 2004). But there is no gender difference in participation in political conversations: other things being equal, men and women talk politics to roughly the same number of people.

Age is related differently to political conversation than to other forms of political participation. In general, older citizens are more active than the young (Franklin, 2004; Pattie, Seyd, and Whiteley, 2004; Putnam, 2000), but the pattern for participation in political conversation is more curvilinear than for other forms of participation. All other age groups report more political discussion partners than do those aged over 65. But the disparity with the retired is greatest for those in early middle age, the age groups with most discussion partners. It is lower (but still positive) for the youngest respondents, those aged 18–24. But it is lowest of all (though again still positive and significant) for respondents in late middle age and approaching retirement, those aged over 55. The most widespread networks of political discussion seem to occur in middle life, therefore.

As discussed above, however, socio-economic factors do not wholly account for political participation. Cognitive engagement and civic voluntarism stress the additional importance of interest, partisanship, and efficacy (Table 4.2: Model II). Political interest is measured by whether individuals cared a great deal who won the 1992 general election (those who did not care much are the comparison group). Partisanship is measured by the strength of partisan attachment. Strong partisans should be very likely to participate, while weaker partisans should be less likely to do so. Respondents are divided into four categories: very strong supporters of a particular party; fairly strong supporters; those who supported a party, but not very strongly; and (the comparison group) those who said they supported no party. Individuals' sense of efficacy was measured using their combined responses to two questions. The first asked whether they agreed that 'People like me have no say in what the government does'; the second whether they agreed that 'Councillors and MPs don't care much what people like me think'. As both questions were measured on a five-point scale (from 'agree strongly' to 'disagree strongly'), adding them together produces a scale running from 2 to 10. A high score on this efficacy scale indicates a strong sense of personal efficacy, since it is achieved by strong disagreement with both statements.

A low score, indicating strong agreement with both statements, shows a weak sense of personal efficacy.[2]

All three factors influence political discussion as expected. For instance, the stronger an individual's sense of partisanship, the more political discussion partners he or she reported. Similarly, those who cared about the result of the election had more discussion partners than those who did not care. And the more people felt they could influence political events (as measured by a high efficacy score), the greater the number of people they talked politics with. As we might expect, therefore, those who were engaged by politics generally, and the general election in particular, were more assiduous political conversationalists than those who were alienated and disinterested. Why talk about something one finds dull or cannot affect? Why not talk about something one is fascinated by and thinks one can influence?

Other, more psychological, issues may also play a part. In conversation, we open ourselves up to challenge and we potentially expose our prejudices, misunderstandings, and shortcomings. It is possible, therefore, that the decision whether or not to engage in a discussion on politics will be affected by levels of political certainty and knowledge. Those who are more certain of their views, and who feel they know more about politics than most, might be more willing to talk about politics than those who are less certain of their views or knowledge. Conover, Searing, and Crewe (2002) show that political discussion in Britain and America is related not only to socio-economic factors and political interest, but also to political competence—the extent to which individuals feel confident in their political judgements. The more political competence individuals display, the more they engage in political discussion.

Again, we can demonstrate the impact of these factors by adding further variables to our model. Political knowledge is measured using the number of correct answers to ten factual questions about contemporary British politics in the 1992 BES.[3] The median score on the quiz was 5. People's confidence in their political judgement is measured using responses to three questions. Individuals were asked whether they agreed with each of the following statements:

---

[2] A factor analysis confirmed that both variables loaded strongly on the same underlying dimension. The scale itself has relatively high internal validity, with a Cronbach's alpha of 0.72.

[3] The political quiz (see Appendix) contained ten statements and respondents were asked to say whether these were true or false. An eleventh statement, 'Neil Kinnock is leader of the Labour party' (true in 1992), was also put to respondents, but so many got it right there was little point in using it in the quiz. The quiz concentrates more on the mechanics than the substance of politics. Even so, quiz scores correlate with actual levels of political understanding and sophistication. For instance, those with high scores are more likely to think of politics in abstract ideological terms (such as left and right) than those who score low (Bartle, 1997; Pattie and Johnston, 2001c; Sniderman, Brody, and Tetlock, 1991).

- 'I think I am better informed than most people about politics and government.'
- 'Sometimes politics and government seem so complicated that a person like me cannot really understand what is going on.'
- 'I feel I could do as good a job as an MP or councillor as most other people.'

As with the personal efficacy measures, responses to each of these statements were coded on a five-point scale, from 'agree strongly' to 'disagree strongly'. They have been combined here to provide a political confidence scale running from 3 (indicating high levels of political confidence) to 15 (indicating low levels of confidence).[4]

Political uncertainty, meanwhile, is potentially harder to measure. Some analysts have tackled it by looking at the time a respondent takes to answer a question, arguing that longer response times indicate greater difficulty in information-processing, decision-making, and recall (Huckfeldt, Sprague, and Levine, 2000). However, the 1992 BES had no facility for recording response times. We have therefore used a different method for measuring uncertainty. BES respondents were asked their opinions on a wide range of attitudinal questions. In each case, the great majority of respondents gave a clear answer, but a small number said they didn't know what they thought on the issue or did not offer an answer. We use this to develop an attitude uncertainty scale, by summing the total number of 'don't know' and 'no answer' responses each respondent gave to each of 33 attitude questions.[5] The scale itself therefore ranges from a theoretical minimum of 0 (complete certainty: 50 per cent of respondents achieved this score, by never giving a 'don't know' response and never refusing to answer) to a maximum of 33 (complete uncertainty: in fact, the least certain respondent scored 30).

In a different vein, political conversation provides an analogue to Habermas's ideal speech situation, and is implicated in models of deliberative democracy (Fearon, 1998; Fishkin, 1995; Habermas, 1984). These theories rest on notions of tolerance, openness, and rationality. Effective conversations, those which might inform, change minds, and develop ideas, require

---

[4] Responses to each of the statements were coded so that the least confident response scored 5, and the most confident 1. Factor analysis confirmed that all three questions were related. The political confidence scale was then constructed by adding together each individual's responses to each of the three statements. Cronbach's alpha for the scale is 0.55.

[5] Far more respondents gave 'don't know' responses (48 per cent said they didn't know what they thought on at least one attitude measure) than refused to answer (only 3.5 per cent refused to respond to at least one attitude question). We include 'no response' answers on the grounds that such responses will, for the most part, indicate that the respondent has no opinion on the issue. There will be occasions, however, when the respondent may have an opinion but be unwilling to share it with the interviewer. We have therefore rerun both the scale and the subsequent analyses, just concentrating on the genuine 'don't know' responses.

that the partners in a conversation are willing to listen to what each other has to say and are ready to rethink their own views in the light of what they hear. Tolerance should therefore be positively associated with the incidence of political discussion. As a final test of who talks politics, therefore, we add measures of social and political tolerance to the regression model. Three questions in the 1992 BES survey measure different aspects of tolerance. Two tap into dimensions of social tolerance, and the third measures political tolerance. The first two questions have been combined into a social tolerance scale, which runs from 2 (very tolerant) to 10 (very intolerant). The third (political) tolerance question has been retained as a separate item, and is scored from 1 (high tolerance) to 5 (low tolerance).[6]

When added to the regression model, these variables prove to be related to the number of political discussants a person names in the expected ways (Table 4.2: Model III). The greater an individual's factual knowledge of British politics, the more people he or she reported talking to about politics. But the less confidence individuals had in their political abilities, and the less certainty they had in their attitudes, the fewer people they talked to. The regression model also bears out the argument that tolerance is an important correlate of political talk. The relevant coefficients are negative and significant, indicating that the higher an individual scores on the tolerance measures (and hence the less tolerant they are), the fewer political discussants they have. The more socially and politically tolerant individuals were, the more political discussants they had.

One further factor is worth discussing here. On the whole, variables that had previously been entered into the equation continued to prove significant, and in the expected direction. But this was not true in every case. Once we control for the effects of political knowledge, political confidence, attitude uncertainty, and tolerance, partisanship ceases to be significant and gender becomes important. The former reflects a tendency for the more partisan to be the most confident, knowledgeable, and opinionated about politics. And the latter suggests that the absence of gender effects in earlier models reflects gender differences in these factors. Other things being equal, women have more political conversation partners than do men.

---

[6] Respondents' social tolerance was assessed by whether they agreed or disagreed with each of the statements: 'Homosexual relations are always wrong'; and 'People in Britain should be more tolerant of those who lead unconventional lives'. Political tolerance, meanwhile, was measured by individuals' agreement or disagreement with the statement: 'People should be allowed to organize public meetings to protest against the government'. In all cases, responses were recorded so that the highest scores were given to the most intolerant responses. Responses to the social tolerance questions are closely correlated with each other (confirmed by a factor analysis) and so have been added together to produce a summary social tolerance scale (Cronbach's alpha = 0.51). Responses to the political tolerance question were only relatively weakly related to the social tolerance measures, and so we have kept that aspect of tolerance distinct in our analyses.

And How Often Do They Talk?

Thus far, we have concentrated on the size of individuals' political conversation networks. But this is only one facet of political conversation. Even if one has many people with whom one discusses politics, this may be relatively unimportant if one seldom talks to them. Equally, even those with just one political discussant may be substantially influenced by that person if they discuss politics with them very frequently. What, therefore, of the frequency with which politics is discussed? Who are the high-intensity political conversationalists? We can obtain some idea by looking more closely at the three individuals named by each 1992 BES respondent as their discussion partners. Respondents were asked to say how often they discussed politics with each of these individuals. Of those who named at least one person with whom they discussed important issues, around 6 per cent said they never talked politics to one of their discussants. A further 15 per cent said that, while they did talk politics to their discussion partners, this happened seldom. Two-thirds (67 per cent) said they discussed politics at most occasionally. And a hyper-active 11 per cent claimed to have a political conversation almost every time they met at least one of their named discussion partners.

To uncover the correlates of frequency of political conversation, we repeat the analyses reported in Table 4.2, concentrating solely on those individuals who named at least one person with whom they discussed important matters. Individuals who did not name a discussant are excluded from this analysis, since their inclusion would lead to confusion over whether the analyses reported on who talked politics at all, or the frequency with which politics was discussed. The results are similar, but not identical to, those for the number of political discussants (Table 4.3). Age is much less important as an influence on the frequency of political discussion than it was on the number of political discussants, and it seems to work in a different way. Only the very youngest respondents, those aged 18–24, were significantly different from the oldest in the frequency of political discussions. Although the young had more political discussants than the old, they talked politics less frequently with their discussants. Women, too, discussed politics less frequently than did men (although this difference disappeared when political knowledge and tolerance measures were added to the equation).

Other socio-economic influences on the frequency of political discussion were more in keeping with patterns for the number of discussants. Middle-class individuals not only talked politics to more people than members of the working class, but they did so more frequently. Similarly, those with educational qualifications (and particularly those with degrees) talked politics more frequently with their discussants than did those with no formal qualifications (though, like gender, education was no longer significant after the addition of the political knowledge and tolerance measures). And, as with

Table 4.3. Who talks politics, and how frequently? OLS regression models of maximum frequency of political discussion

Independent variables	Model I	Model II	Model III
Age (comparison group = aged 65+)			
18–24	−0.19	−0.16	−0.20
25–34	—	—	—
35–44	—	—	—
45–54	—	—	—
55–59	—	—	—
60–64	—	—	—
Gender (comparison = male)			
Female	−0.10	−0.09	—
Class (comparison = working class)			
Salariat	0.21	0.17	0.12
Routine non-manual	0.15	0.12	0.11
Petty bourgeoisie	—	—	—
Foremen and supervisors	—	—	—
Education (comparison group = no qualifications)			
Degree	0.23	0.18	—
Post-school	0.16	0.13	—
School	0.16	0.13	—
Strength of partisan identification			
(comparison group = no party ID)			
Very strong		0.41	0.30
Fairly strong		0.38	0.31
Not very strong		0.26	0.22
Cared who won the election			
(comparison = did not care very much)			
Cared a good deal		0.28	0.21
Personal efficacy scale		—	—
Political knowledge score			
Political confidence scale			−0.05
Attitude uncertainty scale			−0.03
Social tolerance scale			−0.08
Allow anti-government meetings			−0.02
Constant	2.72	2.11	3.07
R^2	0.04	0.10	0.15
N	1683	1683	1683

Note: Only significant coefficients are shown.
Source: BES data files (1992).

the number of political discussants, the frequency of political discussion was related to individuals' sense of political confidence (the more confident, the more frequent the incidence of political conversation), their certainty over political issues (the more uncertainty they showed, the less frequently they discussed politics), and their levels of tolerance (tolerant individuals discussed politics more frequently than the less tolerant).

As these analyses confirm, political conversation is a form of participation that mirrors and reinforces other patterns of political participation. It is the resource-rich, the politically motivated, and the tolerant who are most likely to have numerous discussion partners, while the resource-poor, the less motivated, and the less tolerant have fewer. The number of political discussants one has does not compensate for other inequalities in access to politics.

And Who Do They Talk To?

Thus far, we have seen that many—indeed most—people do engage in political conversations with others. But who do they talk to? This is important in two senses. First, the neighbourhood effects literature in particular places great emphasis on conversations within circumscribed communities. Do people talk mainly to others in their home neighbourhoods? Or do political conversations occur over a wider range of locales (such as the workplace)? Secondly, do people talk mainly to others like themselves? If this is the case, political conversations are likely to reinforce views. Or are discussion networks more heterogeneous? If so, individuals are likely to encounter diverse and potentially challenging views.

As we might expect, many political conversations take place within families (Stoker and Jennings, 2005; Zuckerman, Fitzgerald, and Dasović, 2005). Of the 4283 conversation pairs reported by 1992 BES respondents, for instance, over 60 per cent were with spouses and partners or other relatives (Table 4.4: there were considerably more conversation pairs than there were respondents who reported conversation partners, as many individuals reported more than one significant conversation partner). Spouses and partners were the first people most respondents with conversation partners named as a discussant, although just over a third named some other person as their primary discussion partner (splitting almost 2:3 between relatives and non-family members, respectively). Not surprisingly, spouses and partners were much less likely to be named as the second- or third-most important discussant, and other relatives or non-family members came much more to the fore. Overall, just under a third of all discussion partnerships reported

Table 4.4. Who do people talk to? (Percentages of discussion pairs)

Discussant	1st discussant	2nd discussant	3rd discussant	Total
Spouse	63.8	5.1	3.6	30.1
Other relative	15.9	48.8	34.5	31.8
Friend	11.8	24.1	31.4	20.3
Workmate	5.7	15.7	23.4	12.9
Neighbour	1.0	2.8	2.3	1.9
Same church	0.9	1.6	1.5	1.3
Same club	0.9	1.9	3.3	1.7
N	1842	1581	860	4283

Source: BES data files (1992).

were with spouses or partners, almost another third were with other family members, and the remainder were with non-family members. Many, though not all, of these within-family conversations will take place within the same household unit, perhaps the most intimate 'neighbourhood' in which most voters live (Johnston et al., 2005b).

Outside the family, friends were the most frequently named discussion partners (named in one in every five of the reported discussion partnerships). They were followed by workmates, who were cited in 13 per cent of all discussion pairings. What is striking, however, is that, with the exception of the (unknown but large) number of family discussions within households, very few conversations are with people who clearly live in the respondent's neighbourhood. Only 2 per cent of all conversation partners were neighbours, and only 1 per cent were members of the same church (in most cases this will be located near an individual's residential neighbourhood). It may be the case that friends and workmates also live in or near respondents' home neighbourhoods, and this has not been picked up. However, the growth of substantial commuting to work and inter-regional migration in modern societies means we cannot take this for granted. The rise of the car culture and of commuting means many individuals now live in 'communities without propinquity', not in tightly knit traditional neighbourhood communities (Webber, 1963). Our friends and workmates may live in very different parts of the city to us, or even in different cities. Transport and communications technologies now allow long-distance friendships to be conducted relatively easily. The authors of this book, for instance, have written together for twenty years, and have discussed politics together for longer, but for most of that time have worked in different cities: frequent telephone and email conversations have taken the place of face-to-face encounters. Community without propinquity can also occur within families: many now live in different cities than their siblings, even though contact may remain frequent.

Actually many of these non-family conversations are genuinely local. Respondents to the 1987 BES were asked how nearby the people they talked politics with lived. Around a third of all non-family discussion partners lived in the same neighbourhood as the respondent naming them (Curtice, 1995, Table 11.7); just over half lived in the same town or city. But only 14 per cent of non-family discussion partners lived further away than this. Similarly, the 1992 British Household Panel Survey (BHPS) asked respondents how far their best friends' houses were from their homes. Around a third lived less than a mile away, and almost another third lived within 5 miles of their friends (Pattie and Johnston, 2000). And, in a re-analysis of Huckfeldt and Sprague's (1995) survey of South Bend, Indiana, Eagles, Bélanger and Calkins (2004) showed that, on average, discussion partners identified in that study lived 2.76 miles apart. So many political conversations do take place in the local areas within which people live—if not in their immediate neighbourhood.

What of the diversity of discussion networks? Whether discussion networks are homogeneous (comprising similar and like-minded people) or heterogeneous (made up of people from a wide variety of backgrounds and opinions) has implications for the impact of political conversations, since this will determine whether individuals only encounter their own opinions (in which case conversation with others will tend to reinforce their pre-existing views) or come across divergent opinions (which may cause them to reassess and perhaps change their beliefs). One of the apparent puzzles in the analysis of discussion networks is the persistence of disagreement (Huckfeldt, Johnson, and Sprague, 2004). If people interact regularly with one another, and if that interaction leads, as the neighbourhood effects literature suggests, to 'conversion by conversation', then we might expect that, over time, homogeneity should increase within discussion networks, and heterogeneity between them should increase as people come to agree with those they talk to. But if this occurs, then there is a limit to the operation of 'conversion by conversation' effects—although, of course, friendship networks are not permanent: some people are 'dropped' and others join over time!

Part of the answer lies in the nature of friendship and acquaintance circles. Friendships might form around common interests, say a sport or hobby. They may form around a shared sense of humour. Most people will form friendships for a variety of different reasons—one friend may be a squash partner, another the parent of our child's schoolmate, another might be someone we see at work every day, and so on. Few, if any, choose friends purely on the basis of their political views. Furthermore, friendship networks are rarely self-contained and hermetically sealed, with everyone within the network knowing and interacting with everyone else in the network and with no one else. Some of our friends may know each other and may meet regularly, independently of their association with us. Others of our friends will not: we may be the only point of contact between them and, indeed, they may never meet each other at all.

We can think of two hypothetical and relatively intense conversation networks (Figure 4.1). The first involves individuals *A*, *B*, *C*, and *D*, most of whom talk to every other person in the group: only individuals *C* and *D* have no direct contact with each other. The second group, of individuals *W*, *X*, *Y*, and *Z*, is even more closely interlinked: everyone talks to everyone else. Both these groups are like the hermetic, closed systems discussed above. And, if conversion by conversation really does take place, we would expect to see increasing agreement and conformity within these networks. However, note that one individual in each group talks to someone from the other group: *D* and *W* are friends. This link exposes each group to the opinions of the other. If the two groups hold different opinions, then the *D–W* link will help maintain a situation in which individuals are continually exposed to a diversity of opinion. In reality, there are likely to be many more such links, with many more conversation networks. Our discussion networks are not

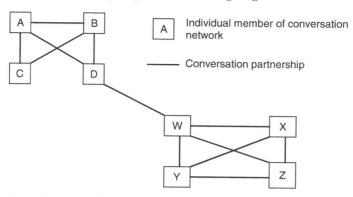

Fig. 4.1. Hypothetical political conversation networks

tidy and self-contained: they are leaky, made up of a range of contacts from intimate to casual, frequent to occasional, and often link us to several non-overlapping groups. Such non-overlapping links between relatively contained networks have considerable theoretical importance. For Granovetter (1973), such 'weak ties' are a means by which new ideas and information can enter our social networks. For Putnam (1993), they create 'bridging' social capital, fostering the tolerance and trust that he argues are essential for an effective community.

Work on American and Dutch elections has demonstrated the importance of cohesive social groups and weak ties linking different social groups for the transfer of political ideas between citizens (Huckfeldt, Johnson, and Sprague, 2002, 2004; Huckfeldt et al., 1995; Nieuwbeerta and Flap, 2000). The less individuals remain solely within tightly knit acquaintance circles, and the more they interact with individuals from a range of different social networks, the more they are likely to encounter diverse opinions, and the more likely they then are to reassess their own views. Even in the Netherlands, where social networks remain relatively homogeneous and hence many conversations lead to conformity, weak ties do widen individuals' horizons (Nieuwbeerta and Flap, 2000). That said, the extent to which weak ties expose voters to diverse opinions is partly culturally determined. For instance, whereas American voters readily acknowledge and express divergent opinions, Japanese voters are much more averse to the public expression of disagreement (Ikeda and Huckfeldt, 2001). The transfer of different political views between voters is facilitated in the former environment but inhibited in the latter. It is likely that British voters are closer to America than to Japan in this regard.

Such cultural differences notwithstanding, however, the diversity of voters' discussion networks remains important. Those most exposed to views from the wider environment tend to be the best educated and to have the greatest civic capacity—that is, they are the people who get most involved in local communities and organizations (Huckfeldt et al., 1995). As we have seen, education is also an important correlate of the size and intensity of individuals' political discussion networks in the UK. This is not to say that social cohesion is not important (Kenny, 1998). We tend to interact with people we think are like us, but few of us can limit our interactions just to the like-minded—and some are less limited in this regard than others.

An alternative approach is to think of how the environments within which we live structure opportunities for finding different opinions in conversation (Huckfeldt and Sprague, 1988, 1995). Few of us live in thoroughly mixed environments. Residential segregation means that we generally live in communities comprising people who, on the whole, share our general level of prosperity and, perhaps, our general lifestyle and outlook. And, because of the geography of party support, most of us live in areas in which one party or another is locally dominant. Unless we wish to be uncommonly selective, therefore, many of our friends and acquaintances are likely to be drawn from locally dominant groups, whether in our home neighbourhoods, our work-places, or our social networks. Huckfeldt and Sprague (1995, 128) put it graphically: 'a Mondale voter will be unable to discuss politics with another Mondale supporter if she resides in a context where all other individuals support Reagan'. People who find themselves in such situations have two choices if they wish to remain in the context (and in some cases, like the workplace, they may have little choice): silence or accommodation. Finifter's (1974) study of American car-workers showed that Republicans in a predominantly Democrat workplace tried to remain aloof from the Democrats among whom they worked. For Cox (1969a), on the other hand, those entering a new neighbourhood where their views were in the minority were likely to change their minds to fit in with local norms— especially when they themselves were not strong partisans.

But even in highly 'coerced' environments, it is not inevitable that all our encounters must be with people holding the locally dominant view. (Finifter's Republican car-workers did find a few other Republicans to talk to in their factory, for instance.) Probability theory shows why (using an example adapted from Huckfeldt, Johnson, and Sprague, 2004). Assume people choose their acquaintances more or less at random, and assume that they do so in an area where 70 per cent of all adults are Conservatives. There is therefore a 0.7 probability that the first acquaintance they make will be a Conservative. But if they make two new friends in the area, the chance that both will be Conservatives is $0.7 \times 0.7 = 0.49$—or just about 50:50! And the chance that three new friends will all be Conservatives is $0.7^3 = 0.343$—just one in three! Diversity is likely to persist in most circumstances. Of course in practice we do not choose friends randomly, but the point remains: unless individuals are highly selective, or live and work in remarkably uniform environments, or are just very reclusive, they are likely to encounter at least some diversity of opinion and disagreement.

With the data available to us, we cannot fully investigate the diversity of individuals' discussion networks. For instance, we have no way of knowing, from the BES surveys, how closed or open discussion networks are. To find this out, we would have to investigate not only respondents' discussion networks but also the networks of those with whom they discuss politics. However, we are able to look at the social and political diversity of the partial networks revealed by the BES conversation questions. Respondents who named a conversation partner were asked what sort of work each discussant did, so we can compare respondents' social class with that of their discussants. If discussion networks are homogeneous, then people are likely to talk to others in a similar social location. But if they are heterogeneous, networks should be more socially diverse. The evidence suggests heterogeneity (Table 4.5). For instance, two-thirds of individuals in the salariat reported at least one discussion partner who was in a different social class. A similar pattern emerges for working-class respondents too. Members of the smaller routine non-manual class (clerical and sales staff) and the petty bourgeoisie (largely the self-employed) were even less likely to talk only to others from their own class. This almost certainly reflects the coercion of minorities discussed by Huckfeldt and Sprague (1988): since these are the smallest classes, people in these groups are the least likely randomly to encounter only people in the same social location, and are the most likely to meet people from different classes. In fact, whatever their own social class, around half of all respondents had discussion networks which took in people

Table 4.5. Social diversity in discussion networks

| Discusant's class | Respondent's social class (%) | | | | |
	Salariat	Routine non-manual	Petty bourgeoisie	Working class	Total
All salariat	**31.8**	21.6	7.6	7.7	19.8
All routine non-manual	6.3	**5.8**	7.6	6.6	6.3
All petty bourgeoisie	4.0	6.2	**13.4**	4.4	5.3
All working class	4.1	12.0	13.4	**35.3**	16.7
Salariat + RNM	15.1	14.0	4.2	4.6	10.7
Salariat + PB	13.6	7.8	9.2	2.9	8.4
Salariat + WC	7.8	6.7	6.7	11.5	8.6
RNM + PB	3.0	4.2	15.1	2.6	4.0
RNM + WC	3.8	10.9	4.2	10.8	7.9
PB + WC	2.6	4.0	10.9	8.2	5.3
Salariat + RNM + WC	4.0	2.0	3.4	0.5	2.3
Salariat + RNM + WC	2.0	2.7	0.0	2.6	2.2
Salariat + PB + WC	1.8	1.3	2.5	1.3	1.6
RNM + PB + WC	0.2	0.9	1.7	1.1	0.8
N	604	450	119	547	1720

Key: RNM = routine non-manual; PB = petty bourgeoisie; WC = working class.
Source: BES data files (1992).

from several different classes: for instance, just under 16 per cent of all members of the salariat named at least one member of the salariat and one member of the working class within their discussion network. Most conversation networks are socially heterogeneous, therefore.

That said, it is important not to overstate this. For instance, around three-quarters of all respondents from the salariat talked to at least one other person from the same class as themselves (even though most also talked to another person from a different class). And around 70 per cent of working-class respondents talked to at least one other working-class person. Again, members of the two smaller classes were the least likely to encounter others from their own class: only 40 per cent of routine non-manual workers and 53 per cent of the petty bourgeoisie reported talking to one or more members of their own class.

The BES data also provide evidence of political diversity in discussion networks. Respondents were asked not only their own partisanship (i.e. which party they would normally consider themselves as supporting, as opposed to the party they voted for in 1992) but also their judgement of the partisanship of each of their named discussants. Around three in five respondents who named a discussant said that all of the discussants whose partisanship they felt they knew supported the same party (Table 4.6).[7] But

Table 4.6. Political diversity in discussion networks

Discussion network partisanship	Respondent's partisan identification (%)					
	No ID	Con	Labour	Lib Dem	Other party	Total
All Conservative	53.1	**60.0**	3.8	16.5	2.3	34.8
All Labour	10.2	3.8	**59.2**	10.0	16.3	21.8
All Lib Dem	10.2	2.4	2.4	**18.4**	7.0	5.2
All other	2.0	0.5	1.0	0.8	**23.3**	1.3
Con–Lab	12.2	16.5	16.5	10.7	14.0	15.4
Con–Lib Dem	4.1	11.3	2.2	20.3	0.0	9.5
Con–other	0.0	1.3	0.0	0.4	9.3	1.0
Lab–Lib Dem	6.1	1.3	11.0	15.7	0.0	6.5
Lab–other	0.0	0.2	1.6	0.8	16.3	1.1
Lib Dem–Other	0.0	0.1	0.2	1.1	7.0	0.5
Con–Lab–Lib Dem	2.0	2.4	1.8	5.4	0.0	2.6
Con–Lab–other	0.0	0.1	0.4	0.0	4.7	0.3
N	49	826	502	261	43	1681

Source: BES data files (1992).

[7] Discussant partisanship in Table 4.6 is measured on the basis of respondents' own perceptions. We have concentrated only on declared partisanships. Where respondents do not know the partisanship of a discussant, or feel that he or she does not support any particular party, we have treated that discussant as missing. Hence, for instance, the 'all-Conservative' group contains not only situations where all named discussants are thought to be Conservatives, but also situations where at least one is a Conservative and the partisanship of the remainder is unclear or unknown.

almost 40 per cent said that they talked to at least two individuals who held different views from each other. People who themselves identified with Labour or the Conservatives were by far the most likely to talk only to people they thought held a similar view: around 60 per cent in each case did so. In part, this may reflect selective memory effects (as discussed above). However, while this undoubtedly applies for some respondents, it is unlikely to apply to all. In fact this almost certainly also reflects, once again, the coercive effect of large majorities for some parties. In 1992, Conservatives and Labour together took 78 per cent of the vote. As the two largest parties, they won most seats, and they took a majority of votes in a sizeable number of constituencies. The chances of Labour voters living in Labour-dominated environments, or Conservative voters living in Conservative-dominated environments, were high, as was the chance of encountering other like-minded individuals.

This interpretation is reinforced when we consider those respondents who identified with the Liberal Democrats. If the high preponderance of Labour or Conservative identifiers reporting that all their discussants supported the same party was a selective memory effect, with people assuming others agree with them, we would expect to see a similarly high figure for Liberal Democrat supporters reporting solely Liberal Democrat discussion networks. But we do not: only 18 per cent said that all their discussants whose political preferences they knew were also Liberal Democrats. The Liberal Democrats are the third party in British politics, with only 18 per cent of the vote nationally in 1992. Their supporters were less likely, therefore, to encounter only like-minded people than were supporters of the Labour or Conservative parties.

Looked at more broadly, a majority of identifiers with each of the three main parties reported talking to at least one other supporter of the same party (just over 90 per cent of Conservative and Labour identifiers did so, as did 61 per cent of Liberal Democrat identifiers). But large numbers (around 40 per cent of Conservative and Labour identifiers, and over 80 per cent of Liberal Democrats) also reported talking to supporters of other parties. Around half of all those who identified with one of the three main parties reported talking to a supporter of a different party. Large numbers of voters, therefore, do encounter different political opinions to their own in their conversations with their friends and acquaintances.

The Impact of Political Conversation

The key question, however, is whether political conversations reinforce existing opinions or whether voters change their minds on the basis of what they hear and learn from others. Much of the neighbourhood effects literature assumes a 'conversion by conversation' effect, but until the 1990s there was little attempt to analyse this empirically.

One attempt at such an analysis was provided in Fitton's (1973) study of social interaction in three Manchester streets during the 1970 general election. The research charted patterns of sociability in each street, recording which neighbours talked to each other, and which did not, and investigated whether individuals' political views were influenced by their neighbours' views. The results were mixed. Patterns of sociability varied from street to street. In one street, neighbourliness was in short supply: few talked to other members of the community in which they lived. Not surprisingly, therefore, few knew their neighbours' political opinions, and there was little evidence of people changing their opinions to fit in with the locally dominant view. In the other two streets, however, there was both greater sociability and more evidence that individuals were changing their opinions to fit in with those of their friends. In the most friendly street of all, nine individuals changed their vote choice prior to the election, with six coming to agree with the views of the neighbours they talked to. And in the third street, where there was some community interaction, five out of the six who changed their vote choice moved in the direction of the locally dominant opinion. Of course, many local residents did not change their views at all, no matter how sociable they were. But, as Fitton noted, most of those who changed switched to the views of those neighbours they talked to most. Conversation within communities seemed to influence at least some voters' opinions, almost certainly enhancing the majority opinion there.

More recent research also demonstrates that conversations can have political consequences (Bennett, Flickinger, and Rhine, 2000; Curtice, 1995; Huckfeldt and Sprague, 1995; Zuckerman, Valentino, and Zuckerman, 1994). Using data drawn from the 1992 BES, Pattie and Johnston (1999, 2000) showed that individuals who had talked to supporters of a particular party were more likely to switch their vote to that party in an election than were people who had not talked to supporters of the party. In the USA, Beck (2002) found that voters who talked to Perot supporters in the 1992 presidential election were more likely to defect to Perot than were those who did not talk to his supporters, even after controlling for individual partisanship, evaluations of the candidates, and so on. And Robert Huckfeldt and his colleagues have shown, in a variety of American electoral contexts (but most famously in their study of the 1984 presidential election in South Bend, Indiana), that voters do pay heed to the views of those they talk to, and can be influenced by those views (Huckfeldt and Sprague, 1987, 1988, 1995; see also Kenny, 1994, 1998). Nor are conversation effects simply an artefact of Anglo-American politics. Similar findings have been reported for Japanese, Dutch, and German electorates (Ikeda and Huckfeldt, 2001; Nieuwbeerta and Flap, 2000; Pappi, 1996).

We can get some idea of the strength of conversation effects by looking at the extent to which British voters changed their votes between 1987 and 1992 to fit in with the opinions of their discussion networks. If conversation does make a difference, then among those who did not vote for a party at the first election, those who have talked to supporters of that party should be more likely to vote for it at the second election than should individuals who have not talked to supporters of the party. Data are taken once again from the 1992 BES. We have calculated how many of each individual's discussion partners supported the Conservatives, Labour, or the Liberal Democrats. The data are constrained as individual respondents could only name a maximum of three discussants. However, within that they can range from having no discussants supporting a particular party to having all three supporting the same party. By counting the number of Conservative, Labour, and Liberal Democrat discussants each respondent named, we obtain an idea of the intensity of partisan bias within their discussion networks.

Among BES respondents who identified with one of the three main UK parties in 1992, and who also reported talking to at least one other supporter of these parties, 82 per cent talked to at least one other supporter of their favoured party. This would be likely to reinforce their own views. But 43 per cent reported that at least one of their conversation partners supported a party other than the one they themselves identified with (the percentages do not add to 100 because many individuals spoke to supporters of both 'their' and other parties). A large proportion of those with political discussants found themselves exposed to heterodox views, therefore. While their views were reinforced by some of their conversation partners, they were challenged by others. Large numbers of voters routinely engage in political discussions, and are often exposed to views that are different from their own, therefore.

We expect that the more supporters of a particular party a person talks to regularly, the more likely he or she should be to come to support that party too. Conversations should have a stronger influence on individuals' political choices when all conversation partners are sending the same message regarding which party to support than when conflicting cues are given by different discussants. With very few exceptions, the data confirm this. Table 4.7a, for instance, looks at those 1992 BES respondents who said they had not voted Conservative in 1987, the previous general election. How many switched to the Conservatives in 1992? The more Conservative supporters they remembered talking to, the greater their chance of switching to the Conservatives. While only 8 per cent of those who spoke to no Conservatives switched to the party in 1992, 52 per cent of those who spoke to three Conservatives did so. But the more Labour or Liberal Democrat supporters our 1987 non-Tory voters talked to, the fewer of them switched to the Conservatives in 1992. Almost one in every five of those who did not talk to any Labour supporters switched to the Tories between 1987 and 1992. But among those who spoke to three Labour supporters, only 2 per cent switched to the Conservatives. The only exception to this pattern occurs among those who did not vote Conservative in 1987 and who talked to three Liberal Democrats: here 22 per cent switched to the Tories. But this latter group is a very small one. Few

Table 4.7. Voter defection and intensity of partisan reinforcement in conversation networks

(a) Percentage of respondents switching to the Conservatives in 1992

	No. of discussants supporting party			
Party supported by discussants	0	1	2	3
Conservative	8.5	26.0	45.5	51.7
Labour	19.4	12.0	5.8	2.1
Liberal Democrat	15.1	15.7	8.9	22.2

Note: Respondents had not voted Conservative in 1987.

(b) Percentage of respondents switching to Labour in 1992

	No. of discussants supporting party			
Party supported by discussants	0	1	2	3
Conservative	16.8	8.1	2.7	2.1
Labour	6.9	15.3	37.3	66.7
Liberal Democrat	12.0	6.5	6.2	0.0

Note: Respondents had not voted Labour in 1987.

(c) Percentage of respondents switching to the Liberal Democrats in 1992

	No. of discussants supporting party			
Party supported by discussants	0	1	2	3
Conservative	10.5	9.9	8.6	2.1
Labour	9.0	13.6	8.3	6.4
Liberal Democrat	6.5	28.8	40.0	57.1

Note: Respondents had not voted Liberal Democrat in 1987.
Source: BES data files (1992).

respondents reported talking to as many as three Liberal Democrat supporters (a function of that party's small size). There is, therefore, a very large margin for error in this particular estimate.

Similar patterns hold for the other parties. Table 4.7b shows that voters who had not voted Labour in 1987 became more likely to do so in 1992 as the number of Labour supporters they talked to rose. Only 7 per cent of those who had no Labour-supporting conversation partners switched to Labour in 1992, compared to fully two-thirds of those who talked to three or more Labour supporters. And their chances of switching to Labour dropped as the number of supporters of other parties in their conversation networks grew. While 17 per cent of those with no Conservative-supporting conversation partners switched to Labour in 1992, only 2 per cent of those with three or more did so. Table 4.7c shows the same pattern for the Liberal Democrats. The proportion of those who had not voted Alliance in 1987 but who switched their vote to the Liberal Democrats in 1992 went up from just 6 per cent of those who reported no Liberal-Democrat-supporting discussion partners to 57 per cent of those who said they had three or more.[8]

Conversation is associated with conversion, therefore: talking to supporters of a party encouraged individuals to switch to that party; talking to opponents discouraged them from doing so. But this is only half the story. Loyalty to a party over time is also encouraged by talking to other supporters of that party (Table 4.8). Among those who voted Conservative in 1987 (Table 4.8a), continued loyalty to the party in 1992 was highest among those with most Conservative discussion partners: 91 per cent of this group voted Conservative again. Conversely, it was lowest among those who reported no conversations with Conservatives: 71 per cent of this group

Table 4.8. Voter loyalty and intensity of partisan reinforcement in conversation networks

(a) Percentage of 1987 Conservative voters remaining loyal to Conservative in 1992

	No. of discussants supporting party			
Party supported by discussants	0	1	2	3
Conservative	70.7	81.3	88.1	91.3
Labour	82.0	76.0	50.0	20.0
Liberal Democrat	82.1	68.8	52.6	25.0

(b) Percentage of 1987 Labour voters remaining loyal to Labour in 1992

	No. of discussants supporting party			
Party supported by discussants	0	1	2	3
Conservative	80.6	72.4	68.8	50.0
Labour	73.9	76.7	87.9	90.9
Liberal Democrat	80.9	64.4	60.0	—

(c) Percentage of 1987 Liberal Democrat voters remaining loyal to Liberal Democrats in 1992

	No. of discussants supporting party			
Party supported by discussants	0	1	2	3
Conservative	64.7	61.5	50.0	—
Labour	62.2	60.0	73.9	—
Liberal Democrat	51.6	73.3	83.9	—

— = insufficient data.
Source: BES data files (1992).

[8] At the 1983 and 1987 elections, the Liberals fought in an Alliance with the Social Democratic Party, with which it merged in 1988; after a brief period when they were known as the Social and Liberal Democrats, they took on their current name of Liberal Democrats.

voted Tory again. But the more Labour or Liberal Democrat supporters they talked to, the less likely they were to remain loyal to the Conservatives. While 82 per cent of those 1987 Conservatives who talked to no Labour supporters voted Conservative again in 1992, only 20 per cent of those who talked to three or more Labour supporters did so. Very similar patterns held for Labour and Liberal Democrat loyalty between 1987 and 1992 (Table 4.8b and c). Among those who had voted for a party in 1987, the more supporters of that party they talked to, the more likely they were to vote for it again in 1987; and the more supporters of other parties they talked to, the less likely they were to remain loyal.

As we have seen, however, many individuals inhabit politically diverse discussion networks, talking to supporters of several different political parties. In their work on American voters, Huckfeldt, Johnson, and Sprague (2002, 2004) showed that the influence of each conversation partnership is affected by all the other conversation partnerships an individual is engaged in. If I talk solely to Labour voters, I am likely to pay attention to the views of another Labour voter. However, if only one of my discussion partners supports Labour while the rest support the Conservatives, I might discount the views of the Labour voter and take the views of the Conservatives more seriously. We can demonstrate this by examining how influential the views of individuals' first-named respondents were, depending on the views of other respondents in their conversation networks (Table 4.9).

Consider first those BES respondents who did not vote Conservative in 1987 (Table 4.9a). Once again, we can see whether their conversations influenced their vote choice in 1992 by looking at the percentage who transferred their vote to the Conservatives in that year. In line with the findings reported earlier, when the first-named discussant was a Conservative, the individual was more likely to switch to the Conservatives in 1992 than were individuals who either reported no discussants or whose primary discussant was not a Conservative. Of those who said their first-named discussant was a Conservative, 44 per cent switched to the Conservatives, compared to just 11 per cent of those with no discussant, 5 per cent of those with a Labour primary discussant, and 9 per cent of those whose primary discussant was a Liberal Democrat. And, as we would expect from Table 4.7, those who reported other Conservatives in their discussion network were more likely again to switch to the Tories in 1992 than were those who did not. So, for instance, while 38 per cent of individuals whose only Tory discussant was their primary discussant switched to the Conservatives, over half (53 per cent) of those with at least one more Conservative discussant did so.

So politically homogeneous discussion networks reinforce the 'conversion by conversation' effect. But politically heterogeneous networks, where there are divergent opinions, attenuate it. For instance, among those who did not vote Conservative in 1987, but whose primary discussant was a Conservative, those whose discussion networks also contained a Labour voter were less

Table 4.9. Intensity of partisan reinforcement in conversation networks

(a) Percentage of respondents switching to the Conservatives in 1992

| | | No. of other discussants supporting: | | | | | |
| | | Conservative | | Labour | | Lib Dem | |
Party supported by first discussant	All respondents	0	1+	0	1+	0	1+
No discussants	11.3						
Conservative	44.4	37.7	53.3	51.6	29.5	44.5	44.2
Labour	4.6	2.7	12.7	6.0	3.8	4.6	2.1
Liberal Democrat	8.6	7.3	13.0	11.0	4.8	9.2	9.3

Note: Respondents had not voted Conservative in 1987.

(b) Percentage of respondents switching to Labour in 1992

| | | No. of other discussants supporting: | | | | | |
| | | Conservative | | Labour | | Lib Dem | |
Party supported by first discussant	All respondents	0	1+	0	1+	0	1+
No discussants	13.3						
Conservative	3.1	4.2	2.4	1.9	8.1	3.1	2.9
Labour	38.0	44.5	23.9	23.3	52.3	40.8	25.7
Liberal Democrat	4.8	6.3	2.7	2.1	11.1	3.9	5.4

Note: Respondents had not voted Labour in 1987.

(c) Percentage of respondents switching to the Liberal Democrats in 1992

| | | No. of other discussants supporting: | | | | | |
| | | Conservative | | Labour | | Lib Dem | |
Party supported by first discussant	All respondents	0	1+	0	1+	0	1+
No discussants	6.8						
Conservative	5.1	4.6	5.1	4.2	7.6	4.3	10.5
Labour	8.4	8.3	8.6	9.4	7.5	6.6	22.4
Liberal Democrat	43.7	46.5	39.3	43.3	44.4	41.3	51.5

Note: Respondents had not voted Liberal Democrat in 1987.
Source: BES data files (1992).

likely to switch to the Tories in 1992 (only 30 per cent did so) than were those whose networks contained no Labour voters (52 per cent of whom voted Conservative in 1992). Similar effects occur for switching to Labour or the Liberal Democrats too (compare Tables 4.9b and c). Voters are more influenced by opinions that are common in their discussion networks than by opinions that are heterodox.

North American work has also demonstrated the relative importance for vote choice of political discussions between voters (Beck et al., 2002). In an analysis of voting at the 1992 presidential election, information received from personal discussion networks proved a more powerful predictor of vote, at least for those interested in politics, than information gained from the mass media or from political parties. Conversations are not trivial, therefore. They can have substantial political consequences.

But is the conversation effect equally strong for everyone? Cox's (1969a) study of the neighbourhood effect in Columbus, Ohio, gives some insights. Recent arrivals in a community were more likely to switch their political allegiances to fit in with local majority opinion than were longer-established residents (presumably because those long-term residents likely to change had already done so). Those whose main contacts were within the local community were more likely to agree with the community norm than were those whose contacts came from outside the community. Partisanship (or its absence) was important too: those who were not strongly committed to a political party were more likely to switch to the local majority view than were those who strongly supported a particular party.

Strength of partisanship also influences the impact of conversations in Britain. The first two columns of Table 4.10 concentrate on those 1992 BES respondents who said they had not voted Conservative in 1987 and who did not identify with the Conservative party. Respondents are divided into two conversation groups (those who talked to no Conservative supporters and those who talked to at least one), and three partisanship groups (very strong supporters of a—non-Conservative—party, fairly strong party supporters, and those with only weak or no party identification). How many of them voted for the Conservatives in 1992? Not surprisingly, the weaker their (non-Conservative) party identification, the more likely they were to

Table 4.10. Strength of partisanship and the influence of conversation on vote-switching, 1992

Strength of party identification	% respondents[a] switching to Conservative in 1992 who had:		% respondents[b] switching to Labour in 1992 who had:		% respondents[c] switching to Lib Dem in 1992 who had:	
	No Con discussants	1+ Con discussants	No Lab discussant	1+ Lab discussants	No LD discussants	1+ LD discussants
Very strong	0.5	0.9	0.8	0.0	1.0	5.0
Fairly strong	2.1	2.7	1.8	2.7	3.1	11.3
Weak/none	5.1	23.6	4.7	13.9	6.1	22.1

[a] Respondents did not identify with Conservatives or vote Conservative in 1987.
[b] Respondents did not identify with Labour or vote Labour in 1987.
[c] Respondents did not identify with Liberal Democrats or vote Liberal/SDP Alliance in 1987.

Source: BES data files (1992).

switch to the Conservatives in 1992. But the effect was much stronger among those who had some Conservative conversation partners than among those who had none. Not surprisingly, hardly any of those with a strong sense of loyalty to another party voted Conservative in 1992, whether or not they had talked to Conservative supporters. But among those with only weak or non-existent attachments to other parties, only 5 per cent of those with no Conservative discussants switched to the Tories in 1992, compared to almost 24 per cent of those with at least one. As the subsequent pairs of columns in the table show, similar patterns hold, *mutatis mutandis*, for Labour and the Liberal Democrats. The politically committed are hard to sway; but floating voters can be influenced by their peers' opinions.

Similarly, the more knowledgeable individuals are about politics, as measured by the political knowledge quiz scores discussed above, the less influenced they are by their conversations with others (Table 4.11). For instance, among individuals who had not voted Conservative in 1987 and who scored low on the quiz, just over 8 per cent who knew no Conservative discussion partners switched to the Tories in 1992, compared to over 40 per cent of those who knew and talked to at least one Conservative supporter. Among 1987 non-Conservatives who scored high on the quiz, however, the gap was narrower: an almost identical percentage of those with no Conservative discussant switched to the Tories in 1992, compared to just over 25 per cent of those talking to at least one Conservative voter. Again, similar (though not as pronounced) patterns also hold for switching to Labour and Liberal Democrats between 1987 and 1992. That said, it is also worth noting that while increased knowledge of the political system lessens the effect of conversations with others, it does not remove it entirely: in all cases, those talking to supporters of a party they had not previously voted for were still more likely to switch to it than were those who did not talk to that party's supporters.

What is more, people are selective in who they listen to. The views of some individuals are listened to carefully, either because we generally agree with

Table 4.11. Political knowledge and the influence of conversation, 1992

Political knowledge score	% respondents[a] switching to Conservative in 1992 who had:		% respondents[b] switching to Labour in 1992 who had:		% respondents[c] switching to Lib Dem in 1992 who had:	
	No Con discussants	1+ Con discussants	No Lab discussant	1+ Lab discussants	No LD discussants	1+ LD discussants
Low (0–5)	8.5	43.8	10.7	26.8	6.1	38.0
High (6–10)	8.4	26.5	3.7	23.1	7.0	27.6

[a] Respondents did not vote Conservative in 1987.
[b] Respondents did not vote Labour in 1987.
[c] Respondents did not vote Liberal/SDP Alliance in 1987.

Source: BES data files (1992).

them on most matters, or because we recognize they have some expertise in the particular subject on which they are expressing a view. The views of others may be discounted, either because we feel they are generally wrong on other matters, or because they are not seen as experts on the specific topic under discussion. And other things being equal, perceptions of expertise do influence electoral choice. Whether or not they think they will disagree with them, people seek out the views of those they consider to have political expertise or knowledge (Huckfeldt, 2001; Huckfeldt, Ikeda, and Pappi, 2000). Not only that, but they tend to be right in their assessments of expertise. Those judged as politically expert generally do have greater knowledge of politics than average, do tend to be better educated on the whole, and also tend to be strong supporters of a political party. And where people know they often disagree with the individuals they talk to, they are less influenced by those individuals' views; they are more influenced by the opinions of those they feel they do often agree with (Pattie and Johnston, 2002b).

To illustrate this, we return to our 1992 BES respondents. Those who named discussion partners were asked how often they disagreed with each discussant when they discussed politics. For simplicity, we consider here whether individuals agreed or disagreed with their first-named discussant. Among those who had not voted for a party in 1987, the probability of switching to the party in 1992 was much higher for individuals whose primary discussant not only supported that party but was also someone the respondent felt they generally agreed with than where the discussant supported the party, but was a person the respondent often disagreed with (Table 4.12). And the impact of agreement was substantial. For instance, individuals who had not previously voted Conservative and whose first-named discussant was a Conservative were almost ten times more likely to switch to the Tories in 1992 if they seldom or never disagreed with their conversation partner (just under three-quarters in this group went on to vote

Table 4.12. The effect of disagreement in political conversations, 1992

Frequency of disagreement with discussant	% respondents[a] switching to Conservative in 1992		% respondents[b] switching to Labour in 1992		% respondents[c] switching to Lib Dem in 1992	
	1st discussant not Con	1st discussant is Con	1st discussant not Lab	1st discussant is Lab	1st discussant not LD	1st discussant is LD
Often	13.0	7.8	11.9	15.1	10.7	38.1
Sometimes	8.9	45.8	4.2	32.6	10.3	33.3
Seldom/never	3.0	74.0	3.4	63.6	4.7	62.5

[a] Respondents did not vote Conservative in 1987.
[b] Respondents did not vote Labour in 1987.
[c] Respondents did not vote Liberal/SDP Alliance in 1987.

Source: BES data files (1992).

Conservative) than if they often disagreed (only 8 per cent in this group switched to the party). Although not as dramatic, levels of agreement in discussion partnerships also had large impacts on switching to Labour and the Liberal Democrats.

It is also worth noting, however, that agreement between discussion partners did not have to be near-total for conversations between the individuals to influence vote choice. So, for instance, only 11 per cent of those who did not vote Conservative in 1987, and who named no individuals with whom they talked politics, switched to the party in 1992. But among those who named as their first conversation partner a Conservative supporter with whom they sometimes disagreed, fully 46 per cent switched to the party five years later. Again, similar patterns hold for vote transfers to Labour and Liberal Democrat. The more we generally agree with our discussion partners, therefore, the more likely we are to be influenced by their views. But near unanimity of view is not necessary: as long as the person we talk to is someone we agree with at least sometimes, we are open to their influence.

A final factor that might affect how much individuals are influenced by their conversations is their relationship with the person they are talking to. As already noted, many discussion partners are family members. And intimacy matters: the closer our relationship with people, the greater their influence on us. We pay more attention to (and are more likely to be influenced by) the views of our relatives (especially partners and spouses) than to the opinions of our other acquaintances (Huckfeldt and Sprague, 1991, 1995; Johnston et al., 2005b; Stoker and Jennings, 2005; Zuckerman and Kotler-Berkowitz, 1998; Zuckerman, Fitzgerald, and Dasović, 2005). This is not to say that there is complete homogeneity of views within households, or even within marriages; clearly disagreements can still persist (Zuckerman, Fitzgerald, and Dasović, 2005). Furthermore, while household members are more likely than others to share the same vote decision, they can still hold divergent political attitudes: vote choice is more amenable to influence than deep-seated beliefs (Zuckerman and Kotler-Berkowitz, 1998).

But while we are most likely to be influenced by those we are most closely related to, that does not mean that conversations with people outside the family unit have no influence. Even if not so strongly as in the case of relatives, voters' decisions are influenced by the views of people outside the family (Huckfeldt and Sprague, 1991; Pattie and Johnston, 1999). Once again, the 1992 BES data illustrate the relative importance of conversations with family and non-family members (Table 4.13). For ease of presentation, this analysis concentrates once again on individuals' first-named discussants. As before, we are concerned with those who did not vote for a particular party in 1987 and examine whether their conversations influenced their chances of switching to that party in 1992. The patterns revealed are straightforward. For instance, how likely were those who had not voted Conservative in 1987 to switch to the party in 1992 (Table 3.13a)? We already know

Table 4.13. The impact of intimacy in political conversations

(a) Percentage of respondents switching to the Conservatives in 1992

		Discussant is:	
Party supported by first discussant	All respondents	Relative	Non-relative
No discussants	11.3		
Conservative	44.4	46.8	37.0
Labour	4.6	3.2	9.6
Liberal Democrat	8.6	8.0	16.0

Note: Respondents had not voted Conservative in 1987.

(b) Percentage of respondents switching to Labour in 1992

		Discussant is:	
Party supported by first discussant	All respondents	Relative	Non-relative
No discussants	13.3		
Conservative	3.1	2.9	3.9
Labour	38.0	44.3	24.2
Liberal Democrat	4.8	5.2	3.2

Note: Respondents had not voted Labour in 1987.

(c) Percentage of respondents switching to the Liberal Democrats in 1992

		Discussant is:	
Party supported by first discussant	All respondents	Relative	Non-relative
No discussants	6.8		
Conservative	5.1	4.7	6.2
Labour	8.4	9.0	5.9
Liberal Democrat	43.7	43.2	45.8

Note: Respondents had not voted Liberal Democrat in 1987.
Source: BES data files (1992).

that those who talked to a Conservative supporter were more likely to switch to the Conservatives themselves than were those who talked to supporters of other parties or who had no discussants. More importantly, this remained true whether or not their conversation partners were relatives. For instance, the proportion of individuals who switched to the Conservatives in 1992 was highest among those whose primary discussant was a Conservative, whether or not that discussant was a family member. Similarly, voters were more likely to switch to Labour or the Liberal Democrats if their primary discussant supported that party than if their discussant did not, irrespective of their relationship to their discussant (Tables 4.13b and c).

However, it is also worth noting that, at least for switching to Labour or the Conservatives, conversations with family members had a greater impact than conversations with non-relatives. Among those who had not voted

Conservative in 1987, 47 per cent of those whose primary discussant was a Conservative-supporting relative switched to the party in 1992. But this dropped to 37 per cent of those whose primary discussant was a Conservative but not a family member. And while 44 per cent of those who had not previously voted Labour but who talked to a Labour-supporting relative themselves switched to the party, only 24 per cent of those who talked to a Labour supporter who was not a family member did so. There was no equivalent difference between discussion with a relative and a non-relative for switching to the Liberal Democrats, but since few respondents reported a non-relative Liberal Democrat primary discussant, this may well be the result of small numbers.

The views of all those we talk to are influential in our vote choices, therefore. But we are particularly attentive to those we are related to, and to those we generally agree with.

Political Conversation and Attitude Change

The preceding discussion has demonstrated that vote choices can be influenced by the opinions of those we live among and talk to. However, the vote decision is a short-term choice which can be shaped by a variety of factors. Some individuals may transfer their votes from one party to another based on deep-seated and substantial changes in their political beliefs. But others may change votes for different, more short-term and contingent reasons. For instance, I may think a tactical vote for party X is the best way of unseating party Y in my constituency, even though my true preference remains for party Z. Or I may decide that, while my long-term preference is for party X, it has temporarily lost its way and hence I will vote for party Y until X recovers. And so on. All these decisions can be influenced by a range of things, including in principle our conversations with other voters. Does who we talk to make a difference to how we think?

One way of finding out is to interview the same group of people at two different points in time. This has the great advantage that we know that differences in responses at different times are the result of changes in peoples' views, not just sampling error (a risk when we rely on two separate cross-sections). The 1992–7 British Election Panel Study (BEPS) provides just such an opportunity. A group of respondents to the 1992 BES were re-interviewed five years later, just after the 1997 general election, and were asked many of the same questions on a range of political issues on both occasions. We can therefore look at attitude change over time. And because the BEPS respondents were asked about their political discussion networks in 1992, we can investigate whether conversations have an impact on attitude change. Do people change their opinions in ways that are predictable from the nature of their conversation networks (Pattie and Johnston, 2001d)?

Political opinion in Britain is structured around two main axes (Evans and Heath, 1995; Evans, Heath, and Lalljee, 1996; Heath, Evans, and Martin, 1993). The first is a left–right dimension, which assesses the traditional battleground of British politics—the permissible extent of wealth redistribution and the balance between state and market in the provision of goods and services. The second, the libertarian–authoritarian dimension, measures attitudes towards law and order, permissiveness, and civil liberties. These dimensions are unrelated to each other and therefore measure very different constructs: an individual's location on the left–right dimension is no guide to that person's position on the libertarian–authoritarian axis.

Both dimensions can be measured using the 1992–7 BEPS survey.[9] And since the questions were repeated in both the first and the last wave of the survey, it is possible to look at how individuals' positions on each dimension have changed over time. The scales are constructed so that high scores reflect relatively right-wing and authoritarian views, while low scores reflect left-wing or libertarian views. We proceed by regressing respondents' scores on each dimension in 1997 on their scores on the same dimension five years earlier, and on the number of Conservative, Labour, and Liberal Democrat conversation partners they reported in 1992 (Pattie and Johnston, 2001d). Controlling for how left or right wing, or how libertarian or authoritarian, an individual was in 1992 both takes into account the extent to which people's attitudes are stable over time, and also in effect controls for many of the personal factors that might account for an individual's political views. Furthermore, it means that the regression coefficients for other variables in the equation tell us about the extent to which those variables account for change over time in political attitudes.

Not surprisingly, people's attitudes in 1997 were strongly related to what they had thought in 1992 (Table 4.14). The coefficients for the 1992 left–right and libertarian–authoritarian scales were positive and significant, indicating that (for instance) those who had started out holding opinions on the left of the political spectrum tended to stay relatively left wing in their views, and those who had started out on the right, were likely to remain right wing in outlook. However, in both cases, the coefficients are substantially less than 1.0, suggesting that, overall, people became more left wing and libertarian in their views between 1992 and 1997.

---

[9] The scales are defined following Heath, Evans, and Martin (1993). Both scales sum respondents' answers to six questions: in each case, respondents were asked if they agreed with a proposition (with responses coded from 'agree strongly' to 'disagree strongly'). Responses were coded so that the most left-wing responses scored 1 and the most right-wing responses scored 5. Similarly with the libertarian–authoritarian dimension, with the most libertarian coded as 1, and the most authoritarian coded as 5. Principal components analyses for 1992 and 1997 responses confirm that the left–right and libertarian–authoritarian dimensions are internally coherent and are clearly distinct from each other. Cronbach's alpha for the left–right scale was 0.73 in 1992 and 0.64 in 1997, and for the libertarian–authoritarian scale it was 0.66 in 1992 and 0.69 in 1997.

Table 4.14. Political conversations and attitude change, 1992–7:
OLS regression models

Independent variables	Left–right scale 1997	Libertarian–authoritarian scale 1997
Left–right scale 1992	0.53	
Libertarian–authoritarian scale 1992		0.79
Number of Conservative discussants 1992	0.40	−0.19
Number of Labour discussants 1992	−0.24	−0.29
Number of Lib Dem discussants 1992	—	−0.25
Constant	7.49	6.62
R^2	0.46	0.60
N	1585	1544

Note: Only significant coefficients are shown.
Source: 1992–7 British Election Panel Study.

But we are interested here primarily in the impact of conversation on attitude change. And the evidence is clear: the more Conservatives a person reported having talked to in 1992, the more right wing their attitudes became over time (indicated by the positive and significant coefficient for Conservative discussants in the left–right equation). And the more Labour supporters they talked to then, the more left wing their views became over the next five years (shown by the significant negative coefficient). Conversational context was related to attitude change, with people moving in the direction favoured by their conversation partners.

The pattern for the libertarian–authoritarian dimension also suggests that conversation helps to change minds, though the detail here is rather different. Once again, it is the number of Conservative and Labour discussants that makes a difference (though the coefficient for the number of Liberal Democrat discussants was only just short of conventional levels of statistical significance).[10] But what is striking is that both the Labour and the Conservative discussant coefficients are negative, indicating that the more supporters of each party a person talked to in 1992, other things being equal, the more libertarian their views became between 1992 and 1997. Talk broadens the mind!

Our conversations with others can influence how we change our minds on political issues, therefore, but engaging in political discussion also makes people more aware citizens. In a survey of American adults, those who engaged in frequent political conversations were able to give more reasons for their own views on a range of issues than were those who engaged in few or no conversations, even when other factors were taken into account (Price, Capella and Nir, 2002). They were also able to suggest more reasons why others might disagree with them. But frequency of political discussion, while

[10] $p = 0.052$.

important, was not the only aspect of conversation that mattered here. Disagreement was important too. Those who reported that they often disagreed with those they talked to were able to give more reasons in justification of their own opinions, and to ascribe more reasons to those who disagreed with them, than were those who seldom disagreed. Discussions with people who hold different views might not force us to change our minds but they do encourage us to think more clearly about what we believe. As the proponents of deliberative democracy suggest, discussion leads to better understanding. For Habermas (1984), rationality is a precondition of the ideal speech situation; but it seems also to be a consequence of deliberation and discussion.

Finally, what of tolerance? We argued earlier that a tolerant attitude towards others and towards politics helps to encourage political conversation. Those who are more tolerant are more willing to talk to others about politics (and do so more frequently) than those who are intolerant. But the relationship between political conversation and tolerance might run in the opposite causal direction too. Political conversation, especially when it involves cross-cutting discussions across diverse opinions and acquaintance circles, can itself foster greater political tolerance among citizens (Mutz, 2002a, 2002b; Mutz and Mondak, 2006). The results reported above for change in libertarian–authoritarian attitudes are consistent with this interpretation, since they show that the more political discussants an individual had, the more accepting they became of diversity, and the less they sought to punish others. It is also worth pointing out that the libertarian–authoritarian scale itself contains responses to all the questions we used above to develop our social and political tolerance scales. But to confirm whether tolerance is indeed affected by conversation, we have repeated our tolerance scales based on respondents' views in 1997 as well as their views in 1992.

As before, we regress attitudes in 1997 on the same attitudes in 1992, and on measures of the conversational context. Here, we are particularly interested in the size of individuals' political conversation networks. Our hypothesis is that the more political conversation an individual is exposed to, the more tolerant he or she should become. So we focus on the number of discussants they report, irrespective of which parties these discussants support. As expected, levels of tolerance in 1992 were a strong and direct influence on tolerance five years later: the relevant coefficients were both significant and positive (Table 4.15). On the whole, the more tolerant people were in 1992, the more tolerant they were in 1997. But in both equations, the coefficients for number of political discussants were significant and negative. Since the tolerance scales are constructed so that low scores indicate high tolerance and high scores high intolerance, this means that the more political discussants individuals had in 1992, the more tolerant they became between 1992 and 1997. Political discussion is not only fostered by a spirit of tolerance, therefore, but it also helps foster tolerance.

Table 4.15 Political conversations and changing tolerance, 1992–7: OLS regression models

Independent variables	Social tolerance scale 1997	Political tolerance scale 1997
Social tolerance 1992	0.64	
Political tolerance 1992		0.47
Number of political discussants 1992	−0.09	−0.04
Constant	2.03	1.28
R^2	0.40	0.26
N	1607	1612

Note: Only significant coefficients are shown.
Source: 1992–7 British Election Panel Study.

Conclusions

Political conversations between citizens do make a difference, therefore. They are mainly (though not exclusively) relatively local, they do lead to people changing their vote choice, and they can influence whether individuals change their opinions. And political conversations are not only fostered by tolerance, they also help to encourage tolerance. People who talk together are more understanding and accommodating of others than are people who do not. Conversation does indeed lubricate social capital (Putnam, 1993, 2000). To that extent, political conversation between citizens is a social good. But it is also worth noting that, like other political resources, political conversation is a resource that is not evenly spread through the population. The generally resource-rich—the affluent, the well educated—are also the most likely to engage in political conversation and to benefit from its positive impacts.

Most interest, perhaps inevitably, has focused on the electoral impacts of conversation, however. As the neighbourhood effects literature suggests, people who talk together do vote together (or at least do so more than those who do not talk). But is political conversation the key to understanding geographical variations in voting behaviour? The evidence is that it is not the whole explanation. For instance, Curtice (1995) reported similar findings to those reported here, but he questioned whether political conversations are the underlying mechanism accounting for the neighbourhood effect, since inter-community differences in voting behaviour persist even after conversation effects are taken into account. That said, conversation is not the only means by which the neighbourhood effect might operate. Voters can also make judgements based on their observations of the local economy, for instance, or may be influenced by political parties' local campaign activities. We examine these in more detail in the following chapters.

5

The Local Economy and
the Local Voter

The previous chapter examined the influence of voters' conversations with friends and families. However, voters are also exposed to other spatially structured sources of political information. For instance, most of us are aware of the state of our localities: are the roads repaired, do local services work well or badly, and how is the local economy performing? Even those with few local friends or contacts are exposed to this information, through the local media and through their daily lives.

Information about social and economic conditions carries potentially powerful political cues, and claims about parties' abilities to deliver prosperity are a regular feature of election campaigns. Conservative Prime Minister Harold Macmillan rode the post-war boom to re-election in 1959 by claiming Britain had 'never had it so good'. In 1979, another Conservative, Margaret Thatcher, fought a successful campaign that emphasized the Labour government's economic failings: the Conservative's most noted advertising poster depicted a long queue of the unemployed and the slogan 'Labour isn't working'. More recently, in 1997, New Labour played successfully on discontent over the competence of the Conservative government, claiming (in their campaign song) 'things can only get better' (an assertion they claimed to have fulfilled in their 2001 and 2005 re-election campaigns: Dorling et al., 2002).

What is more, social and economic conditions vary from place to place: some regions are more affluent than others. Even within towns and cities, some neighbourhoods are well off while others are poor. A resident of a depressed inner city is likely to have a rather different perspective on life—and on the relative strengths and weaknesses of political parties—than someone who lives in an affluent suburb. Economic geography is likely to be associated with the political geography of party support. It is that association we investigate in this chapter. To do so, we begin by setting the discussion into the general context of the wider economic voting literature. That then provides the basis on which we can discuss the effects of geographical economic variations.

It's the Economy, Stupid: Economic Voting

Economic performance is one of the touchstones of modern elections: the state of the economy is held to determine the fate of governments. The 1992

US presidential election provides a striking example. President Bush Senior was confident of re-election. He had fought a short, successful, and domestically popular war in the Gulf. Historical precedent was also in his favour: presidents seeking re-election tend to win (only 4 of his 15 twentieth-century predecessors had lost a re-election battle). But he was defeated by Bill Clinton, a relatively unknown Democrat. What was the secret of Clinton's success? He appealed to growing disquiet in America. As the 1992 presidential election approached, the American economy was entering recession and many Americans felt threatened by unemployment for the first time in over a decade. Japan and West Germany were challenging the USA's position as the world's leading economy. The Clinton campaign focused on Bush's domestic record. Clinton campaign workers adopted a slogan to remind them of this: 'It's the economy, stupid'! He rode the wave of economic discontent all the way into the White House.

Clinton's 1992 campaign is an example of economic voting, a subject of academic interest since the 1950s. Early rational choice theories saw voting as an economic transaction in which consumers try to maximize benefits while minimizing costs (Downs, 1957). This was echoed in Key's (1966) empirical analysis of American presidential elections. Voters, according to Key, used a simple reward–punishment model to decide how to vote. Administrations that delivered good times were deemed successful and were supported. Conversely, those administrations presiding over more troubled times were punished, as voters abandoned them.

This begs a question: why should economic performance in particular influence voting? In part, the answer is obvious. Economic policy is one of the most important areas of government activity. Inevitably, therefore, any evaluation of government performance is very likely to take economic performance very seriously. There is also a subtler reason. Governments do many things. Many government decisions are routine—whose vote will be influenced by food standards rules? Some decisions are hard for lay audiences to evaluate—few voters truly understand the pros and cons of a new EU constitution. And other decisions affect only some voters—students and parents are likely to be concerned about education policy, but pensioners and childless adults outside education are less likely to be worried. And inevitably, given the range of issues with which a government must deal, few, if any, voters are likely to approve or disapprove of every action a government takes.

Evaluating government performance in the round places very high demands on voters, since it requires them to obtain and process vast amounts of information. One audit of the 1997–2001 New Labour government ran to over 250 pages, covering its record on redistribution, education, economic performance, the health service, foreign affairs, European policy, the environment, and the constitution. It utilized thousands of pieces of information drawn from over 40 bodies (Toynbee and Walker, 2001). But, as rational choice theorists point out, the costs to the voter of obtaining so much information are prohibitive, especially compared to the very low probability that an individual's vote will be decisive in any election. A rational voter will not invest the effort and expense required to keep abreast of the necessary information. Heuristic shortcuts that allow voters to evaluate government performance at minimal cost are therefore essential (Lupia and McCubbins, 1998; Popkin, 1994; Sniderman, Brody and Tetlock, 1991). The state of the economy is one such heuristic. Is my job secure? Will my mortgage payments rise or fall? Will my pension be eroded by inflation? Economically driven questions affect people's quality of life and are experienced first hand by everyone. I may not know much about the details of public policy but I do know whether I feel better or worse off. And, goes the economic vote argument, governments that deliver prosperity must be doing something right, while those that deliver recessions must be doing something wrong, even if I am not sure exactly how they achieve those results.

Economic voting is now one of the dominant accounts of voting behaviour. Part of the reason for its success has been its potential as an alternative to another heuristic, partisan identification. In the original Michigan model, partisan identification described a voter's long-term, stable, and deep-seated attachment to a party (Butler and Stokes, 1969; Campbell et al., 1960). However, from the 1970s onwards, dealignment meant voters no longer identified as strongly with particular parties, and were becoming increasingly volatile in their voting behaviour (Clarke et al., 2004; Crewe, Särlvik, and Alt, 1977; Dalton, 2000; Dalton, McAllister, and Wattenberg, 2000; Särlvik and Crewe, 1983). Between 1964 and 2005, the proportion of the British electorate saying they identified with a named political party fell from 98 per cent to 79 per cent, according to British Election Study (BES) data. The strength of partisan attachment fell even more steeply. In 1964, 43 per cent said they identified strongly with a particular party; by 2005 only 10 per cent did so.

As voters dealigned, they began to use other means of deciding which party to support (Franklin, 1985; Rose and McAllister, 1986, 1990; Särlvik and Crewe, 1983). They became more instrumental and judgemental, voting for the party they felt would best serve their interests. Economic voting is a case in point: parties' ability to deliver prosperity is the issue being judged. This shift was already evident in the 1960s: the 'affluent worker' study reported a generational shift in the political attitudes of working-class voters in Luton (Devine, 1992; Goldthorpe et al., 1968). Older workers, who remembered the pre-war Depression, voted Labour because they saw it as the party of the working man. Younger workers, who had entered the workforce during the post-war boom, had no experience of hardship. They still intended to vote Labour, but their support was premised on the party continuing to deliver high living standards. If it failed to deliver, they were quite prepared to vote for another party. While their elders were partisans, they were instrumental voters. In the late 1970s and 1980s, many of these southern manual workers did, in fact, abandon Labour for the Conservatives, judging the former party no longer able to deliver prosperity, while the latter was able to do so (Johnston and Pattie, 1992a).

The relationship between partisanship and economic voting goes still deeper. Contrary to the Michigan model, a number of researchers have argued that partisanship was, in fact, volatile: measurement errors notwithstanding, voters could and did change their partisan attachments over time (Clarke et al., 2004; Green and Palmquist, 1990, 1994; Johnston and Pattie, 1996, 1997a, 1999a; MacKuen, Erikson, and Stimson, 1989; Schickler and Green, 1997). An alternative interpretation of partisanship, consistent with evidence of volatility, is that voters see their attachment to a party less as a lifelong commitment than as a contingent act, a 'running tally' of evaluations of party effectiveness (Fiorina, 1981). Individual voters monitor government performance over time, updating their evaluations in the light of new evidence. Partisanship is not completely volatile, as new evaluations do not totally replace past ones. A few mistakes might be ignored if the party's record is generally good. But voters who build up sufficient negative evaluations of a party they previously identified with might shift their allegiance to another party. And the state of the economy shapes trends in partisanship. If most voters feel the government has handled the economy well, a relatively high proportion of voters will identify with the governing party, and a lower proportion will identify with opposition parties. But if public perceptions of the government's economic record become predominantly negative, identification with the governing party will drop, while identification with opposition parties will rise (Clarke et al., 2004; Erikson, MacKuen, and Stimson, 1998; MacKuen, Erikson, and Stimson, 1989).

Measuring the Economic Vote: Which Economy?

How do economic trends influence party choice? Do voters respond to shifts in the objective economy, or are they influenced by their perceptions of the health of the economy? Are voters forward or backward looking when they think about the economy? And do voters pay more attention to their personal circumstances or to society-wide trends when they think about voting?

Take the first question. It seems obvious that the actual state of the economy might influence voting. Unemployment, inflation rates, and living standards are well publicized measures of economic health and early analyses therefore correlated them with levels of party support. A pioneering study of economic voting in the UK reported a negative correlation between government support in monthly opinion polls between 1947 and 1968 and the numbers unemployed six months previously, and with the inflation rate at the time of the poll (Goodhart and Bhansali, 1970). Between 1961 and 1968, support for the government dropped by one percentage point for every extra 10,000 individuals unemployed, while a one-percentage-point increase in the inflation rate would see government popularity drop by almost two percentage points.

Goodhart and Bhansali's results show the strengths and limitations of objective economic measures. Public sensitivity to objective economic indicators can change over time. Goodhart and Bhansali studied the post-war boom years, a period of generally low unemployment and inflation. In June 1968, 503,000 people were unemployed and inflation was 4.7 per cent. But stagflation during the 1970s and early 1980s radically changed people's expectations. In 1975, inflation peaked at 24 per cent and unemployment passed the 1 million mark. By 1983 over 3 million were out of work. If Goodhart and Bhansali's equation for the 1961–8 period had still held in 1983, it would have implied a vote share for the incumbent Conservative government of −200 per cent, which was clearly impossible. Even so, from the perspective of the late 1960s, the government should have suffered a crushing defeat in 1983. In fact, the Conservatives were re-elected in a landslide victory, with a barely changed vote share.

This did not mean that economic voting failed in 1983, however. Concentrating on objective economic indicators is only one aspect of economic voting; at least as important is how voters perceive the economy. Also writing in the late 1960s, Butler and Stokes (1969) used the British Election Studies (BES) to demonstrate that voting was influenced not only by the actual economy, but also by how voters felt about their own circumstances. Those who felt they had become more affluent were more likely to vote for the government than those who felt they had become worse off.

Crucially, individuals' perceptions can change, and are also conditioned by context. Unemployment and inflation rates that seemed unacceptably high during the post-war boom would have seemed a significant improvement on the much worse rates suffered after 1970. Before 1975, unemployment had been below 1 million since 1940. After then, it did not drop below 1 million until 2001. But the economy was not recession-bound for 26 years: between 1975 and 2001, there were periods of (sometimes prolonged) economic boom. Inflation and unemployment trends still affected government popularity in the 1980s, but voters were less sensitive to relatively small shifts than they had been in the 1960s (Whiteley, 1984, 1986).[1]

A striking illustration of the importance of economic perceptions was provided by Sanders, Ward, and Marsh's (1987) analysis of government

---

[1] In addition, natural turnover alters voters' collective memory, as older voters die and younger individuals join the electorate. By 2005, only voters aged 60 and over could have voted in 1966, the last UK general election of the post-war boom. Among those under 49, only those entering the electorate for the first time after 2000 would have done so at an election where unemployment was under 1 million.

popularity between 1979 and 1983 (dubbed the Essex model, as the authors were based in that university). As discussed in Chapter 1, their results suggested the recovery in personal economic expectations underpinned the Conservatives' recovery, not the Falklands War.[2] Personal economic expectations were influenced by real economic factors such as levels of consumer spending, taxation, interest rates, and short-term working, all of which therefore affected government popularity indirectly. Exchange rates, unemployment levels, and the public sector borrowing requirement all had a direct influence on government popularity, but personal expectations were the main driver.

This raises an important issue: how much do voters know about the economy? On some measures, the answer is 'remarkably little'. Few Danish voters in the early 1990s knew the current level of inflation, the national balance of payments, or the public sector balance, though around half had some idea of unemployment levels (Paldam and Nannestad, 2000). But the same study found that voters became better informed as the election approached. And while most voters have few incentives to gain accurate information, for some doing so is worthwhile (Aidt, 2000). A small core of economically knowledgeable voters would be sufficient to move overall economic perceptions among the electorate in line with economic trends, with knock-on consequences for government support (MacKuen, Erikson, and Stimson, 1989). But while voters may not know exact trends in economic performance, they do seem to have enough idea to reach sensible overall judgements. They may not recall exact inflation rates or recent stock market trends, but they can tell good times from bad (Sanders, 2000).

Sanders, Ward, and Marsh's Falklands claim was criticized. Others, using different methods, have 'reclaimed' the 'Falklands factor' (Clarke, Mishler, and Whiteley, 1990; Norpoth, 1987, 1992). However, they all agree that economic recovery helped the Conservatives' re-election (Clarke and Stewart, 1995; Clarke, Ho, and Stewart, 2000; Clarke, Stewart, and Whiteley, 1997; Clarke et al., 2004; Sanders, 1991, 1994, 1996). Similar analyses have demonstrated that trends in economic perceptions are also related to opposition support: when voters feel the economy is performing poorly, support for the main opposition party increases, and when they feel the economy is going well, it falls (Clarke, Stewart, and Whiteley, 1998).

Analysing voters' economic perceptions has proved very fruitful. However, as discussed in Chapter 1, there are debates over which perceptions matter, when and how. Voters can be either retrospective 'peasants' or prospective 'bankers' when deciding how to vote (Erikson, MacKuen, and Stimson, 2000; MacKuen, Erikson, and Stimson, 1992). Such thinking

---

[2] War can have long-lasting political consequences, however. The controversial invasion and occupation of Iraq in 2003 contributed to a decline in Labour support which persisted up to the 2005 election (Sanders, 2005a, 2005b).

underpinned the Conservatives' 1992 election victory. The UK entered recession in the late 1980s, and the economy was still in poor shape when the 1992 election was called. So why were the incumbent Conservatives re-elected? It seems that enough voters recognized the pre-conditions for recovery (such as falling interest rates). Some 18 months before the election, when many anticipated a Conservative defeat, Sanders (1991) used the 'Essex model' to predict trends in Conservative support in the run-up to the election, based on assumptions of trends in interest rates, inflation, and personal expectations. The model was remarkably accurate, predicting a Conservative vote share of 42 per cent (almost spot on), and an 8-seat Commons majority (close to the actual 21-seat majority). The optimistic bankers among the electorate were right: within a year of the 1992 election, the UK economy had begun to recover strongly, and continued to boom for the next decade.

Similarly, at what scale do voters think when they consider the economy? For egocentric voters, the key question is 'Am I better or worse off?' (Clarke and Stewart, 1995; Lewis-Beck, 1985; Romero and Stambough, 1996). These 'pocketbook' voters either assume their own experiences are universal ('If I am doing well, so is everyone else') or are consciously self-serving ('I'm all right, Jack'). Sociotropic voters, meanwhile, are more concerned about what is happening society wide: 'Irrespective of how I am doing personally, is the country as a whole getting better off?' (Kinder and Kiewiet, 1979, 1981; Lewis-Beck, 1988).

Obviously, time and scale dimensions overlap. Voters can use egocentric retrospective evaluations to judge governments ('Am I better off now than I was in the past?'), or they can use egocentric prospective evaluations ('Do I expect to be better off in the future?'). Alternatively, they might employ sociotropic retrospective ('Has the country become better or worse off?') or prospective ('Will the country become better or worse off?') evaluations. Egocentric prospective evaluations feature strongly in research analysing aggregate time series of government popularity: voters are more likely to support the government if they expect to become better off in the future than if they think their living standards will fall (MacKuen, Erikson, and Stimson, 1992; Price and Sanders, 1995; Sanders, Ward, and Marsh, 1987).

In pre-election interviews immediately before the 2005 general election, the BES asked respondents to think about both their household finances and the general state of the national economy over the previous and the next 12 months.[3] As the UK economy was in good shape in 2005, voters' responses indicated broad satisfaction (Table 5.1). Nearly three-quarters felt their

---

[3] Each respondent was asked four questions: 'How does the financial situation of your household now compare with what it was 12 months ago?' (egocentric retrospective); 'How do you think the financial situation of your household will change over the next 12 months?' (egocentric prospective); 'How do you think the general economic situation in this country has changed over the last 12 months?' (sociotropic retrospective); and 'How do you think the general

Table 5.1. Egocentric and sociotropic economic evaluations at
the 2001 and 2005 general elections

Evaluation	Retrospective (%)		Prospective (%)	
	Egocentric	Sociotropic	Egocentric	Sociotropic
2001				
A lot worse	7.5	5.5	3.2	6.1
A little worse	19.9	24.9	14.6	29.6
The same	43.4	32.3	50.6	36.2
A little better	24.3	33.5	28.2	26.3
A lot better	4.9	3.8	3.4	1.8
N	2277	2186	2166	2095
2005				
A lot worse	8.5	9.0	4.2	4.8
A little worse	24.2	32.7	20.9	26.6
The same	43.8	38.1	50.2	44.6
A little better	19.4	18.7	21.8	22.7
A lot better	4.1	1.4	2.9	1.2
N	2941	2888	2886	2804

Source: BES face-to-face surveys (2001 and 2005).

household finances had remained the same or improved (in a strong economy, most who maintain their income are relatively affluent). Similarly positive evaluations also held for sociotropic retrospective, egocentric prospective, and sociotropic prospective evaluations.

Individuals tend to think in similar ways about their personal finances and the state of the national economy: of those who in 2005 felt they personally had become worse off over the previous year, for instance, 62 per cent felt the national economy had also worsened, 46 per cent expected they personally would also become worse off over the following year, and 42 per cent felt the national economy would also worsen in future. However, while individuals' egocentric, sociotropic, retrospective, and prospective views are undoubtedly related, they are not identical. All four measures correlate positively and significantly with each other, indicating they trend in the same directions. But the correlations are weak: the average correlation coefficient between different economic evaluations in 2005 is 0.32, and the strongest correlation—between egocentric and sociotropic prospective evaluations—is 0.43. Of those respondents who answered all four economic evaluation questions in 2005, only 15 per cent gave identical answers to each question. Although some of the variation is the result of random sampling error, a substantial amount is also due to genuine differences in how people evaluate different scenarios ('I might be personally worse off, but still recognize that the national economy is booming').

economic situation in this country will develop over the next 12 months?' (sociotropic prospective). In each case, respondents were asked whether they thought things had (or would) become a lot worse, a little worse, a little better, a lot better, or had stayed (would stay) the same.

Peoples of
perceptions best
the party to deal
equipped the economy
with the

Economic Evaluations and the Economic Vote

The four economic evaluation measures therefore tap into different, though related, judgements, and they also influence vote choice. But there are grounds for suspecting that the economy failed to move British voters in 2005. Sanders' model of government popularity, so successful throughout the 1980s and 1990s, began to fail in the early 2000s. The previously close relationship between government popularity and aggregate personal expectations became much less pronounced after Labour's 1997 victory. While aggregate personal expectations remained almost unchanged between then and 2005, Labour's support slipped in the polls (Sanders, 2005a, 2005b). And despite Labour's attempts to keep the economy on the news agenda throughout the 2005 election (given the generally strong performance of the economy), the issue was much less noticeable during the campaign than expected (Smith, 2005). Other issues, such as government policy over Iraq, were much more to the fore.

Even so, there is a clear correlation between how individuals perceived the economy and how they voted in 2005 (Figure 5.1). The more optimistic people were about future economic prospects, or the better they felt the previous year had gone, the more likely they were to vote for the Labour government and the less likely to vote for the Conservative opposition. For instance, among those who felt they personally had become worse off in the year before the 2005 election, only 19 per cent voted Labour and 33 per cent voted Conservative. But among those who felt better off, 39 per cent voted Labour, while only 14 per cent voted Conservative. The economic vote is limited to support for the government and the largest opposition party (and hence the most likely alternative government), however. Support for the third party in UK politics, the Liberal Democrats, is not influenced by voters' economic perceptions. In 2005, for instance, 13 per cent of those who felt they personally had become worse off during the preceding year voted Liberal Democrat, as did 19 per cent of those who felt their personal circumstances had not changed, and 16 per cent of those who felt they had become better off.

The economy may not have featured heavily in the 2005 campaign, therefore, and the link between expectations and party support may have broken down in the years before the election. But when they cast their ballots, voters acted on the whole in line with their economic evaluations. In this respect, the 2005 election was similar to previous contests. For instance, the 1992 election was similar to 2005 as the incumbent government (Conservative rather than Labour) was seeking re-election after several full parliaments in office. In that election, too, voters had acted in line with their retrospective economic evaluations (Figure 5.2).[4] In 1992 BES respondents were asked how they

---

[4] As the 1992 BES interviewed respondents after the election, prospective economic evaluations were contaminated by the election result. Conservative supporters, whose party won, would be likely to be more optimistic about the future than would Labour voters. But the 2005 BES asked all the economic evaluation questions before the election, when there was still uncertainty about the overall result.

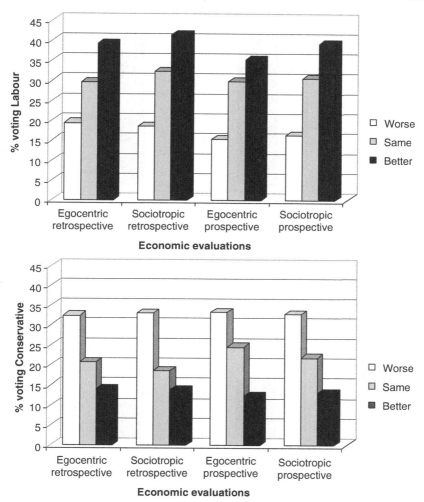

Fig. 5.1. Economic evaluations and voting at the 2005 general election
Source: BES data files (2005).

felt the economy had changed over the five years since the previous election, while in 2005 they were asked how things had changed over the preceding year. Even so, as in 2005, the better people thought the economy had performed prior to the election, the more likely they were to vote for the government (Conservative), and the less likely to vote for the main opposition (Labour).

The economy is just one issue, albeit an important one, on which voters assess governments (Blount, 2002; Clarke et al., 2004; Johnston and Pattie, 2001a; Key, 1966; Whiteley et al., 2005). The 1997 BES asked respondents for

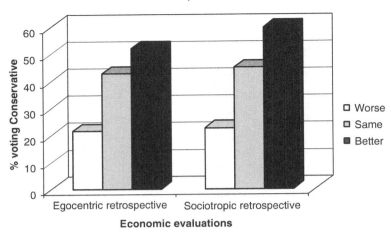

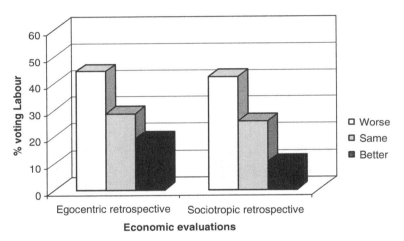

Fig. 5.2. Retrospective economic evaluations and voting at the 1992 general election
Source: BES data files (1992).

their retrospective evaluations not only of economic conditions but also of trends in unemployment, prices, taxes, NHS standards, crime levels, education standards, and also of their own and general living standards since the previous (1992) election. For unemployment, prices, taxes, and crime, a perceived increase meant voters felt the relevant indicator had worsened over time, whereas a decrease meant they felt it had improved. For the other issues, NHS and education standards, and personal and general living standards, a perceived increase represented an improvement, whereas a decrease represented a worsening of standards. In every case, the better individuals felt things had become over the previous five years, the more likely they were to vote for the incumbent Conservative government (Table 5.2). For instance, while only 7 per cent of those who felt unemployment had increased since 1992 voted Conservative in 1997, almost 40 per cent of those who felt it had decreased did so.

The effect of retrospective evaluations across different policy domains is cumulative. Across all eight issues in Table 5.2, the average 1997 BES respondent felt things had worsened over time in five areas and had improved in two. But the more negative assessments individuals made, the less likely they were to vote for the incumbent Conservative government (Figure 5.3). While 63 per cent of those who felt things had become worse in just one area voted for the government in 1997, only 5 per cent of those who felt things had worsened in six or more areas did so. And the more areas individuals felt had improved over time, the more likely they were to vote for the government. Among those who felt that only one out of the eight areas had improved, only 14 per cent voted Conservative in 1997; but among those who saw improvements in six areas or more, 84 per cent voted for the government. Good times favour incumbents' re-election chances and bad times damage them.

Government Responsibility and the Economic Vote

If economic perceptions had no impact on government support in opinion polls between 2001 and 2005, why did they influence voting decisions at the 2005 election? An important part of the answer lies in views of government responsibility for, and competence in, economic management. To vote in line with their economic evaluations, voters need to make two further connections. First, they should think governments can influence the economy. Secondly, there has to be some relational judgement between parties.

Table 5.2. Conservative vote in 1997 (percentages) according to evaluations of change on eight issues

Issue	Change since last election		
	Increased	Same	Fallen
Unemployment	6.8	16.7	39.3
Prices	20.6	31.2	37.6
Taxes	17.5	33.0	37.7
Crime	20.4	27.4	34.7
NHS standards	53.3	40.0	15.0
Education standards	38.3	34.3	14.4
Respondent's standard of living	33.2	23.0	10.0
General standard of living	41.4	23.1	5.8

Source: BES data files (1997).

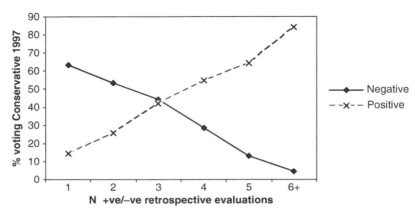

Fig. 5.3. Conservative voting, 1997, and number of positive and negative retrospective evaluations
Source: BES data files (1997).

The economy might be in a mess, and I may think government policy has a lot to do with it. But if I expect the opposition will be even more inept, I might still vote for the government as the lesser of two evils.

Attributions of Government Responsibility

We begin by examining whether the relationship between economic judgements and vote choice depends on whether individuals think governments can influence the economy. Making the connection between government performance and the health of the economy requires some political sophistication. While governments can affect some aspects of the national economy, globalization makes it difficult for any government to steer the national economy against international trends. Governments can try to play this to their advantage. If the national economy is lifted by an international boom, the government might claim the credit. But if recession strikes, the government might argue that this was an inevitable consequence of global forces. Whether voters believe such tactics is another matter.

Further complications arise when political accountability is unclear. In federal and presidential political systems, several different government bodies all may have some capacity to affect the economy. In the USA, the president and Congress can both influence economic policy, and Congress is often controlled by a party other than the president's. The more politically sophisticated American voters are, the less likely they are to see the presidency alone as responsible for economic policy, and the more likely they are to attribute some of the responsibility to other bodies (Gomez and Wilson, 2001). Meanwhile, in countries using proportional representation, elections are likely to produce coalition or minority government, rather than single-party majority government. One potential effect of this is that lines of accountability can become blurred. As a result, economic voting is weaker in countries where responsibility for economic policy within the governing coalition is not clear than in countries where it is clear (Anderson, 2000; Lewis-Beck, 1986, 1988; Nadeau, Niemi, and Yoshinaka, 2002; Powell and Whitten, 1993; Whitten and Palma, 1999).

By international standards, lines of government accountability in the UK are clear and simple. Single-party majority government is the norm and there is no division between executive and legislature. The Treasury controls economic issues and the Chancellor of the Exchequer is invariably a senior member of the ruling party. The incumbent government carries the can for the state of the economy. The decisions facing British voters are whether and how the government influences the economy. British votes are relatively realistic, expecting neither too much nor too little from the government. The 2005 BES respondents were asked whether they felt the government was responsible for the overall performance of the British economy and their household finances.[5] Few thought government was all-powerful: only a quarter felt that the government had a great deal of influence over either the national economy or their household's prosperity (Table 5.3). Similarly, however, only a minority felt it had little or no economic influence. A majority (52 per cent) of voters felt the government had a fair amount of influence over the national economy, and a substantial plurality (45 per cent) felt the same about their personal circumstances. In general, voters felt that governments had a larger impact on the national economy than on their personal circumstances: while 22 per cent felt the government had little or no impact on the national economy, 32 per cent felt the same about its influence on household finances.

The more influence individuals believe government has over the economy, the more their economic evaluations guide their vote (Johnston and Pattie, 2002b; Pattie and Johnston, 1995). There are clear effects for sociotropic

Table 5.3. Evaluations of government responsibility for the economy and for household finances, 2005 (percentages)

Government responsibility	British economy	Respondent's household finances
A great deal	25.9	23.2
A fair amount	52.1	44.6
Not very much	19.3	27.4
Not at all	2.7	4.8
N	2840	2896

Source: BES data files (2005).

[5] While the attribution questions cover both sociotropic and egocentric dimensions, neither contains a temporal dimension. We therefore use the attribution questions to refer to both prospective and retrospective evaluations.

economic evaluations (Figure 5.4a and b). Economic voting was strongest among individuals who thought the government had a great deal of influence over the state of the national economy. Among voters who felt the government had a great deal of responsibility for the estate of the economy, only 16 per cent of those who felt that the national economy had become worse over the preceding year voted Labour in 2005, compared with 55 per cent of

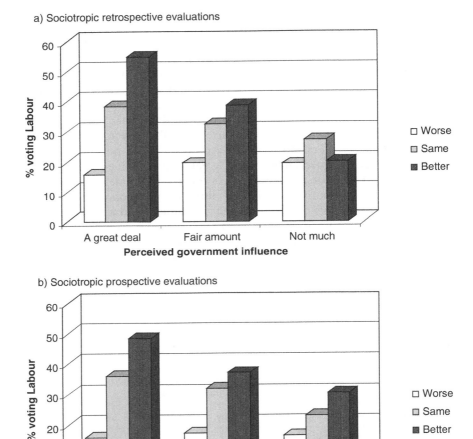

Fig. 5.4. Economic evaluations, attributions of responsibility, and vote choice at the 2005 general election
Source: BES data files (2005).

those who thought the economy had improved. But the less responsibility people felt the government had for the state of the national economy, the smaller was the differential in Labour support between those who thought the economy was doing badly and those who thought it was doing well. Among those who felt the government had little or no influence over the national economy, 19 per cent of those who thought things had become worse over the previous year voted Labour—as did 20 per cent of those who felt things had become better. A similar pattern held for prospective sociotropic

c) Egocentric retrospective evaluations

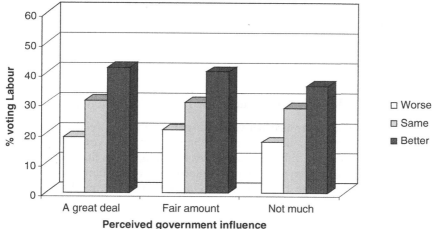

d) Egocentric prospective evaluations

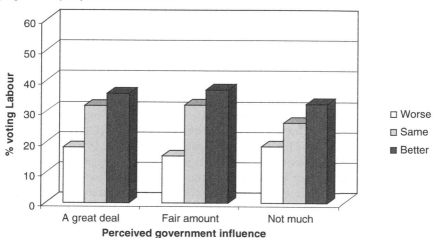

Economic evaluations

Gvt responsibility: parties + handling of econom
e.g. look at 2010 survey,
after financial crisis

160   *The Local Economy and the Local Voter*

economic voting. The interaction between attributions of government responsibility for the state of the national economy and individuals' evaluations of the health of the national economy was significant.

But the attribution of responsibility had almost no effect on egocentric voting in 2005 (Figure 5.4c and d). Among those who felt government had a great deal of influence over their household incomes, 19 per cent of those who felt they had become worse off over the previous year voted Labour in 2005, compared to 42 per cent of those who felt they had become better off. But the figures were almost identical for those who felt the government had little or no influence on their household income: 17 per cent of those who felt things had worsened voted Labour, as did 36 per cent of those who felt things had improved. That said, sociotropic economic evaluations had a greater impact on vote choice overall than did egocentric evaluations, and rather more people felt the government could influence the national economy than felt it had any impact on their personal circumstances.

Relative Judgements of Policy Competence

Do voters see a difference between the parties in their relative abilities to handle the economy? This reflects debates over how voters think about political issues. Two different perspectives dominate the literature: the positional (or spatial) view, which can be traced back to Anthony Downs (1957), and the valence perspective, originating in the work of Donald Stokes (1963; see also Merrill and Grofman, 1999). Positional issues are those where parties take an ideologically distinctive line on a topic. Voters choose the party whose stance best reflects their own ideological preferences. If one party advocates tax and public spending cuts, while another believes in increased public spending and higher tax burdens, then voters' attitudes towards taxation and public spending might become positional issues. Valence issues, on the other hand, are those on which most people agree on the desired outcome. Few wish for corrupt government and almost everyone wants affluence. However, what we want and what we get can be very different. With valence issues, the key electoral decision is which party is most likely, or most competent, to deliver. Although there is often an implicit assumption that ideological factors drive voting, it is valence issues that turn out to be most important in influencing electoral choice in Britain (Clarke et al., 2004; Whiteley et al., 2005). This is especially true when, as in the 1950s and 1960s, or again after 1992, the major parties converge on the ideological middle ground.

There is a grey area between positional and valence issues. If one party becomes clearly associated in the public mind with the effective delivery of a valence issue, while another party is seen as ineffective, then particular parties can own valence agendas in the same way as they own positional agendas. Traditionally, for instance, more voters felt Labour was better able to protect the welfare state and to fight unemployment than the Conservatives. Conversely, the Conservatives have generally enjoyed leads over Labour on issues such as inflation, public order, and economic management. In 1983, the two major economic issues facing the country were inflation and unemployment. But voters differed in which party they felt was best able to handle each issue: according to the 1983 BES data, 48 per cent felt the Conservatives were the party best able to keep prices down, while only 26 per cent favoured Labour on this issue. On the other hand, Labour was thought to be the party most likely to cut unemployment: on this issue it was preferred by 50 per cent of voters, compared to just 18 per cent for the Conservatives. Similarly, more voters felt the Conservatives would prevent strikes than felt Labour would do so (46 per cent compared to 28 per cent). But more felt Labour would look after health and social services best (54 per cent agreeing, compared to 20 per cent favouring the Conservatives).

Ownership of valence issues can change, however, even when one party has held a long-term advantage over its rivals. Economic performance is a clear example. For as long as opinion polls had asked the question, more British voters felt the Conservatives to be the party better able to handle the UK economy compared with Labour. Economic performance, though a valence issue, was a Conservative issue. However, the 1992 crisis over the European Exchange Rate Mechanism (ERM) produced a sea change in public attitudes (Sanders, 1996, 1999). Having previously argued that ERM membership was crucial to Britain's future prosperity, and having spent £10 billion and raised interest rates to 15 per cent to protect the pound, John Major's Conservative government was forced out of the ERM on Black Wednesday, 16 September 1992. The government's hard-won reputation for economic competence was shattered overnight. Things were not helped when, within days of Black Wednesday, senior members of the government claimed that being forced out of the ERM was the best thing that could have happened to the UK economy. Ironically, they were probably right. After the crisis, the UK enjoyed a period of strong economic growth well into the new millennium, while many EU states that had stayed in the ERM and its successor, the Euro, stagnated. But an almost overnight shift in government opinion on the ERM (from the cornerstone of national prosperity to an impediment best abandoned) did not enhance the government's reputation for knowing what it was doing.

Not only did the Conservative government face an economic crisis in 1992, but its main rival was becoming electable. After four successive defeats, Labour came to terms with the Thatcher reforms of the 1980s (Gould, 1998; Riddell, 2005; Shaw, 1994) and began abandoning unpopular left-wing positions in the mid-1980s. But the process was accelerated by its 1992 defeat, which many in the party blamed on the 'Shadow budget' put forward prior to the election, opening the door to Conservative claims that Labour would raise taxes. A key element of Labour's strategy after 1992, therefore, was to reassure voters and markets that it was no longer the 'tax and spend' party of the 1960s and 1970s, and that it now embraced the free market. The new Shadow Chancellor, Gordon Brown, adopted 'Prudence' as his watchword.

The combination of Conservative disarray over the ERM and Labour's re-branding abruptly changed the ownership of economic competence. After the ERM crisis, voters were much more likely to see Labour as the most competent economic manager, not the Conservatives (Sanders, 1996, 1998). Labour's lead over the Conservatives on economic competence persisted through to the 2005 election. Before that election, BES respondents were asked how they thought the Labour government had handled the economy: almost 58 per cent felt the government had handled it well and only 16 per cent thought it had done badly. They were then asked how they thought a Conservative government would have fared: only 39 per cent thought it would have done well, with 24 per cent thinking it would have done badly. When asked whether they felt Labour or the Conservatives would cope best if Britain's economy hit difficulties, just over 50 per cent chose Labour, compared to just under 40 per cent for the Conservatives.

This is particularly striking since, by 2005, public discontent with Labour was growing. After eight years in office, the government had delivered less than hoped on public services, and was embroiled in an unpopular conflict in Iraq. BES respondents in 2005 were also asked how they felt the Labour government had handled (and a Conservative government would handle) a range of other issues, including crime, education, asylum, the health system, terrorism, railways, Iraq, taxation, and pensions. The relative public percep-tions of the two parties on these issues can be gained by coding the responses such that an individual who thinks a party has done (or would do) very well on a subject is coded 5, someone who thinks they would do fairly well is coded 4, and so on, down to individuals who think they would do very badly (coded 1), and then comparing each party's average score on each issue (Table 5.4). The closer an average is to 5, the more people think the party is handling (or would handle) the issue very well: the closer the average is to 1, the more individuals think the party is doing (or would do) very badly. Evaluations of Labour and Conservatives were actually very close on most of these in 2005 and there was a substantial Conservative lead on some, notably asylum (Whiteley et al., 2005). Only the economy was a clear 'win' for Labour.

These evaluations of relative competence affect vote choice in predictable ways, as illustrated by the Labour–Conservative competence differentials for each issue. These are calculated by subtracting an individual's assessment of how well the Conservatives would handle an issue from their evaluation of how well the Labour government handled it. The competence differentials run from a maximum of 4 (someone who thinks Labour handles an issue very well and the Conservatives would handle it very badly) to a minimum of -4 (an individual who thinks Labour handles the issue very badly and the Conservatives would handle it very well).

Table 5.4. Public evaluations of Labour and Conservative ability to handle problems at the 2005 general election

Issue	Average score[a]		
	Labour	Conservatives	t–test
Crime	2.67	3.24	21.87
Education	2.95	3.17	8.77
Asylum	1.94	3.13	38.16
Health system	2.78	2.90	4.22
Terrorism	3.15	3.23	3.22
Railways	2.40	2.73	14.29
Economy	3.49	3.12	14.16
Iraq	2.22	2.90	25.03
Taxation	2.76	2.94	6.21
Pensions	2.49	2.95	17.10

[a] 5 = handled very well, 1 = handled very badly.
Source: BES face-to-face survey (2005).

Logistic regression models evaluate the impact of voters' competence differentials on the chances of voting Conservative or Labour in 2005.[6] Table 5.5 reports the exponents of the significant coefficients. Exponents greater than 1 indicate that the more individuals favoured Labour on an issue, the more likely they were to vote for the party analysed in each equation. And exponents less

Table 5.5. Policy evaluations and votes for Labour and Conservative, 2005: logistic regressions

Policy preference	Vote 2005	
	Labour	Conservative
Crime	—	0.73
Education	1.17	0.84
Asylum	—	0.79
Health	1.25	0.88
Terrorism	—	—
Railways	—	—
Economy	1.25	0.71
Iraq	1.19	—
Taxation	1.32	0.79
Pensions	1.12	0.87
R^2	0.31	0.37
% correctly classified	77.4	79.5
N	2055	2055

Note: Only significant exponents are shown. Positive values indicate that Labour is favoured on a policy.
Source: BES face-to-face survey (2005).

[6] In each case, the dependent variable is coded 1 if the individual respondent voted for the relevant party, and 0 if he or she did not. All variables named in the tables were entered into the models.

than 1 indicate that the more respondents favoured Labour on the issue, the less likely they were to vote for the party being modelled. Judgements of relative competence on crime, asylum, terrorism, and railways had no impact on the chances of voting Labour. But support for the government was influenced by judgements of whether it or the Conservatives was better for education, health, the economy, Iraq, taxation, or pensions: the more individuals favoured Labour over the Conservatives on these issues, the more likely they were to vote Labour. Support for the Conservatives was influenced by competence differentials on education, health, the economy, taxes, and pensions. The more respondents felt the Conservatives were competent on these issues relative to Labour, the more likely they were to vote Conservative. In addition, the better they felt the Conservatives would handle crime and asylum compared to Labour, the more likely they were to vote Conservative—though these issues had no bearing on Labour voting.

The 2005 election was notable for the ability of an unpopular government to be re-elected. Part of the explanation can be found in voters' judgements of the relative competence of the two parties most likely to form a government. On two of the issues on which the Conservatives enjoyed a large lead over Labour in public judgements of party competence (crime and asylum), the Tories benefited, but Labour did not suffer. On the third issue (Iraq), Labour lost ground, but the Conservatives did not make ground. On most other issues, the economy excepted, public judgements of the two parties' relative competence were quite close, providing neither with a substantial advantage. The only subject that affected both parties' votes and on which there was a large competence differential was the economy—on which the balance of public opinion substantially favoured Labour.

during 2005

Endogenous Economic Voting?

One further question must be addressed before we consider the geographical implications of economic voting. Are voters' evaluations of the state of the economy a cause or consequence of their vote choices? Are they exogenous or endogenous? Thus far, we have assumed the former. But the causal direction might run in the opposite direction: people who support the government might feel that most of its major decisions—including those on the economy—are correct, and hence feel that the economy will continue to perform well if their party stays in power. Conversely, people who do not support the government may believe that it does little right. Hence their negative view of the governing party leads them to pessimism about the economy. If this is so, voters' party loyalties cause their economic evaluations, not vice versa.

Individuals do use their partisan loyalties as a short cut to decide how well, or badly, the country is doing. In 2005, for instance, 45 per cent of those who felt their personal circumstances had improved over the preceding year were

Labour identifiers, compared to just 25 per cent of those who felt their personal circumstances had worsened. Similar patterns hold for the other economic evaluation measures too (Table 5.6). For some analysts, this endogeneity substantially accounts for the correlation between economic evaluations and vote (Anderson, Mendes, and Tverdova, 2004; Evans, 1999a; Evans and Andersen, 2004, 2006; Johnston et al., 2005a). This is a major challenge to the economic voting literature, as it implies economic voting is tautological: people think 'their' party will handle the economy best, so a correlation between economic evaluations and vote merely means individuals are voting for the party they support.

But is this the whole story? Our first line of inquiry is to examine the relationship between economic evaluations and voting Labour or Conservative at the 2005 election, controlling for partisan identification. Since the dependent variables are binary (did/did not vote Labour, and did/did not vote Conservative), we use logistic regression (Table 5.7). Two models are fitted for each party's vote. The first contains only the four economic evaluation variables; the second introduces a control for partisan identification (from the pre-election wave of the BES). For ease of presentation, the economic evaluation variables are fitted as continuous variables, ranging in value from 1 (for individuals who felt things had or would become much worse) to 5 (for those who thought things had or would become much better). Exponents greater than 1 indicate that increasing economic optimism is associated with an increased chance of voting for the relevant party, while exponents smaller than 1 mean that the more economically optimistic voters are, the less likely they are to vote for the party. In each case, the first model confirms that the better voters felt about the state of the economy in 2005, the

Table 5.6. Partisan identification and economic evaluations, 2005

Party identification	Retrospective (%)			Prospective (%)		
	Worse	Same	Better	Worse	Same	Better
Egocentric evaluations						
None	24.0	20.6	18.8	25.4	19.3	21.1
Labour	24.8	35.1	44.9	22.7	35.6	42.0
Conservative	32.7	25.1	21.0	32.2	27.1	20.1
Liberal Democrat	12.0	12.6	11.2	11.9	12.4	11.9
N	932	1265	686	708	1422	700
Sociotropic evaluations						
None	24.2	21.4	13.5	23.8	20.5	20.1
Labour	24.2	35.5	51.5	21.1	34.4	50.9
Conservative	35.1	22.1	19.8	36.6	24.2	17.7
Liberal Democrat	10.0	15.0	10.2	11.7	14.3	7.9
N	1175	1083	571	863	1233	656

Note: Column percentages do not sum to 100 per cent as minor party identifiers are omitted.
Source: BES face-to-face survey (2005).

Table 5.7. Economic evaluations, partisan identification and voting, 2005: logistic regressions

	Vote 2005			
	Labour		Conservative	
Independent variables	Model I	Model II	Model I	Model II
Economic evaluations (5 = a lot better)				
Egocentric retrospective	1.25	1.19	0.84	0.82
Sociotropic retrospective	1.39	1.25	0.68	0.75
Egocentric prospective	—	—	0.87	2.25
Sociotropic prospective	1.36	—	0.82	—
Partisan identification (comparison = none)				
Labour		7.17		0.16
Conservative		0.33		12.94
Liberal Democrat		0.63		0.36
Other		—		0.53
R^2	0.09	0.38	0.08	0.53
% correctly classified	71.5	80.2	76.7	86.6
N	2747	2697	2746	2696

Note: Only significant exponents are shown.
Source: BES face-to-face survey (2005).

more likely they were to vote for the government and the less likely they were to vote for the opposition. The only exception was that voters' egocentric prospective expectations had no significant impact on the chances of voting Labour, once their other economic evaluations had been taken into account.

It is the second model, controlling for partisan identification, that we are most interested in. Labour partisans were much more likely than non-partisans (and Conservative and Liberal Democrat partisans were much less likely) to actually vote Labour in 2005. And Conservative partisans were more likely (and Labour and Liberal Democrat partisans less likely) to vote Conservative than were non-partisans. More interestingly, both egocentric and sociotropic retrospective economic evaluations continued to have a significant effect on the chances of voting Labour and Conservative in 2005, even when individuals' prior partisanship was taken into account. The endogenous relationship between partisanship and retrospective economic evaluations does have an effect. Three of the four exponents are noticeably closer to 1 (implying smaller effects) in the equation that controls for partisanship than in that with no control, indicating that the differences between the most and the least economically satisfied individual in the chances of voting Labour or Conservative are reduced once we take partisanship into account. (The exception is the exponent for egocentric retrospective evaluations in the Conservative equation, which is very slightly further from 1 after controlling for partisanship.) But partisanship alone cannot explain away the retrospective economic vote.

Things are different when we look at prospective evaluations. Whereas three of the prospective evaluation exponents (sociotropic evaluations in the Labour equation, and egocentric and sociotropic evaluations in the Conservative) are significant when there is no control for partisanship, only one (egocentric evaluations in the Conservative model) remains significant once partisanship is controlled. These results imply that economic evaluations are partially endogenous to vote choice. However, endogeneity seems a far greater problem for prospective than for retrospective evaluations. This makes intuitive sense, since voters have independent information on how circumstances have changed in the past. (Has my disposable income grown? Is unemployment going down?) Voters can draw on their direct experience or on news reports to form an opinion independent of their partisan inclinations. So evaluations of past economic performance are not simply an artefact of partisan leanings, and still have an influence on vote. But how will things change in the future? Few voters are likely to know for sure. Much might depend on who I think is likely to win the election, and whether or not I support them. If my party is likely to win, I might feel optimistic about the future. But if another party is the likely winner, I might feel pessimistic. Partisan preferences become a guide to expectations for an uncertain future (and hence prospective evaluations are no longer significant predictors of voting when partisanship is controlled).

Retrospective economic evaluations do have an independent effect on vote choice. However, there is a further complication. As discussed above, the nature of partisanship itself is open to question. Is partisanship a deep-seated and long-term attachment to party (in which case it might affect how people see the economy)? Or is partisanship a running tally of evaluations, in which case economic evaluations, over time, can cause partisanship (Fiorina, 1981). If the latter is true, the correlation between partisanship and economic evaluations does not mean the former is caused by the latter, but rather that the latter is caused by the former (Lewis-Beck, 2006)!

A second line of inquiry into whether economic evaluations are endogenous to vote choice examines change over time. Voters can change their minds over the course of a parliament, voting differently in adjacent elections. If economic evaluations influence voters' decisions, then economic evaluations should be correlated with changes in vote behaviour (Evans, 1999a, 1999b; Johnston and Pattie, 1999c; Pattie, Johnston, and Sanders, 1999). The 1992–7 British Election Panel Survey (BEPS) interviewed a group of voters after the 1992 election, then re-interviewed them again annually throughout the parliament, contacting them for the last time after the 1997 election. The BEPS therefore gives an accurate picture of how individuals changed their votes between 1992 and 1997. Each year, BEPS respondents were also asked how they felt their personal living standards and the general standard of living had changed since the previous election. It is possible to look at respondents' perceptions (at the time of the 1997 election) of economic change since 1992. However, there is a clear risk of endogeneity in doing so, since economic evaluations in 1997 might have been brought into line with their 1997 vote, rather than vice versa. We therefore measure changes in economic evaluations using respondents' answers to the same questions in 1996, a year before the election took place. The economic evaluation variables are coded so that 5 indicates a perception that conditions had improved greatly between 1992 and 1996, and 1 a perception that things had become a lot worse. Only retrospective economic evaluations are analysed.

Logistic regression modelled voting in 1997 for the Conservatives (the incumbent government at that election) and Labour (the main opposition). Two models were fitted for each party (Table 5.8). The first looks at all voters, and controls for vote at the previous (1992) election. Not surprisingly, many voters supported the same party at both elections, so 1992 vote was a good guide to 1997 vote. By controlling for past vote, we can see how economic evaluations were related to 1997 vote decisions, net of individuals' voting histories. The second model investigates whether voters' 1996 economic evaluations had any effect on their chance of switching their 1997 vote to a party they had not voted for in 1992. In both models, voters' perceptions of changing economic conditions between 1992 and 1996 were related to how they voted a year later. The more individuals felt that general living standards had improved between 1992 and 1996, the more likely they were to vote for the (Conservative) government a year later (the exponents are greater than 1). And the more they felt general living standards had improved over the same

Table 5.8. Economic evaluations and long-term vote change, 1992–7: logistic regressions

	Vote 1997			
	Conservative		Labour	
Independent variables	All voters	1992 vote not Conservative	All voters	1992 vote not Labour
Economic evaluations since last general election, 1996 (5 = a lot better)				
Egocentric retrospective	—	—	—	—
Sociotropic retrospective	1.45	3.32	0.73	0.62
Vote in 1992 (comparison = abstained)				
Conservative	6.23		0.39	
Labour	0.11		10.70	
Liberal Democrat	0.33		—	
Other	—		—	
R^2	0.48	0.11	0.44	0.03
% correctly classified	79.3	94.9	80.7	80.7
N	1313	756	1313	913

Note: Only significant exponents are shown.
Source: 1992–7 British Election Panel Study.

period, the less likely they were to vote for the main opposition party (Labour: exponents less than 1). Their evaluations of how their personal standards of living had changed were unrelated to vote choice, however, other things being equal. Because these analyses are based on actual opinions at different points in time and also control (in different ways) for previous vote, it is not plausible to suggest that vote choice 'causes' economic evaluations. Rather, it is more likely that economic evaluations affect vote choice.

What of short-term change during an election campaign? The design of the 2005 BES helps investigate this, since respondents were asked about their vote intentions and their economic evaluations at the start of the campaign and were then re-interviewed and asked about their actual voting after the election had taken place. As with the analysis of vote change between 1992 and 1997, we use logistic regression to model voting for the Labour government and the Conservative opposition and look at vote change in two different ways (Table 5.9). First, we control for respondents' self-reported vote intention at the start of the campaign; and secondly, we limit the analysis to those individuals who did not, at the start of the campaign, intend voting for each party. As before, we limit the analyses to retrospective evaluations.

Once again, the models of vote change over the course of a campaign confirm the importance of retrospective economic evaluations. Looking at all voters, and controlling for vote intention at the start of the campaign, perceptions of change over the previous year in both personal circumstances and in the state of the national economy are related to vote choice. Those who felt things had got better were more likely to switch to the government

Table 5.9. Economic evaluations and short-term vote change, 2005: logistic regressions

	Vote 2005			
	Labour		Conservative	
Independent variables	All voters	Intention not Labour	All voters	Intention not Conservative
Economic evaluations (5 = a lot better)				
Egocentric retrospective	1.15	—	0.86	—
Sociotropic retrospective	1.26	1.27	0.75	0.56
Vote intention (comparison = don't know/abstain)				
Labour	8.41		0.02	
Conservative	0.09		15.03	
Liberal Democrat	0.21		0.12	
Other	0.42		0.03	
R^2	0.38	0.02	0.48	0.06
% correctly classified	81.3	82.8	86.2	88.3
N	2838	2286	2838	2322

Note: Only significant exponents are shown.
Source: BES face-to-face survey (2005).

and less likely to switch to the opposition than were those who felt things had become worse. And when we concentrate only on those individuals who had not expressed a clear intention of voting for Labour (in the government vote model) or the Conservatives (in the opposition vote model) at the start of the campaign, we find that sociotropic retrospective evaluations helped voters change their minds, in the same sensible ways.

The above analyses imply that endogeneity is a problem in the economic vote literature: voters' economic perceptions are to some extent shaped by their partisan leanings. However, they also show that even when endogeneity is taken into account, evaluations of economic performance (particularly retrospective evaluations) do still influence vote choices (Clarke et al., 2004). The economic vote does not disappear.

Economic Geography and Economic Voting

Economic voting also has implications for electoral geography. There can be substantial variations in the economic fortunes of different areas. One region (or even part of one city) might be in the economic doldrums while another is enjoying a substantial boom. This is a potential influence on electoral geography because it affects the range of contexts from which an economic voter gathers information. Sociotropic voters are contextual voters as they have to be aware of the wider economy and vote accordingly. But what is the appropriate context within which they form judgements about the state of the economy? Thus far we have concentrated on the national economy, but a sociotropic voter might also use more local cues when assessing economic performance.

Local and regional economies can be in phase with the national economy, growing when the national economy grows, and entering recession when the national economy does. Where this is true, it does not matter whether a sociotropic voter uses the national or the local economy to form economic judgements, since both will point to the same conclusion. But economies can also be out of phase, the regional economy growing when the national economy is struggling, or vice versa. In such circumstances, it is harder to see, *a priori*, which scale (national or regional) is the most appropriate. A voter who is a 'banker', to use the terms of MacKuen, Erikson, and Stimson (1992), could argue that the national economy is the most important, since it affects most people, and trends in the national economy will eventually percolate into all regions. But for 'peasants', the national economy can seem rather remote, compared to the knowledge that a local factory has been forced to lay off workers. Voters' evaluations of economic performance may be influenced by what they see and experience in their immediate local or regional environments as well as by national trends.

Supporting evidence can be found in Britain's changing economic and electoral geographies. For instance, during the 1980s, many accounts of

Britain's economic geography discussed the north–south divide, which widened throughout the decade (Hudson and Williams, 1989; Lewis and Townsend, 1989; Martin and Rowthorn, 1986; Massey and Meegan, 1982). Older urban and industrial regions in the north of the country suffered serious job losses as manufacturing took the brunt of the early 1980s recession. Simultaneously, the service-based finance and banking economy of the south-east boomed in the deregulated free market ushered in by the Thatcher government. While one part of the country became poorer, another became richer: Britain was becoming increasingly economically polarized. At the same time, Britain's electoral geography was also polarizing, in ways that closely matched the changing economic geography (Johnston and Pattie, 1987, 1989a, 1989b, 1989c, 1989d; Johnston, Pattie, and Allsopp, 1988; Martin, 1988). As discussed in Chapter 3, the north and the industrial cities swung increasingly to Labour, while the south and suburbs swung to the Conservatives. Voters in growth regions turned to the government, while those in declining regions turned to the opposition.

The regional economic divide that had opened early in the 1980s narrowed in the late 1980s and early 1990s as northern regions recovered and the south was hit by a services-based recession (Pattie and Johnston, 1990). And, consistent with this shift in the national economic geography, Britain's electoral geography also became less polarized between 1987 and 1992, as the Conservatives lost ground to Labour in the south and gained (slightly) from them in the north (Johnston and Pattie, 1992b; Pattie, Johnston, and Fieldhouse, 1994). Fluctuating economic geographies are associated with fluctuating electoral geographies of government support.

Geographical variation in economic circumstances across Britain is consistent with the geography of electoral dealignment. Analyses of class voting reveal that class dealignment has been uneven across the country (Johnston, Pattie, and Russell, 1993). Over the period between 1964 and 1987, the relationship between class and voting weakened substantially. But how it weakened depended on where individuals lived. For instance, skilled manual workers were traditionally strong Labour voters, and remained so in the northern industrial regions of Britain, despite dealignment. But in the south of the country, they swung increasingly away from Labour to the Conservatives in the 1970s and 1980s. This was a consequence of the rise of the affluent worker, discussed above (p. 146). Skilled manual workers in the boom regions of the 1980s saw their living standards rise, often substantially. 'Essex man'—the stereotypical affluent manual worker of the 1980s—voted for Mrs Thatcher because she delivered economic prosperity in the south-east. Skilled manual workers in northern regions, while in the same class position, were in a different economic environment, one of increasing economic uncertainty and unemployment as the 1980s recession hit the region. They may have been no less dealigned than their southern counterparts, in the sense that their voting choices were increasingly based on government performance. But for them, regional economic trends in the 1980s suggested the government was failing, and they were therefore more likely to vote Labour than Conservative.

Local Unemployment Rates

This can be demonstrated by correlating constituency voting patterns with constituency unemployment rates. Several studies during the 1980s and 1990s made use of this measure, all producing similar results (Johnston and Pattie, 1992c; Johnston et al., 2000a; Owens and Wade, 1988; Pattie, Dorling and Johnston, 1997; Pattie, Fieldhouse and Johnston, 1995). The higher the unemployment rate in a constituency (other things being equal), the better the opposition (Labour) did there and the worse the government (Conservative) fared.

There is a complication, however. Unemployment is both an economic indicator and a positional issue. More voters see Labour as the best party to handle unemployment than think another party can handle it better, irrespective of who is in office. Not only that, but unemployment tends to be concentrated in less affluent, more working-class communities—the bedrock of Labour's electoral support. A positive correlation between local unemployment rates and Labour support when (as in the papers discussed above) Labour is the opposition party, while consistent with an argument that economic voters respond to their environments, is not conclusive, therefore, since exactly the same pattern can result from non-economic factors such as issue ownership and the social correlates of the vote.

The difficulty is clear in the relationship between Labour voting and local unemployment rates at the 2005 election, when Labour was the incumbent government, defending its economic record. The economic vote argument implies that Labour's 2005 vote share should be lower in areas where unemployment is high than where it is low. However, the actual relationship between constituency unemployment and Labour support in 2005 is the opposite of this expectation and is, in fact, entirely consistent with the positional expectation that unemployment is a Labour issue (Figure 5.5). The higher the constituency unemployment rate in June 2005, the higher Labour's vote share in that contest. The relationship is non-linear: unemployment has to be logged to make it so. The rate at which unemployment translates into Labour voting is rapid when local unemployment is relatively low, but slows down at higher levels of unemployment. The main factor underlying the pattern is the social base of Labour support. The significant relationship between Labour vote share in 2005 and (the log of) the local unemployment rate disappears when we control for Labour strength locally at the previous (2001) election (Table 5.10: compare Models I and II). In other words, poorer areas are those where many Labour voters live.

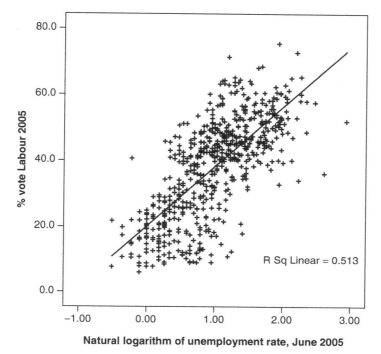

Fig. 5.5. Constituency unemployment and support for the government, 2005

This does not mean that the local unemployment rate is a purely positional issue, however. If we look at change in unemployment, a rather different story emerges. One of Labour's most striking successes in office after 1997 was reducing unemployment: between 1997 and 2005, the numbers unemployed fell everywhere.[7] But the falls were not uniform. In some places, such as Bath and Sheffield Hallam, the drop in the number of people registered unemployed in the constituency was over 70 per cent of the number unemployed there in 1997. In other areas, like Birmingham Northfield, the decline in unemployment was much smaller, just 1.4 per cent of the number unemployed in 1997. Controlling for Labour's vote in each seat in 2001 (and hence for the tendency for a party to do well where it previously performed well, and badly where it was previously weak), the relationship between Labour's 2005 vote share and the percentage change in the numbers unemployed between June 1997 and June 2005 is negative and significant. In other words, the bigger the proportionate drop in unemployment in an area, the better Labour did in 2005. Unemployment is a positional issue, therefore, and Labour's heartland support, even under New Labour, is in the working-class industrial communities where

---

[7] Because of boundary changes to Scottish constituencies prior to the 2005 election, it is not possible to make comparisons between 1997 and 2005 for Scottish seats. These comments are therefore limited to England and Wales.

Table 5.10. Labour support and constituency unemployment, 2005: OLS regressions

Independent variables	Labour vote 2005		
	Model I	Model II	Model III
Unemployed (%) June 2005[a]	18.08	—	
Change unemployed % June 1997–2005			−0.03
Labour vote 2001 (%)		0.88	0.89
Constant	20.13	−0.88	−2.28
R^2	0.51	0.95	0.95
N	626[b]	626[b]	568[c]

[a] Natural log.
[b] Great Britain (excluding Glasgow North East and Blaenau Gwent).
[c] England and Wales only (excluding Blaenau Gwent).

Note: Only significant coefficients are shown.

unemployment tends to be highest. But voters are also responsive to how the local economy is changing. The greater the fall in unemployment locally, the more the government was rewarded.

Local Housing Markets

Other local economic indicators tell similar stories. If unemployment is a marker of economic failure, the health of local housing markets is a marker of economic success. Housing is political in Britain. For some, the public sector's role as a landlord for a substantial minority of British households underpinned a new consumption cleavage in post-war politics (Duke and Edgell, 1984; Dunleavy, 1979; Dunleavy and Husbands, 1985). Support for Labour, the party traditionally associated with state intervention, was higher among public sector tenants than among homeowners, and support for the pro-free-market Conservatives was lower. But the predominant trend in UK housing since the early twentieth century has been the expansion of owner-occupation, a process given a boost in the 1980s when the Conservatives gave council tenants the right to buy their homes. By the early 2000s, around 70 per cent of British households were owner-occupiers. This has a direct political effect: more homeowners implies more pro-Conservative voters. But this effect can be exaggerated. While those tenants who bought their council houses in the 1980s were more Conservative-inclined than other council tenants, they did not become even more pro-Conservative after making their purchases, and they were less pro-Conservative than other homeowners (Garrett, 1994; Heath et al., 1991). The other parties responded to changing circumstances by also articulating homeowners' wishes: as New Labour recognized, failure to do so when the great majority either were, or aspired to be, homeowners was potentially suicidal (Heath, Jowell, and Curtice, 2001).

Housing also has economic effects. Since most home-buyers need a mortgage, homeownership is associated with a substantial, long-lasting debt burden. Homeowners are sensitive to the health of the economy since this can affect their ability to keep up mortgage payments, through earnings and interest rate fluctuations, which can very substantially raise or lower monthly mortgage costs. On the other hand, the general (though not inexorable) trend for house prices to rise over time means that homeownership is also a substantial investment. Over the long term, most homeowners will see the value of their property rise, often very substantially (Hamnett, 1999). Between 1997 and 2004, average house prices in the UK more than doubled—a faster rate of increase than for most other investments over that period.[8]

Homeownership can be a route to considerable wealth, therefore, but how much depends on housing market conditions, which vary markedly over time and space. During the 1980s, house prices grew rapidly in the south of the country as the regional economy boomed. This represented a substantial reward to homeowners in the region, since the value of their major investment grew quickly. House price inflation was weaker in more depressed regions. But in the late 1980s and early 1990s, recession in the south-east produced substantial falls in house prices there (Hamnett, 1989, 1993, 1999). Some homeowners, especially in the south-east, found themselves with negative equity, owing more on their mortgage than they could recoup by selling their homes (Dorling, 1994; Dorling and Cornford, 1995; Gentle, Dorling and Cornford, 1994). In much of the north, however, house prices continued to rise as the region recovered from the early 1980s' recession. Since then, housing markets have recovered strongly throughout the country: house prices grew steadily from the mid-1990s onwards. Housing markets can also vary within a city: in late 2005, someone looking for a two-bedroom semi-detached house in the Sheffield area could choose from properties ranging in value from a £64,000 home in a run-down inner-city area to a £300,000 home in the Peak District National Park.

Evidence from the early 1990s suggests that voters are sensitive to these temporal and geographical housing market fluctuations (Pattie, Dorling, and Johnston, 1995, 1997). The 1992 election was a good example of how housing market fluctuations affected government support, as housing markets in some parts of the country boomed, while they declined elsewhere. Data are available for every constituency in 1992 for three housing-market-related variables: the average constituency house price in 1991 (in thousands of pounds); the change in average house price between 1989 and 1992 (as a percentage of the 1989 house price); and the percentage of mortgage holders in each constituency with negative equity. Controlling for Conservative

---

[8] Data are from the Council of Mortgage Lenders and the Halifax house price index. A house that would have been worth £100,000 in 1997 would, on average, have sold for £229,000 in 2004.

support in the previous (1987) election, regression analyses clearly show that the government's 1992 constituency vote share was affected by local housing market conditions (Table 5.11). The higher house prices were in a constituency in 1991, the better the government performed there. Similarly, the more local house prices grew in the years before the election, the higher was the Conservatives' share of the vote (or, given the market slump of the early 1990s, the more prices fell in an area, the lower was the government's 1992 vote share). And negative equity damaged the government: the higher the proportion of mortgage holders affected by negative equity in an area, the lower the Conservatives' 1992 vote share there.

However, like unemployment, local housing market conditions may be related to Conservative and Labour support for reasons other than economic voting. House prices are highest, unsurprisingly, in areas dominated by the affluent, professional, middle classes, precisely the groups who are usually most likely to vote Conservative and least likely to vote Labour. So a positive correlation between house prices and Conservative vote share in 1992 may reflect little more than this underlying sociological (rather than economic) relationship. Is the relationship between government support and house prices the same when governments change? Repeating the analyses for Labour support at the 2005 election tells the story (Table 5.12, excluding negative equity, which had ceased to be a problem by the late 1990s).[9] Because of constituency changes in Scotland before the 2005 election, no house price data were available there, and the analyses reported here are for England and Wales only. Even so, the story is clear. Although the period after 1997 was marked by generally high house prices, the Labour government did not benefit directly. The higher house prices were locally in 2003 (the closest year to the election for which data were available), the lower was

Table 5.11. Housing market conditions and government constituency support, 1992: OLS regression models

Independent variables	Conservative constituency vote share		
	Model I	Model II	Model III
Conservative vote 1987 (%)	0.94	0.97	0.98
Average house prices 1991 (£000s)	0.03		
Change in house price 1989–91(%)		0.01	
Negative equity 1993 (% with)			−0.04
Constant	0.54	0.86	1.07
R^2	0.97	0.97	0.97
N	633	633	633

Note: Only significant coefficients are shown.

[9] We are grateful to Danny Dorling and Bethan Thomas for access to their data on housing markets since the early 1990s.

Table 5.12. Housing market conditions and government constituency support, 2005: OLS regression models

Independent variables	Labour constituency vote share	
	Model I	Model II
Labour vote 2001 (%)	0.84	0.86
Average house prices 2003 (£000s)	−0.02	
Change in house price, 2001–3 (%)		0.09
Constant	3.88	−3.85
R^2	0.95	0.95

Note: Only significant coefficients are shown.

Labour's vote share in 2005. This is the opposite of what an economic vote model would predict: it reflects the Conservatives' continuing relative strength in deeply middle-class affluent areas.

But the percentage change in house prices between 2001 and 2003 tells a different story. The more house prices rose locally, relative to their levels in 2001, the better Labour did in 2005. As with unemployment, absolute house prices locally are positional goods: the Conservatives do well, and Labour badly, in areas where house prices are high. But rates of change are associated with a clear economic vote: irrespective of which party is in office, the government does better in areas where house prices are growing relatively rapidly than in areas where they are not. Voters reward success and punish failure. And these results are very robust: they survive even when we take into account other factors associated with voting for a party by controlling for past party strength locally. The changing geography of government support is related to the changing economic geography.

Local Economic Geographies and Perceptions of Economic Performance

This section investigates whether these aggregate patterns reflect processes occurring among individual voters. Are voters' economic evaluations related to the local and regional economic contexts within which they live? Do they think of regional economic success or failure separately from either their own individual economic fortunes or from national economic trends? And is there an individual-level correlation between vote and perception of regional economic performance?

Answering these questions requires information on individuals' perceptions not only of their own and of the national economic situation, but also of their local economies (Johnston and Pattie, 1997b, 2001a, 2001b, 2002b; Johnston et al., 2000a; Pattie and Johnston, 1995, 1997b, 1998a, 2001c; Pattie, Dorling, and Johnston, 1997). Suitable questions were asked in the

1992 and 1997 BES. Respondents were asked whether they felt their region had become more or less prosperous over time, compared to other parts of Britain. In 1992, they were asked to think about how their region had fared over the previous ten years; in 1997, the point of comparison was the previous (1992) election. What constituted a region was left up to respondents (with the exception of the Scottish and Welsh, who were asked to compare the prosperity of Scotland and Wales, respectively to that of the rest of the UK). We cannot be certain of the specific geographies most voters had in mind when they answered the question, therefore. Some may have been thinking about relatively local scales—a city or a county; others may have been thinking more regionally—the north of England or the south-east. Be that as it may, respondents were being asked to think about sub-national economic change.

Clearly we would expect some relationship between actual local conditions and perceptions of regional economic performance: it would be odd if voters in poorer areas felt no different about the state of their region's economy than voters in affluent areas. But we might also expect local economic conditions to echo voters' evaluations of their personal circumstances and of the national economy. People living in depressed regions are themselves more likely to face unemployment, to be in insecure and poorly paid jobs, or to have limited housing equity than are otherwise similar individuals who live in more affluent regions. And it is plausible that local conditions are used as short-cut indicators of how the national economy is faring.

We examine this by comparing individuals' regional, personal, and national retrospective evaluations in 1997 with constituency-level indicators of the actual economic circumstances they would experience in their local areas.[10] Actual local economic conditions are measured using data on the percentage change in the number unemployed in each constituency between January 1996 and April 1997 (Table 5.13) and the percentage change in average constituency house prices between 1995 and 1997 (Table 5.14). Those who felt things were getting better in 1997—whether for themselves, for their region, or for the country—tended on average to live in those constituencies that had seen the largest proportional falls in unemployment, and the biggest proportional increases in house prices. By contrast, those who felt things had become worse at each of the three scales lived in constituencies whose average percentage decrease in unemployment was lowest, and whose average house prices had fallen (or, at best, had not increased as much, proportionally, as elsewhere).

Local economic conditions were most strongly related to evaluations of regional economic performance. The ranges in average percentage change in constituency unemployment and in constituency house price between those

---

[10] We concentrate on retrospective judgements since the 1997 BES was a post-election survey: prospective evaluations are contaminated by knowledge of the election result.

Table 5.13. Retrospective economic evaluations and local economic conditions, 1997: mean percentage change in constituency number unemployed, 1995–7

Economic condition	Situation got:			F	p
	Better	Same	Worse		
Area prosperity since last election	−30.32	−28.99	−25.39	83.37	0.00
UK economic situation last year	−30.08	−27.30	−26.66	44.97	0.00
Household financial situation last year	−29.36	−27.96	−27.28	11.74	0.00

Source: BES data files (1997) and constituency data.

who felt things had improved and those who felt they had worsened was greatest for regional economic evaluations and least for household finance evaluations. And those who felt their regional economy had improved were more likely to live in areas where house prices, on average, had increased by more, and unemployment had fallen more, than those who felt the national economy or their personal circumstances had improved. And the corollary is also true. Those who felt their regional economy had done badly were more likely to live in constituencies that were on the average less economically successful than those who felt the national economy or their personal circumstances had worsened. Finally, analysis of variance tests produced much larger F-values for regional economic evaluations than for either national or personal circumstances (the smallest F-values): local economic conditions were more consistent with individuals' evaluations of regional prosperity than with their evaluations of national or personal circumstances.

But do individuals' regional economic evaluations simply reflect their evaluations of personal circumstances and of the national economy? People may elide all three scales, perhaps using their own circumstances as an indicator of what is happening at other levels of the economy. If this were the case, then those who felt they personally were doing well would assume that everyone else in the area and in the country as a whole was doing well too (and those who were struggling personally might assume that the regional and national economies were also performing poorly). That said, there is a

Table 5.14. Retrospective economic evaluations and local economic conditions, 1997: mean percentage change in average constituency average house prices, 1995–7

Economic condition	Situation got:			F	p
	Better	Same	Worse		
Area prosperity since last election	6.38	2.62	−2.14	13.66	0.00
UK economic situation last year	5.78	0.15	−0.50	4.77	0.01
Household financial situation last year	4.24	0.91	2.32	2.46	0.09

Source: BES data files (1997) and constituency data.

wide range of different information sources open to individuals. Someone viewing the main evening news on television might be exposed, in the same broadcast, to 'good news' stories about the national economy and 'bad news' stories about their locality. Much was made before the 2005 election of the Labour government's economic successes—low unemployment, low inflation, rising incomes, and so on. But voters in the West Midlands also had bad local economic news when the closure of the MG-Rover car plant, with associated job losses, was announced during the election campaign (though as a local MP pointed out, the closure was less damaging than it would have been in the past because the local economy was no longer as dependent on one car manufacturer as it had once been: Wright, 2005, 93). It is therefore plausible that, while views of personal, regional, and national economic circumstances are related, they are not identical. Voters should be able to differentiate between economic fortunes at different geographical scales.

The 1997 BES data support this latter interpretation. Individuals' evaluations of their regions' economic performance are not identical to their evaluations of either their personal circumstances or of the performance of the national economy. The correlation coefficient between respondents' evaluations of how their personal circumstances had changed over the previous year and of how their region's economy had performed was significant and positive, indicating that the better people felt their personal circumstances had become, the more likely they were to feel that their region had become better off too.[11] But the correlation was weak: individuals' views of their personal circumstances accounted for only 4 per cent of the variation in their views regarding their region's economy. The relationship between perceptions of national and regional economic performances (also significant and positive) was stronger but was still far from overwhelming: national economic perceptions accounted for just under 10 per cent of the variation in regional economic perceptions.

Voters' perceptions of the state of their region's economy are not divorced from their personal circumstances or their perceptions of the state of the national economy, therefore. But, importantly, nor are they the same. Voters receive different cues regarding the economy depending on the scale at which they assess it. Someone who has become personally more affluent, but who lives in a declining region and who thinks the national economy is neither growing nor declining, is faced simultaneously with three very distinct potential choices when deciding whether to vote for the government. Personal circumstances encourage a vote for the government; regional circumstances might point to a vote for the opposition; national circumstances might leave our voter indifferent to either the government or the opposition.

---

[11] All three questions were coded on a five-point scale: a value of 1 indicated substantial improvement ('things got a lot better') and a value of 5 indicated substantial decline ('things got a lot worse').

Local Economic Evaluations and Electoral Geography

If some voters at least are faced with divergent voting cues based on different perceptions of their personal circumstances, of the regional economy, and of the national economy, how do they decide who to support? Are cues at some scales ignored while those at other scales are heeded? Or do voters try to take into account their perceptions of economic performance at a variety of scales, offsetting perceived good performances at one scale with perceived poor performance at another?

Regional economic perceptions are correlated with vote choice. A cross-tabulation of vote in 1997 with regional economic evaluations at that date shows much the same pattern as seen already for voting and both personal egocentric evaluations and national sociotropic evaluations (Figure 5.6). The more prosperous individuals thought their region had become over time, the more likely they were to vote for the Conservative government in 1997, and the less likely they were to vote for the Labour opposition. While 29 per cent of those who felt their region had become more prosperous over time voted Conservative, for instance, only 12 per cent of those who felt it had become less prosperous did so. Similarly, the less prosperous they felt their region had become, the more likely they were to vote for the Labour opposition: 30 per cent of those who in 1997 said their region had become more prosperous were Labour voters, compared to half of those who felt their region had become less prosperous.

One feature of Figure 5.6 demands further comment. Support for the Conservative government in 1997 was lower than support for the Labour opposition in all groups. This is not some peculiarity of how regional economic perceptions affect voting, however. In 1992, 52 per cent of those who felt their region's economy had improved voted for the Conservative

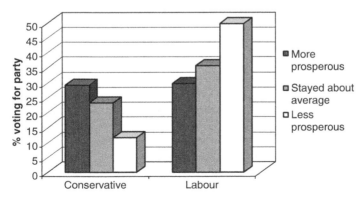

Fig. 5.6. Perceptions of regional prosperity and voting for the government and opposition, 1997

Source: BES data files (1997).

government and only 17 per cent voted for the Labour opposition. Of those who felt their region had become relatively worse off, 40 per cent voted Labour and 29 per cent supported the Conservatives. This is much more in keeping with the patterns for personal and national economic perceptions at the 2005 and 1992 elections, respectively (Figures 5.1 and 5.2). Furthermore, the relationships between individuals' vote choices and their evaluations of their personal circumstances and the national economy in 1997 display similar patterns to those for regional perceptions and vote in that year: the government did better and the opposition did worse among those who felt things had improved than among those who felt things had worsened—but more people in every group voted Labour than voted Conservative (with the sole exception of those who felt the general economic situation had improved, 35 per cent of whom voted Conservative and 26 per cent Labour). The major difference between the 1997 election on the one hand, and the contests of 1992 and 2005 on the other, was that the former involved a landslide defeat for the incumbent government while the 1992 and 2005 contests resulted in its re-election. As discussed above, such was the unpopularity of the Conservative government in 1997 that economic performance was not enough to rescue its fortunes (Sanders, 1999).

Voters' regional economic perceptions influence their voting decisions in the same way as their evaluations of personal circumstances and of the national economy. But do voters make use of their potentially divergent perceptions at all three scales simultaneously when deciding how to vote, or do they privilege evaluations at some scales over those at others? We investigate this through a multivariate analysis of vote choice in 1997, with perceptions at all three scales included in the same model (Table 5.15). Since the dependent variables are whether or not an individual voted Conservative or voted Labour, we use binary logistic regression. The impact of the objective economic geography on individual vote choice is assessed through the inclusion of two measures for the constituency in which each BES respondent lives: the percentage change in the number unemployed locally between January 1996 and April 1997, and the percentage change in average constituency house prices between 1995 and 1997. In addition, we control for how individuals voted at the previous election in 1992, based on their recall of that vote in 1997.

Even when past vote and evaluations of personal and national circumstances are taken into account, regional and local economic perceptions and conditions have an independent effect on vote choice. The exponent for regional economic perceptions (labelled 'sociotropic regional' in the table) is significant and of the correct relative size in both equations. Irrespective of how affluent or poor people felt personally, of how well they felt the national economy was performing, or even of how they had voted in 1992, the more prosperous they felt their region had become over time, the more likely they were to vote for the Conservative government and the less likely they were to

Table 5.15. Economic evaluations, partisan identification, and voting, 1997: logistic regressions

Independent variables	Vote 1997	
	Conservative	Labour
Retrospective economic evaluations (5 = a lot better)		
Egocentric	1.230	—
Sociotropic national	1.630	0.790
Sociotropic regional	1.190	0.840
Change in unemployed 1996–7 (%)	0.970	1.030
Change in house price 1995–7 (%)	—	1.002
Vote, 1992 (comparison = abstained)		
Conservative	12.550	0.650
Labour	0.210	10.800
Liberal Democrat	0.380	—
Other	—	—
R^2	0.54	0.42
% correctly classified	85.1	80.1
N	3198	3198

Note: Only significant exponents are shown.
Source: BES cross-section survey (1997).

vote for the Labour opposition. And, controlling for past vote and economic perceptions at all three scales, the greater the percentage increase (or the smaller the percentage decrease) in the number unemployed in a constituency in the year before the 1997 election, the smaller the chance that a voter living there would vote Conservative then, and the higher the chance that he or she would vote Labour. Changing local housing market conditions present a partial anomaly, however. As we have seen, government and opposition constituency vote shares are both affected by housing market dynamics. But at the level of individual voters, housing market movements had no independent effect on an individual's chances of voting Conservative in 1997. And their impact on individuals' chances of voting Labour, while significant, were weak (as indicated by the closeness of the relevant exponent to 1) and counterintuitive: the greater the percentage growth in average house prices in a constituency since 1995, the higher the chances that an individual living there would vote for the Labour opposition in 1997—the opposite of what we might expect.

The analyses reported in Table 5.15 also confirm once again that individual voters were also influenced independently—and in theoretically consistent ways—by their perceptions of their personal circumstances and of the state of the national economy in 1997. Voters are able to differentiate between economic performance at a variety of scales, and do balance up these evaluations in their minds when deciding how to vote. As with voters' egocentric and national sociotropic evaluations, some individuals hold the government responsible for the state of their region's economy while others do not. In 1997, for instance, 55 per cent of those who expressed a view felt that government policies were responsible for regional prosperity. However, there were regional variations. In Scotland and Wales, 69 per cent of voters in 1997 held the government responsible for the state of the region's economy. In the north of England, this dropped to 62 per cent. But in the midlands and the south of England (excluding London), voters were more evenly split in their opinions: around 48 per cent held the government responsible.

And as with personal and national economic evaluations, whether an individual feels the government is responsible for a region's economic health affects whether the economic judgement influences voting (Johnston and Pattie, 2002b; Pattie and Johnston, 1995). There was a significant relationship between vote choice in 1997 and evaluations of the regional economy for those who hold the government responsible for regional prosperity.[12] For instance, almost 60 per cent of those who felt their region had become much more prosperous since 1992, and who felt the government was responsible for that, voted for the Conservative incumbents in 1997. This compares to just 6 per cent of those who felt it was the government's fault that their region had become much less prosperous. But among those who did not hold the government responsible for the state of their region's economy, there was no relationship at all between their evaluations of regional prosperity and their vote choice.[13] Among those who felt regional prosperity was not the government's responsibility, and who felt their region had become much more prosperous, 23 per cent voted for the Conservative government in 1997— almost the same as the percentage of Conservative voters among those who felt their region had become less prosperous, but who felt the government was not to blame (21 per cent).

How Local is Local?

Other things being equal, therefore, those who live in affluent areas are more likely to vote for the government than those from less-prosperous areas, especially if they feel the government is responsible for local conditions. However, thus far the scale at which local economic patterns influence voters has been left vague. Aggregate analyses can only delve down to the constituency level, since that is the smallest unit for which UK general election results are released. And, as noted above, survey questions on perceptions of regional prosperity leave the definition of 'region' open to the respondent. But how local are people's local economies?

Some insights can be gleaned using the bespoke neighbourhoods discussed in Chapter 3 (see also Johnston et al., 2000a). To recap, 1991 census data

---

[12] The chi-square test is significant at $p = 0.000$.
[13] The p-value for the relevant chi-square test is 0.253.

were used to provide social data for the local neighbourhoods in which 1997 BES respondents lived: all the neighbourhoods were smaller than a parliamentary constituency, ranging in size from the 10,000 residents living closest to each BES respondent down to the nearest 1000 residents. Using these data, we can examine unemployment rates at very local levels indeed. And the story is consistent at all scales. The worse local economic conditions are, the worse the governing party does, even at the most local scale we can measure with the available data. For instance, among those respondents who felt their personal standard of living had increased a lot prior to the 1997 election, almost 50 per cent voted for the government in the 1000 neighbourhoods where unemployment was lowest (between 3 and 5.9 per cent). But in the 1000 neighbourhoods with the highest unemployment levels (over 15 per cent), government support was much lower: even among those who felt their own standard of living had improved a great deal, only 20 per cent voted Conservative in 1997. What is more, these variations persist even after other factors are taken into account. Voters are influenced by economic circumstances in their localities—and that goes down to very local levels indeed. Someone living in an affluent suburb of a generally depressed town is liable to have a different view of government performance than someone who lives in a less-well-off neighbourhood.

Conclusions

Voters are responsive and evaluative individuals, weighing up the successes and failures of governments and the potential strengths and weaknesses of oppositions. Tribal party loyalties based on long-term partisanship and social cleavages have weakened substantially and have been replaced by valence politics (Clarke et al., 2004). Increasingly, voters look for results. Although not the only factor that affects political fortunes, prosperity matters: governments that deliver prosperity have a powerful weapon in their electoral armoury; governments that are blamed for recessions are at a substantial electoral disadvantage. Clinton's 1992 presidential campaign mantra remains true: 'It's (still) the economy, stupid!'

Valence politics involves the processing of contextual information. To make sense of how the government is performing, we need to know something of what is happening 'out there'. Are the public services working well or badly? Is taxation too high or too low? Is public order being maintained effectively? And (the major theme of the chapter) is the economy performing well or badly? But there is no privileged context for these evaluations. People use what they see around them to form their views, from their personal experiences, through what they see in their local neighbourhoods, in their towns and cities, and in their regions, up to what they see happening at the national scale. Voters are sufficiently sophisticated to recognize that economic change can be moving in different directions at different scales—their city might be facing difficulties even while the national economy is booming—and to balance their evaluation of performance at these different scales simultaneously when they make their vote choices. And they are also sophisticated in that they do not hold the government responsible for everything. For instance, as we have seen, fewer voters think the government is responsible for the state of their personal circumstances than hold it responsible for regional or national economic performance.

But the costs to individual voters of keeping track of economic performance are relatively low, since information is widely available. Whether it be news reports, observations of new developments or plant closures in one's locality, or direct personal experience, information on economic performance at a variety of spatial and temporal scales is almost impossible to miss. And the economy changes rapidly over both time and space. Valence voters are therefore likely to change their opinions over time and depending on where they live. Local economic contexts do much, therefore, to help us understand the underlying forces shaping the geography of the vote.

6

Party Campaigns and their Impact

Thus far, we have examined contextual effects created either by direct inter-actions among voters or by voters' reactions to events and trends in their regions. In this chapter, we look at effects created by political parties through their campaigning. Political campaigns aim to achieve a number of ends. First, a party must mobilize its own supporters, ensuring that as many vote as possible. But no party can rely solely on this to deliver victory as none commands majority support in the electorate. All parties—especially those in opposition—need to try and win over new supporters at each election. Persuasion tactics are also required. Identifying supporters and ensuring they vote is primarily a local process, carried out by local and regional parties through canvassing activities. Winning over new converts takes place at all scales, from local canvassing efforts through to the national campaign. Perhaps the most easily persuaded are individuals who are likely to vote but have not made up their minds which party to support. Surprisingly many voters are undecided at the start of an election campaign, or change their minds during the campaign. At the start of the 2005 general election cam-paign, only 47 per cent of respondents to the 2005 British Election Study (BES) said they had already decided which party they would vote for in the upcoming election and 46 per cent said they had not yet decided (Table 6.1).

We can see how many people changed their minds during the campaign by using the 2005 BES, which interviewed a group of voters at the start of the campaign and re-interviewed them after the election. Post-election, just over eight out of every ten who said at the start of the campaign they would definitely vote actually had voted, as had seven in every ten of those who had not yet chosen a party at the outset of the campaign, and just under one out of every five of those who originally said they would abstain (Table 6.1). Almost 20 per cent of all those who thought they knew for sure who they would vote for when the election was called changed their minds and actually abstained. Among those who initially said they had definitely made their choice and who did go on to vote, almost 10 per cent changed their party choice before polling day. Similarly, of those who at the start of the campaign thought they would vote but had not yet decided who to vote for, 28 per cent abstained. In total, an astonishing 60 per cent of those who took part in the 2005 survey were, in effect, floating voters. Some of these floating voters may have been influenced by the campaign.

Table 6.1. Change in intention to vote during the 2005 UK general election campaign

Decision at start of campaign	%	Actually voted (%)
Yes, decided how to vote	46.7	81.2
No, not decided yet	46.2	71.5
Will not vote	7.0	16.8
N	2959	2136

Source: BES face-to-face panel (2005).

But are campaigns effective and how do they contribute to the geography of the vote? *A priori*, campaigning should have an influence, since the campaign takes place at a variety of scales, from the national to the local. It matters how many voters a party can persuade to vote for it, and how many of its own supporters it can encourage to turn out. But it also matters where they do so. Votes are always valuable for parties, but in first-past-the-post elections, where they are cast can be just as important as the fact they are cast at all. There are therefore grounds for expecting party campaigning to take into account not only the national but also the local situation. Parties might well campaign differently—and with different effects—in safe seats compared with marginals, since the outcome in the latter is much more in the balance than in the former. So how do parties campaign, and with what (geographical) effect? We address these questions in the remainder of the chapter.

The National Campaign

The nature of electoral campaigning has changed over time as parties have actively responded to new opportunities and methods for getting their message across to voters. Election campaigning since the Second World War has resembled an information technology 'arms race', with parties competing to make the most effective use possible of each successive innovation. It is instructive to compare election campaigns in the first half of the twentieth century with more recent competitions. Up until the 1950s, elections were mainly fought using similar techniques to those prevalent in the nineteenth century. Parties made widespread use of posters and leaflets, while newspaper reports and mass meetings were voters' main sources of information on election campaigns. Party leaders had to travel widely during the campaign to put their message across, covering large distances day after day to get from one mass meeting or rally to another. Even in an age when attendance at political rallies was much higher than it is now, this inevitably limited the ability of party leaders to appeal directly to the majority of voters, since most voters would have been unable to attend the relevant meetings. They therefore relied strongly on the press to report on their activities (Rosenbaum, 1997). Access to other media was limited. Pre-war, cinema and radio enjoyed mass audiences, and parties used both in their campaigns (Rosenbaum, 1997, 80). However, much of the effort of campaigning fell on individual candidates fighting in local seats.

Contrast this with the most dramatic change in modern electioneering—television's emergence as the major medium for party communication and electoral news. It lets modern political leaders speak directly to almost all electors simultaneously in their own homes. The net result has been the nationalization of the campaign, with far more attention paid to the activities and utterances of party leaders, and far less being given to local candidates. Attendance at local election meetings fell steeply as television took over as the main communication medium.

Party Election Broadcasts and Media Coverage

Most directly in a party's control is the party election broadcast (PEB). PEBs are made by the parties and are not subject to normal advertising rules (that the content be 'legal, truthful, and decent'), but they are rationed by broadcasters so all parties get (roughly) equal access to the medium.[1] Since the initial PEBs in the early 1950s, they have become (on the whole) slicker and better produced, with a move away from 'talking heads' to mini-dramas, some expounding a party's proposals, others attacking its rivals (though few have achieved the notoriety of American 'attack ads': Ansolabehere and Iyengar, 1995; Jamieson, 1992a).

PEBs are widely watched: 70 per cent of respondents to the 2005 BES reported having seen at least one during the course of that year's election campaign. But do they change voters' opinions and vote intentions? If voters were selectively attentive, watching only the broadcasts of parties they already supported, a correlation between seeing a party's PEB and voting for it would tell us only that party supporters tend to vote for their party! However, if a party's broadcasts are also seen by supporters of other parties and of none, then they have the potential to influence vote decisions. Evidence from the 2005 election tests whether voters are selectively attentive to PEBs. Before the election, BES respondents were asked which party they generally identified with. After the election, they were asked which parties' PEBs they could remember seeing during the campaign. On the whole, respondents did not just pay attention to their own party's broadcasts (Table 6.2). Labour and Conservative partisans were more likely to have seen their own parties' PEBs than to have seen those of rival parties. But more Liberal Democrat identifiers saw a Labour or a Conservative broadcast than saw a Liberal Democrat one. Opportunity certainly played a part here: the Liberal Democrats had fewer

---

[1] They are in theory subject to advertising standards legislation, but challenges are rare.

Table 6.2. Partisan viewers or attentive citizens? Attention to party election broadcasts in the 2005 general election campaign by prior partisanship

Declared party identification before the campaign	Saw party election broadcast from:			
	Labour (%)	Conservative (%)	Lib Dem (%)	N
None	46.6	43.0	38.8	618
Labour	68.0	59.3	52.5	982
Conservative	66.5	69.0	58.2	770
Liberal Democrat	63.4	60.3	59.5	347
Other	53.4	46.9	51.5	176
All	61.6	57.8	51.9	2893

Source: BES face-to-face panel (2005).

PEBs during the campaign than either Labour or the Conservatives. But in almost every case, irrespective of their initial partisanship, a majority of respondents reported seeing a PEB from each of the largest three parties in the election. Just over two-thirds of those who, before the campaign started, said they were Labour partisans reported seeing a Labour PEB; 59 per cent saw a Conservative PEB too, and 52 per cent saw a Liberal Democrat broadcast. Similar patterns also hold for Conservative and Liberal Democrat partisans. Only among those who said they did not generally support any party did a majority not see PEBs from each of the parties.

PEBs reach beyond those who already support a party. But how effective are they as a means of electoral communication? They have a beneficial effect on voters' perceptions of parties and party leaders (Pattie and Johnston, 2002a). Before the 2005 campaign, for instance, BES respondents were asked to rate their feelings towards the party leaders and the parties on an 11–point scale, with 0 indicating a strong dislike, and 10 strong liking. They were asked the same question again after the election. We can therefore examine whether changes in their views were influenced by whether they had seen PEBs (Table 6.3). Not surprisingly, the more favourably an individual felt towards a party or its leader at the outset of the campaign, the more favourable they felt at the end (the relevant coefficients are positive and significant). But, other things being equal, seeing a party's broadcast was almost always associated with feeling more favourable towards the party or its leader at the end of the campaign. And in some cases, seeing another party's PEB made one less likely to feel well-disposed to a party or its leader. For instance, people who had seen a Liberal Democrat PEB were less well-disposed to the Conservative leader, Michael Howard, at the end of the campaign than were those who had not seen such a broadcast. Similarly, compared to those who had not seen a Conservative PEB, those who had seen one thought less well of the Liberal Democrat leader, Charles Kennedy. The only exception to the general ability of PEBs to affect evaluations of parties and their leaders is in the case of feelings about the

Table 6.3. The impact of party election broadcasts on feelings towards parties and leaders in the 2005 general election: OLS regressions

	End-of-campaign feelings about:					
	Tony Blair	Michael Howard	Charles Kennedy	Labour	Conservatives	Liberal Democrats
Feelings at the start of the campaign about:						
Tony Blair	0.72					
Michael Howard		0.66				
Charles Kennedy			0.54			
Labour				0.75		
Conservatives					0.69	
Liberal Democrats						0.55
Watched Labour PEB	0.39	—	—	0.44	—	—
Watched Conservative PEB	—	0.31	−0.23	—	—	—
Watched Lib Dem PEB	—	−0.23	0.32	—	—	0.39
Constant	1.26	1.47	2.71	1.20	1.36	2.51
R^2	0.59	0.43	0.31	0.59	0.52	0.33
N	2923	2718	2680	2889	2823	2775

Note: Only significant coefficients are shown.
Source: BES face-to-face panel (2005).

Conservative party, which were not influenced by PEB viewing. 'Affect', or feelings towards parties, can be important factors in elections and parties ignore this emotional aspect of politics at their peril (Clarke et al., 2004). PEBs' beneficial effects on party affect are good news for parties, therefore.

Do PEBs affect votes (Pattie and Johnston, 2002a)? Once we control for their reported vote intention at the start of the campaign, the odds that BES respondents who saw a Liberal Democrat broadcast in 2005 would actually vote for the party were 2.7 times greater than for respondents who had not seen a broadcast (though those who had seen either a Conservative or a Labour broadcast were less likely to do so: Table 6.4). But PEB viewing had no discernible effect on the chances of voting either Labour or Conservative (apart from a weak, though surprising, increase in the chances of voting Conservative among those who saw a Liberal Democrat PEB). As the two largest parties, Labour and the Conservatives are exposed to constant media coverage throughout the lifetime of a parliament, not just during elections: PEBs do little to raise their already high profiles. But smaller parties, which struggle to be noticed outside election campaigns, do gain both attention and votes from their PEBS. That said, neither Labour nor the Conservatives can afford to abandon PEBs. Giving the other party a clear run by unilaterally stopping PEBs might prove very damaging, since it would provide the party's main rivals with unchallenged supremacy over the only area of broadcasting that parties can influence directly. PEBs in some form are therefore likely to remain an important component of all parties' electoral armouries.

Table 6.4. The impact of party election broadcasts on voting,
2005: logistic regressions

Independent variables	Vote 2005		
	Labour	Conservative	Lib Dem
Vote intention at start of campaign (comparison = undecided/will not vote)			
Labour	9.78	0.01	0.09
Conservative	0.08	15.18	0.16
Liberal Democrat	0.24	0.11	11.13
Other	0.43	0.14	—
Labour PEB (comparison = did not watch)			
Watched	—	—	0.64
Conservative PEB (comparison = did not watch)			
Watched	—	—	0.62
Lib Dem PEB (comparison = did not watch)			
Watched	—	1.43	2.69
R^2	0.38	0.47	0.30
% correctly classified	81.4	86.3	86.9
N	2917	2918	2919

Note: Only significant exponents are shown.
Source: BES face-to-face panel (2005).

PEBs are not the only means by which parties can get media coverage. They also vie for attention on news broadcasts and in the press. Although the UK press is highly partisan, television and radio news are both subject to strict rules on political neutrality. That said, television news does reach a large audience and the political parties cannot ignore it. Over time, they have increasingly attempted to influence how they are presented on both television and radio news. They do this by setting up pre-planned media events and photo-opportunities, carefully 'scripting' campaign efforts to focus on themes they wish to emphasize, and working on the representation (or 'spin') of news stories.

This is all part of the increasing professionalization of party election campaigning (Kavanagh, 1995; Rosenbaum, 1997; Scammell, 1995). The 1979 UK general election was a watershed, with the Conservative campaign closely coordinated by Saatchi and Saatchi, a major advertising company. Throughout the early 1980s, the contrast between the professional Conservative and amateurish Labour campaigns (culminating in their inept 1983 campaign) was stark. But by the late 1980s Labour too had begun to professionalize. After Tony Blair became leader in 1994, New Labour came to represent the new approach to campaigning (Gould, 1998): tight central control meant spokespeople stayed 'on message'; policies and advertising were tested via private polls and focus groups; relations with the news media were handled by spin doctors; and the party moved to a semi-permanent campaign footing. Campaigning no longer focused solely on elections but was planned for the entire parliament, with intensive campaigning beginning over a year before an election.

New Technologies: from Telephone Campaigning to the Internet

Modern campaigners have been quick to exploit new technologies. Telephone campaigning (increasingly through call centres: Labour established one in North Shields prior to the 2001 election) allows parties to talk directly to voters without having to rely on traditional doorstep canvassing (the latter having become more difficult in many areas as numbers of party activists decline: Fisher, 2000b; Pattie and Johnston, 2003a). Some calls are focused on known supporters, asking for donations and support, but many are aimed at voters in target seats, identifying who will vote for a party, who will not, and who is wavering. Almost 70 per cent of Constituency Labour Parties (CLPs) in Labour's target marginals in 2001 reported carrying out a substantial amount of telephone canvassing during the year before the election: only 15 per cent of CLPs in safe seats made the same claim, as did 7 per cent in seats where Labour stood no chance of winning (Denver et al., 2002a, 172). At that election, neither the Conservatives nor the Liberal Democrats made as much use of telephone canvassing, but they too concentrated their efforts in marginals: 37 per cent of Conservative associations in Conservative targets reported substantial telephone canvassing in the year before the election, compared to 16 per cent of those in safe seats and 8 per cent of those in seats where the Tories could not win. The equivalent figures for Liberal Democrat local parties were 27 per cent in target seats and 1 per cent in seats where the party could not win (the Liberal Democrats had relatively few safe seats in 2001). Information from the telephone canvass can be fed into targeted mailing activities, concentrating particular messages on particular types of voters. By facilitating the central coordination of efforts focused on particular seats, telephone campaigning links the national and the constituency campaign.

The rapid expansion of the internet during the late 1990s has provided parties with another campaigning tool (Ward and Gibson, 1998; Ward, Gibson, and Lusoli, 2003). In both 2001 and 2005, Labour's website provided information on what the party had done for voters while in office. By entering their constituency name or postcode, voters could access official statistics showing what the government had done in their area. All the statistics reported were positive, implying the Blair government had done a uniformly good job everywhere. But this was achieved in 2001 by the careful manipulation of the geography or the time scales (or both) over which information was reported (Dorling et al., 2002).[2] The party mounted a

---

[2] Things really did improve between 1997 and 2001 (Toynbee and Walker, 2001). How the statistics were reported was cynical, but the story they told was true.

similar exercise on its website in the 2005 election campaign, but the spatial and temporal manipulation of data were far less overt.

The proportion of the population using the internet to obtain political information has grown with the general rise of internet usage. Whereas only 7 per cent of voters said they had visited a website to obtain election information in 2001, 17 per cent did so in 2005 (Lusoli and Ward, 2005). However, the number of voters using the party websites remains small, especially compared to the numbers using television (90 per cent of voters used it for election news in 2005), newspapers, and party literature (each used by 70 per cent of voters), radio (51 per cent), and friends and families (42 per cent). And internet users are not a random cross-section of the public: they tend to be younger, more highly educated (students make up a particularly large proportion), and more affluent than the public at large. As a means of narrowcasting to younger 'opinion-formers' the net seems a useful tool, but as a device for broadcasting information to the public at large, it still has a way to go.

Inevitably, some of the novelty of these developments has worn off since 1997 (when Labour's efforts yielded an electoral landslide). Not only have the other parties caught up with Labour, but Labour has increasingly had to concentrate on governing, with less time and energy to focus on campaigning than when it was in opposition. And voters and the media are now more aware of, and more cynical about, the new campaign techniques. Even so, contemporary campaigns remain much more professional and nationally coordinated activities than was the case a generation ago.

Resourcing the Campaign

Substantial resources are deployed nationally during a modern election. Since the passage of the Political Parties, Elections and Referendums Act in 2000, national campaign expenditure has been legally capped. During the year prior to polling day 2005, parties could spend no more than £30,000 per constituency contested on national campaigns, up to a ceiling of £18.8 million. Of course, the ability to spend at this level depends substantially on a party's fundraising ability. Some parties have deeper pockets than others, and hence come closer to reaching the legal national campaign spending limit. The Conservatives, traditionally the richest party, spent just over £17.85 million in 2005. Labour had traditionally relied on trades union donations but after 1992 had diversified fundraising to take in large personal and business donations. It was therefore able to more than match Conservative expenditure for the first time in 2005, laying out over £17.94 million on its national campaign. The Liberal Democrats, meanwhile, are the poorest of the three main parties, relying primarily on membership fees and smaller donations. They spent only £4.32 million nationally in 2005.

Most national expenditure goes on advertising, election broadcasts, campaign staff, and market research. In 2005, advertising accounted for

46 per cent of the Conservatives' campaign spending, 30 per cent of Labour's, and 37 per cent of the Liberal Democrats'.[3] All three also spent heavily on unsolicited materials for electors: the Conservatives spent £4.45 million, compared to Labour's £2.70 million and the Liberal Democrats' £1.24 million.[4] And Labour and the Conservatives also spent over £1 million each on rallies and public events (almost £3 million and £1.1 million, respectively). Reflecting the importance for the modern campaign of knowing voters' views, market research accounted for around £1.5 million of both the Labour and Conservative budgets. The Liberal Democrats could not afford so extensive a market research effort, spending both a smaller absolute amount (£165,000) and a smaller proportionate share of their overall budget on this than the other two parties (just 3.8 per cent, compared to 7.2 per cent for the Conservatives and 8.8 per cent for Labour).

Is the effort expended on the national campaign worth it? As we have already seen, election broadcasts only benefit the Liberal Democrats and press influence is notoriously hard to measure. After the Conservatives' unexpected 1992 win, the Conservative-supporting *Sun*'s front page boasted that it was 'the *Sun* wot won it': more *Sun* readers supported the Conservatives (38 per cent) than voted Labour (29 per cent).[5] When the *Sun* switched allegiance in 1997 to New Labour, the partisanship of the paper's readers changed too: 21 per cent voted Conservative and 36 per cent Labour.[6] But did the readers follow their paper's lead, or was the paper reacting to its readers' views (a sensible strategy in a highly competitive market)? Research during the 1987 general election campaign suggested that some of the largest swings of opinion towards the Conservatives occurred among readers of Conservative-supporting tabloids (Miller, 1991). But later work on the 1992 and 1997 campaigns heavily downplayed the influence of the press on vote choice (Curtice and Semetko, 1994; Norris et al., 1999).

Television coverage, meanwhile, does have a small potential effect. An ingenious experiment tested the effects of different television stories in 1997 by surveying randomly selected members of the public before showing them a 30-minute television news broadcast into which had been inserted either material with a partisan bias in one direction or another, or material with no bias (Norris et al., 1999). The researchers could vary the contents of this section at random. The subjects were then interviewed again after the broadcast, when changes in their attitudes could be attributed to the material they had just watched. Although the effects were small, exposure to positive

---

[3] The biggest change in spending patterns between 2001 and 2005 was for the Liberal Democrats, whose 2001 advertising expenditure covered just 14 per cent of their budget.

[4] These increasingly include media other than printed leaflets. In 2001, for instance, Labour sent out over a million videos targeted at new voters (Ballinger, 2002, 214).

[5] Data are from the 1992 BES post-election cross-section survey.

[6] Data are from the 1997 BES post-election cross-section survey.

stories about a party did increase levels of support for it (though how long-lasting or cumulative these effects might be remains to be seen).

The Permanent Campaign?

One of the features of the modern campaign is its semi-permanent nature. Parties campaign throughout the parliamentary cycle, not just at election time, and much of the 'work' of campaigning may have been done by the time an election is called. One means of capturing the 'long campaign' empirically is to look at how much each party spends nationally every year. Since much expenditure is ultimately aimed at campaign efforts, this is a rough, though far from ideal, campaigning indicator. If the 'long campaign' has an effect, we would expect trends in expenditure to influence trends in opinion poll standing: parties spending more should, other things being equal, be more popular in the polls than parties that spend less. However, a study of party expenditure between 1959 and 1994 shows few consistent effects on opinion poll ratings (Fisher, 1999b). In part, this may be because of limitations in the key measures: annual expenditure is a crude measure, especially when public opinion can be volatile over much shorter periods of time. Also, parties do not campaign in a vacuum. If one party launches a campaign that seems to be effective, its rivals respond. And, if their responses are effective too, one campaign will cancel out the other. However, the results do suggest we should be cautious in over-stressing the effectiveness of the long campaign.

Gelman and King (1993) identified a long-campaign paradox. Long-range forecasts of American presidential elections, made well in advance of the poll and based on factors such as the state of the national economy, are generally (though not always: see Lewis-Beck, 2005) very accurate. Yet opinion polls suggest voter volatility during the campaign, often influenced by campaign events (Holbrook, 1996). Why did voters take so long to recognize the apparently inevitable? Gelman and King argued that the campaign itself, by focusing voters' attention on politics, meant they paid greater attention to the media and so became more informed on both party platforms and on how those platforms related to their own views and preferences. The campaign informed voter opinion and sharpened voter choice. More recent British research strongly supports this interpretation (Andersen, Tilley, and Heath, 2005). British voters' knowledge of parties' political platforms was higher in election than in non-election years, and party choice was more predictable in election years than mid-cycle. The national campaign, especially as the election approaches, serves a function even if no voters change their minds as a result, since it fosters an informed electorate. However, much of this gain seems to occur close to the election. Despite the long campaign, public awareness and knowledge drops off when an election is not in the offing. Parties may be talking to the electorate during the parliamentary mid-term, but it would appear that few are listening.

The permanent campaign is primarily fought by parties nationally, since they have the necessary personnel and resources. Local parties, by contrast, are run by volunteers, few of whom have the time, energy or resources for a local permanent campaign. However, in strategic locations, where a party is building support and hopes to win the parliamentary seat, a local permanent campaign can develop. The Liberal Democrats (and the Liberals before them) have been particularly adept at this grassroots activity. Research on Liberal Democrat campaigning in Bath showed how the party ran what were in effect permanent campaigns in a few key local government wards in order to keep itself in the electorate's eye (Cutts, 2006a).

The Constituency Campaign

UK elections are not simply national competitions: each constituency is a separate contest. Before radio and television, most elections were local affairs, with limited national coordination. Candidates and their local activists in constituencies campaigned largely on their own, issuing election addresses to constituents, holding meetings in local halls and public places, and canvassing voters at home. And before 1970, British ballot papers printed only the candidates' names. To know how to vote, electors had to at least know the name of their preferred party's candidate: only the local campaign made the connection between candidate and party. The need to know candidate names was removed by the 1969 Representation of the People Act, which, for the first time, allowed candidates to give their party affiliation on the ballot paper. Modern voters need only know which party they support when they vote.

But the emergence of the television-driven national campaign changed electioneering. Increasingly, voters' contact with the election has come through the national electronic media rather than through the constituency campaign. As early as 1950, while only 7 per cent of voters in Greenwich had attended a local election meeting, 70 per cent had heard at least one radio PEB (Benney, Gray and Pear, 1956). In addition, at elections throughout the 1950s and 1960s, most constituencies throughout the country saw vote changes of roughly the same size (Butler, 1963; see also Chapter 3, p. 74). If there was no variation from seat to seat in the swing, it was argued, then variations in local campaign intensity from constituency to constituency made little real difference to electoral outcomes. Not surprisingly, therefore, an orthodox view developed regarding the limited impact of constituency campaigning. The orthodoxy was enshrined most clearly in the Nuffield election studies, which have covered every UK general election since 1945. For instance, in their analysis of the 1992 election, Butler and Kavanagh (1992, 245) argued that it was 'hard to pinpoint any constituencies where the quality of one side's efforts made a decisive difference'.

For Kavanagh (1970), the constituency campaign was largely irrelevant: 'democratization and modernization of the social and political systems has enervated the local campaign' (p. 10) and 'the political swing during a campaign is negligible and what change does occur is only slightly related to exposure to campaign propaganda' (p. 87). He concluded that the benefits of constituency campaigns were more psychological than political. They were of more use to the parties in keeping local activists busy, and giving them a stake in the party's campaign, than in affecting the result of the election.

But modernization *per se* is not a sufficient reason to suggest that constituency campaigning is an anachronism. Campaign modernization began earlier, and is more advanced, in the USA than in the UK (Jamieson, 1992b). But far from spelling the end of local campaigning, the modernization of American elections has gone hand in hand with very visible and effective candidate-centred electioneering in congressional districts. An extensive literature attests that the more candidates for elected office spend on their campaigns, other things being equal, the more votes they win (Engstrom and Kenny, 2002; Green and Krasno, 1988, 1990; Jacobson, 1978, 1990; Kenny and McBurnett, 1994; Partin, 2002; Thielemann, 1993).

Of course, individual candidates' campaigns in the USA differ substantially from those in the UK. For instance, legal spending restrictions on American candidates are very generous by UK standards. At the 2004 US House of Representatives election, incumbents raised, on average, $1.1 million each, while the average challenger raised $260,000 (Stratmann, 2005). In the UK, candidate expenditure is still governed by the 1883 Corrupt and Illegal Practices Act. At the 2005 UK general election, the maximum a candidate could spend on his or her campaign in a county (rural) constituency was £7150 plus 7p for every registered elector in the constituency, while in borough (urban) constituencies, candidates were limited to £7150 plus 5p per elector (Electoral Commission, 2004b, 34). As there were 68,882 registered electors in the average constituency in 2005, the average candidate was restricted to spending no more than £11,971 in a county or £10,594 in a borough constituency.

In addition, some of the factors that sustained the orthodoxy regarding constituency campaigns in modern British elections are themselves now in question. National uniform swing disappeared in the 1970s. Regional voting trends diverged, often substantially, from the national pattern (see Chapter 3). Part of the reason lies in regional economic divergence (see Chapter 5), but part might also lie in local campaign efforts. It can be argued that local campaigns should have electoral effects, even in (post-)modern campaigns. Theoretical expectations for local campaigning can be developed by thinking of campaigning as using scarce resources (political, financial, and personnel) in the pursuit of winning as many MPs for one's party as possible. On that basis, a rational party in a plurality election system like the UK's will know there is little point in spreading scarce campaign resources widely. Some seats are safe: one's party will win them no matter what. In other seats, one's party has no realistic chance of victory. Of course, parties tend to have few members or resources in seats where they are electorally weak, so their chances of putting on a strong campaign there will be small in any case (Johnston, McAllister, and Pattie, 1999). But even so, campaign resources expended in either of these environments will be largely wasted, since they can have no real effect on the election outcome. However, some seats are marginal, and might be lost or won on relatively small swings of the vote. A rational party should concentrate its campaign resources more on marginals than on either safe or no-hope contests.

Having identified its target seats, a rational party must think about what it wants its campaign to achieve. It will want to win converts among swing voters. But probably more important is the need to identify potential supporters and ensure that as many as possible turn out to vote. Studies of political participation show clearly that being asked to participate is a powerful incentive: people are more likely to do something if they are asked to than if they are not asked, even if they are already predisposed towards it (Parry, Moyser, and Day, 1992; Pattie, Seyd and Whiteley, 2004; Verba, Schlozman and Brady, 1995). The implication for electioneering is clear—if parties want voters to vote for them, it helps to ask them. And since in systems like that of the UK, it matters where votes are won because that affects whether or not they elect MPs, this provides another incentive for parties to concentrate campaign resources in marginals. Local campaigning might still matter, therefore, if it serves to both persuade and to mobilize voters in the marginals.

Evidence of this emerged even as the orthodox view of constituency campaigns' redundancy was becoming established. Bochel and Denver (1971) conducted an experiment in two socially identical tower blocks in a safe Dundee Labour ward during the 1970 local election. One block was canvassed intensively for the Labour party. The other was not subject to an intense canvass. The experimental canvass aside, no other canvassing took place in either tower block, and the only other campaign activity experienced by the residents was the receipt of party campaign literature. Turnout was higher in the canvassed experimental tower block than in the uncanvassed control. And, reflecting the fact that the extra canvassing activity was on behalf of the Labour party, the Labour vote was also higher in the experimental than in the control block (80.5 per cent compared to 76.5 per cent—not a large difference, but sufficient to affect the result of a closer contest). Later research in Dundee and Lancaster confirmed these results: canvassing does seem to get the vote out (Bochel and Denver, 1972).

Measuring Constituency Campaigning

Groundbreaking though Bochel and Denver's work was, however, their results suffer from one limitation: they are based on (quasi-experimental) case studies. As such, they are unable to escape the possibility either that there was something *sui generis* about the areas studied, or that some uncontrolled and unanticipated local factor other than canvassing effort might have produced the better than expected Labour performances and turnouts in the canvassed areas. More systematic evidence has been supplied in recent years from four different sources:

1. analyses of constituency campaign spending (Johnston, 1979a, 1987; Pattie and Johnston, 2003b; Pattie, Dorling and Johnston, 1995);
2. surveys of local party members (Seyd and Whiteley, 1992, 2002; Whiteley and Seyd, 2002, 2003a; Whiteley, Seyd and Richardson, 1994);
3. surveys of party election agents (Denver and Hands, 1992, 1997b, 2004; Denver et al., 2002a, 2002b);
4. surveys of individual voters (Clarke et al., 2004; Pattie and Johnston, 2003b).

All these sources exploit data available simultaneously for numerous constituencies and (in most cases) for several parties.

Each of these more extensive information sources has strengths and weaknesses. Constituency campaign spending data have the considerable advantage of universality. All election candidates in the UK are required by law to declare their campaign expenditure, and the data are publicly available. However, since much constituency campaign activity relies on uncosted factors such as the number of volunteers and party members (and their enthusiasm), constituency campaign expenditure (mainly on printing leaflets and posters: Johnston, McAllister, and Pattie, 1999) misses important aspects of the campaign (Gordon and Whiteley, 1980; Johnston, 1981a). And candidates' expenditure returns may be inaccurate or misleading, especially if there is a risk that actual expenditure exceeds the constituency legal limit (Crick, 1998). Finally, the legal limit on constituency spending (even if sometimes ignored in practice) means there is also an upper limit to the ability of expenditure to capture the most intense campaigns: if we have two campaigns, both of which spend to their limits, but one of which is more actively pursued than the other, we have no way of differentiating between them.

Other researchers have sought more direct measures of campaign intensity. Surveys such as the BES, which ask individual voters whether they were canvassed during the election, give an indication of how the public is affected by or even notices the constituency campaign. However, such data cover only some constituencies: many contain no BES respondents and hence provide no data. Furthermore, responses are based on recollections, which can be inaccurate. Respondents may remember being canvassed by the party they eventually voted for, but forget being canvassed by other parties, for instance. Surveys of party members, meanwhile, have the considerable advantage of talking directly to campaign activists. However, they are expensive and relatively rare events. As such, they cannot provide simultaneous data on several parties' efforts, they do not cover all elections, and, even for one party, they do not provide data on all constituencies. Secondly, the surveys do not necessarily coincide with elections. Seyd and Whiteley's (1992) survey of Labour members was carried out in 1989 and asked about activities during the 1987 election, two years previously. Finally, the surveys of party agents by Denver and Hands deal with two of these problems very effectively. Like party member surveys, their data came from the coalface. But unlike party member surveys, party agent surveys focus solely on campaigning, occur soon after elections (minimizing memory effects), and also contact activists from all parties in all seats. However, response rates are highly variable, both across parties and between seats: in some constituencies, agents of all major parties reply; in others only one or two—or no—parties provide responses. The data are patchy.

In fact, all the various measures are strongly correlated with each other (Denver and Hands, 1997b, 254; Pattie et al., 1994; Whiteley, Seyd and Richardson, 1994, 199). At the 2001 general election, for instance, we have information from three of the four possible sources outlined above. Constituency spending data are available for each party in every constituency, expressing each party's spending in a seat as a percentage of the legal maximum permitted there. Denver and Hands' campaign intensity indices are available for Labour in 443 seats, for the Conservatives in 375, and for the Liberal Democrats in 432.[7] And finally, we have BES-derived measures of how much contact the average respondent had with each party's campaign in 108 seats.[8] The BES contact measure for each party was created by summing the number of ways each respondent had been contacted by a party during the constituency campaign (respondents were asked whether they were canvassed, whether they were telephoned, and whether they were contacted by a party on polling day) and then calculating the average number of contacts per respondent in each constituency for each party.

Constituencies providing data from all three sources allow us to evaluate whether the various constituency campaign measures are all assessing the same thing. Three principal components analyses (PCAs, which search for underlying patterns of correlation between variables), one for each party's constituency campaign, are used. Each PCA produces a one-component solution, lending strong support to the claim that all three measures are measuring the same underlying thing (Table 6.5). In all cases, the component loadings are positive and strong, with loadings of around 0.8 or better.

---

[7] Their index is based on electoral agents' reports of constituency campaign organization, the number of campaign workers available to the local party, and the extent of activities such as canvassing, using computers and telephones, leafleting, and activities on polling day itself (for details, see Denver and Hands, 1997b, 246–52; Denver et al, 2002b, 82–3).

[8] Following Denver and Hands (2004, 715), analysis is restricted to those constituencies with ten or more BES respondents.

Table 6.5. Comparing alternative measures of constituency campaigning: principal components analyses

	Principal components		
Campaigning measure	Labour	Conservative	Lib Dem
Expenditure (%)	0.90	0.89	0.88
Denver/Hands campaign index	0.92	0.90	0.92
BES contact index	0.82	0.78	0.79
% variance accounted for	77.74	73.58	74.71
Eigenvalue	2.33	2.21	2.24
N	74	60	72

Sources: BES face-to-face panel (2001); Denver and Hands (2001) constituency campaign study (data available from the ESRC); Electoral Commission (2002a).

And each of the components identified gives a good summary of the original variables, accounting for three-quarters of the original variance. Similar results can be achieved using estimates of campaign activity drawn from party member surveys (Denver and Hands, 1997b, 2004; Pattie et al., 1994; Whiteley, Seyd and Richardson, 1994). The conclusion is clear: the more intense a party's campaign in a constituency, the more that party will spend there, the more its electoral agent will report doing, the busier its local members will report being, and the more local voters will be contacted. All measures of the constituency campaign are robust indicators of local electoral campaign activity.

The Impact of the Local Campaign

We turn next to the impact of constituency campaigns on voting. Since a party's campaign efforts are expected to influence both its own support and support for other parties, we must examine all major parties' campaigning simultaneously. We therefore use constituency spending to measure local campaigning, since data are available for all parties in all seats. Regression analysis of constituency vote shares for each of the three major parties in 2001 reveal the impact of constituency campaigning (Table 6.6).[9] Each of the models includes the relevant party's local vote share at the preceding (1997) general election. This controls for the wide range of other factors that influence constituency voting trends, including the fact that many voters are habitual supporters of a particular party and are not likely to be swayed by campaigning. In addition, it means that the slope coefficients for the campaign measures indicate the change in party support associated with constituency campaigning.

[9] Constituency campaign spending data for the 2005 election were not available at the time of writing.

Table 6.6. Comparing alternative measures of constituency campaigning and voting, 2001: OLS regressions

Independent variables	Vote share 2001		
	Labour	Conservative	Lib Dem
Labour vote 1997 (%)	0.81		
Conservative vote 1997 (%)		1.03	
Lib Dem vote 1997 (%)			0.73
Labour campaign spend 2001 (%)	0.04	−0.02	−0.02
Conservative campaign spend 2001 (%)	—	—	−0.03
Lib Dem campaign spend 2001 (%)	−0.05	−0.02	0.10
Constant	6.23	1.12	5.93
R^2	0.96	0.95	0.89
N	640	640	640

Note: Only significant coefficients are shown.

Not surprisingly, the coefficients for party vote share at the 1997 election are positive and highly significant. Parties did well in 2001 where they had done well in the past, and badly where their 1997 support had been weak. But our main interest is in the effect of constituency campaign spending. All the relevant coefficients for each party's campaign spending are correctly signed, positively in the model for its own 2001 vote share, and negatively in the models for the other parties' vote shares. And (with the exception of Conservative campaign spending in the models for Conservative and Labour vote shares) all the campaign coefficients are statistically significant. The more a party spends on its constituency campaign, the better it does locally and the worse its rivals fare, other things being equal.[10] But, strikingly, Conservative campaigning in 2001 had no discernible effect on the Conservative vote (see also Denver and Hands, 1996). The party's failure to benefit from its own local campaign effort is a puzzle we return to below.

The equations give an idea of the impact of constituency campaigns. Take two hypothetical constituencies. We assume Labour won identical vote shares in both in 1997 but made no campaign effort whatsoever in 2001 in one constituency, and spent nothing, while it was more enthusiastic in the other seat, mounted its strongest possible campaign, and spent 100 per cent of its allowance. Also assume that the other parties did not campaign in either seat in 2001. Labour's vote share would have been 4 percentage points

---

[10] Similar results have been reported for other UK elections using all the indicators of local campaigning discussed above (e.g. Clarke et al., 2004; Denver and Hands, 1992, 1996, 1997a, 1997b, 2004; Denver, Hands and McAllister, 2004; Denver et al., 2002a, 2002b, 2003; Johnston, 1979a, 1987; Johnston and Pattie, 1996, 1998a; Johnston, Pattie and Johnston, 1989; Pattie and Johnston, 2003b; Pattie, Johnston, and Fieldhouse, 1995; Seyd and Whiteley, 1992; Whiteley and Seyd, 1994, 2003a, 2003b), and for other countries such as Australia, New Zealand, and Canada (Carty and Eagles, 1999, 2000; Eagles, 1993; Forrest, Johnston and Pattie, 1999; Johnston and Pattie, 1999b, 2002a, 2003c).

(0.04 × 100) higher in the seat where it campaigned hard than where it did not try at all. A vote differential of this size could have been enough to make the difference between victory and defeat in a marginal constituency.

The Local Campaign: Locally or Nationally Controlled?

Constituency campaigning remains effective, therefore. But far from being a bastion of local independence, it is now an integral part of parties' national strategies, controlled and scripted by national campaign headquarters (Denver and Hands, 2004; Denver et al., 2003). Some of the links between national and constituency campaigns are low-key. For instance, Liberal (and more recently Liberal Democrat) party headquarters have, for many years, provided local parties with *pro forma* guidelines for the production of leaflets and *Focus* newsletters outlining the activities of their local candidates (Russell and Fieldhouse, 2005). Labour's national website of statistics showing what the party had achieved in local communities, discussed earlier, is another example. Its largest audience in 2001 and 2005 was local Labour parties, using it to provide local copy for campaign leaflets. The professionalization of campaigning during the 1990s saw growing national control of constituency campaigns, in part by providing information for dissemination to local voters via faxes, pagers, emails, and the internet (Denver and Hands, 1997b).

The national campaign can give local activists a song to sing. But the process can also work in reverse. For instance, building a local profile by campaigning on local issues is a strong part of the Liberal Democrats' strategy as it provides a means of establishing the party's credibility (always the major challenge facing a third party in UK politics). This provides a platform from which the party can get local councillors elected. That in its turn provides a campaigning base from which to tackle other, surrounding, areas. As we saw in Chapter 3, Liberal Democrat success in local government elections tends to spread like a contagious disease. First one ward falls to the party, then surrounding wards fall, and so on (Dorling, Rallings and Thrasher, 1998). Having built a base of local government councillors in an area, the party then moves on to win MPs (Cutts, 2006a, 2006b, 2006c; Russell and Fieldhouse, 2005). National success is built on local success.

Targeting

Constituency campaigns are also integrated into parties' national campaigns in more direct ways. To win a first-past-the-post election, a party must win enough constituency contests to give it an overall majority in Parliament. Maximizing the party's overall national vote share is not necessarily the most important goal in achieving this (though clearly it would be in a pure proportional representation election). A plurality of votes is sufficient to win a seat: a true majority of votes is, in most circumstances, overkill. As discussed above. in a first-past-the-post election a rational party concentrates its local campaign efforts in marginal seats. Targeting campaign efforts in marginal seats also helps modern parties in another way. The constituency campaign depends on local party workers and volunteers, who canvass, deliver leaflets and newsletters, and so on. But party membership is in decline, reducing the pool of volunteers that can readily be drawn on (Fisher, 1999a, 2000a, 2000b; Seyd and Whiteley, 2002 ; Whiteley, Seyd and Richardson, 1994). This makes it all the more imperative that they use their grassroots activists as effectively as possible—and seat targeting is one means of doing so.

Targeting has been a major feature of constituency campaigning in recent British elections. The Liberal Democrats cannot afford to fight strong campaigns in all seats and so must be selective. In some seats, the party does little more than put up a candidate. Others where it might win are part of a 'Key Seats Initiative'. In 2001, around 60 seats were targeted for special attention (Russell and Fieldhouse, 2005, 208). They received visits from the party leader during the campaign, help and advice from party headquarters, access to a full-time field officer, and so on. In seats where the Liberal Democrats were the leading challenger, much effort went into encouraging anti-incumbent (and, in 1992, 1997, and 2001 especially, anti-Conservative) tactical voting. The message was simple: to oust the (Conservative) incumbent MP, vote Liberal Democrat (a claim supported in party leaflets by bar charts of previous election results in the seat). In 2005, the party's target seats campaign was more varied, involving an ultimately unsuccessful 'decapitation' strategy, which tried to unseat prominent Conservative front-bench MPs (including Conservative leader Michael Howard).

Labour deemed its 1992 targeting experiment a success in an otherwise disappointing election, and the strategy has been adopted at all subsequent elections (Hill, 1995). In 1997 the party targeted 57 seats needed for an overall majority (virtually all of which it went on to win), a further 22 marginals where victory was possible, and 11 Labour-held seats where there was no sitting MP.[11] In 2001 it targeted around 148 seats that it had won four years earlier, many unexpectedly (Denver et al., 2002b). In 2005, around 110 marginals were targeted, with an inner core of 45 earmarked for special attention (Fisher et al., 2005). These seats were the primary focus of the party's telephone canvassing. Activists in non-target seats were encouraged to campaign in target seats rather than their own. And, like the Liberal Democrats, Labour nationally provided extra resources in the form of advice, expertise, and information to support campaigns in its target seats.

---

[11] Because of boundary reviews between the 1992 and 1997 elections, marginality is based on estimates of what the 1992 result would have been in the 1997 constituencies.

Once in power after 1997, Labour also used its MPs as part of its target seats strategy, especially those elected in seats won from other parties in 1997. Soon after the election, Labour asked them to enter into a contract with the party. Their seat would be designated a 'key seat' and would receive additional help and support from the national party in any upcoming election campaign. In return, the MP agreed to a programme of local constituency activism for the duration of the parliament, with targets for the number of constituents the MP and local party should contact each week, the amount of time to be spent canvassing, the amount of direct mailing to be undertaken, and so on.

The Conservatives, too, claim to have operated target seats strategies in recent elections. However, their party structure makes it difficult for the party centrally to operate truly effective targeting: constituency Conservative associations are independent of the party nationally. There is little correlation, for instance, between the strength of the Conservative party in a constituency and the amount the local association raised for the national party (Pattie and Johnston, 1996, 1997a). There is little the party nationally can do to dissuade Conservative associations in its safe seats from campaigning hard there, or to encourage activists in these safe seats to campaign in marginals instead.

Targeting can be illustrated by plotting the amount each party spends on its constituency campaigns (as a percentage of the maximum permitted expenditure in each seat) against the marginality of the seat for the party at the previous election. Figure 6.1 does this for Conservative constituency campaigning in 2001.[12] Where the Conservative party won in 1997, marginality is the difference between its 1997 percentage vote share and that of the second-placed party. Where the party lost, its marginality is the gap between its vote share and that of the winner. So marginality figures close to 0 indicate highly marginal seats: the more positive the marginality, the safer a seat is for the party; and the more negative the marginality, the more hopeless the seat is. As expected, given the party's structure, the Conservatives conformed only weakly to the 'rational party' constituency campaign strategy. They spent little on campaigns in seats where they stood no chance of victory (though in many cases these constituencies had moribund local associations and few resources to expend on campaigning). And they spent at or very close to the legal maximum in their marginals. Not surprisingly, given they were in opposition, spending began to hit the legal limit in marginals the party needed to win (where the party was less than 20 percentage points behind the winner). Rather less rational, however, is what happened in seats the party held, where there was little fall-off in campaign spending. The Conservatives put almost as much effort into their safest seats as into their most marginal. This is not what would be expected from a party concentrating its campaign resources on marginal seats alone.

---

[12] The crosses on the graphs in Figures 6.1–6.3 represent individual constituencies, and the lines are a loess nearest-neighbour regression lines.

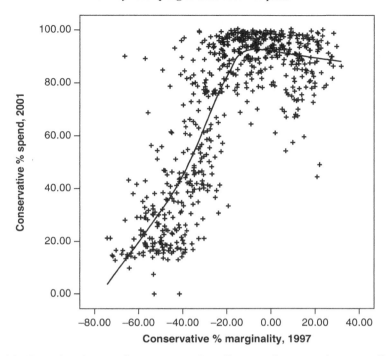

Fig. 6.1. Targeting the constituency campaign: Conservative campaign expenditure and constituency marginality at the 2001 general election

One might argue that this reflects the Conservatives' difficult situation in 2001—they had suffered a catastrophic defeat in 1997 and could not dent Labour's poll lead during the 1997–2001 parliament. Local activists might have thought no seat was safe in 2001, hence the need to campaign hard even in apparently secure constituencies. However, this argument, though plausible, is wrong. The chances of either Labour or the Liberal Democrats increasing their seat haul substantially in 2001 were small. More telling, the pattern of Conservative constituency campaigning had been the same in earlier elections too, even when the party won elections. For instance, the Denver/Hands campaign index (Table 6.7) shows that while Labour and the Liberal Democrats concentrated their efforts most intensively in their target seats in 1992, 1997, and 2001, the Conservatives always campaigned just as hard in their safe seats as in their marginal ones (Denver and Hands, 1997a, 1998; Denver et al., 2002b, 2003).

The pattern of Conservative constituency campaigning helps explain the puzzle identified above: why was the party's local campaign in 2001 so ineffective? Failure to concentrate campaigning in the marginals meant that much effort was put into talking to the already converted in areas where the party had few more votes to win. Campaigns in safe seats may make local

Table 6.7. Mean Denver/Hands constituency campaign intensity scores, 1992–2001

Party	Held, not targets	Targets	Not held, not targets	All
Conservative				
1992	139	134	94	124
1997	127	127	91	110
2001	128	127	83	110
Labour				
1992	114	143	93	112
1997	114	141	107	115
2001	105	126	83	106
Liberal Democrat				
1992	—	123	79	82
1997	—	146	78	83
2001	113	133	76	81

Source: Denver et al. (2003).

activists feel good, but they do comparatively little to win new Conservatives voters, as there are relatively few new voters left to win!

There is clearer evidence that Labour and the Liberal Democrats not only talked the talk of constituency targeting, but walked the walk too. The relationship between Labour constituency marginality in 1997 and its campaign spending there in 2001 is curvilinear (Figure 6.2). The party's expenditure was lowest where it stood little chance of winning and highest in the most marginal constituencies. In seats Labour held, the safer the seat, the less on average the party spent on its campaign there (though there is noticeable spread around this trend, with some high spending in some very safe Labour seats).

One feature of Labour campaign spending in 2001 that bears additional comment is that the peak of the curve is to the right of zero marginality: the party spent most in marginals it held. Labour was defending a huge landslide in 2001 and did not expect to win additional seats, but it did need to retain its 1997 gains. The constituency campaign strategy it adopted in 2001 was adapted to this goal. Contrast Labour constituency campaign spending in 2001 with the pattern at the 1987 election, when the party was in opposition and needed to gain marginals it did not hold (Figure 6.2). Once again, the curvilinear trend is clear: the party campaigned hardest in its most marginal seats. But in 1987 (and in 1983, 1992, and 1997), the peak of Labour's spending distribution was just to the left of zero marginality: the party spent most in marginals it had to win, and slightly less, on average, in marginals it held. In both cases, Labour campaigning was focused on the seats that mattered most to the party.

The Liberal Democrats, too, allocate constituency campaign resources and efforts rationally. The greatest effort is concentrated in the most marginal seats, and (even more so than for either Labour or the Conservatives)

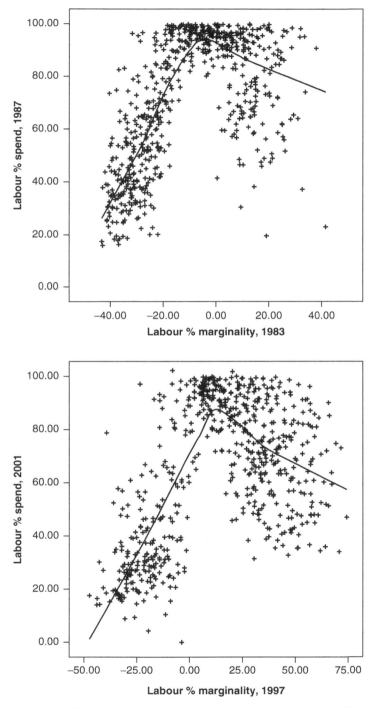

Fig. 6.2. Targeting the constituency campaign: Labour campaign expenditure and constituency marginality, 1987 and 2001

virtually no campaigning occurs in seats where the party has little chance (Figure 6.3). Given their lack of funds, using resources with care makes good sense. Unlike their rivals, however, and despite the advances the party has made in recent elections, the Liberal Democrats have very few truly safe seats, so there is no evidence of declining spending with declining marginality in seats the party holds.

Two controversies surround target seat strategies and constituency campaigning, however. Both are at root concerned with the effectiveness of a centrally governed constituency campaign. The first concerns whether target seat strategies actually work. The second concerns whether effective constituency campaigning is an expression of local party autonomy and grassroots activism or the result of a well-coordinated electoral strategy organized and operated by the national party. Not surprisingly, party strategists make strong claims for their target seats efforts (Cook, 2002). Labour's Director of Campaigns in 1992 felt that election 'vindicate[d] one of the key decisions that [Labour] made early on, to have an organisational system which concentrated on key marginals' (Hill, 1995, 40). And commenting on their 1997 performance, the Chair of the Liberal Democrats' general election campaign team argued: 'The policy of targeting [seats] . . . was

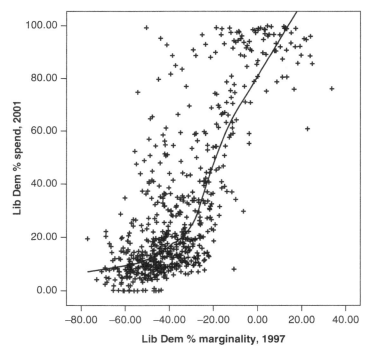

Fig. 6.3. Targeting the constituency campaign: Liberal Democrat campaign expenditure and constituency marginality, 2001

wholeheartedly pursued and served us well. The party's coefficient of seats won to votes cast has steadily improved in general elections' (Holme and Holmes, 1998, 26; see also Rennard, 2002). But in 1997 Labour not only won almost all of its 90 target seats; it also won a further 65 seats not on its target list, with similar swings to those achieved in the target seats. This led some to suggest that Labour's key-seats strategy had failed: the party would have won the target seats whether or not they had received special treatment (Curtice and Steed, 1997).

Doubts have also been raised with respect to the second controversy, whether constituency campaigns are best conceptualized as part of a national strategy or have more to do with grassroots activism. For Seyd and Whiteley (2002; see also Whiteley and Seyd, 2003a), it is grassroots campaigning, carried out by committed party members in constituencies, that produces results, not top-down centrally administered key-seat campaigns. They point out that local Labour parties in many seats where Labour was the challenger in 1997 campaigned hard even though they were not target seats. Hence the benefits of campaign effort were not restricted to the target seats. They further argue that parties nationally do not have sufficient control over their constituency organizations to move resources around the electoral map from safe and no-hope seats to marginals. Local parties may not want to cooperate, preferring to expend their efforts in their own seat than to campaign in a (perhaps distant) marginal, and, as in those seats Labour won unexpectedly in 1997, may be right to do so. The argument can be taken further, to support claims about the importance of a healthy and independent grassroots party organization and the limitations to over-zealous central control of campaigning.

Both claims—that targeting does not work, and that grassroots activism is more effective than central control—can be challenged. Although most party activists do campaign in their own constituencies, there are substantial transfers of help into target seats: 97 per cent of local Labour parties in Labour's target seats received volunteer workers from elsewhere on polling day in 1997, compared to just 6 per cent of parties in non-target seats (Denver and Hands, 2004). And in both 1997 and 2001 Labour mounted more intense campaigns, including telephone canvassing, in target than in non-target seats. Whereas (as Whiteley and Seyd suggest) there were no differences in 1997 between target and non-target 'possible' seats (i.e. those Labour had some chance of winning on a large swing) in traditional grassroots activities such as doorstep canvassing and leafleting, by 2001 these activities too were concentrated on the target seats. And the party did better in its target seats in both 1997 and 2001 than it did elsewhere (Denver and Hands, 2004, 723–4).

Furthermore, it is possible to differentiate between centrally and locally organized features of the constituency campaign. Fisher, Denver and Hands (2006) examined central involvement in local campaigns by Labour, the Conservatives, and the Liberal Democrats at the 1992, 1997, and 2001 general elections. Their measures are based on three factors: how much contact national and regional party offices had with local electoral agents before and during the election campaign; whether party headquarters assigned a special officer to work on the local campaign; and whether the local party was supplied with election software by party headquarters. In addition, they also looked at other, more local, factors such as canvassing, and analysed variations in local party membership (the key local campaign resource according to Whiteley and Seyd). By correlating these measures with changes in party vote share over time, they were able to analyse the relative importance of nationally coordinated and locally driven constituency campaigns. The positive correlation between local campaigning and party performance (Conservatives excepted) was not only the result of local efforts. National support for local campaigns was important too, and became more important as time went on. The greater the assistance a constituency party received from its national headquarters, the better it tended to do, other things being equal.

Constituency campaigning is not just an expression of local party activism, therefore. It is also an important tool in the armoury of the modern, nationally coordinated election campaign.

Constituency Campaigning and the Individual Voter

The chapter has concentrated thus far primarily on aggregate trends at the constituency level and on changes in voting between elections. But does the constituency campaign affect individual voters? To answer this, we turn to the 2005 BES, which lets us examine short-term changes in vote over the course of the campaign. BES respondents were asked about their experience of the constituency campaign: whether they had been canvassed at home during the campaign, whether they had been phoned by a party during the campaign, and whether any party worker had contacted them on election day itself to check whether they had voted or intended to vote. In each case, those who reported some form of contact were also asked which party had made the contact. We therefore have two measures of traditional constituency campaigning (doorstep canvassing and election-day contacting) and a measure of the modernized, more centrally controlled constituency campaign (telephone contact).

Only a minority of respondents were contacted by the parties during the 2005 constituency campaign. Overall, just over one in every five remembered being canvassed by at least one party, and only 5 per cent recalled being contacted by a party on election day itself (Table 6.8). Some of those who reported being canvassed also reported an election-day contact. The double counting means that, overall, just under a quarter reported some face-to-face contact. Rather fewer, just 7 per cent, remembered being telephoned by a political party.

Table 6.8. Contacting voters in the constituency campaign during the 2005 general election campaign

Contact type	Voters contacted (%)			
	All	Labour	Conservative	Lib Dem
Canvassed	21.7	8.7	11.5	6.0
Contacted on election day	5.4	2.8	1.3	1.0
Any face-to-face	23.8	10.0	12.2	6.5
Telephoned	7.4	2.8	3.5	1.0

Source: BES face-to-face panel (2005).

Contact rates by particular parties were lower. Just under 9 per cent of respondents remembered being canvassed by Labour, for instance, and 12 per cent recalled being canvassed by the Conservatives. Not surprisingly, given their smaller number of party members to draw on, the Liberal Democrats contacted substantially fewer voters than either Conservative or Labour. Individual parties' use of telephone canvassing was limited: only around 3 per cent of respondents remembered being phoned by Labour or the Conservatives, and just 1 per cent were called by the Liberal Democrats. Labour was the most active in contacting voters on polling day in 2005. Around 3 per cent of voters reported that the party had contacted them, compared to around 1 per cent reporting polling-day contacts from either the Conservatives or the Liberal Democrats. The patterns of constituency campaigning revealed by voters' recollections in the 2005 BES suggest few real changes between 2001 and 2005. The only statistically significant shift was a decline in Labour's doorstep canvassing effort: in 2001, 10.4 per cent of voters recalled being contacted by the party, compared to 8.7 per cent in 2005.[13] As a result, the Conservatives overtook Labour in the doorstep canvassing 'race' in 2005, having 'drawn' with them four years before (when 10.6 per cent of BES respondents had reported being canvassed by the Conservatives).

While the number of BES respondents reporting being contacted by the parties is small, this does not mean the constituency campaign was limited. First, as seen earlier, constituency campaigning was targeted in relatively few marginal seats. In large swathes of the country, there was minimal party activity as the constituency result was not in question. Secondly, much telephone canvassing takes place before the election is called: parties use their telephone campaigns for voter identification—sorting voters into supporters, opponents, and potentially floating voters—and then using this information to direct campaign materials accordingly. Voters' recollections

---

[13] The change between 2001 and 2005 in the proportion reporting being canvassed by Labour is statistically significant ($\chi^2 = 4.72$, $p = 0.03$). No other comparison between 2001 and 2005 reported levels of constituency campaigning was significant.

of being telephoned during the campaign itself are therefore likely to under-estimate the telephone canvass. Thirdly, much of the constituency campaign involves the delivery of printed material such as leaflets and newsletters, not direct face-to-face (or telephone) contact with voters. Even in marginals, many more voters see party literature delivered through their letterbox than are contacted directly by party workers.

Even so, the BES data do give insights into the impact of constituency campaigns on voters' decision-making in 2005. Logistic regression models are used to account for whether individuals voted Labour, Conservative, or Liberal Democrat in 2005 (Table 6.9). The models control for vote intention at the start of the campaign, so the coefficients for the remaining variables indicate whether exposure to each party's constituency campaign made individuals change their vote intention during the campaign (as before, we report only the exponents for significant coefficients). The vote intention measure contrasts those who at the start of the campaign had a clear

Table 6.9. The electoral impact of face-to-face and telephone constituency campaigning, 2005: logistic regressions

Independent variables	Vote 2005		
	Labour	Conservative	Lib Dem
Vote intention at start of campaign (comparison = undecided/will not vote)			
Labour	10.07	0.01	0.08
Conservative	0.09	16.12	0.15
Lib Dem	0.24	0.11	11.47
Other	0.43	0.15	—
Labour face-to-face contact (comparison = no contact)			
Contacted	1.90	—	—
Conservative face-to-face contact (comparison = no contact)			
Contacted	—	3.10	—
Lib Dem face-to-face contact (comparison = no contact)			
Contacted	0.55	—	1.82
Labour telephone contact (comparison = no contact)			
Contacted	2.86	—	—
Conservative telephone contact (comparison = no contact)			
Contacted	—	1.77	—
Lib Dem telephone contact (comparison = no contact)			
Contacted	—	—	6.17
R^2	0.39	0.49	0.29
% correctly classified	81.7	86.3	87.0
N	2885	2885	2886

Note: Only significant exponents are shown.
Source: BES face-to-face panel (2005).

intention of voting for each party against those who either had not yet decided who to vote for or intended to abstain. The explanatory variables include measures for BES respondents' exposure to constituency campaigning in 2005. The first set of measures indicate whether an individual was canvassed in person or was contacted on polling day. One such variable is used for each party, and is coded 1 if a respondent remembers being canvassed on the doorstep or was contacted on polling day by the party, and 0 if he or she does not recall a contact. We combine both aspects into one variable to give a measure of face-to-face contact for the constituency campaign. If constituency campaigning does have an effect, individuals who are contacted by a party should be more likely to vote for it (and less likely to vote for its rivals) than individuals who are not contacted. A second set of constituency campaign variables measures whether individuals were telephoned by each party (coded 1 if they had been telephoned during the campaign and 0 if they had not). Although few BES respondents were telephoned in 2005, telephone and face-to-face contact are analysed separately, since this allows an assessment of the relative impact of traditional and modern constituency campaign techniques.

Vote intention at the start of the 2005 campaign was the strongest guide to how people actually voted. Compared to those who either had not yet made up their minds or who intended to abstain at the start of the campaign, those who said they would vote for a party were very likely actually to do so (the relevant exponents are all large, much greater than 1 and highly significant), and were also very unlikely to vote for another party (the coefficients for initial support for one party in the equation accounting for actual vote for another are considerably smaller than 1 and significant). But some changed their minds during the campaign, either switching from one party to another, or going from indecision or a resolve to abstain to support for a party.

As for constituency campaigning, it not only has an aggregate effect on electoral outcomes, but also influences individual voters' decisions over the short-term period of the campaign itself. In each equation, the exponent for face-to-face contact by the party whose vote is being modelled is always significant and greater than 1. Compared to those who had not been contacted face-to-face by a party (that is, either canvassed on the doorstep or contacted on polling day), those who had been were more likely to switch to the party. And the effects can be substantial. To get a sense of their relative size, we calculate hypothetical individuals' probabilities of voting for a party, depending on whether or not they have been contacted by the party during the campaign.[14] Consider, for example, someone who at the start of the campaign had either decided to abstain or was undecided on which party to support, and was neither contacted face-to-face nor telephoned by any party. There is a 14 per cent chance of such an individual actually voting

---

[14] These estimates are based on the full equations, not reported here.

Labour in 2005, a 12 per cent chance of voting Conservative, and a 28 per cent chance of voting Liberal Democrat. But had this individual been canvassed face-to-face by Labour and nothing else, then his or her chance of voting Labour would almost double, to 24 per cent. Similarly, if this person had only been contacted face-to-face by the Conservatives, his or her chance of voting for that party would have gone up to 30 per cent. And if this individual's only contact had been a face-to-face canvass by the Liberal Democrats, his or her chances of voting for them would have risen to 42 per cent.

What about the telephone canvass? If it proves as effective as traditional doorstep canvassing, then it may provide a way of dealing with the grassroots decline in party organizations. But the jury is still out on this. American studies of voter mobilization efforts suggest voters are more responsive to personal face-to-face contact with campaigners than with relatively impersonal phone calls, especially when the latter are automated (Gerber and Green, 2000, 2001; Green and Gerber, 2004). Similarly, analysis of canvassing at the 1997 UK general election (the first UK election in which telephone canvassing was used extensively) shows that while doorstep canvassing did influence individual vote choice in 1997, telephone canvassing did not (Pattie and Johnston, 2003a). The personal touch of face-to-face contact had a greater impact than the more impersonal and anonymous telephone techniques.

The results for 2005 (by which time both parties and voters had greater experience of telephone campaigning) show these early dismissals of telephone canvassing to have been premature (see Table 6.9). Unlike 1997, telephone canvassing did make a difference in 2005, even when face-to-face canvassing and prior vote intention are taken into account. In the models for each party's vote, the exponent for telephone canvassing by the party is greater than 1 and significant. Being telephoned by a party during the 2005 election made those so contacted more likely to vote for it. Indeed, for both Labour and the Liberal Democrats, the relevant coefficient is larger than the equivalent for exposure to that party's face-to-face canvassing efforts. If our hypothetical undecided voter had only been telephoned by Labour, and had no other contact with another party, then his or her chances of voting Labour in 2005 would have been 32 per cent. The equivalent chances of voting Conservative if our individual had only been exposed to their telephone canvass would have been 19 per cent. And if only exposed to a phone call from the Liberal Democrats, his or her chances of voting for that party would have been an impressive 71 per cent. Of course, very few individuals were telephoned by any party, so we should keep the impact of phone calls in proportion. But phone calls can be a highly cost-effective campaign tool.

However, as noted above, reliance on individual voters' recollections of being contacted during the campaign exposes us to two risks: fallible human memory and the inability to assess the impact of aspects of the local campaign, such as leafleting, which reach many more voters in a constituency than canvassing ever can. As we have seen, constituency spending is a useful surrogate measure for these wider aspects of local campaigning. Adding data on party spending in each of the BES respondents' home constituencies to their individual responses allows us to analyse the impact of the wider local campaign on individuals. At the time of writing, constituency campaign spending data were not available for the 2005 general election, but we can repeat the analyses reported in Table 6.9 for the 2001 general election.

Table 6.10 gives the results. Two models are fitted for each party. The first replicates the 2005 analyses using 2001 data: the results are clearly comparable to those for 2005. It is the second model, including measures of constituency campaign spending at the 2001 election, which is of most interest. It confirms the importance of the wider constituency campaign. Almost all the spending exponents are correctly signed (greater than 1 in equations predicting whether individuals vote for the spending party, less than 1 in equations predicting whether individuals vote for the party's rivals). And most are significant: the more a party spent on its 2001 constituency campaign, the more likely individual voters living there were to vote for it. And individuals' chances of voting either Labour or Conservative in 2001 were negatively related to the amount spent locally by the other parties. Constituency campaigning works partly through individual contact and also through activities such as leafleting.

Who Benefits from Constituency Campaigning: Incumbents or Challengers?

Is the effect of constituency campaigning the same for all candidates? There is some dispute in the North American literature over who benefits from campaign effects. For some, all candidates benefit (Gerber, 1998; Goldstein and Freedman, 2000; Green and Krasno, 1988, 1990). Others argue that incumbents receive little or no benefit, since they already have local recognition through their activities in office, whereas challengers, who do not have the publicity-generating advantages of office, do benefit since their campaigns raise their profiles with the electorate (Jacobson, 1978, 1990). Of course, North American trends need not be replicated in the UK. However, it is worth asking whether constituency campaigning works better for a party when it is defending a seat or when it is attacking. This can be investigated by repeating the regression models reported in Table 6.6, splitting constituencies into those held by a party before an election (where campaigning will be focused on maintaining its hold) and those seats where the party was a challenger (and where it might campaign to gain the seat, or to increase its vote share in preparation for a win at a subsequent election).

Table 6.10. The electoral impact of local and national campaigning,
2001: logistic regressions

| | Vote 2001 | | | | | |
| | Labour | | Conservative | | Lib Dem | |
Independent variables	Model I	Model II	Model I	Model II	Model I	Model II
Vote intention at start of campaign (comparison = undecided/will not vote)						
Labour	14.44	15.80	0.03	0.04	0.23	0.24
Conservative	0.07	0.08	15.64	15.33	0.21	0.17
Lib Dem	0.10	0.11	0.06	0.05	20.91	20.70
Other	0.09	0.06	—	—	0.06	0.06
Labour face-to-face contact (comparison = no contact)						
Contacted	1.58	—	—	—	—	—
Conservative face-to-face contact (comparison = no contact)						
Contacted	—	—	2.12	1.86	—	0.57
Lib Dem face-to-face contact (comparison = no contact)						
Contacted	—	—	—	—	2.25	—
Labour telephone contact (comparison = no contact)						
Contacted	2.69	2.41	—	—	0.05	0.04
Conservative telephone contact (comparison = no contact)						
Contacted	—	—	—	—	—	—
Lib Dem telephone contact (comparison = no contact)						
Contacted	—	—	—	—	—	—
Constituency campaign spending (%)						
Labour spend 2001		1.01		0.99		—
Conservative spend 2001		0.99		1.02		—
Lib Dem spend 2001		0.99		0.99		1.02
R^2	0.57	0.61	0.58	0.60	0.35	0.39
% correctly classified	81.1	82.2	86.2	86.0	84.7	85.7
N	1592	1592	1593	1593	1592	1592

Note: Only significant exponents are shown.
Source: BES face-to-face panel (2001).

The results suggest that the value of local campaigning depends strongly on the nature of the tactical battle facing a party in a particular seat (Table 6.11). In seats that a party won in 1997, and was defending in 2001, its local campaign spending had no impact on its 2001 vote share. However, where a party was a challenger in 2001, its local campaign expenditure boosted its 2001 vote share. The more it spent on its local campaign in these seats, the better it did, other things being equal. This even held true for the Conservative party's constituency campaigns, which had no aggregate effect when all seats were considered simultaneously. Challengers get more out of local campaigning than do incumbents.

Table 6.11. The impact of party incumbency on constituency campaign effectiveness, 2001: OLS regressions

	Vote share 2001					
	Labour		Conservative		Lib Dem	
Independent variables	Incumbent	Challenger	Incumbent	Challenger	Incumbent	Challenger
Lab vote 1997 (%)	0.72	0.70				
Con vote 1997 (%)			0.55	0.98		
Lib Dem vote 1997 (%)					0.38	0.63
Lab campaign spend 2001 (%)	—	0.05	−0.03	—	—	−0.02
Con campaign spend 2001 (%)	—	—	—	0.02	—	−0.02
Lib Dem campaign spend 2001 (%)	−0.02	−0.08	−0.04	−0.02	—	0.10
Constant	15.20	10.18	23.45	0.99	25.72	7.09
R^2	0.82	0.90	0.56	0.92	0.06	0.83
N	415	221	164	472	45	590

Note: Only significant coefficients are shown.

Several factors help create this asymmetry between incumbents and non-incumbents. Incumbent MPs receive more publicity than do their challengers, simply because they are in office (though, given the more restricted profile of a British MP compared to an American Congressman, it is important not to exaggerate this). That said, most MPs' behaviour in the House of Commons rarely deviates from party lines, even on free votes, and there is little evidence that MPs who develop a reputation for rebelliousness fair any better or worse at the polls than their more sedate peers (Cowley, 2002; Pattie, Fieldhouse, and Johnston, 1994; Pattie, Johnston, and Stuart, 1998). Most voters pay little attention to the details of who does or says what in the Commons. But MPs do benefit from another of their roles, dealing with constituents' problems (Cain, Ferejohn and Fiorina, 1984, 1987; Heitshusen, Young, and Wood, 2005; Searing, 1985; Wood and Norton, 1992). Good constituency MPs, especially those recently elected, are more successful in winning votes than are those who put less effort into their constituencies. It hardly needs saying that challengers, who do not have even the limited powers of being an MP to draw on, cannot benefit from constituency activism in the same way. Challengers can try to build a local profile by leading local campaigns: Liberal Democrat candidates have been particularly effective in this way (Russell and Fieldhouse, 2005). But it is an uphill struggle to fight a record of actual achievement.

Finally, being an MP gives incumbents a platform for long-term local campaigning which is harder for challengers to achieve. Labour's contract with its new 1997 MPs is a case in point (see p. 206). As part of that contract, Labour MPs were expected to campaign visibly in their constituencies as the

2001 election approached. Did they do so? No data are available on how much time MPs spent in their seats. However, we do know something about their presence in the House of Commons. All Commons votes (or divisions) are recorded, with individual MPs named. The number of divisions each MP takes part in can then be calculated and so, by extension, can the number of divisions in which he or she does not vote. An MP might have to miss a vote in the Commons because he or she is campaigning in his or her constituency. If the party requires some MPs, especially those defending marginal seats, to campaign harder than average, then such MPs are likely (other things being equal) to miss more Commons votes than their peers in seats where less effort is being expended on the local campaign.

There are many reasons for not voting in the House of Commons: MPs may be incapacitated; they may have pressing engagements that require their absence from the chamber (often the case for front-benchers); they may disagree with their party's policy but not wish to rebel openly, in which case recording a *de facto* abstention by missing the vote will allow them to square the circle of individual conscience and party discipline; and so on. It is, however, unlikely that many backbench MPs will absent themselves too frequently from Commons divisions without good reason. It is a reasonable assumption that regular absentees who are not seriously ill are, at least part of the time, working in their constituencies. What is true of all backbench MPs is even more likely to be true of those defending highly marginal seats. MPs in marginals are no more prone to illness, or rebellious behaviour, than those in safe seats (Cowley, 2002, 114). But they are more likely to lose their seats if there is a swing against their party. As such, they have a particularly strong incentive to campaign hard for re-election. So if MPs in marginals are absent from the Commons more frequently than MPs in safer seats, then involvement in local campaigning is a plausible reason for at least some of those absences.

Using *Hansard* records of Commons voting, Johnston et al. (2002b) calculated the participation rate for every MP in each of the 244 divisions of the 1999–2000 parliamentary session, and in the 209 divisions of the 2000–2001 session (the session preceding the 2001 general election). This provided an estimate of how often Labour backbenchers were absent from the Commons. In the 1999–2000 session, the average backbencher voted in around 70 per cent of divisions. During the following (and pre-election) 2000–2001 session this dropped to voting in around 64 per cent of divisions. But there were notable changes in the relationship between the marginality of MPs' constituencies and how often they voted in the Commons. In the 1999–2000 parliamentary session, seat marginality made little difference to Labour backbenchers' propensity to vote in the Commons (Table 6.12). Contrast that with the pre-election 2000–2001 session. Commons attendance dropped dramatically for Labour backbenchers in the most marginal seats, down to participation in just over 53 per cent of divisions on average. But the

Table 6.12. Average percentage of divisions voted in by backbench Labour MPs standing for re-election in 2001, by constituency marginality

Marginality (%)	Parliamentary session		
	1999–2000	2000–2001	Difference
0.0–4.9	75.2	53.2	−22.0
5.0–9.9	69.8	59.3	−10.5
10.0–14.9	67.1	56.8	−10.3
15.0–19.9	70.3	65.1	−5.3
>20.0	69.8	67.9	−1.9

Source: Johnston et al. (2002b).

less marginal a Labour backbencher's constituency was, the smaller the average drop in his or her participation in Commons votes. Indeed, participation by backbenchers in the safest seats hardly changed at all. In other words, those Labour backbenchers who absented themselves from the Commons most frequently as the 2001 election approached were precisely the individuals who were facing the hardest fights to win re-election. They almost certainly spent much of the time freed by not voting in the Commons on campaigning in their constituencies.

Did it make a difference? An assessment is complicated by two factors. First, Labour's key-seats campaign in 2001 concentrated extra efforts in those marginals the party had to hold to retain power. Secondly, because most Labour MPs were relatively frequent Commons voters who represented very safe seats, any analysis of the electoral fortunes of Labour MPs who represented marginals and who were relatively infrequent Commons voters in the 2000–2001 session will inevitably be based on small numbers. Bearing those caveats in mind, however, Johnston et al.'s (2002b) analyses do suggest some interesting trends. It is possible to look at how much, on average, Labour's vote share changed between 1997 and 2001 in those seats defended by a Labour MP, broken down according to how marginal the seat was in 1997 and the proportion of divisions the MP voted in during the 2000–2001 session (Table 6.13).

Clear patterns are hard to discern in the most marginal seats. But these were precisely the constituencies into which Labour was already throwing considerable campaign resources in 2001. Whether the sitting MP had a lot or a little time available for campaigning made little additional difference to the party's performance there in 2001. But in seats that were not the focus of the key-seats campaign, but which were still relatively marginal (those with margins of between 10 and 19.9 per cent), the less time a Labour MP spent in the Commons in the session before the election and hence, by implication, the more time he or she spent campaigning in the constituency, the better Labour's performance in 2001. Where, as in Labour's most marginal seats in 2001, there were plenty of campaign resources to go round, therefore, the

Table 6.13. Change in Labour share of the vote, 1997–2001, in seats where Labour MPs stood for re-election in 2001, by marginality and by MPs' voting records

Marginality (%)	Divisions voted in, 2000–1 session (%)			
	<55	56–66	67–76	>77
0.0–4.9	+2.0 (9)	+2.1 (10)	+5.3 (2)	+2.3 (21)
5.0–9.9	+1.7 (11)	+2.8 (17)	−1.0 (8)	+1.4 (2)
10.0–14.9	−0.7 (10)	−1.3 (13)	−4.8 (4)	+0.2 (1)
15.0–19.9	+1.2 (4)	−2.5 (12)	−3.5 (4)	−0.6 (10)
20+	−3.9 (51)	−4.6 (46)	−3.5 (67)	−3.7 (247)

Note: Number of MPs in parentheses.
Source: Johnston et al. (2002b).

sitting MP might feel obliged to campaign hard (for fear of losing the seat). But his or her campaign participation locally did not affect the result. However, in seats where fewer central resources were available, the amount of time the local MP could devote to campaigning really did make a difference. In the (relative) absence of central campaign resources, a party's local campaign can benefit from the active involvement of its sitting MP.

Knowledge about Local Candidates

The analyses reported here suggest that one beneficial impact of constituency campaigning is to raise the individual candidate's profile locally, therefore. This is not new, of course. As we have seen, one of the original aims of the constituency campaign was to impart information to voters regarding the candidates (Kavanagh, 1970). In particular, before 1969 the constituency campaign served to inform voters of candidates' names, since only these, and no party affiliations, appeared on the ballot paper. Of course, since the early 1970s, ballot papers have carried party affiliation, so it is no longer imperative that voters know the names of the individuals seeking their support. But British MPs do not see their role (and are not seen by voters) purely as party representatives. They are also in the Commons to represent their constituents. The notion of a personal relationship between MPs and constituents remains a central feature of the Westminster system (Heitshusen, Young and Wood, 2005). Even though there is no longer an absolute need for voters to know the names of the candidates standing in their seats, therefore, achieving name recognition among voters might still confer some advantage on candidates since it could contribute to that sense of personal representation.

Does the local campaign still help to inform voters of who, personally, their candidate are, therefore? The 1997 BES provides an opportunity to find out (Pattie and Johnston, 2004). In that survey, respondents were asked to name the candidates standing for each party in their seat. We can differentiate, therefore, between those who could name a party's local candidate correctly and those who could not (the latter group, of course, combines those who came up with the wrong name and those who had no idea at all). Data on constituency campaign spending at the 1997 election in each respondent's constituency give measures of the intensity of the local campaign. If campaigns do increase voter recognition of candidates as individuals, then voters should be more likely to name a candidate correctly if that candidate has fought an intense campaign than if the candidate has not. But we would also reasonably expect voters to be more attentive to, and more knowledgeable about, the candidate of the party they would normally support than of candidates of other parties. We therefore take selective attention into account by controlling for individual party identification.

The logistic regression results fit our expectations well (Table 6.14). Partisan identification structures voters' knowledge of local candidates. Voters were more likely to correctly name the candidate of the party they normally supported than they were to name other parties' candidates. Interestingly, compared to non-partisans and minor-party supporters, Labour and Liberal Democrat identifiers were also more likely to name their local Conservative candidate correctly, and Liberal Democrats were more likely to name their Labour candidate correctly too. In 1997, tactical voting between Labour and Liberal Democrat candidates in order to oust Conservative incumbents was a major feature of the election (Johnston et al., 1997). Liberal Democrats' knowledge of Labour candidates may well be a result of their search for the best anti-Conservative tactical option in their seat.

But even when the propensity of individuals to recognize 'their own' candidates is taken into account, constituency campaigning influences voters'

Table 6.14. Constituency campaigning and knowledge of local party candidate, 1997: logistic regressions

	Correctly named constituency candidate for:		
Independent variables	Conservative	Labour	Liberal Democrat
Party identification (comparison = other/none)			
Conservative	3.97	—	—
Labour	1.51	2.18	—
Liberal Democrat	2.48	1.68	2.53
Constituency campaign spending 1997			
Conservative % spend	1.03	0.99	—
Labour % spend	0.99	1.02	—
Lib Dem % spend	—	0.99	1.03
R^2	0.21	0.15	0.17
% correctly classified	69.6	64.7	84.5
N	2405	2406	2406

Note: Only significant exponents are shown.
Source: BES cross-section survey (1997).

knowledge of who the candidates are. As the logistics regression models show, the more each party spent on its local campaign in a seat at the 1997 general election, the more likely were individuals living there to know the name of the party's candidate. And there is also evidence of a 'crowding-out' effect. The more other parties spent locally, the less likely were voters to know the names of their Labour or Conservative candidate. Once again, these effects can be substantial. The chances that a hypothetical individual who did not support any of the three major parties in 1997 and who lived in a seat where no party campaigned would correctly name the Conservative candidate locally was just 5 per cent. The probability of them knowing who the Labour candidate was would be just 33 per cent. And their probability of naming the Liberal Democrat candidate would be only 13 per cent. But if the Conservatives spent up to the local maximum on their constituency campaign while the other parties still spent nothing, such an individual's chance of correctly naming the Conservative candidate would rise to 52 per cent. The equivalent probability of naming the Labour candidate correctly had Labour spent to its limit and had no other party spent on the local campaign is 79 per cent. And assuming the Liberal Democrats spent as much as possible while the other parties spent nothing, the equivalent chance of correctly naming the Liberal Democrat candidate would be 76 per cent.

But does this matter? Even though British elections are primarily party-centred events, and even though voters no longer need to know who their party's local candidate is in order to cast their vote successfully, voters who can name a party's local candidate are, in fact, more likely to vote for that party. Logistic regression models predicting whether or not individual BES respondents voted Conservative, Labour, or Liberal Democrat in 1997 show the size of the effect (Table 6.15). The models control for voters' prior party identification, which operates in exactly the way one might expect: Conservative partisans were most likely to vote Conservative, Labour partisans to vote Labour, and Liberal Democrat partisans to vote Liberal Democrat. However, controlling for party identification takes into account many of the underlying factors that influence vote decisions, and means that any effects of candidate knowledge on vote choice are unlikely to be the spurious outcome of the propensity, discussed above, for partisans to be most knowledgeable about their own party's candidates.

Having taken partisanship into account, it is clear that knowledge about candidates does influence vote choice. Other things being equal, individuals who could correctly name the Conservative candidate in 1997 were more likely to vote Conservative and less likely to vote Labour than were individuals who could not name the candidate. Compared to those who could not name the Labour candidate, meanwhile, those who could were more likely to vote Labour and less likely to vote Conservative or Liberal Democrat. And those who knew the name of their Liberal Democrat candidate were more likely to actually vote Liberal Democrat and less likely to vote either Labour

Table 6.15. Constituency campaigning, candidate knowledge, and vote choice, 1997: logistic regressions

	Vote 1997		
Independent variables	Conservative	Labour	Liberal Democrat
Party identification (comparison = other/none)			
Conservative	44.26	0.11	0.16
Labour	0.06	26.58	0.24
Liberal Democrat	0.32	0.43	11.13
Candidate correctly named? (comparison = no)			
Conservative candidate	1.92	0.53	—
Labour candidate	—	3.06	0.36
Liberal Democrat candidate	0.41	0.33	3.90
Constituency campaign spending 1997 (%)			
Conservative spend	—	—	—
Labour spend	—	1.01	0.99
Liberal Democrat spend	—	0.99	1.01
R^2	0.80	0.76	0.54
% correctly classified	93.6	90.3	90.0
N	1903	1902	1902

Note: Only significant exponents are shown.
Source: BES cross-section survey (1997).

or Conservative than were those who could not name the candidate. The implication seems clear: other things being equal, the local campaign helps inform voters of who, personally, their candidates are. And, other things being equal, voters are more likely to support candidates they know than candidates they do not. Constituency campaigning helps foster a personal connection between voters and candidates which, if successfully established, helps the latter win support.

But the constituency campaign also influences the vote decision in other ways (almost certainly related to the mobilization of party support). The equations reported in Table 6.15 also contain measures for the amount of campaign spending in 1997 by each party in each respondent's constituency. Even when we control for individual partisanship, and for knowledge of who the candidates were, the intensity of the constituency campaign still influenced individuals' chances of voting Labour or Liberal Democrat in 1997. The more each of these parties spent in a seat, the greater the chance that an individual living there would vote for the party, and the smaller the chance that he or she would vote for the other party.

Conclusions

Campaigning in UK elections has been revolutionized by technology and by the increasing professionalization of the campaign process. Little is left to chance in the modern campaign, and central control of the process has become the sought-after holy grail of campaigning. From the organization of carefully choreographed campaign events, through ever-more sophisticated attempts to communicate with voters, to the relentless drive to ensure that all party activists and spokespeople stay 'on message', modern electoral campaigning resembles a high-tech war, directed by the generals in their national bunker/party headquarters. And, as demonstrated in the case of party election broadcasts, there can be dividends. For large parties, the national campaign provides an opportunity not to slip up (as Labour did spectacularly in its 1983 campaign). For small parties, it can influence voters (as with Liberal Democrat PEBs).

While these trends in electioneering have accelerated noticeably in recent elections, they can be traced back to early television campaigns in the 1950s, and to radio electioneering in the 1930s, both of which allowed party leaders to speak directly to most voters. Early assessments of the impact of the electronic media on campaigning argued that the new media had effectively killed off the local campaign, leaving it as a ritual with little real effect. As we have seen in this chapter, however, that settled post-war orthodoxy no longer holds. A substantial accumulation of evidence has shown that the constituency campaign remains a vital and effective part of the UK electoral process. Parties take trouble to focus their efforts in key marginal seats. And voters respond. Where parties, especially challengers, campaign hard in a seat, they improve their vote; where they put little effort into the local battle, they do not. Of course, the local campaign is not sufficiently powerful to change the overall result of a landslide election. But when the national battle is close, attention to local campaigning may make the difference between forming a government and sitting on the opposition benches. Far from being an anachronism, the constituency campaign is an integral part of the modern election process.

7

To Vote or Not to Vote: The Problem of Turnout

Essentially, voters are faced with two basic decisions. One is obvious, and has been the focus for much of this book: who should I vote for? The second, however, is rather more fundamental: should I vote at all? Deciding whether or not to participate in the ballot is perhaps the most basic political statement of all at election time. In this chapter, therefore, we consider trends over time in electoral participation in the UK, and ask what factors influence the decision whether or not to vote. As in previous chapters, we are interested in the role of contextual effects: is the decision whether to vote influenced by political, social, and economic factors in the individual voter's local environment? To understand this fully, we also need to know something about the personal factors that influence participation. To appreciate contextual effects fully, we have to take into account compositional influences too.

Accounting for change in turnout is not simply an exercise in understanding the factors underlying political participation, however; it is also a pressing issue of practical political concern. In many established democracies (including the UK, the USA, and Canada) turnout has been falling in recent elections, in some cases precipitately (Gray and Caul, 2000: Norris, 2002). In the 2001 British general election, for instance, only 59 per cent of the electorate voted, the lowest turnout since 1918: more electors abstained than voted for the election winners. Turnout increased slightly at the 2005 election, but with only 61 per cent of the electorate voting in that contest, it was still one of the lowest on record, hardly demonstrating a strong recovery in public participation. Under such circumstances, concerns can be raised regarding the ability of an election to represent public opinion accurately, particularly if those who abstain are not a random cross-section of the electorate.

Nor is the problem restricted to elections for national governments. Turnout is routinely even lower at so-called 'second-order' elections, where the contest is for a body subordinate to and less powerful than national government, and where voters feel there is little at stake (Heath et al., 1999; Reif, 1984, 1997; Reif and Schmitt, 1980; Schmitt, 2005). Turnout at UK local elections averaged just 40 per cent in the 1990s (Rallings and Thrasher, 1997, 47), dropping to between 30 and 35 per cent in English local elections after

2000. (Local election turnout was higher in the 2005 county council elections, but as they took place on the same day as the general election, the 'improvement' is more apparent than real.) British voters' participation in voting for the European Parliament is often even more dismal: in 1999, for instance, only 24 per cent voted (Butler and Westlake, 2000, 212). This improved somewhat in 2004, probably thanks in part to the introduction of widespread postal voting (including all-postal ballots in four of the UK's 12 regions) and to that year's co-incidence of local and European elections in many parts of the country. But even so turnout was a dismal 38 per cent, below the overall turnout of 45 per cent across all EU member states. Turnout in elections for the devolved governments of Scotland and Wales was also below general election levels, though participation was higher in the former than in the latter country (for instance, 49 per cent of the Scottish electorate voted in the 2003 Scottish Parliament election, compared to just 38 per cent of voters in the same year's Welsh Assembly contest). The difference between the two devolved bodies reflects differences in their powers (the Scottish Parliament having substantial legislative powers, while the Welsh Assembly does not) and in underlying national support for devolution (still higher north of the border than in the Principality). Even so, turnout seems to be declining in these new bodies too: at the first devolved elections in 1999, turnout was a respectable 59 per cent in Scotland and 46 per cent in Wales.

One can recast the question somewhat, however, and ask not 'Why do so many now abstain?' but rather 'Why do so many vote at all?' Beginning with Downs's (1957) seminal study, rational choice models of political participation have repeatedly identified a 'voting paradox': if all voters are totally rational in their behaviour, none should vote! The theoretical logic depends on an assumption of voter rationality. The rational choice model assumes voters are rational actors who wish to maximize their personal benefits and minimize their personal costs. They will tend to support parties that offer policy packages closest to their own preferences. However, they will also consider the costs of voting. These are numerous, ranging from the costs of gathering information on party platforms (not inconsiderable) to the costs of walking to the polling station. Furthermore, when comparing the costs and benefits of voting, a truly rational voter will discount expected benefits according to the likelihood that his or her personal vote will prove crucial in determining the election result. However, in modern elections thousands vote in individual constituencies and millions vote across the entire country. The chances of any one individual's participation determining the overall result are, therefore, very small indeed. Being intelligent observers of the political scene, our rational voters know this, and therefore calculate that the election result will almost certainly be the same whether or not they personally take part. They will therefore receive any benefits that might accrue from the election irrespective of their own involvement. When the benefits accruing to an individual from voting are discounted by the probability that the individual's participation will be crucial, therefore, the costs of voting, however small, will virtually always outweigh the benefits. Under such circumstances, no rational person should vote at all. Let others carry the costs! But, of course, if everyone is rational, everyone will assume that everyone else will vote, and so will abstain. Everyone depends on the election taking place in order to receive their benefits, but no one wants to bear the costs of participation. No one will vote and the election will fail. And if the election fails, all suffer: by following individually rational courses of action, the theory suggests, voters will damage their collective interests. It is an example of Olson's (1965) celebrated logic of collective action.

There are ways out of the voting paradox. For instance, rational voters know that elections recur regularly. As a result, even if their vote will not make a difference to the result in the current election, it can provide a signal for the next by showing how substantial support for a particular party is (Dunleavy, 1991). Under such circumstances, it can still be rational to vote. And, of course, we know that in practice turnout is not negligible. Most voters do participate in elections. However, the rational choice argument does alert us to the importance of costs and benefits in the voting calculus. Citizens are more likely to participate if their involvement is likely to make a difference than if it is not. Extending this insight, we might expect that (for instance) knife-edge elections (whether nationally or in individual constituencies), which might go either way, should produce higher turnouts than elections where the result is obvious. The closer the competition (and hence the more marginal the constituency), the more likely it is that voters will expend effort in voting and parties will expend effort in encouraging them to do so. Similarly, we might also expect that the more frequently voters are consulted, the lower turnout should be (as more frequent elections, maybe for a variety of different posts, raise the costs of participation substantially). Ironically, too many elections may be bad for democracy!

Trends in Turnout over Time: the Growing Problem of Falling Turnout?

There is evidence to suggest that this is in fact the case. Low turnout is very much a feature of elections in the USA. Even in presidential elections, only around 50 per cent of eligible electors actually vote—and they are dispro-portionately affluent. And in many other US elections, turnout levels are much lower. In part, the problem in America is one of electoral fatigue: elections are frequent and ubiquitous. In addition to the four-yearly ritual of presidential elections, there are also presidential primaries, biennial elections for the Senate and House of Representatives, state-level gubernatorial and legislature elections, elections for county and city governments and mayors, elections for local officials, and, in some states, referendums and voter initiatives. American voters might be forgiven for finding it hard to summon enthusiasm for yet another ballot. And, not surprisingly, the other western country with particularly low electoral turnout is Switzerland, another society where ballots are commonplace and electoral fatigue a factor.

Switzerland and the USA have long been considered exceptional in terms of their low electoral participation rates. Traditionally, election turnout has been relatively higher in most other western countries. In Britain, for instance, between 75 and 80 per cent of all electors turned out for much of the post-war period. However, in British elections from 1997 on, turnout has declined rapidly, approaching North American levels of voter apathy (Figure 7.1). Similar patterns have been reported in a number of other western democracies, though turnout decline is not universal. For Gray and Caul (2000), the decline is both real and caused by the decline of working-class political mobilization via bodies such as trades unions in the face of neo-liberal economic reforms to national economies in the latter part of the twentieth century. For Franklin (2002, 2004), meanwhile, turnout decline in recent years is real and widespread across different countries, but not as dramatic as some critics suggest. For him, the causes of this international decline in electoral participation are to be found mainly in 'the character of elections, not the character of society' (2004, 171). Voters are, he argues, no less civically minded or committed to democracy now than they were in the past.[1] But some elections (and some electoral systems) offer greater incentives for participation than others. In some systems, voting is compulsory; in many it is voluntary. The less competitive an election is, the lower the turnout.

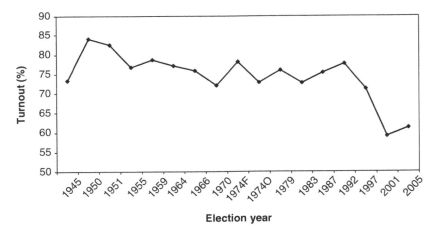

Fig. 7.1. Turnout in British general elections, 1945–2005

[1] To take a recent example from UK elections, Curtice (2005) notes that the percentage of British voters saying they were fairly or very interested in politics in 2005 (61 per cent) was scarcely different from the equivalent percentage in 1973 (60 per cent).

Well-established and cohesive party systems produce higher turnout at elections than weak and fragmented systems.

But Franklin's most striking finding is that the widespread practice of lowering the voting age—commonly from 21 to 18—has a permanent depressing effect on electoral participation. The basic problem is that younger voters, especially those in their teens, are noticeably less likely to vote than older voters. And, since voting is in part an habitual activity—the more one does it, the more one continues to do it—the entry of non-voting 18-year-olds into the electorate is likely to have a long-term as well as a short-term effect. Young electors who do not vote in their first election are less likely to vote in their second, and even less likely to vote in their third, than are their peers who do vote. And having abstained in three elections, they are unlikely ever to gain the voting habit. As older voters die and are replaced by these younger, less-voting-minded electors, so turnout declines—and the process continues for many years after the introduction of the franchise for younger voters, until no electors are left who entered the electorate before the extension of the franchise.

Whatever the reasons adduced, there is a high level of agreement that declining electoral participation is a widespread phenomenon. Norris (2002) is sceptical, however. Based on the analysis of an exceptionally large and wide-ranging elections dataset, drawn from all continents and embracing long-established and new democracies, and rich and poor countries, she demonstrates that turnout is strongly related to socio-economic development. Nor is the relationship a linear one; rather it is curvilinear. From the onset of modernization to the establishment of a fully fledged modern economy, turnout grows. But as national economies develop further, becoming post-industrial, turnout seems to fall somewhat again. In this perspective, whether turnout is declining or not depends on wider social and economic forces. At the same time as it is falling in some—generally older and wealthier—societies, turnout can be rising in others—often those experiencing rapid economic development or where democratic elections have recently taken hold.

Most international studies imply that turnout change is gradual. But while that may be true for overall trends, it can look very different from the perspective of individual countries. In fact, as Figure 7.1 confirms, the decline in turnout has been remarkably recent in Britain. At 77 per cent, turnout was relatively high at the 1992 election. And while it fell to its (then) lowest level since the war in 1997 (71 per cent), that was not much lower than the two previous post-war lows of 1945 and 1987 (both 73 per cent). Not until 2001 did turnout fall well outside the normal range of post-war elections, dropping to 59 per cent, the lowest level of electoral participation since 1918. The recovery to 62 per cent in 2005 was still well below the general post-war range.

A recurrent claim, especially from politicians and journalists, has been that the decline in turnout after 1992 is indicative of a more general political malaise. According to this view, there is a growing gulf between ordinary citizens and politicians, and trust in politicians has declined (Pattie and Johnston, 2001b). Declining turnout, goes the argument, is therefore a symptom of the growing failure of western democracies like Britain's to engage and motivate support. The crisis in turnout is taken to reflect a crisis in democracy itself. But things are not necessarily quite so simple. First, there is little evidence of long-term decline in voters' attitudes towards the political system as a whole (Clarke et al., 2004, ch. 9; Electoral Commission, 2005). For instance, Clarke et al. (2004) show that there was no overall trend, either up or down, in the proportion of the UK electorate declaring at least some interest in politics between 1974 and 2001: on average, 64 per cent of voters report at least some interest. More recent data from the 2005 BES confirms the overall pattern: at that election, 70 per cent of BES respondents claimed some interest in politics. And in some respects, people are actually happier with the political system now than in the past. The Eurobarometer survey has asked about satisfaction with democracy since the mid-1970s, and the question has also been taken up in recent BES surveys (the results for 1974 to 2001 inclusive are reported by Clarke et al., 2004, 293). On a four-point scale (with 4 indicating a great deal of satisfaction with democracy, and 1 indicating very little), average levels of satisfaction in the UK have risen from about 2.3 in 1975 to 2.6 in 2005.

That said, continued support for the political system as a whole does not of itself mean falling turnout is unproblematic. The turnout decline may represent a crisis for electoral participation as a particular mode of political engagement without necessarily implying a more systemic problem. There is ample evidence that voting is only one of many different ways in which citizens can act politically: alternative strategies include such diverse activities as engaging in ethical consumption, contacting politicians and officials, engaging in direct action, and taking part in protest activities (Parry, Moyser and Day, 1992; Pattie, Seyd and Whiteley, 2003, 2004). Many of these other forms of political activism are widespread, especially among younger people. However, if, as Franklin (2004) has argued, there is a particular 'electoral deficit' among younger voters, with fewer gaining the voting habit now than was the case in the past, then a decline in turnout could still be a source for concern, continued high levels of support for the overall political system notwithstanding.

A second strand to the discussion therefore requires a closer inspection of falling turnout in recent elections, therefore (Pattie and Johnston, 2001b). Analysis of trends in turnout between 1950 and 2005 shows a secular decline during that period.[2] A simple bivariate model of turnout regressed on

---

[2] The 1945 election is excluded from the following analyses for two reasons. First, the election was fought before the end of the Second World War. As a result of population displacement (not least because a substantial number of voters who were still serving overseas in the armed forces),

months elapsed since the 1950 election suggests that turnout fell by 0.025 percentage points every month over the period (Table 7.1). Although this sounds small, remember this is a period of 55 years—or 660 months. Over such a period, the model predicts a substantial 16.5-percentage point fall in election turnout (or 0.025 × 660).

Accounting for Trends in Turnout

That said, turnout decline was not constant over time. As Figure 7.1 shows, there are potential start- and end-point effects. At over 80 per cent, turnout was unusually high in the first two truly post-war elections of 1950 and 1951. And, at around 60 per cent, it was unusually low in the 2001 and 2005 contests at the end of the period. The main declines in turnout occurred in the 1950s and in the 2000s, not between the 1960s and 1990s. We can demonstrate this empirically by repeating the regression model for election turnout, and either including dummy variables for particular periods or restricting analysis to subsets of years. For instance, repeating the 1950–2005 model while including a dummy variable for the early 1950s (coded 1 for the 1950 and 1951 elections, and 0 for all subsequent contests) and another for the twenty-first-century elections (coded 1 in 2001 and 2005, 0 otherwise) produces a very strong fit to the data: the model accounts for 95 per cent of the variation in turnout (the equation is reported in the second line of Table 7.1). The dummy variables are significant. Turnout in 1950 and 1951 was around 5.8 percentage points above the post-war average, while in 2001 and 2005 it was around 12.8 percentage points below the average. But the time trend variable, measuring months since the 1950 election, was insignificant. The post-war downward trend in turnout was entirely a product of relatively

Table 7.1. Accounting for trends in turnout at British general elections, 1950–2005: OLS regression models

Period	Constant	Months since 1950 election	Early 1950s	Post-2000	R^2
1950–2005	83.557	−0.025			0.64
1950–2005	77.874	—	5.839	−12.848	0.95
1950–1970	85.009	−0.040			0.83
1950–1970	81.843	—	—		0.88
1974–2005	91.093	−0.038			0.57
1974–2005	77.854	—		−13.169	0.89
1955–1997	77.932	—			0.19

Note: Only significant coefficients are shown.

there is likely to have been more disruption for voters than usual. In addition, again as a result of the war, the electoral register was more out of date than usual, making the calculation of turnout relatively unreliable (McCallum and Readman, 1947, 31).

high turnout right at the start of the period and low turnouts right at the end. In between, turnout fluctuated up and down, but there was no underlying trend whatsoever.

Further analyses confirm this interpretation. If we concentrate solely on the period between 1950 and 1970 (in the third line of Table 7.1), we find, once again, a significant, negative, and strong relationship between the passage of time and turnout (accounting for over 80 per cent of the variation in turnout). But when we include (in the next line) the dummy variable for the first two elections of the 1950s, the coefficient for months elapsed is no longer statistically significant. Similarly, concentrating on the period between 1974 and 2005, there is once again a significant and negative bivariate relationship between time elapsed and turnout (the fifth line of Table 7.1). But adding the dummy variable for the 2001 and 2005 elections makes this time trend insignificant. Finally, the last model in Table 7.1 concentrates only on elections from 1955 to 1997 inclusive: over this period, there was no significant relationship between time elapsed and electoral turnout, and the former accounted for just 19 per cent of the variance in the latter.

These analyses point to two conclusions, therefore. First, commentators who, in 1997, claimed that the 71 per cent turnout represented a crisis were mistaken: it was entirely within (albeit at the lower end of) the normal range of turnout at post-war British elections. General election turnout in the UK displayed trendless fluctuation for much of the post-war period. But, secondly, something more striking has occurred since 1997: turnout in both 2001 and 2005 was significantly lower than in other post-war general elections. Declining turnout in the UK has not been steady, therefore: it has been a rapid and recent fall from generally stable levels of electoral participation in the post-war period. Something has happened to turnout.

But that is not to say that electoral participation rates were totally random between 1955 and 1997. In fact, turnout was relatively predictable over the period. As we might expect from the rational choice model discussed above, the key factor underlying whether participation was high or low at a particular contest was how competitive the election was. Where an election was likely to be a close-run contest (as indicated by the standing of the two major parties in pre-election opinion polls), turnout was high. Where it seemed clear that one party was heading towards an easy victory over the other, turnout was low (Heath and Taylor, 1999; Pattie and Johnston, 2001b; Whiteley et al., 2001). This can be illustrated using opinion poll data on the relative closeness of the Conservatives and Labour. For each election between 1955 and 1997, we have calculated the absolute difference (ignoring minus signs) between percentage support for Labour and the Conservatives in polls. We can then regress turnout at each election on this measure of the gap between the major parties in the run-up to the election (excluding the October 1974 election from our analysis since it was a very unusual one, following hard on the heels of the February 1974 contest. The resulting equation is:

$$\% \ turnout = 78.22 - 0.32 \times polldiff$$

where *polldiff* is the absolute difference between the Conservative and Labour shares of the polls a month before the election. This relationship between turnout and closeness in the polls is highly significant ($R^2 = 0.60$). Furthermore, although turnout in 1997 was low, it was actually quite similar to what might have been expected from the above relationship (Figure 7.2). Only two elections over the period (1959 and 1970) had turnouts that differed markedly from the overall trend, and only one of these, the 1970 election, was significantly different (with a standardized residual of -2.32). The 1970 general election was notable in that most commentators and polls prior to the election predicted the comfortable re-election of the Labour government, but the actual result was a narrow win for the Conservatives. The election was widely seen in retrospect as a very poor one for the polling companies (Butler and Pinto-Duschinsky, 1971, 171ff.). From this perspective, turnout in 1997 was not unusually low.

The reason for the steep decline in turnout between 1992 and 1997, therefore, mainly reflects the very different circumstances of the two elections rather than some deep-seated malaise in democracy (Heath and Taylor, 1999;

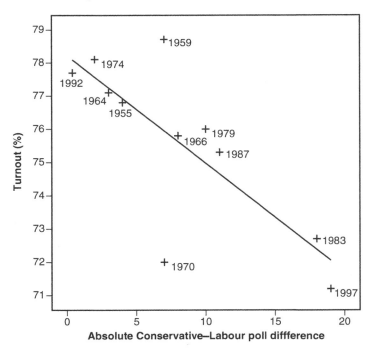

Fig. 7.2. Election turnout and the closeness of the national competition, 1955–97

Pattie and Johnston, 2001b). Most voters and commentators anticipated that the 1992 election would be a very close-run thing, with either Labour or Conservatives possible winners, and a hung parliament widely expected to be a likely outcome. In the run-up to polling day in 1992, therefore, it seemed as though every vote would count: before the event, the election seemed to hang by a thread. Contrast that with the very different context of the 1997 election, when the Conservative party had trailed far behind Labour in the polls for almost five years. Hardly anyone in 1997 expected anything other than a landslide Labour win—and that is exactly what happened. Even the most die-hard political aficionado would have been forgiven for thinking the election was a foregone conclusion: it was! Under such circumstances, a low turnout was hardly surprising.

Following this logic, another low turnout was to be anticipated in 2001. The Conservatives continued to languish in the polls throughout the 1997–2001 parliament, with virtually no signs of any recovery in their support. Labour's poll ratings, meanwhile, remained buoyant. All the evidence, throughout the parliament, was that Labour would maintain not only its grip on government but also much, if not all, of its majority. Another Labour landslide seemed inevitable (and that, of course, is how the election turned out). So the fact that turnout did not recover in 2001 was not surprising. What was striking, however, was the extent to which it fell. The models that had successfully accounted for turnout trends over the 1950–97 period failed in 2001 (Johnston and Pattie, 2003b). The model sketched out above for the 1955–97 period predicted a turnout of 73.7 per cent; in fact, it fell to 59 per cent. While the fall in participation between 1992 and 1997 can be explained away as mainly the result of the shift from a close to a clear-cut election, the even steeper decline between 1997 and 2001 cannot. That does begin to raise concerns over the long-term future of electoral participation in the UK.

Those concerns about long-term trends were reinforced by the 2005 general election. Between 2001 and 2005, New Labour's previously unassailable poll lead was severely diminished, especially in the aftermath of the Iraq invasion. For virtually the first time since 1992, the party looked vulnerable, and the election was certainly rather less predictable than either the 1997 or the 2001 contests. Expectations based on the perceived closeness of the competition would point to an increase in turnout. Had voter participation in 2005 followed the trend for the 1955–97 period, the pre-election poll positions of Labour and the Conservatives would have implied a turnout of 76.5 per cent. Turnout did increase—but only by around 2 percentage points, up to 61 per cent, and well short of what we would expect from the 'normal' post-war trend.

That said, while Labour no longer looked dominant in 2005, its rivals hardly seemed poised to win power. The Conservatives' poll ratings had almost flat-lined since 1992, showing little sign of recovery; and the Liberal Democrats, while doing well, were still clearly in third place. Not only that, but (as we show in the next chapter) the operation of the electoral system gave Labour a very substantial advantage over its rivals after 1992. Although the polls indicated a close contest, therefore, a third successive Labour victory (albeit with a substantially reduced majority) was widely seen as by far the most likely outcome of the competition. And it is also worth reflecting on how unusual the New Labour years after 1997 were in British politics. Normally, even during prolonged periods of one-party dominance (for instance, during the three-term Conservative government of 1951–64, and the four-term Conservative administration of 1979–97), the government has experienced often prolonged periods during which it was behind its main rival in the opinion polls. For post-1992 Labour, this was not the case. By the 2005 election, and apart from a very short-lived 'blip' during the September 2000 fuel crisis, Labour had been consistently ahead of the Conservatives and the Liberal Democrats in the polls for 13 years (albeit only narrowly at times after the onset of the Iraq War). It is hard to overemphasize just what an extraordinary achievement this was in British politics. Labour's 2001 and 2005 re-elections were therefore under rather different circumstances to the Conservatives' re-elections in 1983, 1987, and 1992. Given Labour's long dominance in the polls, the unusually low turnouts of 2001 and 2005 seem rather more in keeping with an 'expected-outcomes' interpretation than the poll gap between Labour and Conservatives immediately before each election would lead us to expect. As Curtice (2005, 781) commented:

The 2005 election appears...to have been similar to 2001 in its failure to provide voters with a stimulus to vote. As in 2001, few saw much difference between the parties, while in practice the message of the opinion polls was still that only one party appeared to have a chance of wining...Certainly, as in 2001, there is little evidence that the low turnout is simply or even primarily an indication of a new disinclination on the part of voters to vote.

Turnout in 2001 and 2005 may have been lower than post-war trends would lead us to expect, therefore. But the jury is still out on whether this represents a long-term crisis of participation. However, as Franklin (2004) reminds us, the more often individuals abstain, the less likely they are to vote again in the future. Furthermore, while turnout rose slightly in most groups of the population between 2001 and 2005, it actually fell further among the youngest voters, those aged between 18 and 24. As we have noted above, lower than average turnout among younger, first-time voters is a long-established feature of electoral participation. But there are signs that the situation is worsening. And, *pace* our comments above about continued high levels of interest in politics, long-term evidence from the British Social Attitudes surveys suggests that, since 1994, young voters' interest in British politics has fallen and they have become less supportive of existing political parties (Park, 2004). This is a source for longer-term concern. Continued low turnouts (especially among first-time voters) may be building a group of individuals who have never voted and may never do so—and that would represent a long-term challenge.

Turnout varies geographically as well as temporally. In 1997, for instance, 71.5 per cent of electors in the average constituency turned out to vote, but the standard deviation around this average was 5.6. The total range in turnout varied from a low of 51.9 per cent in Liverpool Riverside to a maximum of 82.2 per cent in Brecon and Radnorshire. And while overall turnout fell between 1997 and 2001, the range of constituency turnouts actually increased. The standard deviation for constituency turnout in both 2001 and 2005 was 6.4 per cent. With turnouts of just 34.1 per cent in 2001 and 41.4 per cent in 2005, Liverpool Riverside gained the dubious distinction of a hat-trick for the lowest turnout of any British constituency at three successive elections.[3] At the other end of the range, the highest turnout in 2001 outside of Northern Ireland was 72.3 per cent, recorded in Winchester (though note that this was barely higher than the *average* turnout just four years previously), while the highest turnout in 2005, 76.3 per cent, was recorded in Dorset West.

In general, turnout is lower in seats defended by the Labour party than elsewhere. The 2005 election was fairly typical in this regard. At that contest, the average turnout in seats defended by the Conservatives was 65.3 per cent, and in Liberal-Democrat-defended seats it was 65.6 per cent. But in seats Labour was defending, only 58.5 per cent of the electorate voted.[4] Similar relative variations could be reported for most post-war elections. Some of the reasons for lower turnout in Labour than in other seats are explored below.

Who Votes?

So who does vote? At the start of the chapter, we outlined one theoretical approach to this question, the rational choice model, which posits that participation is linked to a calculus of costs and benefits. However, as we saw, rational choice, strictly applied, leads to a paradox of participation: the costs of individual participation so far outweigh the marginal benefits that a rational elector will always abstain. Not surprisingly, then, the rational choice model is not the only account of political participation on offer, even though, as we have seen, it provides insights into why turnout should

---

[3] In fact, Staffordshire South recorded the lowest turnout of any constituency at the 2005 election, at just 37.3 per cent. However, due to the death of a candidate before polling day, this contest was postponed, occurring some weeks after the main general election. Other factors, not least the fact that the national election outcome was no longer in question, therefore account for this low turnout, and it cannot really compare with Liverpool Riverside's performance.

[4] These differences were statistically significant: an analysis-of-variance test produced an *F*-value of 50.88 and a *p*-value of 0.000.

be higher in close contests than in elections where the outcome is in little doubt.

An alternative and widely supported account of participation is provided by the civic voluntarism approach (Brady, Verba, and Schlozman, 1995; Clarke et al., 2004; Parry, Moyser, and Day, 1992; Pattie, Seyd, and Whiteley, 2003; Verba, Schlozman, and Brady, 1995; Whiteley et al., 2001). At the core of this approach sits a socio-economic understanding of participation. The likelihood of involvement in politics is enhanced by the presence of a range of resources and retarded by their absence. Study after study shows that voters tend to be more affluent, better educated, and older than abstainers (Clarke et al., 2004; Crewe, 1981; Crewe, Fox, and Alt, 1977; Leighley and Nagler, 1992; Pattie and Johnston, 1998b; Wolfinger and Rosenstone, 1980).

To some extent, then, turnout is a function of resources, both economic and intellectual. The resource-rich are more likely to participate in elections than the resource-poor. In 2005, for instance, turnout was substantially higher among those with a degree than among those with no educational qualifications (Table 7.2). The table uses self-reported data on turnout in 2005, and hence overstates political participation at that election. The discrepancy between the actual turnout and that suggested by the survey is a consequence of two factors. First, a few non-voters report taking part in the election, presumably to give what they perceive to be a socially normative answer. Secondly, and apparently more common in the BES data used here, there is a differential response effect: people who take part in surveys tend to be those who also vote. Abstainers at election time also tend to avoid

Table 7.2. The demographic correlates of individual turnout, 2005

Socio-economic characteristics	Turnout (%)
Education	
No qualifications	69.0
School qualifications	67.1
Post-school qualifications (sub-degree)	72.1
University degree	84.5
Social class	
Professionals	83.8
Skilled non-manual	71.0
Petty bourgeois	69.8
Foremen and supervisors	73.3
Working class	61.9
Age	
18–25	44.1
26–35	58.6
36–45	76.3
46–55	76.0
56–65	84.9
65 and over	87.2

Source: BES data files (2005).

responding to surveys, and so are under-sampled (Swaddle and Heath, 1989). Even so, there is a significant 16-percentage-point difference between turnout among those with no qualifications and turnout among those with degrees. While around 69 per cent of the former group reported voting in 2005, around 85 per cent of the latter group also did so. There is a similar significant class effect: while 84 per cent of professional workers claimed to have voted, this dropped to just 62 per cent of those in manual jobs. But the largest differential pattern for turnout was age-related: the propensity to vote was considerably higher among older voters, and particularly low among the youngest voters. Among 18–25-year-olds in 2005 (many of whom were first-time voters), only 44 per cent of BES respondents turned out. Among those aged 66 and over (the retired), in contrast, 87 per cent voted. Although the exact figures are specific to the 2005 contest, similar patterns could be reported for most post-war UK elections: the main variation has been in the average levels of turnout, not in which groups tend to vote most and which least.

There is a paradox here, however. In most western democracies (and the UK and USA are no exception) social change means that increasing proportions of people are in middle-class jobs and have university degrees. And demographic change in the west means most states there have ageing populations. Given the individual-level socio-demographic factors underlying turnout discussed in Table 7.2, we might expect turnout to be increasing over time. Yet, even as the socio-demographic picture is apparently increasingly likely to encourage participation, election turnout is, as we have seen, falling (Franklin, 1999, 2004; Norris, 2002; Putnam, 2000). Something else must be involved.

The most plausible explanation for the decline in turnout (other than contextual factors related to the closeness of the competition) involves a general sense of disillusion with the political system. During the 1990s, British politics (like politics elsewhere) had been shaken by a series of recurrent scandals (Ridley and Doig, 1995). At first, these mainly seemed to involve the Conservative party (unsurprising, as it was in government until 1997, and hence in the full glare of media attention). However, after 1997, New Labour too found itself caught up in a series of unsavoury revelations, including apparently delaying a ban on tobacco advertising in Formula-one racing at a time when one of the largest personal donors to the party was Bernie Ecclestone, a major player in the car-racing world. With trust in politicians falling to very low levels (Pattie and Johnston, 2001a), it would hardly be surprising if that were to translate into low turnout. If we look, for instance, at voters' opinions on how fairly they are treated by government, it is clear that in 2005 (as in previous contests) the less fairly they thought they were treated, the less likely they were to vote (Table 7.3). (We must remember that questions about vote turnout were asked after the election, while questions about attitudes towards the political system were asked before.) Not surprisingly, there was a strong correlation in 2005 between voters' normative attitudes to voting and their propensity to turn out. Among those who agreed with the proposition that 'it is every citizen's duty to vote', 81 per cent turned out (Table 7.3), but participation in the election dropped to just 41 per cent of those who disagreed. Rather more striking, perhaps, is the observation that well under half the respondents (only 37 per cent) to the 2005 BES did actually strongly agree with the proposition.

A related factor is the extent to which, during the 1990s, the two major parties in UK politics converged onto much the same middle ground of politics. As the price of winning re-election, New Labour under Tony Blair ditched much of the party's remaining socialist baggage and moved to the right, embracing markets, distancing itself from the unions, and committing itself to tight fiscal policies. Increasingly, voters could see little difference between Labour and the Conservatives. And if there is little ideological distance between the main rivals, on what grounds can one choose? One might as well stay at home. Much of the decline in individual turnout between the 1992 and 1997 British general elections can be accounted for by an increase in the proportion of voters who felt there was no substantial difference between Labour and the Conservatives (Pattie and Johnston, 2001d). In fact, this measure can be related without too much difficulty to the rational choice account outlined above. Rather like the variable measuring the difference between Conservative and Labour opinion-poll positions in the analysis of time trends in election turnout reported above, this variable can be seen as measuring the marginal value of an individual voting. In that earlier analysis, the nearer two parties were to each other in the polls, and hence the closer the contest, the more one individual's vote might count in deciding the overall result. Here, the nearer Labour and Conservatives are perceived to be to each other in ideological space (that is, the more likely voters think it will be that the two parties will offer very similar policy packages to the electorate), the less likely a rational individual should be to

Table 7.3. Individual turnout and attitudes towards the political system, 2005

	Turnout (%)	
Attitude	Government generally treats people like me fairly	It is every citizen's duty to vote in an election
Agree	76.2	80.7
Neither	70.8	53.1
Disagree	69.3	40.6
N	2943	2957

Note: Questions about vote turnout were asked after the election, while questions about attitudes towards the political system were asked before.
Source: BES data files (2005).

vote, since the policy outcomes following the election will be expected to be much the same whichever major party wins.

And this expectation is supported by the evidence. For instance, the 1992–7 British Election Panel Study reveals that whereas in 1992 a majority (56 per cent) of voters felt there was a substantial difference between Labour and the Conservatives, this dropped to just under a third by 1997 (Table 7.4).[5] By contrast, the percentage seeing not much difference between the parties doubled, from just under 10 per cent in 1992 to almost 21 per cent in 1997. And this had consequences for abstention. Concentrating on those panel members who voted in 1992, it is clear that abstention in 1997 was higher among those who felt there was little difference between the two main parties in 1997 than among those who thought there was a considerable difference (Table 7.5). And it was almost twice as high among those who felt that Labour and the Conservatives had become less different from each other between 1992 and 1997 than among those who felt the parties had become more distinctive over time.

The 2005 BES does not contain comparable questions. However, we can use other variables to measure how far apart respondents felt Labour and the Conservatives were in that year. Respondents to the 2005 BES were asked where they would place each party on an 11-point left–right dimension (with 0 as the most left-wing position and 10 as the most right-wing). The measure of perceived distance between Labour and Conservative is obtained by calculating the absolute difference between respondents' perceptions of Labour and Conservative positions on the scale. The closer to 0 the measure is, the closer voters think the two parties are on the left–right dimension. And there is a significant difference between voters' and non-voters' perceptions.

Table 7.4. The effect of perceived differences between major parties on electoral turnout, 1992 and 1997

	Turnout (%)	
Do Conservatives and Labour differ?	1992	1997
Great difference	58.4	31.1
Some difference	32.0	48.1
No difference	9.6	20.7
N	1560	1375

Source: British Election Panel Study 1992–7.

[5] Since this is a panel survey, which interviewed the same individuals at both elections, we can be sure this is true change for those respondents. That said, we cannot be certain the panel data give us a fully representative picture of change in the UK electorate. The well-known consequences of panel attrition and conditioning mean that the panel is more likely to contain individuals who are knowledgeable about, interested in, and thoughtful regarding politics than would be true for the electorate at large.

Table 7.5. The effect of perceived differences between major parties on electoral turnout in 1997 among those who voted in 1992

Perceived differences	Voted 1997 (%)	Abstained 1997 (%)	*N*
Perceived difference between Conservative and Labour, 1997			
Great difference	96.4	3.6	357
Some difference	90.3	9.7	556
Not much difference	82.6	17.4	247
Change in perceived difference between Conservative and Labour, 1992–7			
Less difference	87.8	12.2	534
No change	92.8	7.2	503
More difference	93.2	6.8	133

Source: British Election Panel Study 1992–7.

On average, voters saw a greater difference between the two largest parties than did non-voters: the average difference for the former in 2005 was 3.1, whereas for the latter it was 2.7.[6]

We can obtain some idea of the relative importance of these various factors for an understanding of individual turnout by conducting a regression analysis (this is similar to the analysis reported in Table 1.21, but we are mainly interested here in the party difference measures, which were not part of the earlier analysis). The analysis reported here looks at turnout at the 2005 British general election and draws on data from that year's BES survey. The survey was based on a panel design, with a sample of respondents interviewed before the election took place and then re-interviewed after it. The advantage of this design is that we can use the concept of time's arrow to disentangle cause-and-effect relationships, since opinions held before the election are likely to influence behaviour in the election, but behaviour in the election is unlikely to affect opinions held beforehand.[7] The dependent variable in our model is whether or not each survey respondent voted in the 2005 election (coded 1 if the person voted, 0 if he or she abstained). As this is a binary variable, we employ logistic regression. Needless to say, individual turnout is measured after the election. Deploying the logic of time's arrow just discussed, our independent explanatory variables are all drawn from answers given by the same individuals in the pre-election wave of the survey. In the analysis, we look at two different types of explanatory variables: socio-demographic information (age, class, and education); and attitudes towards the political system (how close the Labour and Conservative parties

---

[6] The difference is statistically significant ($t = 3.5$; $p = 0.000$).

[7] Unlikely, but not impossible: anticipation of future events or behaviours may affect current behaviour. A classic example is the surge in Christmas card sales in the weeks before Christmas. But although they occur first in the temporal sequence, Christmas card sales do not cause Christmas: causality runs the other way round!

were perceived to be in 2005 on the 11-point left–right dimension, how fairly individuals felt government treated them, and whether individuals felt citizens had a duty to vote).

The first model looks just at the socio-demographic variables (Table 7.6, Model I). As the independent variables are categorical, we have compared turnout for each category of each variable to a reference category: voters aged 18–24 for age, middle-class salariat for class, and those with no educational qualifications for education. In each case, we report only the exponents of significant coefficients. An exponent less than 1 indicates that a group is less likely to turn out than its reference group, while an exponent greater than 1 indicates that members of the category are more likely to turn out than their reference group. Not surprisingly, most of the significant relationships work in the expected directions. The older voters are, the more likely they are to vote (with the odds of retired voters turning out being over 12 times greater than the equivalent odds for the youngest voters,

Table 7.6. Summarizing individual turnout: logistic regressions

Independent variables	Voted 2005		Voted 2001
	Model I	Model II	Model III
Age (comparison = 18–24)			
25–34	1.73	—	0.42
35–44	4.22	2.83	—
45–54	4.44	2.77	—
55–64	10.59	5.64	—
65 and over	12.55	6.11	—
Class (comparison = salariat)			
Routine non-manual	0.71	—	—
Petty bourgeoisie	0.53	—	—
Foremen	0.60	—	—
Manual	0.49	0.56	0.68
Education (comparison = no qualifications)			
School qualifications	1.73	1.99	—
Post-school qualifications	1.62	1.80	—
Degree	3.19	2.92	—
Government treats people like me fairly (comparison = agree)			
Neither		—	—
Disagree		—	—
Every citizen has a duty to vote (comparison = agree)			
Neither		0.34	0.54
Disagree		0.21	0.36
Conservative–Labour difference		—	1.14
R^2	0.21	0.24	0.13
% correctly classified	77.6	79.0	78.3
N	2668	2241	1570

Note: Only significant exponents are shown.
Source: BES data files (2001, 2005).

other things being equal). Compared to the core middle classes, all other social classes were less likely to vote in 2005, with manual workers the least likely to do so. And controlling for age and class, education played a significant role in accounting for individual turnout in 2005. Individuals with any formal qualifications were more likely to vote than were people with none, and graduates were the most likely to vote, compared to those with no qualifications.

As the second model indicates, attitudes towards the political system played a role in 2005 (Table 7.6: Model II). Even when socio-demographic factors were held constant, attitudinal factors proved significant. As expected, the less strongly individuals agreed with the normative statement that every citizen has a duty to vote, the less likely they themselves were to turn out. But, other things being equal, whether an individual felt fairly treated by the government made no significant difference; nor did the perceived difference between the Conservative and Labour parties in 2005, once other factors are taken into account. In this regard, turnout at the 2005 election was different from that in 2001. If we repeat the model for the earlier contest, we see that individuals' perceptions of the absolute ideological difference between Labour and the Conservatives were related to whether they voted in 2001, other things being equal: the greater the perceived difference between the parties, the greater the likelihood of voting (Table 7.6: Model III). In other respects, turnout in 2001 was influenced by similar forces to turnout in 2005, though social factors were less of an influence at the earlier contest than at the later (after attitudinal measures were taken into account).

The analyses thus far suggest that both rational choice and civic voluntarism have something to offer in helping us understand the motivations underlying the decision whether or not to vote. However, as discussed in Chapter 1, not all reasons for voting are quite so rationally based. Particularly in systems like that of the UK, where, in most circumstances, voters must present themselves in person at a polling station in order to vote, or must have applied for a postal or proxy vote in advance of the election, some potential voters at least will be prevented from attending their local polling station, and hence from voting, by factors beyond their control. Perhaps they were ill on polling day and so unable to vote. Perhaps their jobs called them away at short notice, making it impossible for them to vote in person. We can therefore, in principle at least, divide non-voters into two distinct groups. One group, involuntary abstainers, are those individuals who intend to vote but are prevented from doing so by circumstances beyond their control. In contrast, individuals in the other group, voluntary abstainers, abstain consciously, either because they are unable to make up their minds or because they object to either the choices on offer or to the concept of elections as a whole (Crewe, 2002; Johnston and Pattie, 1997c; Pattie and Johnston, 1998c).

The proportions of non-voters in each of these categories stayed broadly comparable throughout the late 1980s and 1990s, according to the reasons non-voters gave to the BES for their failure to participate in the election (see Table 1.18). Over that time period, a fairly consistent 60 per cent or so of non-voters gave reasons for abstention that fall into our 'involuntary abstainers' grouping, suggesting that they intended to vote but were prevented from doing so by circumstances beyond their control on polling day itself. And between 43 per cent (1992) and 33 per cent (1997) gave reasons that suggested abstention was thought through and deliberate, a comment on the political system rather than on the vagaries of everyday life: these are our voluntary abstainers.

The picture looks somewhat different in the exceptionally low-turnout elections of 2001 and 2005 (see Table 1.19). While the percentage of non-voters giving 'voluntary' reasons for not taking part in the 2001 election was (at 43 per cent of all non-voters) broadly comparable to the equivalent proportions at previous elections, many more (almost three-quarters) gave voluntary justifications for their abstention in 2005. And far lower proportions of respondents (42 per cent in 2001 and 33 per cent in 2005) gave 'involuntary' reasons at these two elections than had been the case before. In part, the position is muddied here, since the 2001 and 2005 BES used rather different conventions from the 1987, 1992, and 1997 studies for coding the open-survey questions that sought reasons for abstention. The results are not therefore directly comparable, but they do seem to indicate a broad trend. And the proportion giving some other reason for not voting grew from just 4 per cent of all non-voters in 1992 to 25 per cent in 2005. We suspect this growth is fuelled in large part by essentially voluntary abstainers who do not want to declare themselves as such to the BES interviewers. To the extent that this assumption is correct, it would seem that voluntary, deliberate abstention actually rose significantly after 1997, encompassing up to 62 per cent of all non-voters in 2001 and potentially all non-voters in 2005. To return for a moment to our earlier discussion of trends in electoral participation in the UK, this rise in the numbers abstaining on purpose does not bode well for the long-term health of British elections.

Turnout and Local Context

The socio-demographic correlates of individual turnout can, to some extent, help us account for the cross-constituency variations in participation discussed above. We know, for instance, that social class and affluence are not uniformly distributed across the country: some areas are more working class than others, for instance. As a result, we might expect that the correlation between individual class and turnout should translate into a constituency-level geography, with higher turnout in middle-class areas than in predominantly working-class areas. This expectation is amply borne out by the evidence. At the 2005 election, for instance (Figure 7.3), there was a generally positive (though not overwhelmingly strong) association between election turnout and the percentage of a constituency's population employed in professional and managerial jobs (as measured by the 2001 census). With a few exceptions, the more middle class the seat, the higher the turnout. A similar, though stronger, pattern holds when we examine the relationship between owner-occupation and turnout. The higher the proportion of homeowners in a constituency in 2001, the higher the turnout there in 2005 (Figure 7.4).

Deciding to vote is not simply a function of demography and affluence, however. Electors are also influenced by the electoral contexts within which they live. As we have already seen, the overall closeness of the national election is an important factor. However, geographical contexts matter too. In particular, they are influenced by how competitive the local electoral situation is. The logic of the rational choice argument outlined above would suggest that those who live in the most marginal constituencies will be the most likely to vote, while those in very safe constituencies will be the least likely to do so. The votes of individual electors in the former areas have a realistic chance of changing the constituency result; but in the latter seats, the

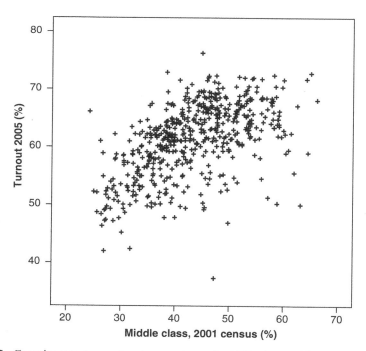

Fig. 7.3. Constituency turnout and percentage of middle-class residents, 2005

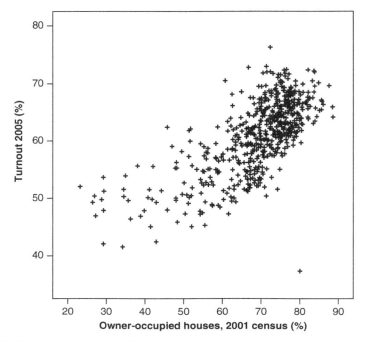

Fig. 7.4. Constituency marginality and owner-occupied housing, 2005

same party is liable to win no matter who votes. In such circumstances, abstention becomes rational—why waste effort on a certain outcome? And, of course, the marginality of constituencies varies substantially from place to place.

Marginality and Turnout

One way to see this is to look at the percentage-point majority obtained by the winner in a constituency over its nearest rival. If the winning party won 50 per cent of the constituency vote, and the second-placed party won 20 per cent, the winner's percentage point majority would be 30 per cent. At each election, the relevant majority in the constituency is that obtained at the preceding contest, since this represents the *status quo ante* of local party competition around which well-informed voters will make their decisions (including, in some cases, the decision whether or not to vote tactically) and parties will organize their campaigns. So for the 2005 general election, we need to look at constituency majorities in 2001. On that basis, the most marginal seat in Great Britain in the run-up to the 2005 election was Cheadle, with a Liberal Democrat majority of just 33 votes over the Conservatives in 2001. By contrast, the safest seat was Bootle, where Labour led the Liberal

Democrats by 69 percentage points in 2001 (Labour having secured 78 per cent of the constituency vote to the Liberal Democrats' 9 per cent).[8]

When we compare constituency marginality in 2001 with turnout in 2005, we find the expected relationship (Figure 7.5).[9] As the winning party's majority at the previous election increased, turnout fell, in a more or less linear fashion. The correlation between 2001 marginality and 2005 constituency turnout is −0.71, strong and statistically very significant. Voters living in seats where there was little doubt about the outcome were harder to persuade to vote than voters who lived in seats where the result was in the balance. It is therefore hardly surprising that Cheadle, as the most marginal seat in 2005, also had a high turnout (70 per cent). Similarly, the seat with the highest turnout of all in 2005 was very marginal: the Conservatives' 2001 lead over the second-placed Liberal Democrats in Dorset West was only 2.9 percentage points. Nor is it surprising that Liverpool Riverside managed to score the worst turnouts in 1997, 2001, and 2005. While not the safest seat in the country, it is an ultra-safe Labour stronghold. In 1997, Labour won the

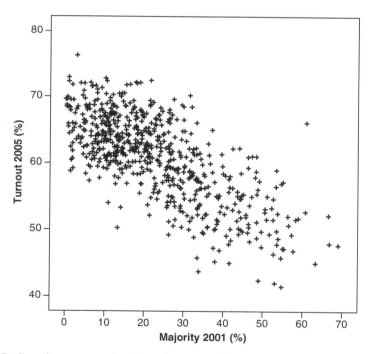

Fig. 7.5. Constituency marginality and turnout, 2005

[8] Bootle was also the least marginal seat in the run-up to the 2001 election. At the preceding 1997 election, Labour had an 83 percentage-point lead over the Conservatives there.
[9] As explained above, Staffordshire South is omitted from this figure.

seat easily with 70 per cent of the vote: its nearest local rival, the Liberal Democrats, won just 13 per cent of the vote, giving Labour a very large 57-percentage-point majority. The party's majority there was also high in 2001, at 55 percentage points.

The relationship between constituency marginality and turnout was not just a feature of the 2005 contest, however. It has been reported at most post-war British elections (Denver, 1995; Denver and Hands, 1974, 1985; Mughan, 1986). Throughout that period, there has been a negative correlation between the winning majority in a seat and the turnout there. As in 2005, the safer a seat in the run-up to an election, the lower the turnout. However, intriguingly, the relationship between constituency marginality and turnout has not been constant over time. Some appreciation of this can be gained by looking at the correlation between the two at each election since 1964 (Figure 7.6). The relationship, quite strong in the 1960s and 1970s, weakened in the 1987 and 1992 elections (Denver, 1995; Pattie and Johnston, 1998c). But it strengthened again after 1997, and continued to be particularly strong at the next two elections: a highly significant -0.69 in 2001 and, as already noted, -0.71 in 2005.

Patterns of turnout, therefore, do seem to be created by voters reacting rationally to their geographical contexts. But what is the mechanism connecting constituency marginality and turnout? Part of the answer can be found among voters themselves. The overall relationship between constituency marginality and turnout masks important variations, for

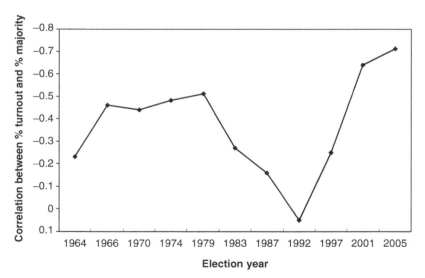

Fig. 7.6. Constituency marginality and turnout since 1964
Source: Data for 1964–92 from Denver (1995).

instance. It is particularly noteworthy that the strength of the relationship depends on which party is defending a seat (Curtice, 2005). Once again, the 2005 election is a convenient, but fairly typical, example. In seats defended by Labour at that election, the correlation between marginality and turnout is strong and statistically significant, at −0.75. In seats defended by the Liberal Democrats, the relationship is still significant, though not so strong, at just − 0.29. But in Conservative seats there was no correlation at all: the coefficient, at −0.06, was not only very weak but fell far short of statistical significance.[10] Similar patterns held at other elections too: in 2001, for instance, the correlation between marginality and turnout was significant in seats defended by Labour and the Liberal Democrats (with coefficients of −0.66 and −0.37, respectively) but insignificant in Conservative-held seats (where the correlation coefficient was −0.10).

Why should this be? In part, it is a function of the different social bases of each party's support. The Conservatives, in particular, are most successful among older, more middle-class groups, precisely those who are most likely to turn out. The corollary is also true: the Conservatives' vote tends to be highest in seats where these groups are locally dominant. Not only that, but Conservative supporters are committed voters. In the run-up to the 2005 election, for instance, the BES asked respondents to assess how likely they were to vote. Self-assessments were recorded on an 11-point scale: those who thought it very unlikely they would vote scored 0, while those who thought it very likely scored 10. These pre-election assessments of the likelihood of voting were related to party identification (Figure 7.7, which shows both the average score for each party identification and the 95 per cent confidence interval around that average, giving some idea of the spread of values around the mean). The averages were statistically different from each other, indicating that whether one identified with a party, and which party one identified with, affected one's probability of voting.[11] Not surprisingly, those who did not identify with a party in 2005 were much less likely to think they would vote in the upcoming election than were those who identified with any party. But Conservative identifiers were significantly more likely than any other group to think they would vote.[12] And they followed through on this: 82 per cent of Conservative identifiers in the BES actually voted in 2005, compared to 75 per cent of Labour identifiers, 76 per cent of Liberal Democrats, and 51 per cent of 'non-identifiers'. Hence turnout tends to be uniformly high in Conservative-held seats, largely because Conservative supporters are from high-turnout groups who will vote come hell or high water.

---

[10] In fact, the associated *p*-value was 0.47.

[11] An analysis-of-variance test on the data in Figure 7.7 produces an *F*-value of 162.17, which is significant at $p = 0.000$.

[12] This is confirmed by a Bonferroni test: Conservative supporters were, on average, significantly more likely to think it likely they would vote than were Labour identifiers, Liberal Democrat identifiers, those identifying with other parties, and those identifying with no party.

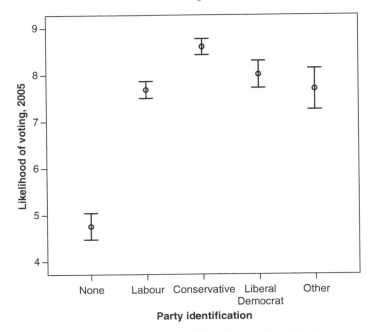

Fig. 7.7. Average likelihood of voting in 2005 and party identification
Source: BES pre-election wave (2005).

Local campaigning

Parties, too, may play a role in encouraging turnout in some seats rather than others. As we saw in Chapter 6, parties allocate their campaign resources rationally, concentrating their efforts in marginal seats where the potential gains are greatest. High turnout in marginals relative to safe seats may, therefore, be a function of more intense party campaigning in the former areas than in the latter. A substantial literature has built up to show that local campaigning, and face-to-face canvassing in particular, does tend to increase turnout, while other forms of campaigning (including telephone campaigns) are much less effective. As discussed in Chapter 6, intensive campaigning can increase turnout (e.g. Bochel and Denver, 1971, 1972). However, Bochel and Denver's study was conducted at a time when the majority of local campaigning was conducted by local party volunteers. Since then, campaign technologies have changed, with the growth of direct mail and telephone canvassing. At the same time, the decline in grassroots party membership has reduced parties' ability to mount doorstep canvasses, thus increasing their reliance on mailshots and telephone canvassing. Some studies suggest telephone canvassing is less effective than face-to-face canvassing in encouraging voters to participate in elections. Gerber and Green (2001; see also Green and Gerber, 2004), for instance, demonstrate that telephone canvassing does not increase voter turnout as effectively as face-to-face canvassing, other things being equal. In a similar vein, Gray and Caul (2000) have argued that the decline in parties' grassroots organizations and the reduction in their capacity for face-to-face mobilization over time have been contributory factors underlying the decline in turnout in many democracies since the 1980s.

However, the evidence is not clear cut: other studies suggest that mobilization efforts have not become any less effective over time (e.g. Goldstein and Ridout, 2002). One factor that may be germane here is that Gerber and Green's experiment was based on a non-partisan telephone call to targeted voters, who are encouraged to vote but are given no guidance on who to vote for. Where partisan cues are offered, it seems all forms of canvassing can improve turnout. At the 2005 British general election, for instance, most if not all canvassing activity was conducted by political parties seeking to maximize their own votes. And survey data from the 2005 BES do indicate that turnout was higher among those who remembered being contacted by a party during the campaign than among those who could not remember such contact (Table 7.7). In fact, if anything, turnout is higher among the (small) group of voters who could remember being telephoned by a party during the campaign than among those who were contacted face-to-face. It does seem as though party activity in constituency campaigns can encourage turnout.

We can get some idea of the size of the effect in Britain by constructing a surrogate measure of the total amount of campaigning going on in each constituency by using the constituency campaign spending measures discussed in Chapter 6. Since, at the time or writing, suitable data were unavailable for the 2005 election, we use equivalent information from the 2001 contest. By summing for each constituency each major party's constituency campaign spend in 2001 as a percentage of the legal maximum there, we can obtain our measure of total campaign intensity. The higher the total value of this surrogate measure, the more intense the constituency campaign. For ease of comparison, we focus here on English constituencies only, where three parties (Labour, Conservative, and Liberal Democrats) dominate the competition. By excluding Scotland and Wales from our example, we avoid the complication of a fourth major party (the nationalists) campaigning

Table 7.7. Individual turnout and exposure to local party campaigning, 2005

Turnout	Canvassed face-to-face		Telephoned by party	
	Yes	No	Yes	No
Voted 2001 (%)	80.1	70.1	84.3	71.3
Abstained 2001 (%)	19.9	29.9	15.7	28.7
N	637	2302	217	2732

Source: BES data files (2005).

there. A graphical presentation (Figure 7.8) shows the underlying relationships. There is a reasonably strong negative correlation between the size of the winning party's majority in each constituency in 1997 and the total amount spent on party campaigns there at the next general election in 2001. Parties were concentrating their attention on the marginals. And, what is more, the higher the total level of party campaigning in a constituency in 2001, the greater the turnout there (Figure 7.9). Much of the relationship between constituency marginality and turnout, therefore, can be accounted for by party activity. Voters are rational, yes, but they discover how competitive their constituency is through their exposure to party campaigns. Where parties fight hard, they encourage participation. Where they put in little effort, electors are less likely to turn out.

Minimizing Participation Costs? Turnout and Distance to Polling Station

It is worth noting that other contextual factors can also influence turnout. One such is the distance voters must travel to cast a vote. Despite some recent experiments with polling stations in shops, and extensive access in some trial areas to internet and postal voting, most British voters are required to vote in person at the designated official polling station that serves their neighbourhood (in New Zealand, in contrast, voters can vote at any polling station anywhere in the country). Each polling district (the smallest electoral unit in the UK) has its own polling station. In towns and cities, a polling station can

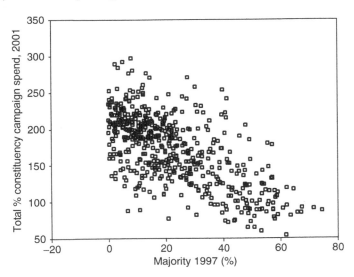

Fig. 7.8. Constituency marginality and party campaign effort, 2001

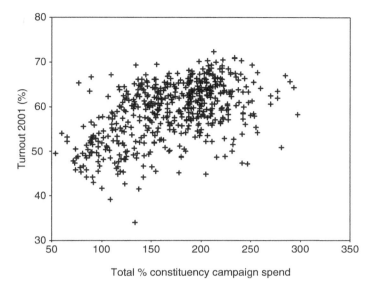

Fig. 7.9. Party campaign effort and constituency turnout, 2001

serve a few streets, so most urban voters live within a short walk or drive of their polling station. In rural areas, the journey to a polling station can be longer, however, particularly for those living in remote hamlets. The polling station itself is usually a school or community hall or other similar establishment, and voters are informed of its location when they receive their polling cards prior to an election. Only those who have applied for a postal vote or a proxy vote prior to the election are exempt from reporting in person to a specific named polling station if they wish to vote and, even though some of the restrictions on obtaining a postal vote in the UK have been lifted, the vast majority of voters still vote in person.

Inevitably, this means that most voters must make a short journey of at least a few minutes' duration in order to cast their votes. That takes time, in addition to the (short) time spent in the polling station itself to collect a ballot paper, fill it in, and deposit it in the ballot box. But time spent travelling to and from the polling station is time that cannot be spent on other activities: it is, therefore, a cost on voting. And, as the rational choice model tells us, when the marginal returns to an individual's personal participation in the ballot are low (as they typically are), then costs will tend to discourage people from voting. We know, for instance, that one of the most common reasons given for not voting is that the person abstaining was too busy on polling day to get to the polling station: as we saw earlier, many non-voters claim that circumstances prevented them from reaching the polling station. Although the BES does not break down what the relevant circumstances might be, it is very likely that the time constraints of busy modern lives played a part in many cases.

We might therefore expect that the further people live from a polling station (and hence the further they have to travel to reach it), the more time it will take them to get there. Hence, the higher will be their costs of voting and the lower their propensity to vote. And there is some evidence to suggest that such an effect does indeed operate, at least in urban areas. Research on turnout patterns at the 1972 local government elections in Swansea's Victoria ward revealed a classic distance-decay pattern (Taylor, 1973). When people vote at a British polling station, a line is drawn through each person's name on the electoral register by one of the election officials at the polling station. Using these marked-up registers, it is possible to see not only who has voted but also (as the register records home address) where they live. Using this evidence, Taylor was able to show that, for instance, while almost 60 per cent of voters living within one minute's travel time of the Vincent polling station turned out, only 41.4 per cent of those living six or more minutes from the polling station voted. However, more recent evidence suggests some more subtle patterns than a simple distance-decay effect. In their study of turnout variations within three Maryland counties, Gimpel and Schuknecht (2003) found that urban voters living closer to the polling station were more likely to vote than those urban voters living further away. Other things being equal, the worst turnout was among suburban residents living between 2 and 5 miles from their polling stations, while turnout was higher among those urbanites living less than 2 miles from a polling station. But turnout was also high among rural voters living more than 6 miles from their nearest polling station. Once again, it seems, the decision on whether or not to vote is affected by context.

Postal and Electronic Voting

If this is indeed a distance-decay effect, then removing the friction of distance should also remove the travel-related differential costs of turnout and so turnout should increase. One way of removing distance effects on voting is to move to all-postal ballots. Experiments in the UK and USA suggest that this does indeed boost turnout substantially. In the late 1990s and early 2000s, a number of experimental schemes specifically designed to boost turnout were piloted in various British local government elections (Electoral Commission, 2002b). In some localities polling stations were provided in unorthodox locations, such as supermarkets; in others, voters were allowed to cast their votes at any polling station in the ward, not just (as is normally the case in the UK) at the polling station nearest their place of residence. In a number of wards, electronic balloting was permitted, using mobile phone text messaging or the internet. And in other areas, all-postal ballots were conducted. In general, the results were mixed: few of the experimental alternatives to traditional voting made a consistent difference to turnout. In some areas, turnout grew; in others it fell or remained static. In the 2002 English local elections, for instance, 16 pilot schemes adopted multi-channel and electronic voting procedures. All the pilot areas also employed conventional voting in person at polling stations. The improvement in turnout overall as a result of adopting electronic voting was modest, up from an average of 29 per cent at the previous comparable local election to just 32 per cent in 2002, roughly in line with the national change in local election turnout since 2000. In four areas, turnout actually fell. But one method, postal balloting, did seem to have a fairly consistent positive effect on electoral participation. Where voters were given the chance to return their vote by mail, turnout increased markedly. In the 2002 local government elections, for instance, experiments with all-postal balloting were carried out in 18 wards throughout England. Turnout in these wards rose from an average of 26 per cent at the previous comparable local election to an average of 42 per cent, an increase of over 50 per cent. In South Tyneside, turnout more than doubled. Only in one locality (Hackney) did turnout fall after the introduction of all-postal voting.

Subsequent experiments have been conducted in both local government and European Parliament elections. Repeated experiments at the 2003 local government elections showed significant improvements in turnout in areas where postal voting was employed. On average, turnout was around 49 per cent in areas where all-postal ballots were used, compared to 35 per cent in England as a whole (Electoral Commission, 2003, 23). At the 2004 European Parliament election, all-postal ballots were employed in four of the 12 regions of the UK. In these all-postal regions, turnout was 42.4 per cent, 5 percentage points higher than in regions where no pilot scheme operated (Electoral Commission, 2004a). However, doubts remained over postal voting in two regards.

First, those applying for a postal vote were more likely to use that vote than were individuals who did not apply, and who would therefore have to vote in person. At the 2005 election, for instance, turnout among those with a postal vote was 76.6 per cent, compared to 59.4 per cent among those without a postal vote (Electoral Commission, 2005, 46). But this dos not mean that postal voting encourages voting among those who would not otherwise do so. People applying for a postal vote are generally relatively more interested in politics than are those who do not apply. As a result, many of those taking up the chance of voting by post were undoubtedly people who would normally vote but who might have been prevented from doing so on polling day by circumstances beyond their control. Without postal voting, such individuals might otherwise have become involuntary non-voters. Research conducted after the 2005 general election seems to confirm this. While not compulsory, it was easier to vote by post in 2005 than in most previous general elections, and many more voters availed themselves of the opportunity than had been the case in the past: whereas 4 per cent of the electorate were issued with a postal vote in 2001, 12 per cent received one in 2005 (Electoral Commission, 2005). But turnout at the 2005 election increased only slightly more in seats where postal voting increased substantially than in seats where the growth in postal voting was lower (Curtice, 2005; Electoral Commission, 2005, 47). Although postal voting meant that fewer of those who intended voting would miss out by accident, it did not bring substantial numbers of habitual non-voters back into the active electorate.

Secondly, a few well-publicized incidents raised the spectre of electoral fraud. After the 2004 local elections in Birmingham, some Labour councillors were accused of forging postal vote ballot papers. In the subsequent well-publicized court case, the judge described postal voting as 'an open invitation to fraud' (see *The Times*, 5 April 2005). The root of the problem was the insecurity of postal ballot papers. It was relatively easy to impersonate others in order to obtain their votes, either by pretending to be another person in order to apply for a postal vote or by filling in someone else's postal ballot with or without their consent. Nor was this the only problem to be widely aired in the media. For a period during the 2005 election campaign, newspapers vied with one another to find examples of children who had wrongly received voting papers, or adults who had applied for postal ballots but who had not yet received them. On election day itself, some voters—including the prominent BBC journalist John Humphrys, who angrily recounted his experience on air in the widely heard Radio 4 *Today* programme—reported being turned away from their polling station on the grounds that they had applied for a postal vote and hence could not vote in person. In practice, only a very few problems were revealed. However, the damage done to perceptions of the integrity of the electoral process was substantial.

Electronic balloting (whether via email, the internet, or telephone text messaging) has also been experimented with, but it is subject to many of the same potential problems as postal voting (Gibson, 2001). Voter impersonation remains a risk for remote internet voting at home, despite the use of PIN technology. Security risks are hard to avoid: election sites may be subject to hacking by unscrupulous individuals who wish to tamper with vote records, parallel sites can be set up to confuse unwary voters, and so on. Some electronic ballot systems do not have robust mechanisms for checking the result in the event of a recount becoming necessary: in the absence of a conventional hard-copy ballot paper showing the vote, it is almost impossible to check for data entry difficulties (or even outright electoral fraud). And the 'digital divide' in internet availability means that poorer voters in particular are less likely than the more affluent to have access to the necessary technology for remote internet voting, potentially exacerbating existing social biases in turnout, though it may prove a means of helping to mobilize younger voters (Solop, 2001). Electronic voting systems, especially those allowing voting from home via the internet, are still far from unproblematic.

The impact of postal voting experiments on turnout is not restricted to the UK. North American studies have reported similar effects. In the state of Oregon, for instance, voting has taken place by mail alone for local elections since 1981, and by the late 1990s, the state was also experimenting with mail-only elections for state-wide elections. Analyses of the effects of the Oregon experience demonstrated that mail-only elections generally have a higher turnout than conventional elections with voting at designated polling places (Berinsky, Burns and Traugott, 2001; Karp and Banducci, 2000). However, the North American studies suggest that all-postal (and internet) ballots are not necessarily a clear-cut panacea to low turnout. Karp and Banducci (2000) showed that the impact on turnout was greatest in low-salience elections such as mid-term primaries, and lowest in high-salience competitions such as presidential elections. Where voters' interest in the election was likely to be low, and hence where we might normally expect turnout to be low too, therefore, a postal ballot encouraged a significant increase in participation. But where the election was likely to engage voters' interests (and so could be expected to have a higher turnout), all-mail ballots had less of a beneficial effect. And Berinsky, Burns and Traugott (2001) showed that all-mail postal ballots were most effective in mobilizing people who normally vote, but who occasionally abstain. They seem much less effective in mobilizing those who seldom or never vote. As we have seen, frequent voters do tend to come from more affluent groups in society, while serial abstainers tend to come from poorer groups. By ensuring that more of the affluent vote while failing to achieve the same effect for the poor, therefore, all-postal ballots may increase turnout, but in doing so could reduce rather than increase the representativeness of the overall election result.

Irrespective of the effects, positive or negative, of postal or e-voting, its opponents argue that voting in person at a polling station is a valuable part of the democratic process. Unlike remote voting, it involves a public act, carried out with other citizens. As argued below, a sense of duty and social pressure are important factors encouraging turnout. We might therefore expect that the more individuals see others voting, the more likely they will be to vote themselves. Since remote voting removes its public visibility, it could be argued that it will also, over time, weaken the social norms that underpin participation (Watt, 2005).

Personal Turnout and the Actions of Others

As we saw in Chapter 4, voters are influenced by the opinions and behaviour of those around them. Does the same hold true when it comes to deciding whether or not to vote at all? *A priori*, we might expect individuals to be strongly influenced by what they see as the prevailing social norms regarding electoral participation. When people discuss voting, it is common to hear them talk in terms of duty. A still-current trope talks of the right to vote as something fought for by previous generations and hence too precious to be thrown away.

Some indication of the extent to which people felt social pressures to vote can be obtained from the 2005 BES. Respondents were asked whether they agreed with a series of statements that tapped into their personal norms regarding electoral participation and their perceptions of how other people think and behave when it comes to voting. Personal norms were tapped by their reactions to the statements 'I would feel guilty if I didn't vote in a general election' and 'I would be seriously neglecting my duty as a citizen if I didn't vote'. Their perceptions of social norms on voting were measured by their responses to the statements 'People are so busy they don't have time to vote' and 'Most people around here usually vote in general elections'. The latter is of particular interest, as it provides a measure of the extent to which individuals think electoral participation is a social norm in their area.[13]

The relationship between turnout and the extent to which individuals feel voting to be a personal or a social norm is much as we would expect (Table 7.8). The guiltier people felt about not voting, and the more they felt it would be a neglect of duty not to do so, the more likely they were to turn out in 2005. The gradient is a steep one. For instance, only just over a third of those who felt strongly that abstention would not make them feel guilty actually did vote in 2005. But among those who said abstention would make them feel very guilty, over 90 per cent voted. And how people thought those around them would think and act also made a difference. Just under 60 per cent of those who felt strongly that people would be too busy to vote turned out themselves, but among those who strongly disagreed with the idea, 89 per cent voted. Similarly, 61 per cent of those who strongly disagreed with the statement that most people in their area would vote turned out themselves, compared with 87 per cent of those who strongly agreed with the

Table 7.8. Perceived social norms and individual turnout, 2005 (percentages)

| | % turnout, 2005 | | | |
Level of agreement	Guilty if don't vote	Not voting a serious neglect of duty	People too busy	Most vote here
Strongly agree	90.7	88.9	58.7	87.0
Agree	84.3	82.0	62.4	78.2
Neither	67.7	60.0	64.8	64.7
Disagree	52.6	44.7	77.6	68.0
Strongly disagree	35.6	29.4	89.2	60.9
N	2951	2953	2923	2557

Source: BES data files (2005).

[13] Similar questions were asked in the 2001 BES, with similar results to those reported here (Clarke et al., 2004).

statement. As with vote choice, so too with the decision to vote itself: social norms in local communities matter. The more individuals think that people around them will vote, the more likely they themselves are to do so (Clarke et al., 2004).

Individuals' decisions on whether or not to vote are also influenced by what the people they live with do. Most voters are politically socialized in the contexts of their families (by their parents) and their households. As research using the British Household Panel Study (BHPS) has demonstrated there is a correlation between household and individual electoral participation (Johnston et al., 2005b). The BHPS data are unusual in that the survey interviews all adult members of a household. It therefore provides very good contextual information about what is happening around individuals at the most local scale of all. After the 1992 general election, 16 per cent of BHPS respondents said they had abstained. If the chance of an individual abstaining was unrelated to whether other members of the household voted, we would expect that the number of households in which all adults abstained would be given by the probability of an individual abstaining raised to the power of the number of adults in a household.[14] Applying this rule of thumb, we can calculate how likely it would be for individuals living in the same household to all abstain if individuals' decisions on whether or not to vote are unrelated to what other household members do. (In other words, we are assuming that we have randomly chosen individuals who happen to live in the same household but who otherwise have no influence on each other's lives and are then calculating the probability that none of them will vote.) In single-person BHPS households, we would expect the chances of abstention in 2001 to be the same as for the sample as a whole, 0.16. But the probability of two otherwise unrelated individuals living in the same household abstaining is $0.16 \times 0.16 = 0.0256$. For a three-person household, the probability drops further, to $0.16 \times 0.16 \times 0.16 = 0.004$, and so on.

Johnston et al. (2005b) compared these expectations with actual levels of abstention in households to obtain a picture of the extent to which the individual decision to vote is influenced by the actions of other household members. In single-person BHPS households, the expected abstention rate is almost identical to the actual rate: with no one else in the household to influence them, these home-alone householders abstain at the same rate as the overall sample. Among two-person households, there were almost three times more examples where both adults actually abstained than expected: those who live with someone who abstains are themselves much more likely to abstain too than we would expect based simply on random chance. Among three-person households, the actual incidence of all three adults abstaining was 12 times more common than random chance alone would lead us to expect. In other words, people tended to behave like the people they lived

---

[14] This is simply a consequence of the multiplication rule of probabilities.

with. Sharing a household with others who have the voting habit rubs off: one is more likely to vote oneself if others in one's household do too. Similarly, those who live with abstainers are themselves more likely than normal to abstain: if one's cohabitees do not vote, that reduces the chances of voting oneself. This may be a result of peer pressure ('If my cohabitees are/ are not voting, I should follow suit so as not to stand out'). It may be a consequence of socialization and shared values ('My cohabitees do/do not think voting is worthwhile, and I agree with them'). But irrespective of the mechanism, it has a strong effect. The implication is that there are 'voting-rich' households, in which most adults vote, and 'voting-poor' households, in which most abstain.

Finally, turnout is related to community stability and social capital (Eagles and Erfle, 1989; Highton, 2000; Putnam, 2000). Strong links between individuals in a community seem to be associated with higher rates of electoral participation: the more cohesive a community, other things being equal, the higher the turnout. Where there is rapid population turnover, however, turnout is low. In part this may reflect the disruption of social ties as a result of relocation. When people move, they uproot themselves from previous local networks of friends and acquaintances. It takes time for these links to be rebuilt in their new home areas, and that can have the effect of depressing electoral participation. However, more important, it seems, is the disruptive effect of migration on voter registration. In systems that relate voting rights to area residence (as in the UK), people are registered at their home addresses: move home, and one needs to re-register to vote. This can take time, not least as voter registration is rarely a top priority for those who have just moved home. Hence areas experiencing rapid population turnover are also likely to see electoral participation fall, purely as an artefact of delays in voter registration: areas losing population are likely to retain the names of no-longer-resident voters on their electoral rolls for some time after these individuals have left the area, for instance, thus decreasing apparent turnout.

Summarizing the Contextual Effect on Turnout

The geography of electoral turnout therefore seems to depend on two sorts of context: the electoral context (constituency marginality and the geography of polling stations within individual electoral districts), and the social context (how affluent and old each constituency's electorate is). We can obtain some impression of how important the various individual factors are by performing a multiple regression analysis.

Our dependent variable is percentage turnout in each constituency in Great Britain. Two models are estimated—one for turnout in 2001 and the other for turnout in 2005. The choice of independent variables is determined in part by theory and in part by the availability of relevant data. It would be prohibitively expensive to produce nationwide data on the distance between voters' homes and their polling stations, so we omit that measure of spatial context. We can, however, estimate constituency marginality using, as before, the winning party's percentage-point majority over its rivals at the previous election (1997 for the 2001 contest, 2001 for 2005). Our measures of social context are provided by data from the 2001 census, giving the percentage of owner-occupied households in each constituency, the percentage of adults employed in middle-class jobs, and the percentage of individuals aged over the retirement age.[15] And, for the 2001 election only, we also include data on the intensity of the local campaign: the variable sums (for each constituency) the campaign expenditures of the Labour, Conservative, and Liberal Democrat candidates as a percentage of the legal maximum in the seat.[16]

The results are as expected at both elections: the safer a constituency is (and hence the larger the winning party's majority), the lower the turnout; and the more affluent and elderly its population, the higher the turnout (Table 7.9). All the coefficients are highly significant and correctly signed and the equation overall can account for just under 70 per cent of the constituency variation in turnout. All our measures of context have individual and separate impacts on local turnout. Social factors all have a distinct influence: the more middle class its population, the greater the proportion of its residents who are homeowners, and the older its population, other things being equal, the higher is its electoral turnout. And local turnout is also

Table 7.9. Constituency turnout and context: a multivariate model

	Turnout (%)	
Independent variables	2001	2005
Constant	27.80	33.10
Majority 1997/2001 (%)	−0.07	−0.14
Owner-occupied housing, 2001 (%)	0.23	0.16
Middle class 2001 (%)	0.13	0.25
Pensioners 2001 (%)	0.42	0.38
Total constituency campaign spend (%)	0.02	
R^2	0.69	0.69

Note: Only significant coefficients are shown.

[15] The analyses for 2001 are restricted to constituencies in England and Wales, as 2001 census data are not available for the Scottish constituencies used at that election. We have repeated the analysis using data from the 1991 census, which does allow us to include the Scottish seats. (Although the absolute social geography of the UK did shift between 1991 and 2001, the relative geography remained quite stable, making the 1991 census data a reasonable approximation of the situation in 2001.) The results are unchanged.

[16] As noted earlier, 2005 constituency campaign expenditure data were not available at the time of writing.

independently affected by political factors: the more marginal the seat, and the more intensively the parties campaign there, the higher the local turnout.

Conclusions

Electoral participation is driven, therefore, by a variety of factors recognizable as features of both rational choice and civic voluntarism. Citizens are more likely to participate when the stakes are high (whether in terms of the marginality of the contest or the size of the perceived ideological gap between the main parties) than when they are low. And the resource-rich are more likely to participate than are the resource-poor. As we have seen, too, context plays an important role in influencing the decision to participate: it makes more sense to take part in an election in some seats than in others.

That said, we have also seen evidence of rapidly declining participation rates in recent British elections—more rapid than contextual explanations alone would suggest. The certainty of a Labour victory in both 1997 and 2001 and also (albeit a less emphatic one) in 2005, and the perceived ideological closeness of Labour and the Conservatives, both undoubtedly helped to create low turnouts in those election years. However, turnouts at the 2001 and 2005 general elections were even lower than this account would lead us to expect. There are signs that all is not well with British electoral democracy.

Should this worry us? We would argue that it should. There is a leap of faith involved in voting. I may be just one of millions of voters, but my vote does, in some sense, matter—my personal participation makes a difference. As long as most voters believe this to be the case, participation in elections should remain high. But if faith in the electoral process (or in the efficacy of individual voters) declines, there is a real risk that participation rates could fall. And that raises a host of questions regarding the legitimacy of election results, their representativeness, and so on. As we have seen, turnout and abstention are not uniformly spread through the population. Some groups— the more affluent, the better educated, the old—are more likely to vote than others—the less well off, the less well educated, and the young. There is, therefore, a real potential risk that substantial parts of the population might effectively cease to be represented, purely because they cease to vote. If elections do not confer legitimacy on governments, and do not provide some form of representative outcome, it is hard to see what purpose they might serve.

The potential problems of permanently low electoral turnout are well captured in J. K. Galbraith's (1992) description of the culture of contentment. In his analysis of contemporary US society, he pointed to the emergence of two communities living in the same country but experiencing very different lives as a consequence of the logic of market capitalism. One community, in the numerical majority, comprises the beneficiaries of the affluent society: their lives are comfortable, their living standards tend to rise, and they tend to favour the current status quo. This contented majority is likely to participate in politics to preserve their privileges. Members of the other community—a large minority in the late twentieth and early twenty-first centuries—are relative losers in the market order. They are the poor, the underclass, the dispossessed. As political parties in electoral systems are in the business of winning more votes than their rivals, argued Galbraith, they are likely to appeal to majority opinion, since that is where most votes are. As a result, the logic of electoral arithmetic points towards adopting policies that will appeal to relatively affluent and contented voters: low taxes, limited public spending, and so on. And all major parties, he argued, are drawn onto this territory if they intend to compete with each other. But in doing so, they neglect the interests of the poorer minority, who may favour (or stand to benefit from) more progressive taxation and enhanced public spending. The affluent majority, therefore, have an incentive to vote, as parties are acting in their interests. But the poor minority lack such an incentive: why should they vote for policies that will not benefit them. They therefore become less likely to vote. And that exacerbates the problem, since rational political parties will not expend effort in appealing to individuals who are unlikely to vote, particularly if the policies most likely to appeal to habitual (poor) non-voters are liable to alienate more-affluent and more-frequent voters. As a result, turnout falls overall, and falls particularly fast among the poor. And, furthermore, party politics becomes skewed towards the interests of the affluent, while the interests of the poor become marginalized. Under such circumstances, low turnout is associated with unrepresentative politics.

8

Votes into Seats

In previous chapters we have demonstrated the importance of geography as the context in which who votes for what, where (as well as who doesn't vote at all) is determined, at a variety of spatial scales. The result is a geography of party support across Great Britain—the typical map dominated by red, blue, and (increasingly) yellow that appears in the media before and after every general election. That geography invariably shows which party wins in each of the parliamentary constituencies. But how is that related to other maps that could be drawn—maps showing, for example, the geography of voting for each of the political parties? Winning votes is basic to winning elections, but winning them in the right places is fundamental too.

The nature of that partial relationship between the geography of voting for each party and the geography of electoral success is readily appreciated through the summary statistics in Table 8.1. This gives the percentage of the votes cast in Great Britain for the winning party at each of the last seven general elections, and the percentage of the parliamentary seats it obtained. Three main features stand out:

- Until 2005 there was a very small range in the percentage of the votes cast that were won by the victorious party (40.7–43.9), and at none of the elections did the winning party obtain a majority of the votes.

- At every one of the elections, the winning party obtained not only a much larger share of the seats than of the votes but also a majority of the seats, despite not getting a majority of the votes.

Table 8.1. Seats and votes won by the victorious party at general elections in Great Britain, 1979–2005

Election	Winner	Votes (%)	Seats (%)	Seats/votes ratio
1979	Conservative	43.9	53.4	1.22
1983	Conservative	42.2	61.1	1.45
1987	Conservative	43.4	57.8	1.33
1992	Conservative	42.3	51.6	1.22
1997	Labour	43.3	63.6	1.47
2001	Labour	40.7	62.6	1.53
2005	Labour	36.2	55.0	1.52

- There was considerable variability in the ratio of seats won to votes won (the final column of the table), indicating that the process of translating votes into seats was inconsistent; furthermore, on average the Labour party got a better return for its vote share (i.e. a higher seats:votes ratio) at the last three elections than the Conservatives did in their victories at the previous four (averages of 1.51 and 1.31, respectively).

Other features of the operation of the electoral system follow from these three. For example, given the large 'winner's bonus' that was typical of every election (the difference between the party's share of the seats and the votes), there must as a consequence also have been a 'loser's penalty'—if one party is gaining a greater share of the seats than it does of the votes, then other parties must be getting a smaller share relative to their vote total.

The pattern of 'bonuses' and 'penalties' can be shown by each party's seats:votes ratio (i.e. its percentage of the seats divided by its percentage of the votes). If all parties were treated equally, then the ratios should be 1.0 (each party gets the same share of the seats as it does of the votes—so-called proportional representation): ratios below 1.0 indicate that the party is under-represented in Parliament relative to its share of votes in the country; ratios greater than 1.0 indicate over-representation. Figure 8.1 shows the ratios for the three main parties that have regularly contested virtually all of the constituencies in Great Britain—Conservative, Labour, and Liberal Democrat[1]—since 1950.[2] This shows that after 1959 Labour has always had a positive ratio, which increased substantially from the 1997 to the 2005 election, exceeding 1.5 in 2001 and 2005, when it was over-represented by 50 per cent relative to its share of the votes. The Conservatives had ratios substantially in excess of 1.0 at most elections prior to 1997 (the sole exception was 1966), but fell well below the 'equal representation norm' at the last three. Finally, the Liberal Democrats have never achieved a ratio as high as 0.5—their share of the seats has always been less than half of their share of the votes. At most elections between 1959 and 1992 (inclusive) their ratio was less than 0.2, but it more than doubled in 1997 and remained at virtually the same level thereafter.

Three main conclusions can be drawn from this graph. The first is that the British electoral system treats parties unequally through a translation process of converting votes into seats that invariably creates a disproportional outcome. The second is that the translation process does not seem to treat

---

[1] Throughout this chapter we use the current name for the country's 'third party': until 1983 it was known as the Liberal party; at the 1983 and 1987 elections, the Liberals fought in an Alliance with the Social Democratic Party; these merged in 1988 and, after a brief period when they were known as the Social and Liberal Democrats, they took on their current name. They only began contesting virtually every seat in 1979.

[2] The reasons for choosing 1950 as the starting date will become clear during this chapter: the new system of drawing up constituency boundaries was first used at the 1950 general election.

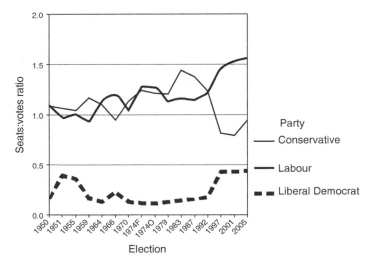

Fig. 8.1. Seats:votes ratios, 1950–2005

the parties in the same way when they get the same share of the votes—the Conservatives and Labour have received a larger share of the seats than of votes at most of the 16 elections during this period, whereas the Liberal Democrats have received a much smaller share. The latter have traditionally received the 'loser's penalty'; the Conservatives have only done so at four elections, those won by Labour with large majorities (1966, 1997, 2001, and 2005). Labour had a 'loser's penalty' at only two elections: in 1951 (when it won a larger percentage of the votes than the Conservatives but obtained 17 fewer seats) and in 1959. From then on, even when Labour's vote share fell precipitately in the 1980s, it still got a larger percentage of the seats than votes, because the 'loser's penalty' was being suffered by the Liberal Democrats.

The third conclusion is clearly demonstrated by two graphs. Figure 8.2 gives the seats:votes ratio for the winning party at each election from 1950 to 2005. This shows a very strong upward trend over the 55 years, as indicated by the best-fit regression line: it averaged 1.12 in the 1950s and 1960s, 1.27 for the elections in the 1970s and 1980s, and 1.45 at the last four elections. In other words, the results of British general elections have become increasingly disproportional in over-representing the winning party. This is shown by Figure 8.3, which uses a simple index of disproportionality: half of the sum of the absolute differences between each party's percentage of the votes and of the seats.[3] It shows the percentage of the seats that would have to be redistributed across the parties so that vote and seat shares were equal, and

---

[3] This is the same as the index of dissimilarity widely used in studies of residential segregation.

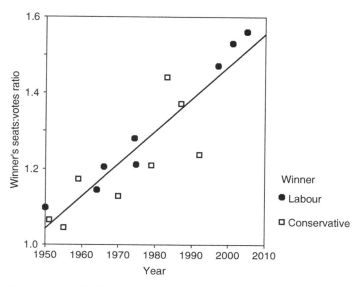

Fig. 8.2. Seats:votes ratio for the winning party, 1950–2005

thus varies between 0.0 (no disproportionality) and 100.0 (total disproportionality). Until the 1970s disproportionality was at a low level—only twice
slightly exceeding 10 percentage points. There was a step-change at the first
of the 1974 general elections, however: from an average of only 6.5 for

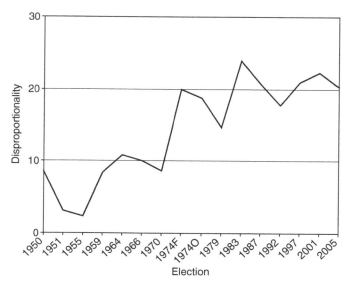

Fig. 8.3. Disproportionality in British general election results, 1950–2005

the first of the eight contests, it increased to an average of 22.4 for the second eight.

Accounting for Disproportionality

Why does the UK electoral system produce disproportional election results, and why has that disproportionality increased over this 55-year period? The answers presented here, as in the rest of the book, bring geography to the foreground. In part, the outcomes of the way votes are translated into seats reflect the geographies discussed in the earlier chapters: parties get more votes in some places than others—at a variety of scales and for a variety of reasons. The key to answering the question, however, is a further geography that has been little remarked-upon so far in this book—that of the spatial containers within which the votes are counted and the election's winners determined. The UK's electoral system is frequently termed a plurality system, because the winner in each constituency is the candidate with a plurality of the votes—the largest number, which may not be a majority; it is also frequently referred to as 'first-past-the-post' (FPTP) for the same reason. To operate this system, the country is divided into a number of spatially demarcated constituencies, each returning one MP to the House of Commons.[4]

Virtually all countries using this electoral system experience disproportional electoral outcomes. This was accounted for statistically in the British case by what was termed the 'cube law', a relationship between the percentages of votes and of seats won by the various parties. This has the form (Johnston, 1979b):

$$S_i/S_j = (V_i/V_j)^3 \qquad (1)$$

where S_i and S_j are the percentages of the seats won by parties i and j; and

V_i and V_j are the percentages of the seats won by parties i and j.

Further, because the formula looks only at the performance of the two main parties, votes won by other parties are excluded from the analysis so that V_i and V_j sum to 100.

If each party obtained 50 per cent of the votes cast, therefore (i.e. half the 'two-party vote', excluding votes won by other parties), then solving the equation would give a result of 1.0: the ratio between the percentage of the seats won by the two parties would be 1.0—each would get 50 per cent of the seats too. However, if one party (i) got 55 per cent and the other (j) got 45 per cent, solving the equation would give

$$(55/45)^3 = 1.22^3 = 1.82$$

---

[4] Multi-member constituencies were abolished before the 1950 election: see Butler (1963) and Rossiter, Johnston, and Pattie (1999).

Equation (1) can be rewritten as

$$S_i = (100 \times V_i^3)/(V_i^3 + V_j^3) \tag{2}$$

which is $(100 \times 55^3)/(55^3 + 45^3) = 64.6$

So with 55 per cent of the votes, according to the cube law party i should get 64.6 per cent of the seats.

Early work using the cube law showed that it produced a good fit to the result of the 1950 election (Butler, 1951; Kendall and Stuart, 1950), and also to elections between then and 1970 (Tufte, 1973), but not thereafter. Figures 8.4 and 8.5 show the difference between the cube law's prediction of a party's percentage of the seats and its actual performance. For the Conservatives (Figure 8.4), there was a close fit between the observed and predicted percentage for every election up to and including October 1974: the largest deviation was only 3.38 percentage points, and the average over all nine elections was only 1.81 points. Thereafter, the cube law substantially over-predicted the Conservative performance by an average of 9.5 percentage points at the final seven elections of the sequence. For Labour (Figure 8.5), all but six of the cube law predictions fall within 5 percentage points of the actual value—with the exceptions occupying the period between the October 1974 and 1997 contests. Most notable in Labour's case, however, are the four fairly substantial positive values—with Labour getting a larger share of the seats than predicted—for the four elections won by the Conservative party between 1979 and 1992, when Labour was at its nadir in electoral support.

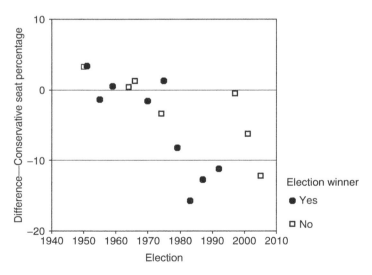

Fig. 8.4. Difference between the percentage of seats won by the Conservatives and that predicted by the cube law

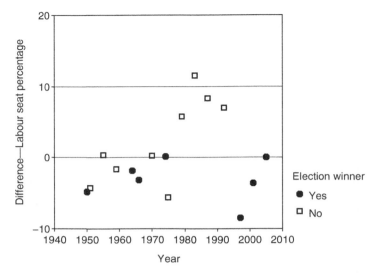

Fig. 8.5. Difference between the percentage of seats won by Labour and that predicted by the cube law

There has been a number of analyses of the cube law's failure to predict British election outcomes successfully from the mid-1970s on. One of the major reasons is that the cube law is nothing more than a statistical peculiarity. It only applies if a number of conditions are met: each of the two main parties has a normally distributed share of the votes cast across all constituencies; the mean of the distribution is close to 50; and the standard deviation of that distribution is close to 13.7. Gudgin and Taylor (1979) showed in a detailed examination of the cube law's applicability that these conditions are rarely met, and that if one or more of them is not, then the law will be a poor predictor of the election outcome: what appeared to be a 'rare jewel [for political science]—a phenomenon that was measurable, regular and susceptible to statistical proof in a manner akin to some of the natural sciences' (Curtice and Steed, 1982, 253; Butler, 1963, 201–2, called it 'one of the more certain things among the uncertainties of politics') turned out to be a special case.

Fitting a statistical relationship does not necessarily provide an explanation, however. Even if the cube law did still fit,[5] this would not provide a reason why the British electoral system produces a 'winner's bias'. That reason is entirely linked to geography, specifically to two geographies—that of the constituencies and how they are defined; and that of who votes for which party, or abstains, where. Exploration of that reason is undertaken here, in the context of another feature of British post-1950 election results—bias.

---

[5] Or some variant on it, such as a square law, in which $(S_i/S_j) = (V_i/V_j)^2$, and the standard deviation is much larger.

Not only Disproportional but also Biased

Table 8.1 suggests that the two main parties were not equally treated by the process of translating votes into seats from 1979 on. The seats:votes ratios show that when Labour won, it obtained a larger share of the seats than the Conservatives did with the same share of the votes at other elections. Compare, for example, 1987 and 1997, when the two parties obtained virtually the same vote share but Labour in 1997 got nearly 6 percentage points more of the seats than the Conservatives had done in 1987. This suggests an unequal—or biased—treatment, favouring Labour.

To measure the extent of that bias we use a method developed by a New Zealand political scientist (Brookes, 1959, 1960), which has a range of advantages discussed later in this chapter—but which also makes an assumption regarding how patterns of voting change across constituencies.[6] The basic argument is that if two parties have the same percentage of the votes then they should have the same percentage of the seats too: if one gets a larger share than the other, then the system is biased in its favour. To inquire whether that is the case, a uniform swing (see Chapter 6) is applied across all constituencies. Table 8.2 illustrates how this is done, using the 2005 general election. The Labour and Conservative parties obtained 36.2 and 33.2 per cent, respectively, of the votes cast in Great Britain, and got the majority of the seats. With equal vote shares each would have 34.7 per cent, so 1.5 percentage points of its votes won are taken from Labour's total in each constituency and re-allocated to the Conservatives. The result of this transfer is far from equality in the allocation of seats: with each party having 34.7 per cent of the votes, Labour would nevertheless have won 111 more seats than the Conservatives. This is the measure of bias: the difference between the two main parties in their shares of the seats if they were to have the same percentage of the votes, with the latter

Table 8.2. Calculating bias at the 2005 general election

Party	Actual result		Equal shares result	
	Vote (%)	Seats	Vote (%)	Seats
Labour	36.2	355	34.7	334
Conservative	33.2	197	34.7	223
Liberal Democrat	22.6	62	22.6	58
Nationalist (PC, SNP)	2.2	9	2.2	9
Other	0.7	5	0.7	4

[6] An alternative procedure to that deployed here, based on different assumptions, has been developed by Blau (2001): with few exceptions, however, the trends it identifies are very similar to those discussed here.

being re-allocated according to a uniform swing from the leading to the
second-placed party across all constituencies. (A fully worked example of
this process is in Johnston et al., 2001a.)

This bias measure for each election since 1950 is shown in Figure 8.6,
in which (as in all further uses of this method) a bias in favour of the
Conservative party is shown as a negative value whereas a bias favouring
Labour is a positive figure. There is a clear trend over the period. At the first
six elections there is a pro-Conservative bias, which stood at 51 and 59 seats,
respectively in 1950 and 1951 but fell to just three in 1966. At the next six
elections the bias was small, averaging 10.5 seats, with Labour benefiting on
three occasions and the Conservatives on the other three. The final four
elections then saw a major change, with the bias not only increasing very
substantially—peaking at 141 seats in 2001—but also favouring Labour.

At the beginning of the sequence of elections studied here, therefore, the
electoral system favoured the Conservative party; it would have won as many
as 59 more seats than Labour would have done if they had achieved equal
shares of the votes. (This was in 1951, when Labour won 49.36 per cent of the
votes and the Conservatives 47.78, so that the equal shares situation had
both with 48.57 per cent—a uniform swing away from Labour across all
constituencies of 0.395 points.) For a sequence of years thereafter there was
relatively little bias, with neither party apparently benefiting greatly from
the way in which votes are translated into seats. Finally, the last four
elections—three of which were won by Labour—saw the bias figures increase

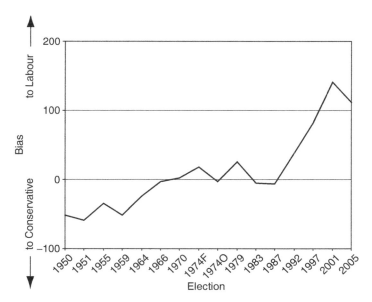

Fig. 8.6. Biases in British general election results, 1950–2005

again, to an extent not previously encountered. Labour was a major beneficiary of that shift in the translation process. Even in 2005, when it had a
lead of only three percentage points over the Conservatives in the vote share,
it had a favourable bias of 111 seats.

Not only did the outcome of British elections become more disproportional over the period 1950–2005, therefore, it also became more biased. The
allocation of seats to parties was increasingly further away from the ideal of
proportional representation (each party getting the same percentage of the
seats as of the votes), and that disproportionality increasingly favoured one
of the main parties—Labour. What changed: was it the electoral system? The
answer is 'no': as described in the next section, the procedure for defining
parliamentary constituencies in the United Kingdom has remained virtually
the same since the 1940s and the small alterations cannot account for the
major shifts noted so far in this chapter.

The Making of a Geography: Constituency Definition in the UK

Bounded territories—spatially defined constituencies—are the fundamental
organizing units for UK general elections. Their use for the election of MPs
has a very long history. Until the nineteenth century, Parliament comprised
representatives (usually two each) elected from the shire counties and the
parliamentary boroughs (independent settlements within those counties), the
units of local government. By then, however, the pattern of representation
was extremely disproportional, because of population growth in some areas
and decline in others. Some very large towns, notably those growing rapidly
during the industrial revolution, had no separate representation and were
part of very large county constituencies, whereas many small settlements had
very few electors indeed (the so-called 'rotten boroughs'). Before the first
Reform Act of 1832, for example, 202 separate boroughs returned MPs; 56 of
them had fewer than 50 electors each.

Concern about this clear disproportionality was only a small part of
contemporary political disquiet about representation, which focused on the
very narrow franchise: the vast majority of British adults (all females and
most males—including all those who were not property-owners) played no
part in the election of MPs. (Universal male franchise was only introduced
early in the twentieth century, however, and universal female franchise not
achieved until 1929.) The three main nineteenth-century Reform Acts (1832,
1867, and 1885) focused very largely on that issue, but at the same time
involved changes to the map of constituencies. The creation of those new
geographies involved political exercises, with the parties seeking to maximize
their own benefits from the changes. Single-member constituencies became
the norm at the 1885 redistribution of seats.

As in the nineteenth century, the population continued to grow and move during the first half of the twentieth century: the main cities and towns expanded rapidly, while the countryside became increasingly depopulated. Differences in the sizes of constituency electorates became exaggerated over time, which offended many people's notions of equality of representation (or 'one person, one vote: one vote, one value'): a constituency with 100,000 electors and a single MP was under-represented in the House of Commons compared to another with only 40,000 electors. There was only one redistribution in the first part of the century, however (in 1917) and continued population changes soon generated further representation inequalities.

Tackling these inequalities on a regular basis was not finally addressed until legislation introduced during the Second World War, as part of a wider attempt to regulate the electoral system. The House of Commons (Redistribution of Seats) Act 1944 was based on a small number of principles which had evolved over the preceding century:

- Each constituency should return one MP.
- Each constituency should comprise a contiguous block of territory.
- Constituencies should be delimited so as to reflect 'communities of interest'.
- Each constituency should have the same number of electors—as 'far as is practicable'.

To operate these principles, the Act established four Boundary Commissions (one for each of the UK's constituent countries) to undertake regular reviews (the required frequency of which has been changed twice; at the time of writing it is once every 8–12 years). In particular, those reviews were to take account of the impact of population changes on variations in constituency size.[7] The outcome of a review might involve reducing the number of constituencies in some parts of the country and increasing them elsewhere, as well as changing the boundaries in many areas in order to maintain (approximate) equality of electorates. The requirement that communities should be separately represented is reflected in parts of the legislation that require the Commissions to take account of local government boundaries (by not creating constituencies crossing the boundaries of the major units unless absolutely necessary), and the Commissions themselves have decided to use local government electoral wards as the building blocks for constituencies.[8] In addition, the Act—as amended in the 1950s—requires the Commissions

---

[7] Throughout this chapter, all references to constituency size refer to the number of electors in a constituency, not its area.

[8] There are slight variations among the four countries in the importance given to local government boundaries when defining constituencies: in Northern Ireland, though not in the other three, the use of local government wards as the building blocks is prescribed (although those wards are no longer used for local government elections since the switch to STV).

not to disturb constituencies simply to get slightly greater equality of electorates: MPs prefer continuity in the areas/populations they represent. (For full details of the various Acts and amendments, plus their interpretation by the Commissions, see Rossiter, Johnston, and Pattie, 1999a.)

This system was put into operation in the late 1940s, and the first set of constituencies was produced in time for the 1950 general election. Four full reviews have since been reported and implemented—at the 1955, 1974 (February), 1983, and 1997 general elections. (New constituencies were also used in Scotland in 2005, but not in England, Wales, or Northern Ireland— the first time that all four countries have not had new constituencies introduced contemporaneously.[9]) Each review has applied the same principles, with only small changes in procedures—some mandated by Parliament, others introduced by the Commissions themselves. Basically, therefore, the system for revising constituency boundaries has not changed since the Second World War; hence our focus here on all general elections since 1950.

The Boundary Commissions operate by first determining the quota—the average constituency electorate—to be applied in the review, based on the national electorate in the year when the review commenced. It then calculates the number of constituencies to be allocated to each part of the country (such as counties and metropolitan boroughs in England—the major local authorities whose boundaries should not be crossed by parliamentary constituencies save in special circumstances), and proposes constituency boundaries within each area.[10] This is done in an entirely neutral way, with no reference to the political characteristics of an area, let alone the likely electoral consequences of any proposed changes. The provisional recommendations are put out for public consultation. If there is sufficient negative comment about the proposals for any area, a public inquiry is held before an Assistant Commissioner at which interested parties can present their views about the proposals, put forward alternative schemes, and contest what other interested groups and individuals propose. The political parties are the major players at these inquiries, seeking to convince the Commission to adopt a set of recommendations that is to their best advantage: the party with the most convincing case may be able, in effect, to manipulate constituency boundaries to some extent to its own advantage.

On the basis of the Assistant Commissioners' reports, the Commission revisits the recommendations for each area: it may decide to make no changes to its provisional recommendations or it may alter its proposals. If it chooses the latter course, its revised recommendations are again put out

---

[9] There was also one interim review, in 1988, when the rapidly expanding town of Milton Keynes had its number of constituencies increased from one to two.

[10] In this, as in other aspects of the work, the Commissions vary somewhat in their practices, in part as a consequence of legislative changes, some of which affect the four countries differentially.

for public consultation and on very rare occasions a further public inquiry may be held. Normally, however, both the unchanged and the revised recommendations become the final recommendations for that area. When the process is completed for the whole country, the full set of recommendations is forwarded to the relevant Secretary of State for transmission to Parliament for approval. Since the 1950s, Parliament has been able only to accept or reject the recommendations rather than modify them: the Secretary of State can amend recommendations before presenting them to the House of Commons (where they are always submitted first), but this power has never been deployed. Once accepted by both Houses and given the Royal Assent, the new constituencies are introduced for the next general election.

The main change after most of these periodic reviews is that variations in constituency size are reduced: they can never be entirely removed because of the other rules and the use of wards as the building-blocks. Because constituencies rarely cross major local government boundaries, differences in their total electorates will generate differences in average constituency size. For example, the quota for the review that began in 2001 in England was 69,934. Somerset had a total electorate of 380,651 and was allocated five constituencies, with an average of 76,130 electors each; South Gloucestershire, on the other hand, with a total electorate of 186,555, was allocated three constituencies, whose individual electorates averaged 62,185. Some size differences are thereby built in to the system. This is exacerbated by the situation within local authorities. Birmingham, for example, has 40 wards, to be allocated among ten constituencies, comprising contiguous ward groupings. It may not be possible to achieve electoral equality with these, because of the size and location of the individual wards. The Commission's provisional recommendations produced constituencies there ranging in size from 65,061 to 76,482 electors, for example, and after the public inquiry the range was cut only slightly (to 65,061–75,563).

A further cause of constituency-size variations is that Scotland and Wales were guaranteed at least 70 and 36 seats, respectively by the 1944 Act (their allocations then). Continued population growth in England relative to those two countries, each of which were allocated additional seats at various reviews (in 2001 Scotland had 72 and Wales 40), meant a growing disparity in relative average constituency electorates. Northern Ireland was initially allocated 12 seats, but after suspension of the Stormont Assembly in the early 1970s, was allocated between 16 and 18 in 1977, so that its average constituency electorate is now close to that in England. After the Fourth Periodic Review, which reported in 1994–5, the average constituency electorate in England was 68,626 and in Northern Ireland, 64,082; for Scotland and Wales the comparable figures were 54,569 and 55,559, respectively.

As part of the 'devolution settlement' of 1998, Scotland's quota at the next review was to be the same as England's, which led the Boundary Commission for Scotland to reduce the country's constituencies and MPs from 72 to 59. No such change was made for Wales, however, whose Assembly has fewer powers than the Scottish Parliament. Scotland's new constituencies were introduced early enough to be deployed in the 2005 general election, when the total number of MPs in the UK was reduced from 659 to 646 (628 in Great Britain).

Geography, Disproportionality, and Bias

Given this system of producing constituencies with approximately equal electorates, at least within each country, why does the British electoral system result in disproportional and biased outcomes, as the data examined earlier indicated? Such outcomes are generally associated with electoral abuses—such as malapportionment and gerrymandering.[11] These are/have been common in the USA: malapportionment was outlawed in the 1960s, but gerrymandering is increasingly common (see Monmonier, 2002). Such abuses do not characterize the British system, however: although a small amount of malapportionment is built into the system, the Boundary Commissions are independent and there is no evidence that the political parties can influence the outcome of their deliberations to a great extent. (Labour is widely agreed to have been much more successful in influencing the Commissions during their Fourth Reviews, which ended in 1994, but this probably only gained it a handful of extra seats at the next general election in 1997: Rossiter, Johnston, and Pattie, 1999a.[12])

To illustrate how a non-partisan system of drawing constituency boundaries can nevertheless advantage one party over others we use simple hypothetical examples. Take a place with 25 equal-sized wards each having 100 voters (Figure 8.7). There are only two parties—*X* and *Y*: everybody turns out at an election, with *X* winning 1290 of the 2500 votes (51.6 per cent of the total) and *Y* 1210 (48.4 per cent). The vote totals are shown in Figure 8.7(A), with party *X*'s votes as the top figure in each ward. The 25 wards have to be combined into five equal-sized constituencies. Figure 8.7(a)–(f) shows five different ways in which these could be created: in each case, the constituencies are the same size and comprise contiguous blocks of territory (some more 'shapely' than others). Some disproportionality is almost

[11] Gerrymandering is the deliberate drawing of electoral district boundaries to produce an electoral advantage for an interested party. The term was coined by enemies of Massachusetts Republican Governor Elbridge Gerry who created a district in 1812 that his party would win: it was shaped like a salamander, hence the neologism and the widespread (if false) belief that gerrymandering necessarily involves odd-shaped district boundaries. Although gerrymandering has long been practiced in the USA, it has only recently—and in specific conditions—been interpreted by the courts there as a constitutional violation

[12] Similarly in Northern Ireland the various parties had different impacts on determining both the number of seats and their boundaries—and hence the election results (Rossiter, Johnston, and Pattie, 1998).

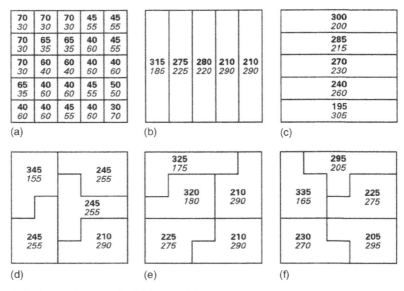

Fig. 8.7. A constituency-definition problem
Source: Johnston et al. (2001b, 25).

certain—after all, X has 51.6 per cent of the votes, but can only win 0, 20, 40, 60, 80, or 100 per cent of the five constituencies—but it is more 'extreme' in some cases than others. For example, in (b) and (c), X wins three of the constituencies to Y's two, so that with 51.4 per cent of the votes X gets 60 per cent of the seats while Y gets 40 per cent of the seats with 48.4 per cent of the votes: this is the smallest amount of disproportionality feasible. In (d), however, X wins only one seat while Y, with a minority of the votes cast, wins four, and in (e) and (f) the seats are split 3:2 in Y's favour, despite it being the 'losing' party in terms of votes cast.

Why can the 'winning' party in terms of votes cast be the loser in terms of seats allocated? The reason lies in the geography of the voting: X is the larger party, but its strength is very much concentrated in the north-west corner of the area. It has a majority of 40 votes over Y in five of the wards there, and of 30 in three others. Party Y is strongest in the south-east, but has a margin as large as 40 votes over its rival in just one ward. Where Y wins, it tends to win by 10–20 votes: its average margin of victory in the 14 wards where it is the leading party is just under 18 votes, compared to X, which wins in ten wards by an average of 33 votes. (There is a tie in one ward.) In other words, Y's votes are more efficiently distributed than X's. In three of the five sets of constituencies it gets a better return on its votes, because of where they were cast and where the constituency boundaries were drawn: as a result it wins a majority of the seats with a minority of the votes.

Of course, these are only five out of a large number of ways in which those 25 wards could be grouped into five equal-sized contiguous constituencies. Using a computer program specifically designed for the purpose (Rossiter and Johnston, 1981), we have identified a total of 4006 different constituency configurations. In 2100 of them, Party *Y* would win three of the seats, whereas in a further 1487 Party *X* would win three and Party *Y* two: in a small number of cases, one of the parties would get four seats to its opponent's one. (For more details, see Johnston et al., 2001b.) Thus, although *Y* is the smaller of the two parties in terms of electoral support, it is more likely to win a majority of the seats than its rival because of the geographies of support for the two parties.

This simple example clearly illustrates the role of the interaction of two geographies—of votes and of constituencies. Party *X* tends to be disadvantaged because too many of its votes are concentrated in one small corner of the map, but whether it is disadvantaged and to what extent depends on which constituency configuration is chosen. Party *Y*, on the other hand, tends to be advantaged: although it is the minority party, in terms of the translation of votes into seats it is more likely than not to be the winner—assuming that each constituency configuration is equally likely to be selected.[13] Where a party's votes are cast is crucial to its electoral success: it will not do well in terms of winning seats if it does not win a substantial proportion of the votes overall, but it will do better with a given percentage of the total if those votes are efficiently distributed. For a party with 51 per cent of the votes, for example, the most efficient distribution would be for it to win by 1 per cent in *every* constituency—100 per cent of the seats with 51 per cent of the votes. Of course, with such a small margin in every constituency, the loss of a few votes everywhere could lead to it losing every seat: it might be better if it won by 57:43 in four of the seats, and 'conceded' the fifth to its opponent by a margin of 27:73.

Because of where they are cast, therefore, some votes are more valuable than others. We can illustrate this by using a simple classification of votes into three types:

- *Wasted votes* are those that have no impact on a party's representation, because they do not help it to win seats: they are cast in the constituencies that it loses.

- *Surplus votes* similarly have no impact on how many seats a party wins, because they are additional to requirements in seats that it wins: if party *Y* gets 100 votes in a constituency, then *X* needs only 101 to defeat it, so if it gets 400, 299 of them are surplus to requirements.

---

[13] This is, of course, unlikely because Boundary Commissions prefer 'shapely' constituencies, on the grounds that these are easier for MPs and parties to service. In Figure 8.7, *X* 'performs' best in the less shapely constituencies in (a) and (b), which a Commission is less likely to favour: its disadvantage may be even greater than the overall pattern for the 4006 'solutions' identified in Johnston et al. (2001b) suggests.

• *Effective votes* are those that help a party to win seats—as with the 101 cited in the example of surplus votes.

For any party, therefore, the more wasted and surplus votes it gets, relative to its effective votes—and to those won by its opponent—the poorer its performance. Too few of its votes are being translated into seats, and in effect bring no returns: the party has campaigned for the votes but they have proved to be worthless.

This simple categorization can be used to analyse the five elections result in Figure 8.7 (b–f). In (b), for example, party X has 186, 226, and 221 effective votes in the five westernmost constituencies, associated with 129, 49, and 59 surplus votes; it has 210 wasted votes in each of the eastern constituencies. On average, it wastes 210 votes per seat lost and has a surplus of 95.3 per seat won: of its total of 1290 votes, 633 (49.1 per cent) are effective. Party Y also wastes an average of 210 votes in the three seats it loses, but averages only 79 surplus votes per seat won. It has 422 effective votes (211 in each of the two seats that it wins), comprising 34.9 per cent of its total, compared to 49.1 per cent for X. Perhaps not surprisingly, therefore, X gets more of the seats in that configuration. In configuration (c) too, X has a much larger share of its votes being effective than Y (50.2 to 36.1 per cent, respectively).

In the other three configurations, however, the situation is reversed: party Y's effective percentage is 78.4, 53.6, and 54.8 per cent, respectively in D, E, and F, compared to X's 12.1, 27.7, and 28.8. With a minority of the votes cast, Y is able to win more seats than X because many more of them are effective: they are in the right places. In (d), for example, Y wins four of the five seats because it has very few surplus votes where it is the victor—9 in three of the four and 79 in the other—whereas X's single victory produces 189 surplus votes and it averages 236 wasted votes in the four that it loses. Party Y wins three of the five seats in (e) and (f), because it has much smaller majorities there than X does in the two that it wins (an average surplus per seat won of 144 for X in configuration (e), for example as against 69 for Y in its three victories). The geography of where a party's votes are cast is therefore crucial to their influence on the electoral outcome.

We can derive a few 'general principles' from these simple illustrations. In a two-party system, a small party with less than, say, 30 per cent of the votes cast wants them to be concentrated in a few parts of the area only, so that it can win at least some seats: if it got 30 per cent of the votes everywhere, it would win nowhere. As a party's vote share increases, however, it needs them to be more evenly distributed across the constituencies: if they are 'piled' up in just one part of the area, then it may win some constituencies by large margins but may lose many more by less substantial percentages of the votes cast (i.e. it needs to be more like Y than X in Figure 8.7). And a larger party may still benefit from having its votes a little more concentrated: winning a clear majority of the seats by considerable margins (and therefore being relatively immune to small shifts in voter choices) and letting its opponent win the remainder fairly comfortably may be preferable to winning nearly all of the seats by smaller margins—and thus being open to losing many of them if there is a swing against the party at an election. In sum, large and small parties both benefit from their support being concentrated spatially; medium-sized parties get a greater advantage from a more even distribution of support. (An excellent full discussion of this argument is in Gudgin and Taylor, 1979.)

The efficiency of a party's vote distribution (its geography) is a key to its relative success or failure in the translation of votes into seats. The efficiency of a party's vote distribution could be deliberately created—by gerrymandering. But a comparable outcome can result through the non-partisan practice deployed in the UK (as described above) if the efficiency of their vote distributions across the constituencies varies by party. That can occur if one party's support is spatially more concentrated than others', because of either or both of compositional effects (parties varying in the extent to which their 'natural' supporters are spatially concentrated) and differential campaigning to make a party's vote distribution more efficient (as discussed further below).

Other factors can influence the efficiency of a party's vote distribution, however, and thereby contribute to disproportionality and bias. The first of these is the major reason why the UK government introduced regular reviews of constituency boundaries—inequalities in the size of constituency electorates. These size differences will not benefit one party over another, however, unless the geographies of party support are related to the pattern of constituency size. If one party is strongest in the areas where constituencies are on average small, then its votes may be more efficiently distributed than those of an opponent whose support is concentrated in areas of large constituencies. It takes fewer votes to win a small constituency than a large one, so a party that is strong in areas with small constituencies needs fewer votes to win than its opponent—it gets a better return (thinking of the seats:votes ratio as a cost:benefit equation) for its vote-winning than its opponent. This is illustrated by Figure 8.8, which uses the same 25 wards for constituency-building as Figure 8.7, but has two large constituencies in the west—where party X is strong—and three small ones in the east—where Y is strong. Party X wins only one seat—the largest, in the north-west: of its 1290 votes, only 301 (23.3 per cent) are effective, with the remainder being either surplus (23.2) or wasted (53.5). Party Y, on the other hand, wins four seats despite having a minority of the votes: of its 1210 votes, fully 57.3 per cent are effective, with 24.8 per cent wasted and 17.9 per cent surplus.

If equality of constituency electorates is one of the criteria that a Boundary Commission must operate, then there should be no long-term advantage for one of the parties as a consequence of it being the stronger in areas with smaller constituencies. It may emerge after each review, however, if

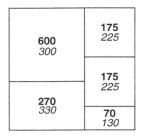

Fig. 8.8. A constituency-definition problem with malapportionment
Source: Johnston et al. (2001b, 42).

population change between elections means that on average the constituencies held by *Y* have fewer voters whereas those held by *X* expand. If this happens, then there is 'creeping malapportionment' whereby *Y* is increasingly favoured over *X* as the constituency boundaries age—something that will continue unless there is a redistribution. But malapportionment that favours one party over others may be built into the electoral system—as in the UK where, as already noted, the guarantee of a certain number of seats for Scotland and Wales for elections during the period 1950–2001 meant that a party that was strong in Scotland and Wales was likely to be advantaged over one that was stronger in England.

A variation on the impact of constituency size differences on an election outcome is produced by the geography of turnout. This may be the same across all constituencies, but it may vary, with the abstention rate greater in some areas than others. The greater the number of abstentions, the smaller the number of votes needed to win a constituency: with 100 voters and two parties contesting the seat, 51 votes are needed for victory if there is 100 per cent turnout; if 20 abstain, however, then only 41 votes are needed for victory among the 80 who do turn out. If abstention rates vary across the constituencies, then some seats will be easier to win than others in terms of vote totals, so that a party which is strong in areas of low turnout will benefit—it will need fewer votes on average to win there than a party whose strengths are in areas with relatively high turnout. The impact of 'third' or 'minor' parties operates in exactly the same way: the larger their support in a constituency, the smaller the number of votes being contested by the two main parties, and the fewer the number of votes needed for victory there. Thus, as with abstentions, a party that tends to be stronger in areas where 'third parties' are also strong will get a better return—in seats—for its vote total than one whose main support is concentrated in areas where 'third parties' attract few votes.

Disproportional election results come about because one party's votes are more effective than another's in the process of translating votes into seats, and that efficacy may be a function not only of where a party's votes are located within the matrix of constituencies but also variations among the constituencies in their size, in their turnout, and in the relative success of 'third parties'. Biased election results—as defined here—come about because one party is advantaged over another in the operation of these various factors. In the remainder of this chapter, we explore the relative importance of these factors in producting the biases identified in Figure 8.6 and how these biases have been produced.

Bias Decomposition and the Geography of the Vote

One of the advantages of the bias measure that we deploy here is that it can be decomposed into various components, which can be deployed to evaluate the relative importance of the size and efficiency elements of the system, and also the sub-components in the case of size—differences in constituency electorates, in abstention rates, and in the impact of 'third parties'. (The methodology was developed by Brookes, 1959, 1960, and adapted for the British situation in Johnston et al., 2001b; Rossiter, Johnston, and Pattie, 1999b) This decomposition can be done for comparisons of the two main parties with any vote share: we can evaluate the relative importance of the components when the parties have equal vote shares, when either gets 45 per cent of the votes cast, and so forth. Here, we concentrate on the situation with equal vote shares as our baseline indicator of the degree of bias in the system: would the Conservatives and Labour have obtained the same number of seats if they had an equal share of the votes cast (assuming a uniform movement of votes from one to the other across all constituencies), and if not, why not?

The Impact of Size

The size of constituency electorates can vary for a number of reasons, as described above. The bias decomposition procedure identifies the impact of each, in terms of the number of seats that one party is advantaged over the other.

Differences in Constituency Size

Looking first at what we term the 'pure size effect' (differences between constituencies in their numbers of electors), in Great Britain this can be split into two sub-components. As already noted, the 1944 legislation establishing the procedures for defining constituencies guaranteed Scotland and Wales a minimum number of seats each, and this was clarified by an amendment to the Act passed in 1958. This does not reflect an explicit decision to allow over-representation for Scotland and Wales relative to England; it was rather based on an initial decision not to reduce the number of MPs from each of those countries relative to the situation before the original legislation (on which see McLean, 1995). Because subsequent population changes have seen England grow relative to Scotland and Wales, the average constituency size in England has increased from 58,734 electors after the first Boundary Commission review in 1947 to 68,626 after the fifth in 1995 (a 17 per cent increase), whereas in Scotland the average constituency increased from 49,620 to 54,569 (a 9 per cent increase) and the comparable figures for Wales were 51,641 and 55,559 (7 per cent). The rules under which the Commissions have to operate meant that, under the 1958 legislation, the gap could not be closed. (On this issue see Butler and McLean, 1996; McLean, 1995; McLean and Mortimore, 1992; Rossiter, Johnston, and Pattie, 1999a.) However, in 2005—the final election in our sequence—the Scottish advantage was removed, with the reduction in the country's constituencies from 72 to 59; the average English constituency then had 70,200 electors and in Scotland the comparable figure was 65,287, as against 55,762 in Wales.[14]

Irrespective of the between-country variations, there are also differences between constituency electorates within each country. The Boundary Commissions conduct their reviews every decade or so to reduce these (it is virtually impossible to eliminate them entirely because of the procedures, as described above). But populations change, through ageing and migration processes. In particular, over the 55-year period being studied here many of the country's largest cities have lost population very substantially, especially from their inner-city areas, whereas the suburban areas and some rural districts, especially those adjacent to the main conurbations (plus other accessible areas), have gained. Because of this, the geography of parliamentary representation has changed: Greater London had 115 MPs in 1945, for example, but only 74 in 1995, whereas the number in the south-east region outside London increased from 53 to 83. Such shifts are episodic, however, whereas population changes are continuous. Thus as constituencies 'age' after a Boundary Commission review, so the variations between their electorates increase. Furthermore, because the Commissions have to use electoral data for a date fixed at the start of a review, which may take up to five years, the constituencies have usually 'aged' long before they are first used. The constituencies first used in the 1997 general election in England were defined using 1990 data, for example, and were still being used, 15 years on, at the 2005 election.

Are these between- and within-country differences important with regard to electoral bias, and which party do they favour? As far as between-country differences are concerned, Labour has been the strongest party in Wales throughout the period studied, with a very clear majority over the

---

[14] Scottish and Welsh constituencies still on average had fewer voters because the Boundary Commissions are allowed to create constituencies with smaller electorates in areas of low population density, such as the Highlands, the Western Isles, and Orkney and Shetland.

Conservatives at every election since 1950, though the gap was much smaller in 1983. It has also been the largest party in Scotland since the 1960s, but for most of the period the difference between the Conservatives and Labour in England has been small. In terms of bias, therefore, Labour should have been advantaged by the smaller electorates in Scottish and Welsh constituencies than in English ones. Within each of the three countries, Labour—with its relative strength among the working class as against the middle classes—has always gained more votes in urban than suburban and rural areas. Given that the former have tended to lose population whereas the suburban and rural areas have gained, then Labour should also have been increasingly advantaged the longer the time gap between a Boundary Commission review and the next election. The older the constituencies, the larger the variation in the electorates and the greater the potential benefit for Labour.

Labour, then, should have an advantage in the translation of votes into seats because of differences in the size of the electorates in the constituencies it represents compared with Conservative constituencies. The basis for this expected advantage is exemplified in Table 8.3, which has two blocks of constituency data for the 2001 election: the first gives averages for the seats that the two parties actually won; the two right-hand columns give averages for the seats that they would have won with equal vote shares (the basis of our bias calculations). In each case, the average Labour-held constituency was several thousand electors smaller than that won by the Conservatives.

The contributions of the two components of constituency size variations to bias over all 16 elections are shown in Figure 8.9. That resulting from differences between Scotland and Wales on the one hand and England on

Table 8.3. Contributors to constituency size bias estimates at the 2001 general election

	Seats won			
	Actual		Hypothetical[a]	
Contributory factors	Labour	Conservative	Labour	Conservative
Average constituency electorate	65,708	72,021	65,155	71,611
Abstainers				
Average	28,412	26,590	28,742	26,327
As % of electorate	43.3	37.0	44.2	36.8
Other party vote				
Average	7632	11,651	7638	11,184
As % of electorate	20.9	25.3	21.4	24.4
Majority over other main party				
Average	10,349	9025	7976	10,921
As % of votes cast	29.8	19.6	23.61	23.81

[a] Seats that would have been won with equal vote shares.

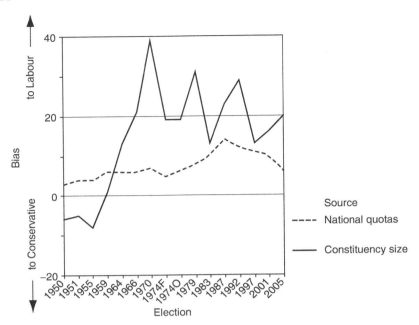

Fig. 8.9. The size bias components in British general election results, 1950–2005

the other—termed national quotas in the graph—has always favoured Labour (a positive figure): it increased until 1992 and then declined somewhat. At the first two elections (1950 and 1951) it benefited Labour by 3 and 4 seats only; it increased to 10 seats by 1983 and peaked at 14 in 1987, before falling back again to 10 in 2001 and then 6 in 2005, when the English–Scottish differential was much reduced. Labour's growing electoral dominance in Scotland over the five decades, along with its continued predominance in Wales, was a major contributor to the increase. Within-country differences in constituency electorates made only a small contribution to the bias in the 1950s, which favoured the Conservatives (Figure 8.9); from then on, however, they favoured Labour, by as much as 39 seats (in 1970). The initial pro-Conservative bias resulted from a decision by the Boundary Commission for England at its early reviews to create constituencies with slightly fewer electors in rural than urban areas—on the grounds that low-density rural areas were harder for MPs to service than more compact, high-density urban constituencies. This practice was discontinued at later reviews, and Labour was then favoured because of its relative strength in the urban areas.

The size of the pro-Labour bias from 1959 on varied over time, with the low points reflecting the reduction in the size variations by the Boundary Commission reviews, which cut the number of constituencies in areas of population decline and increased them in areas of growth. New constituencies were introduced for the February 1974 general election, for example, and the size bias was 20 seats smaller than it had been in 1970. Similarly, the new constituencies in 1983 saw a reduction in the pro-Labour bias from 31 to 13 seats (as always, assuming equal vote shares between Labour and the Conservatives), and those used for the first time in 1997 resulted in a similar reduction from 29 to 13. In 2001, with constituencies that were four years older than in 1997, the pro-Labour bias had grown again by three seats, and in 2005 it increased by a further four.

Since 1959 this bias component has never been less than 13 seats, which was the figure in 1964, and again in 1983 and 1997 (both of which were the first to be fought with new boundaries). This suggests an inbuilt pro-Labour bias of about 13 seats resulting from the Commission's failure to achieve full equality of electorates because of:

- the use of wards as building blocks;
- the need to constrain constituencies within the major local authorities (although the Commissions are increasingly prepared to cross their boundaries—as in London at each of the last two reviews—in order to prevent gross inequalities);
- the ageing of constituency electorates, which comes about because of the Commissions' lengthy timetables—approximately five years in the English case for both of the most recent reviews.

One interesting feature of the saw-tooth trend in the within-country bias figures in Figure 8.9 is that whereas the size of the pro-Labour bias was 31 and 29 seats, respectively at the last election before each of the most recent reviews (the 1979 and 1992 elections, respectively), in 1970 it was 39 seats. This is because the constituencies deployed then were very old, having been used for the first time in 1955. Boundary Commission reviews were completed in good time for the 1970 election to be fought in new constituencies, but although the recommendations were delivered in 1969, they were not implemented. The Labour government had calculated that an election fought on the new set of boundaries could cost it up to 20 seats and so, by a series of parliamentary manoeuvres, it managed to delay their introduction. The election was fought in the 'old' constituencies to Labour's considerable benefit, as Figure 8.9 shows—but Labour lost the election in any case! (For further details on this partisan interference with the redistribution process—and other attempts to influence the process by both main parties—see Johnston et al., 2001b; Rossiter, Johnston, and Pattie, 1999a.)

The Geography of Abstentions and Electoral Bias

The first of the indirect impacts of variations in constituency size to be addressed here concerns abstentions. Chapter 7 showed that turnout tends to be lower in Labour-held than Conservative-held seats, for several reasons.

First, individuals in the social groups that tend to favour Labour rather than the Conservatives are also more likely to abstain because of alienation from the electoral system. Secondly, Labour supporters are traditionally less likely to go out and vote unless pressed to do so by party canvassers; Conservative supporters are more likely to turn out, whatever the nature of the contest in their local constituency. Thirdly, much of the large drop in turnout since 1992 has been in safe Labour-held constituencies, where the party has not campaigned and canvassed hard: victory there is almost certain.

Data from the 2001 election confirm these expected patterns. Table 8.3 identifies some 2000 more abstainers in seats that were won by Labour rather than the Conservatives and also in those that would have been won by Labour rather than the Conservatives with equal vote shares. Furthermore, as already demonstrated, Labour-held constituencies ('actual' and with equal vote shares) tend to have smaller electorates in any case than those won by the Conservatives, and this differential is reflected in the percentages of abstainers in the two types of seats in 2001—the percentage of the electorate not voting was some 6 percentage points higher in Labour- than Conservative-held seats.

Figure 8.10 shows that the geography of abstentions was to Labour's advantage at every election from 1955 on. (Turnout rates were both very high in 1950 and 1951 and varied little across the constituencies.) As turnout fell nationally, so the benefit to Labour increased: by 1964 it was worth 10 seats in the bias calculations and it stabilized at 16–17 seats across the next

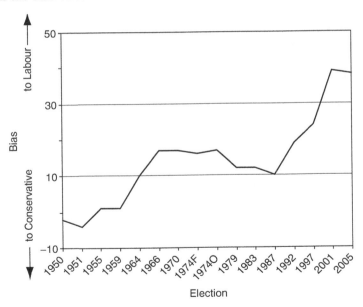

Fig. 8. 10. The abstentions bias component in British general election results, 1950–2005

four elections. There was a drop to an advantage of only 10–12 seats at the three elections won by the Conservatives under Margaret Thatcher's leadership, but it then increased rapidly again, reaching a peak of 39 seats in 2001, more than double the figure only a decade earlier. It fell by just one seat in 2005 (when, because of the reduction of Scottish representation, the total number of constituencies was cut by 13). Labour has thus been a substantial beneficiary of the increasingly low turnouts: as a consequence of more people abstaining, it has gained greater returns from the votes that it gets, relative to the Conservatives.

This substantial return to Labour from the abstentions component—more than one-third of the net bias in 2005 (39 seats out of a net total of 111: see Figure 8.6)—focuses attention on a major contemporary feature of this situation. After the 2005 general election, in which Labour got 36.2 per cent of the votes in Britain and 56.5 per cent of the seats, compared to 33.2 and 31.4 per cent, respectively for the Conservatives, there was considerable public discussion regarding the causes of this obvious bias. Most attention focused on variations in constituency size, it being pointed out that it took on average some 27,000 voters to elect a Labour MP (the party's total vote share divided by its number of seats), as against 44,000 for a Conservative and 97,000 for a Liberal Democrat. (Furthermore, the Conservatives actually outpolled Labour in England by some 66,000 votes but got 92 fewer seats.) The reason, it was suggested, was differences in constituency size, and it was argued that the Boundary Commissions should be directed to ensure greater equality of constituency electorates so as to remove that pro-Labour advantage.

To evaluate whether this was so, the 627 constituencies in Great Britain (excluding that held by the Speaker) were divided into quintiles on both electorate size and turnout, with the number of seats that Labour would have won with equal vote shares indicated (Johnston, Rossiter, and Pattie, 2006). The row totals in Table 8.4 show that Labour would have won 117 of the 126 seats with the lowest turnouts as against only 18 of the 125 with the

Table 8.4. The number of seats that would have been won by Labour at the 2005 general election with equal vote shares, by constituency size and turnout (both in quintiles)

Turnout	Electorate size					
	Smallest	2	3	4	Largest	Total
Lowest	46/49	29/30	21/22	9/11	9/12	117/126
2	23/28	27/31	25/29	6/10	6/10	102/125
3	16/22	16/22	12/21	12/32	12/32	69/126
4	5/13	5/19	8/28	5/31	5/34	28/125
Highest	4/13	4/23	7/26	2/25	1/38	18/125
Total	94/125	81/125	73/126	53/125	33/126	334/627

highest. A similar, if less extreme, pattern emerges with size of electorate as the variable of interest: Labour would have won 94 of the 125 smallest seats and 33 of the 126 largest. Combining the two, the internal cells indicate Labour's predominance in the smallest seats with the lowest turnouts. (There is a correlation between the two variables: there are 49 constituencies in the top-left-hand cell, for example—the seats with the smallest electorates and lowest turnouts—instead of the 25 which would be the case if the two were independent.) The argument was, at best, only partly right, therefore: Labour did benefit from its relative strength in the areas with small constituencies, but benefited much more from being the leading party in nearly all of the constituencies with low turnout.

'Third Parties' and Electoral Bias

Votes for 'third parties' act in the same way as abstentions in their potential impact on electoral bias: if they are concentrated in constituencies where one of the two main parties is stronger than the other, they benefit the former. In Great Britain as a whole, the Liberal Democrats and their predecessors have been relatively strong in some rural and suburban areas, though not all of them by any means: with a few exceptions (such as Southwark, won at a by-election against a divided Labour party in 1983 and retained since) they have not performed well in inner-city areas. As a consequence, the constituencies where they have performed relatively well have tended to be those where the Conservatives were stronger than Labour. This was shown in Table 8.3, which included the average number of votes and share of the vote for 'other parties' (i.e. the Liberal Democrats, Plaid Cymru, the Scottish National Party, and all other parties, including independents) in seats won by the Conservatives and Labour and those that they would have won with equal vote shares in 2001.

The implication is that the larger the share of the vote for 'third parties', the larger the benefit in terms of the bias calculations to the Conservative party. However, if these parties win seats, this should then be at the Conservatives' expense—an argument sustained by the 2001 situation. The Liberal Democrats won 52 seats then, in 43 of which the Conservatives came second; similarly, four of the SNP's five victories were in constituencies where the Conservatives came second. In Wales, however, three of Plaid Cymru's four successes were in seats where Labour occupied second place and the Liberal Democrats came second in the other. Overall, therefore, whereas 'third-party' vote-winning may assist the Conservatives in the creation of a biased outcome, if the 'third parties' start to win seats, this could operate against the Conservatives, to Labour's benefit.

Figure 8.11 traces the impact of these two elements of the third-party effect over the 16 elections and indicates the expected consequences. The 'third-party' share of the vote increased substantially after 1970. At the first seven elections in the sequence, the Conservative and Labour parties together averaged 92.2 per cent of the votes and 98.7 per cent of the seats. From then

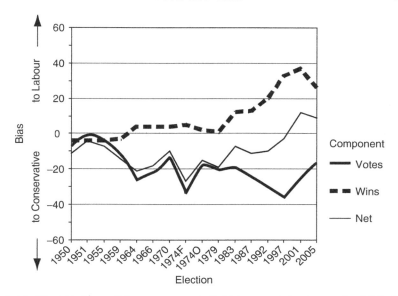

Fig. 8. 11. The 'third party' bias component in British general election results, 1950–2005

on, their combined share of the votes cast only once topped 80 per cent (in 1979) and it averaged 75.7—falling below 70 per cent in 2005. Their share of the seats declined much less, however, averaging 94 per cent over the nine post-1970 elections and falling below 90 per cent only in 2005. Disproportionality increased substantially and provided the potential for an increase in bias, therefore, as the loss of votes was not paralleled by the loss of seats: the latter were made 'cheaper', and it was open to one of the two main parties to benefit more than the other from that. As the 'third-party' vote share increased, this generated a pro-Conservative bias—from just three seats in 1955 to a maximum of 36 in 1997. There were reductions in 2001 and 2005, however, as the Liberal Democrats increasingly targeted Labour-held seats in some major cities (such as Liverpool, and Newcastle-upon-Tyne). This reduced the Conservative advantage to 25 and then 17 seats.

Whereas the geography of 'third-party' votes favoured the Conservatives, 'third-party' wins operated to Labour's advantage: most of the seats won by the 'third parties' would otherwise have been captured by the Conservatives, with equal vote shares, so those losses benefited Labour in the calculation of bias. Figure 8.11 indicates that, as seat-winning by 'third parties' increased from the 1970s on, Labour received an increased bias: this was worth only 4–5 seats in the equal-share calculations up to 1979 (and just one then), but after that the benefit increased rapidly, reaching 37 seats in 2001. 'Third-party' victories, because they tended to be at the Conservatives' expense, substantially increased the pro-Labour bias—until 2005, when several Liberal Democrat victories in seats that would otherwise have been won by Labour (and had been at previous contests) reduced the advantage substantially to 26 seats.

These two bias components work in opposite directions: vote-winning by 'third parties' has helped the Conservatives; their seat winning has assisted Labour. The net impact of the two is shown in Figure 8.11: for most of the 55-year period the advantage lay with the Conservatives, since the 'third parties' were increasing their share of the votes but not winning many seats. As more seats were won by parties other than the main two, however, the pro-Conservative advantage was reduced, so much so that by 2001 the net benefit (of 12 seats) was with Labour. That was reduced four years later to nine seats, indicating that the Liberal Democrats (by far the most important of the 'third parties' across Great Britain as a whole) have begun to erode both of the main parties' hold on some of their seats. If this trend continues, the net impact of the 'third parties' may turn out to be neutral.

Vote Efficiency

Whereas the size component of the bias calculations can be split into several sub-components, the efficiency component remains a single element. As suggested earlier, the main beneficiary will be the party with the smallest number of surplus and wasted votes (once the size effects have been taken into account): having too many of each is inefficient since neither type of vote wins seats. Thus the bias component should favour the party that has relatively few very safe seats and wins a large majority of its constituencies by fairly small majorities—though as noted above, winning by small majorities can be a disadvantage if there is a swing of support against the party.

Of the two main parties, Labour should be the least likely to benefit from an efficient vote distribution: well into the late twentieth century it retained much of the geography of support on which it had built its electoral foundations. As it sought to replace the Liberals as the Conservatives' main opponent in the century's first decades, it benefited from building up a strong support base in Britain's industrial areas, notably the coalfields. These provided it with a solid platform for further development in 1945, when it captured large numbers of votes outside the inner cities, coalfields, and industrial centres, winning its first-ever parliamentary majority. The safe seats in the coalfields and elsewhere remained, however, and Labour continued to recruit large numbers of surplus votes there, with the aid of the trades unions, which mobilized large bodies of voters to go to the polls. At the same time, although it established firm bases in many other parts of the country, these were insufficient to be translated into many constituency victories (at least until 1966, to some extent, and then 1997) and it garnered many wasted votes there: the Conservatives won by comfortable majorities, but not as large as those in many of Labour's heartland seats. Thus Labour had more surplus and wasted votes per seat won and lost, respectively than its main opponent, although the latter were reduced somewhat in the 1980s, when Labour's support dwindled fast in much of southern England, where the Liberal Democrats became the main party of opposition.

The efficiency component of the bias calculations should have favoured the Conservative party, therefore, which is what occurred until 1997 (with one exception—the somewhat anomalous February 1974 election, when Labour won the largest number of seats but the Conservatives got more votes). From then on there was a massive shift (Figure 8.12). In 1997 the component generated 48 seats in the bias calculation to Labour, and in 2001 it generated 72; it was cut in half to 35 seats in 2005, just less than the abstentions component but nevertheless still comprising one-third of the total pro-Labour bias. Why was it that (as we saw in Table 8.3) by 2001 Labour was winning seats with smaller majorities than the Conservatives when they had equal vote shares? (Note, though, that the two parties' majorities were almost the same when expressed as percentages of the votes cast, because the Conservatives tended to win in the larger constituencies with higher turnout.) To a large extent, Labour created its own success. In part this was through its participation in the Boundary Commission process. It had become the received wisdom that the Conservative party was the main beneficiary from each redistribution, largely because of the removal of the constituency size differential. The Conservatives assumed that this would again be the case with the reviews that began in 1990, which produced the constituencies first used at the 1997 contest. But Labour workers realized that the Conservatives'

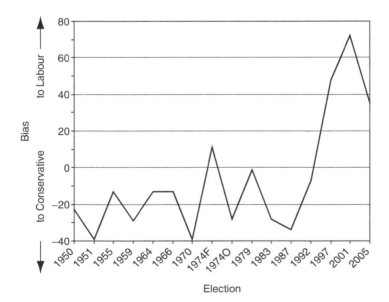

Fig. 8.12. The efficiency bias component in British general election results, 1950–2005

advantage could be nullified somewhat if they put up alternative schemes for each part of the country that would favour Labour's electoral prospects and then supported these with strong arguments at the public inquiries. This strategy succeeded: the Conservatives were outflanked and the new map of parliamentary constituencies was much more favourable to Labour than might otherwise have been the case—in effect, Labour achieved something of a gerrymander in some parts of the country (on which see Rossiter, Johnston, and Pattie, 1999a).

Success with the Boundary Commissions was only worth some 10–20 seats to Labour in the efficiency bias component, however. Much of the rest was generated through the party's campaigning tactics at the 1997–2005 elections. These had two main elements. The first was a function of the party's own efforts: Labour decided to concentrate on the seats that it needed to win in 1997 (and then retain in 2001 and 2005) in order to obtain an overall majority. Hopeless seats where it had no chance of victory were substantially ignored—as shown by the data on campaign spending discussed in Chapter 6. Although the local party organizations there wanted to perform well (as did their candidates), they received little central support: they were lost causes and wasted votes were not worth much effort soliciting. Similarly in Labour's very safe seats: it seemed rather pointless to work hard and turn out a large number of Labour supporters and so garner lots of surplus votes: a solid majority was needed, but no more, and resources were redirected to where they might bring greater benefits. Labour campaigned to make its vote distribution more efficient—and succeeded.[15]

In this, Labour was substantially assisted in many places by the Liberal Democrats through an implicit (more often explicit on the Liberal Democrats' part) policy of promoting tactical voting in many Conservative-held seats. Where it was clear that one of the two opposition parties had a much better chance than the other of unseating a Conservative incumbent and so removing the Conservative government in 1997, supporters of the third-placed party were encouraged to switch to the second-placed. The strategy worked in many places, as discussed in Chapters 1 and 6 (pp. 23 and 205) and shown in Table 8.5. The Conservative share of the vote fell by about the same amount across all constituencies that it held after the 1992 election. The Labour vote also increased by about the same amount (12–13 percentage points) in each of the seats where it came second in 1992, whatever the margin of the Conservative victory; it increased by much less in the seats where the Liberal Democrats occupied second place, and thus were best situated to remove the incumbents, especially those held by the Conservatives by small majorities. And whereas the Liberal Democrat share of the vote fell in all of the Conservative-held seats where Labour

---

[15] See, for example, Johnston et al. (2002b) on the amounts of campaigning done by incumbent MPs in relatively marginal constituencies, and its apparent impact.

Table 8.5. Change in party share of the vote, 1992–7, in Conservative-held seats, by second-placed party in 1992 and margin of victory then

| | Second-placed party 1992 | | | | | |
| | Labour Change in vote, 1992–7 (%) | | | Liberal Democrat Change in vote, 1992–7 (%) | | |
Margin 1992 (%)	Con	Lab	Lib Dem	Con	Lab	Lib Dem
<5	−13	12	−2	−12	5	2
5–10	−11	12	−2	−10	4	3
10–19	−13	13	−4	−12	7	1
20+	−13	13	−3	−13	9	0

occupied second place, it increased in those where it was lying second, especially the most marginal. The strategy worked again in 2001, when many Labour and Liberal Democrat supporters voted for the best-placed candidate of the pair (usually an incumbent) to keep the Conservative candidate out, and was largely repeated in 2005 (Fisher and Curtice, 2005).

Tactical voting contributed substantially to Labour benefiting from the efficiency component of the bias calculation at those three elections because it meant that Labour's wasted vote total shrank considerably. In seats where Labour was likely to come, at best, a reasonable third, if its supporters switched to the Liberal Democrats then Labour would come a poor third, with few wasted votes—but the Liberal Democrats might win. Similarly, where Labour was best placed to defeat the Conservatives, tactical voting defectors from the Liberal Democrats may have made this feasible: instead of perhaps coming a good second, with many wasted votes, Labour was a comfortable winner, with a fairly small number of surplus votes. (For a more technical discussion of this, see Johnston et al., 2002a.)

Tactical voting is only a viable strategy when there are two (or more) parties whose supporters are prepared to combine in order to defeat another. This is not the case for the Conservatives at present: in the early 1980s some Liberal Democrat (then Alliance) supporters voted Conservative tactically in order to prevent a Labour constituency victory—and vice versa. But since the 1990s there has been no party with sufficient support that could act as a partner for the Conservatives: if they were to win elections, it had to be by their own efforts. (Indeed, the Conservatives lost votes to parties on the 'right'—the Referendum party in 1997 and the UK Independence party in 2001 and 2005.) This meant that efficient campaigns along the lines deployed by Labour and the Liberal Democrats had to be designed—focusing on key seats that could be won and lost. This was the party's goal in 2001 and, especially, 2005, but it was not particularly successful.

Overall, the Conservative vote share in 2005 increased by less than 1 percentage point on its 2001 performance, so to increase its share of seats it needed to improve the efficiency of its vote total. Table 8.6 suggests that it was only partly successful in doing this—its share increased by 1.37 and 2.44 points, respectively in the most marginal seats (won by less than 5 percentage points in 2001) held by Labour and the Liberal Democrats, and with the Conservatives in second place. But it also increased its vote share by more than the national average in most of its own safe seats, which—having been won by majorities of 10 percentage points or more in 2001—were not under threat. Increased efficiency in the marginal seats was therefore not matched in the safe seats, where more surplus votes were amassed.

Putting it all Together

Disproportionality and bias in election results come about because a larger percentage of one party's votes is effective than is another's. Each party has two types of ineffective votes: those surplus to requirements in seats that it wins, and those wasted where it loses. The party most favoured by the system is the one that minimizes its surplus and wasted votes. Increasingly over the 55-year period studied here that party has been Labour. It now attracts many fewer surplus and wasted votes than it did earlier in the period and has a much more effective vote total.

Three graphs illustrate this shift. The first (Figure 8.13) shows the average number of surplus votes per seat won across the constituencies where the party would have been victorious with an equal share of the votes. With the exception of 1970, Labour has traditionally garnered many more of these votes because of the large majorities in its safe seats; this was very much the case in 1983 and 1987 when the 'Thatcher landslides' pressed Labour back into its safe-seat heartlands in the coalfields and industrial cities. But by 2001 Labour was getting fewer surplus votes per seat won than the Conservatives,

Table 8.6. Mean change in Conservative share of the vote by constituency, 2001–5 (percentage points), by result of the 2001 election there

	Winner 2001					
	Conservative		Labour		Liberal Democrat	
	Second 2001		Second 2001		Second 2001	
Margin 2001 (% points)	Lab	LD	Con	LD	Con	Lab
0–4.99	—	−1.53	1.37	−1.63	2.44	—
5–9.99	−0.93	1.02	0.78	−3.00	1.76	1.36
10–14.99	−1.05	2.75	−0.12	−1.82	0.63	4.92
15–19.99	0.88	2.68	−0.19	−1.55	−1.10	—
20+	2.10	1.41	−1.20	−0.43	−1.42	−2.97

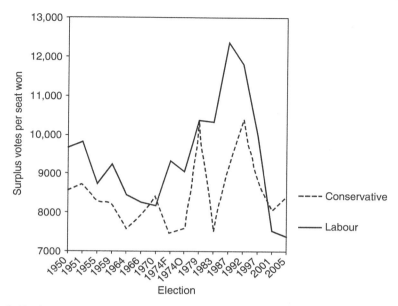

Fig. 8.13. Average number of surplus votes per seat won, with equal vote shares, 1950–2005

and in 2005 the difference between the two was about 1000 votes. Labour had ceased to campaign hard for votes that would be surplus to requirements in its safe seats,[16] and the Conservatives in turn had been pressed back into their safe-seat heartlands, where the absence of much active campaigning by the other parties meant that the Conservative vote share and majority increased (Table 8.6). With regard to wasted votes per seat lost, the difference between the two parties has been small at many of the elections (Figure 8.14)—but where there has been a difference, until 1997 it was largely to Labour's disadvantage.

Effective votes are those that win seats. Figure 8.15 shows each party's number of effective votes with equal vote shares, expressed as a percentage of its total number of votes won (the remainder are surplus and wasted votes). For much of the period, on average some 42 per cent of the Conservatives' votes were effective, whereas for Labour the figure was about four points lower at 38. In the late 1970s and the 1980s, Labour's percentage fell even further, widening the gap between the two parties to over eight points. The gap was then rapidly closed so that by 1997 both parties had the same

---

[16] Labour's campaigning strategy was aided by other changes. With the closure of most of the mines, for example, not only were there very few mining seats to deliver large Labour majorities but the trades unions that had pressed for high turnout in those areas had been largely eliminated.

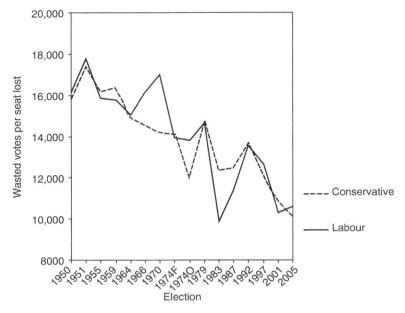

Fig. 8.14. Average number of wasted votes per seat lost, with equal vote shares, 1950–2005

percentage—38. In 2001 it widened again, but in the other direction: the Conservatives had their lowest effective vote percentage and Labour much their highest—with a gap between the two of over six points. In 2005, the Conservatives closed this gap only slightly and Labour retained a substantial advantage.

Bias may be built into the electoral system, therefore, but it may not be consistent in its direction. This is clearly illustrated in Figure 8.16, which shows the separate sum of the bias components that favoured each party across the 16 elections (i.e. the sums of the positive values for Labour and of the negative values for the Conservatives, as explained on p. 274). In the 1950s, there were virtually no benefits for Labour, whereas the Conservatives benefited by an average of some 50 seats. For the next two decades, the two parties benefited almost equally—Labour from constituency size variations (between and within countries) and from differences in turnout, the Conservatives from the efficiency component and the impact of 'third-party' votes. The two groups more or less balanced out. And then there was a further shift: the advantages to the Conservatives fell somewhat whereas Labour's boomed. The total amount of bias (the sum of the biases to the individual parties, irrespective of sign) in the system also increased, with a nearly fivefold increase from the lowest value (43 seats in 1955) to the largest (199

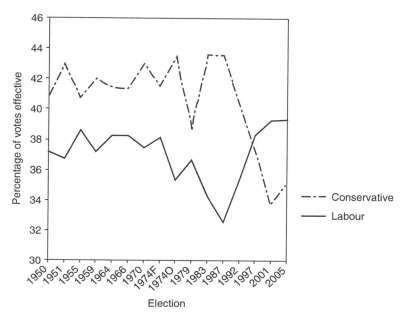

Fig. 8.15. Percentage of each party's votes that were effective, with equal vote shares, 1950–2005

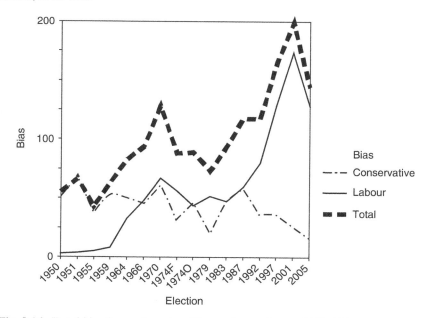

Fig. 8.16. Total bias for each party with equal vote shares, 1950–2005

in 2001). At the beginning of the twenty-first century, the British electoral system is delivering more biased election results than ever before.[17]

Conclusions

Labour's landslide victories of 1997 and 2001 and its substantial majority in 2005 owe much to geography, therefore. This is not because the system is constructed to favour Labour (whether intentionally or not): the system has not changed since 1950 and Labour has only benefited markedly since 1992. Instead, Labour has done much to create the geographical conditions that produced its landslide victories—whether through its influence on the Boundary Commissions, its carefully targeted and spatially focused campaigns, its willingness to accept low turnout in many constituencies (whatever the rhetoric about the challenge to democracy posed by high abstention rates), and its (implicit) preparedness to participate in tactical voting strategies. Labour's victories in 1997 and 2001 would not have happened if it had not won just over two-fifths of the votes and the Conservatives less than a third, and its 2005 success (especially its substantial majority) relied on its winning the largest vote share. But the size of those victories reflected Labour's success in making so many of its votes effective, both more effective than they had been at previous elections and more effective than the votes the Conservatives had for so long enjoyed.

The system certainly assisted Labour to some extent, notably through the variations in constituency size. These have aided Labour since the 1960s, increasingly so as each set of constituencies has aged and variations in their electorates have grown, because much of the core of Labour's electoral support is in those parts of the country that tend to lose electors over time—through a combination of deaths exceeding people reaching voting age and net migration. Until the 1990s, though, this benefit that was apparently built into the system was only sufficient to more or less cancel out the benefits accruing to the Conservatives from other bias components. From then on, Labour 'made its own luck'—with some help from the Liberal Democrats: it focused its vote-winning efforts geographically, and was thus able to ensure that its vote total was not only much more efficiently distributed than ever before, but also that it replaced the Conservatives—for long lauded as the best 'electoral machine' in the country—as the most efficient party.[18]

Geographies don't exist, they are made. From the mid-1990s on the Labour party was involved in the creation of a new geography—of voter

---

[17] Bias was generally low in the first half of the century, but did reach 100 in 1929 (Johnston et al., 2003).

[18] All the analyses presented here to sustain that conclusion are based on analyses of biases at the equal vote share point: however, evaluations of the robustness of the findings indicate that whereas the bias tends to be largest at that point, it is also large at other vote shares (Johnston et al., 2002a).

support. Until then, the geography of voting Labour was inefficient—it had too many votes in the wrong places; since 1992, it has generated an efficient distribution—it has many more votes in the right places (Johnston et al., 2002a). It is thus inaccurate to blame the system for Labour's electoral successes since 1997, particularly the size of its majorities. It has been helped by the system—particularly by the size differences among constituency electorates—but much of its success must be put down to its ability to operate within the system to its great advantage, whereas its main opponent has not been able to. Small changes to the current system would thus not remove the potential for Labour—or any other party—to benefit from the potential advantages that its geography offers. Larger changes—such as compulsory voting—might remove some of them, as, of course, might more sweeping electoral reform, involving a totally new system. None is entirely geography-free, however.

APPENDIX: THE BRITISH ELECTION STUDY

Political Knowledge

Political knowledge was assessed using responses to the following true/false statements:

- The number of MPs in the House of Commons is about 100. (false)
- The longest time permitted between general elections is four years. (false)
- Great Britain's electoral system uses proportional representation. (false)
- MPs from different parties sit on parliamentary committees. (true)
- No individual can be on the electoral roll in two different places. (false).
- Great Britain holds different elections for the Euro and British parliaments. (true)
- Women are not allowed to sit in the House of Lords. (false)
- The Queen appoints the British prime minister. (true)
- No one is allowed to stand for Parliament unless they pay a deposit. (true)
- A Minister of State is senior to a Secretary of State. (false)

Political Attitudes

The following questions were used to assess political attitudes:

- Do you think Britain should continue to be a member of the European Community or should it withdraw?
- On the whole, do you think Britain's interests are better served by closer links with Western Europe or closer links with America?
- Do you think Britain's long-term policy should be to leave the European Community, to stay in the EC and try and reduce its powers, to leave things as they are, to stay in the EC and try to increase its powers, or to work for the formation of a single European government?
- Here are three statements about the future of the pound in the EC. Which one comes closest to your view?
- Replace the pound by a single currency.
- Use both the pound and a new European currency in Britain.
- Keep the pound as the only currency for Britain.
- (agree/disagree) If we stay in the EC, Britain will lose control over decisions that affect Britain.
- (agree/disagree) The competition from other EC countries is making Britain more modern and efficient.
- (agree/disagree) Lots of good British traditions will have to be given up if we stay in the EC.
- Government (definitely should/shouldn't) get rid of private education in Britain.
- Government (definitely should/shouldn't) spend more money to get rid of poverty.

- Government (definitely should/shouldn't) encourage the growth of private medicine.
- Government (definitely should/shouldn't) put more money into the NHS.
- Government (definitely should/shouldn't) spend more money on education.
- Government (definitely should/shouldn't) introduce stricter laws to regulate the activity of trade unions.
- Government (definitely should/shouldn't) give workers more say in running the places where they work.
- (agree/disagree) Income and wealth should be redistributed towards ordinary working people.
- (agree/disagree) The government should give more aid to poor countries in Africa and Asia.
- (agree/disagree) If you want to cut crime, cut unemployment.
- (agree/disagree) Britain should bring back the death penalty.
- (agree/disagree) People who break the law should be given stiffer sentences.
- (agree/disagree) The middle classes and the working classes will always be on opposite sides in politics.
- Do you think that local councils ought to be controlled by central government more, less, or about the same as now?
- Thinking about the poll tax, or community charge, which of these statements comes closest to your view? The poll tax was: a good idea and should never have been abandoned; a good idea, but was too unpopular to keep; a bad idea and should never have been introduced.
- (Gone too far/not gone far enough) the welfare benefits that are available to people today.
- (Gone too far/not gone far enough) attempts to give equal opportunities to women in Britain.
- (Gone too far/not gone far enough) the right to show nudity and sex in films and magazines.
- (Gone too far/not gone far enough) the building of nuclear power stations.
- (Gone too far/not gone far enough) attempts to give equal opportunities to black people and Asians in Britain.
- (Gone too far/not gone far enough) allowing the sale of council houses to tenants.
- (Gone too far/not gone far enough) the availability of abortion on the NHS.
- (Gone too far/not gone far enough) attempts to give equal opportunities to homosexuals,
- (Gone too far/not gone far enough) privatization of industries.
- 'Do you think that trade unions have too much power or not?
- 'Do you think that big business in this country has too much power or not?'

The Left–Right Scale

The following propositions were used to assess respondents' positions on the left–right scale:

- Ordinary people get their fair share of the nation's wealth.
- There is one law for the rich and one for the poor.
- There is no need for strong trade unions to protect employees' working conditions.
- Private enterprise is the best way to solve Britain's economic problems.
- Major public services and industries should be in state ownership.
- It is the government's responsibility to provide a job for everyone who wants one.

The Libertarian–Authoritarian Scale

Respondents' positions on the libertarian–authoritarian scale were gauged from their response to the following propositions:

- Young people today don't have enough respect for traditional British values.
- Censorship of films and magazines is necessary to uphold moral standards.
- People should be allowed to organize public meetings to protest against the government.
- Homosexual relations are always wrong.
- People in Britain should be more tolerant of those who lead unconventional lives.
- Britain should bring back the death penalty.
- People who break the law should be given stiffer sentences.

REFERENCES

Agnew, J. A. (1987) *Place and Politics: The Geographical Mediation of State and Society*. Boston, MA: Allen and Unwin.

Agnew, J. A. (1990) From political methodology to geographical social theory? A critical review of electoral geography, 1960–1987. In R. J. Johnston, F. M. Shelley, and P. J. Taylor, editors, *Developments in Electoral Geography*. London: Croom Helm, 15–21.

Agnew, J. A. (1996a) Mapping politics: how context counts in electoral geography. *Political Geography* 15: 129–46.

Agnew, J. A. (1996b) Maps and models in political studies: a reply to comments. *Political Geography* 15: 165–7.

Agnew, J. A. (2002) *Place and Politics in Modern Italy*. Chicago, IL: University of Chicago Press.

Agnew, J. A. and Duncan, J. S., editors (1989) *The Power of Place: Bringing Together Geographical and Sociological Imaginations*. Boston, MA: Unwin Hyman.

Aidt, T. S. (2000) Economic voting and information. *Electoral Studies* 19: 349–62.

Akerlof, G. A. (1997) Social distance and social decisions. *Econometrica* 65: 1005–27.

Alford, R. R. (1964) *Party and Society*. Chicago, IL: Rand McNally.

Andersen, R. and Heath, A. (2002) Class matters: the persisting effects of contextual social class on individual voting in Britain, 1964–97. *European Sociological Review* 18: 125–38.

Andersen, R., Tilley, J. and Heath, A. F. (2005) Political knowledge and enlightened preferences: party choice through the electoral cycle. *British Journal of Political Science* 35: 285–302.

Anderson, C. J. (2000) Economic voting and political context: a comparative perspective. *Electoral Studies* 19: 151–70.

Anderson, C. J. and Paskeviciute, A. (2005) Macro-politics and micro-behaviour: mainstream politics and the frequency of political discussion in contemporary democracies. In A. S. Zuckerman, editor, *The Social Logic of Politics: Personal Networks as Contexts for Political Behavior*. Philadelphia, PA: Temple University Press, 228–48.

Anderson, C. J., Mendes, S. M. and Tverdova, Y. V. (2004) Endogenous economic voting: evidence from the 1997 British election. *Electoral Studies* 23: 683–708.

Ansolabehere, S. and Iyengar, S. (1995) *Going Negative: How Political Advertisements Shrink and Polarize the Electorate*. New York: The Free Press.

Ballinger, C. (2002) The local battle, the cyber battle. In D. Butler and D. Kavanagh, editors, *The British General Election of 2001*. Basingstoke: Palgrave, 208–34.

Bara, J. and Budge, I. (2001) Party policy and ideology: still New Labour? In P. Norris, editor, *Britain Votes 2001*. Oxford: Oxford University Press, 26–42.

Barnett, M. J. (1973) Aggregate models of British voting behaviour. *Political Studies* 21: 121–34.

Bartle, J. (1997) Political awareness and heterogeneity in models of voting: some evidence from the British Election Studies. In C. J. Pattie, D. T. Denver, J. Fisher, and S. Ludlam, editors, *British Elections and Parties Review* 7. London: Frank Cass, 1–22.

Bartolini, S. (2000) *The Political Mobilization of the European Left, 1860–1980: The Class Cleavage*. Cambridge: Cambridge University Press.

Bealey, F., Blondel, J. and McCann, W. (1965) *Constituency Politics*. London: Faber and Faber.

Beck, P. A. (2002) Encouraging political defection: the role of personal discussion networks in partisan desertions to the opposition party and Perot votes in 1992. *Political Behavior* 24: 309–37.

Beck, P. A., Dalton, R. J., Greene, S. and Huckfeldt, R. (2002) The social calculus of voting: interpersonal, media and organizational influences on Presidential choices. *American Political Science Review* 96: 57–73.

Bennett, S. E., Flickinger, R. S. and Rhine, S. L. (2000) Political talk over here, over there and over time. *British Journal of Political Science* 30: 99–119.

Benney, M. and Geiss, P. (1950) Social class and politics in Greenwich. *British Journal of Sociology* 1: 310–27.

Benney, M., Gray, A. P. and Pear, R. H. (1956) *How People Vote: A Study of Electoral Behaviour*. London: Routledge and Kegan Paul.

Berelson, B., Lazarsfeld, P. F. and McPhee, W. N. (1954) *Voting*. Chicago, IL: University of Chicago Press.

Berinsky, A. J., Burns, N. and Traugott, M. W. (2001) Who votes by mail? A dynamic model of the individual-level consequences of voting-by-mail systems. *Public Opinion Quarterly* 65: 178–97.

Berrington, H. (1965) The British general election of 1964. *Journal of the Royal Statistical Society Series A (Statistics in Society)* 128: 17–66.

Birch, A. H. (1959) *Small Town Politics*. Oxford: Oxford University Press.

Blau, A. (2001) Partisan bias in British general elections. In J. Tonge, L. Bennie, D. Denver, and L. Harrison, editors, *British Elections and Parties Review Volume 11*. London: Frank Cass, 46–65.

Blount, S. (2002) Unemployment and economic voting. *Electoral Studies* 21: 91–100.

Bochel, J. M. and Denver, D. (1971) Canvassing, turnout and party support: an experiment. *British Journal of Political Science* 1: 257–69.

Bochel, J. M. and Denver, D. (1972) The impact of the campaign on the results of local government elections. *British Journal of Political Science* 2: 239–44.

Bogdanor, V. (1983) *Multi-Party Politics and the Constitution*. Cambridge: Cambridge University Press.

Bogdanor, V. (1986) Letter to the Editor. *Environment and Planning A* 18: 1537.

Books, C. L. and Prysby, J. W. (1991) *Political Behavior and the Local Context*. New York: Praeger.

Brady, H. E., Verba, S. and Schlozman, K. L. (1995) Beyond SES: a resource model of political participation. *American Political Science Review* 89: 271–94.

Brookes, R. H. (1959) Electoral distortion in New Zealand. *Australian Journal of Politics and History* 5: 218–23.

Brookes, R. H. (1960) The analysis of distorted representation in two-party, single-member elections. *Political Science* 12: 158–67.

Buck, N. H. (2001) Identifying neighbourhood effects on social exclusion. *Urban Studies* 38: 2251–75.

Budge, I. (1999) Party policy and ideology: reversing the 1950s? In G. Evans and P. Norris, editors, *Critical Elections: British Parties and Voters in Long-Term Perspective*. London: Sage Publications, 1–21.

Burbank, M. J. (1995) How do contextual effects work? Developing a theoretical model. In M. Eagles, editor, *Spatial and Contextual Models in Political Research.* London: Taylor and Francis, 165–76.

Butler, D. (1951) The results analysed. In H. G. Nicholas, editor, *The British General Election of 1950.* London: Macmillan, 333.

Butler, D. (1963) *The Electoral System in Britain since 1918.* Oxford: The Clarendon Press.

Butler, D. and Kavanagh, D. (1988) *The British General Election of 1987.* London: Macmillan.

Butler, D. and Kavanagh, D. (1992) *The British General Election of 1992.* Basingstoke: Macmillan.

Butler, D. and Kavanagh, D. (2002) *The British General Election of 2001.* London: Macmillan.

Butler, D. and McLean, I. (1996) The redrawing of Parliamentary boundaries in Britain. In I. McLean and D. Butler, editors, *Fixing the Boundaries: Defining and Redefining Single-Member Electoral Districts.* Aldershot: Dartmouth, 1–38.

Butler, D. and Pinto-Duschinsky, M. (1971) *The British General Election of 1970.* Basingstoke: Macmillan.

Butler, D. and Stokes, D. (1969) *Political Change in Britain: Forces Shaping Electoral Choice.* London: Macmillan.

Butler, D. and Stokes, D. (1974) *Political Change in Britain: The Evolution of Electoral Choice.* London: Macmillan.

Butler, D. and Westlake, M. (2000) *British Politics and European Elections 1999.* Basingstoke: Macmillan.

Cain, B. E., Ferejohn, J. A. and Fiorina, M. P. (1984) The constituency service basis of the personal vote for US Representatives and British Members of Parliament. *American Political Science Review* 78: 110–25.

Cain, B. E., Ferejohn, J. A. and Fiorina, M. P. (1987) *The Personal Vote: Constituency Service and Electoral Independence.* Cambridge, MA: Harvard University Press.

Campbell, A., Guerin, G. and Miller, W. E. (1954) *The Voter Decides.* Evanston, IL: Row, Peterson.

Campbell, A., Converse, P., Miller, W. E. and Stokes, D. E. (1960) *The American Voter.* New York: John Wiley.

Carty, R. K. and Eagles, M. (1999) Do local campaigns matter? Campaign spending, the local canvass and party support in Canada. *Electoral Studies* 18: 69–88.

Carty, R. K. and Eagles, M. (2000) Is there a local dimension to modern election campaigns? Party activists' perceptions of the media and electoral coverage of Canadian constituency politics. *Political Communications* 17: 279–94.

Clarke, H. D. and Stewart, M. C. (1995) Economic evaluations, prime ministerial approval and governing party support: rival models reconsidered. *British Journal of Political Science* 25: 597–622.

Clarke, H. D., Ho, K. and Stewart, M. C. (2000) Major's lesser (not minor) effects: prime ministerial approval and governing party support in Britain since 1979. *Electoral Studies* 19: 255–73.

Clarke, H. D., Mishler, W. and Whiteley, P. (1990) Recapturing the Falklands: models of Conservative popularity, 1979–1983. *British Journal of Political Science* 20: 63–81.

Clarke, H. D., Stewart, M. C. and Whiteley, P. F. (1997) Tory trends: party identification and the dynamics of Conservative support since 1992. *British Journal of Political Science* 26: 299–318.

Clarke, H. D., Stewart, M. C. and Whiteley, P. F. (1998) New models for New Labour: the political economy of Labour party support, January 1992–April 1997. *American Political Science Review* 92: 559–75.

Clarke, H. D., Sanders, D., Stewart. M. C. and Whiteley, P. F. (2004) *Political Choice in Britain*. Oxford: Oxford University Press.

Conover, P. J., Searing, D. and Crewe, I. (2002) The deliberative potential of political discussion. *British Journal of Political Science* 32: 21–62.

Cook, C. and Ramsden, J. (1997) *By-Elections in British Politics*, 2nd edn. London: UCL Press.

Cook, G. (2002) The Labour campaign. In J. Bartle, R. Mortimore, and S. Atkinson, editors, *Political Communications: The General Election Campaign of 2001*. London: Frank Cass, 87–97.

Cowley, P. J. (2002) *Revolts and Rebellions: Parliamentary Voting under Blair*. London: Politico's.

Cowley, P. J. (2005) *The Rebels: How Blair Mislaid his Majority*. London: Politico's.

Cowley, P. J. and Stuart, M. (2005) Being policed, or just pleasing themselves? Electoral rewards and punishment for legislative behaviour in an era of localised campaigning—the case of the UK in 2005. Paper presented at the annual conference of the Political Studies Association Specialist Group on Elections, Public Opinion and Parties, University of Essex, September 2005. Available at http://www.essex.ac.uk/bes/EPOP%202005/index.htm

Cox, K. R. (1968) Suburbia and voting behavior in the London metropolitan area. *Annals of the Association of American Geographers* 58: 111–27.

Cox, K. R. (1969a) The voting decision in a spatial context. In C. Board, R. J. Chorley, P. Haggett and D. R. Stoddart, editors, *Progress in Geography* 1. London: Edward Arnold, 83–117.

Cox, K. R. (1969b) The spatial structuring of information flow and partisan attitudes. In M. Dogan and S. Rokkan, editors, *Quantitative Ecological Analysis in the Social Sciences*. Cambridge, MA: MIT Press, 157–85.

Cox, K. R. (1969c) Voting in the London suburbs: a factor analysis and a causal model. In M. Dogan and S. Rokkan, editors, *Quantitative Ecological Analysis in the Social Sciences*. Cambridge, MA: MIT Press, 343–69.

Cox, K. R. (1970a) Geography, social contexts and voting behavior in Wales, 1861–1951. In E. Allardt and S. Rokkan, editors, *Mass Politics*. New York: The Free Press, 117–59.

Cox, K. R. (1970b) Residential relocation and political behavior: conceptual model and empirical tests. *Acta Sociologica* 13: 40–53.

Crewe, I. (1973) The politics of 'affluent' and 'traditional' workers in Britain: an aggregate data analysis. *British Journal of Political Science* 3: 29–52.

Crewe, I. (1981) Electoral participation. In D. Butler, H. R. Penniman, and A. Ranney, editors, *Democracy at the Polls*. Washington, DC: American Enterprise Institute, 216–63.

Crewe, I. (1986) On the death and resurrection of class voting: some comments on *how Britain votes*. *Political Studies 35*: 620–38.

Crewe, I. (2002) A new political hegemony? In A. King, editor, *Britain at the Polls, 2001*. New York: Chatham House, 207–32.

Crewe, I. and King, A. (1995) *SDP: The Birth, Life and Death of the Social Democratic Party*. Oxford: Oxford University Press.

Crewe, I. and Payne, C. (1971) Analysing the census data. In D. Butler and M. Pinto-Duschinsky, editors, *The British General Election of 1970*. London: Macmillan, 416–36.

Crewe, I. and Payne, C. (1976) Another game with nature: an ecological regression model of the British two-party vote ratio in 1970. *British Journal of Political Science* 6: 43–81.

Crewe, I., Fox, T. and Alt, J. (1977) Non-voting in British general elections, 1966–October 1974. In C. Crouch, editor, *British Political Sociology Yearbook 3*. London: Croom Helm.

Crewe, I., Särlvik, B. and Alt, J. (1977) Partisan dealignment in Britain, 1964–1974. *British Journal of Political Science* 7: 129–90.

Crick, M. (1998) Statement to the Neil Committee. Memorandum 16/386. *Neill Committee on Standards in Public Life, 5th Report: The Funding of Political Parties in the United Kingdom. Volume 2, Written Evidence and Other Material*. London: HMSO, Report CM 4057–II.

Curtice, J. (1995) Is talking over the garden fence of political import? In M. Eagles, editor, *Spatial and Contextual Models in Political Research*. London: Taylor and Francis, 195–209.

Curtice, J. (2005) Turnout: electors stay home—again. *Parliamentary Affairs* 58: 776–85.

Curtice, J. and Park, A. (1999) Region: New Labour, new geography? In G. Evans and P. Norris, editors, *Critical Elections: British Parties and Voters in Long-Term Perspective*. London: Sage Publications, 124–47.

Curtice, J. and Semetko, H. (1994) Does it matter what the papers say? In A. Heath, R. Jowell, J. Curtice, and B. Taylor, editors, *Labour's Last Chance? The 1992 Election and Beyond*. Aldershot: Dartmouth, 43–64.

Curtice, J. and Steed, M. (1980) The results analysed. In D. Butler and D. Kavanagh, editors, *The British General Election of 1979*. London: Macmillan, 390–431.

Curtice, J. and Steed, M. (1982) Electoral choice and the production of government: the changing operation of the electoral system in the United Kingdom since 1955. *British Journal of Political Science* 12: 249–98.

Curtice, J. and Steed, M. (1984) The results analysed. In D. Butler and D. Kavanagh, *The British General Election of 1983*. London: Macmillan, 333–73.

Curtice, J. and Steed, M. (1988) Analysis. In D. Butler and O. Kavanagh, *The British General Election of 1987*. London: Macmillan, 316–62.

Curtice, J. and Steed, M. (1997) The results analysed. In D. Butler and D. Kavanagh, *The British General Election of 1997*. London: Macmillan, 295–325.

Curtice, J. and Steed, M. (2002) An analysis of the results. In D. Butler and D. Kavanagh, *The British General Election of 1983*. London: Macmillan, 304–38.

Cutts, D. J. (2006a) Continuous campaigning and electoral outcomes: the Liberal Democrats in Bath. *Political Geography* 25: 72–88.

Cutts, D. J. (2006b) Did Liberal Democrat activism really matter? *British Journal of Politics and International Relations* 8: in press.

Cutts, D. J. (2006c) 'Where we work we win': examining Liberal Democrat campaigning at the sub-national level using a case study approach. *Journal of Elections, Public Opinion and Parties* 2: in press.

Dalton, R. J. (2000) The decline of party identifications. In R. J. Dalton and M. P. Wattenberg, editors, *Parties Without Partisans: Political Change in Advanced Industrial Democracies*. Oxford: Oxford University Press, 19–36.

Dalton, R. J. (2002) *Citizen Politics*. New York: Seven Bridges Press.

Dalton, R. J. and Wattenberg, M. J. (2002) Unthinkable democracy: political change in advanced industrial democracies. In R. J. Dalton and M. J. Wattenberg, editors, *Parties without Partisans: Political Change in Advanced Industrial Democracies*. Oxford: Oxford University Press, 3–18.

Dalton, R. J., McAllister, I. and Wattenberg, M. P. (2000) The consequences of partisan dealignment. In R. J. Dalton and M. P. Wattenberg, editors, *Parties Without Partisans: Political Change in Advanced Industrial Democracies*. 37–63.

Deakin, N. (1965) *Colour and the British Electorate 1964: Six Case Studies*. London: Pall Mall Press.

Denver, D. T. (1995) Non-voting in Britain. In J. Font and R. Virós, editors, *Electoral Abstention in Europe*. Barcelona: Institut de Ciènces Politiques i Sociale, 181–98.

Denver, D. T. (2001) The Liberal Democrat campaign. In P. Norris, editor, *Britain Votes 2001*. Oxford: Oxford University Press, 74–85.

Denver, D. T. (2003) *Elections and Voters in Britain*. London: Palgrave Macmillan.

Denver, D. T. and Halfacree, K. (1992) Inter-constituency migration and turnout at the British general election of 1983. *British Journal of Political Science* 22: 248–54.

Denver, D. T. and Hands, G. (1974) Marginality and turnout in general elections. *British Journal of Political Science* 4: 17–35.

Denver, D. T. and Hands, G. (1985) Marginality and turnout in general elections in the 1970s. *British Journal of Political Science* 15: 381–88.

Denver, D. T. and Hands, G. (1992) Constituency campaigning. *Parliamentary Affairs* 45: 528–44.

Denver, D. T and Hands, G. (1996) Constituency campaigning in the 1992 General Election: the peculiar case of the Conservatives. In D. M. Farrell, D. Broughton, D. Denver, and J. Fisher, editors, *British Elections and Parties Yearbook 1996*. London: Frank Cass, 85–105.

Denver, D. T. and Hands, G. (1997a) Challengers, incumbents and the impact of constituency campaigning in Britain. *Electoral Studies* 16: 175–93.

Denver, D. T. and Hands, G. (1997b) *Modern Constituency Electioneering: Local Campaigning in the 1992 General Election*. London: Frank Cass.

Denver, D. T. and Hands, G. (1998) Constituency campaigning in the 1997 general election: party effort and electoral effect. In I. Crewe, B. Gosschalk, and J. Bartle, editors, *Political Communications: Why Labour Won the General Election of 1997*. London: Frank Cass, 75–92.

Denver, D. T. and Hands, G. (2004) Labour's targeted constituency campaigning: nationally directed or locally produced? *Electoral Studies* 23: 709–26.

Denver, D. T., Hands, G. and Henig, S. (1998) Triumph of targeting? Constituency campaigning in the 1997 Election. In D. Denver, J. Fisher, P. Cowley, and C. Pattie, editors, *British Elections and Parties Review 8: the 1997 General Election*. London: Frank Cass, 171–90.

Denver, D. T., Hands, G. and McAllister, I. (2004) The electoral impact of constituency campaigning in Britain, 1992–2001. *Political Studies* 52: 289–306.

Denver, D. T., Hands, G., Fisher, J. and McAllister, I. (2002a) Constituency campaigning in 2001: the effectiveness of targeting. In J. Bartle, R. Mortimore, and

S. Atkinson, editors, *Political Communications: The General Election Campaign of 2001*. London: Frank Cass, 159–80.

Denver, D. T., Hands, G., Fisher, J. and McAllister, I. (2002b) The impact of constituency campaigning in the 2001 General Election. In L. Bennie, C. Rallings, J. Tonge, and P. Webb, editors, *British Elections and Parties Review 12: The 2001 General Election*. London: Frank Cass, 80–94.

Denver, D. T., Hands, G., Fisher, J. and McAllister, I. (2003) Constituency campaigning in Britain, 1992–2001: centralization and modernization. *Party Politics* 9: 541–59.

Devine, F. (1992) *Affluent Workers Revisited: Privatism and the Working Class*. Edinburgh: Edinburgh University Press.

Dorling, D. (1994) The future negative equity map of Britain. *Area* 26: 327–42.

Dorling, D. and Cornford, J. (1995) Who has negative equity? How house price falls have hit different groups of buyers. *Housing Studies* 10: 151–78.

Dorling, D., Rallings, C. and Thrasher, M. (1998) The epidemiology of the Liberal Democrat vote. *Political Geography* 17: 45–70.

Dorling, D., Eyre, H., Johnston, R. and Pattie, C. (2002) A good place to bury bad news? Hiding the detail in the geography on the Labour party's website. *Political Quarterly* 73: 476–92.

Downs, A. (1957) *An Economic Theory of Democracy*. New York: Harper & Row.

Duke, V. and Edgell, S. (1984) Public expenditure cuts in Britain and consumption sectoral cleavages. *International Journal of Urban and Regional Research* 8: 177–99.

Duncan, G. J. and Raudenbush, S. (2001) Neighbourhoods and adolescent development: how can we determine the links? In A. Booth and N. Crouter, editors, *Does it Take a Village? Community Effects on Children, Adolescents, and Families*. Mahwah, NJ: Lawrence Erlbaum Associates, 105–36.

Duncan, G. J., Magnuson, K. A. and Ludwig, J. (2004) The endogeneity problem in developmental studies. *Research in Human Development* 1: 59–80.

Dunleavy, P. J. (1979) The urban basis of political alignment: social class, domestic property ownership and state intervention in consumption processes. *British Journal of Political Science* 9: 409–43.

Dunleavy, P. J. (1980) The urban basis of political alignment: a rejoinder to Harrop. *British Journal of Political Science* 10: 398–402.

Dunleavy, P. J. (1991) *Democracy, Bureaucracy and Public Choice: Economic Explanations in Political Science*. London: Harvester.

Dunleavy, P. J. and Husbands, C. T. (1985) *British Democracy at the Crossroads: Voting and Party Competition in the 1980s*. London: George Allen & Unwin.

Eagles, M. (1990) An ecological perspective on working class political behaviour: neighbourhood and class formation in Sheffield. In R. J. Johnston, F. M. Shelley, and P. J. Taylor, editors, *Developments in Electoral Geography*. London: Croom Helm, 100–20.

Eagles, M. (1993) Money and votes in Canada: campaign spending and parliamentary election outcomes 1984 and 1988. *Canadian Public Policy – Analyse de Politiques* 19: 432–49.

Eagles, M. and Erfle, S. (1988) Community cohesion and working class politics: workplace–residence separation and Labour support, 1966–1983. *Political Geography Quarterly* 7: 229–50.

Eagles, M. and Erfle, S. (1989) Community cohesion and voter turnout in English parliamentary elections. *British Journal of Political Science* 19: 115–25.

Eagles, M., Bélanger, P. and Calkins, H. W. (2004) The spatial structure of urban political discussion networks. In M. F. Goodchild and D. G. Janelle, editors, *Spatially Integrated Social Science*. Oxford: Oxford University Press, 205–18.

Electoral Commission (2002a) *Election 2001: Campaign Spending*. London: The Electoral Commission.

Electoral Commission (2002b) *Modernising Elections: A Strategic Evaluation of the 2002 Electoral Pilot Schemes*. London: The Electoral Commission.

Electoral Commission (2003) *The Shape of Elections to Come: A Strategic Evaluation of the 2003 Electoral Pilot Schemes*. London: The Electoral Commission.

Electoral Commission (2004a) *Delivering Democracy? The Future of Postal Voting*. London: The Electoral Commission.

Electoral Commission (2004b) *Election Expenditure and Donations: Guidance for Candidates and Election Agents*. London: The Electoral Commission.

Electoral Commission (2005) *Election 2005: Turnout. How Many, Who and Why?* London: The Electoral Commission.

Engstrom, R. N. and Kenny, C. (2002) The effects of independent expenditures in Senate elections. *Political Research Quarterly* 55: 885–905.

Erikson, R. S., MacKuen, M. B. and Stimson, J. A. (1998) What moves macropartisanship? A response to Green, Palmquist and Schikler. *American Political Science Review* 92: 901–12.

Erikson, R. S., MacKuen, M. B. and Stimson, J. A. (2000) Bankers or peasants revisited: economic expectations and Presidential approval. *Electoral Studies* 19: 295–312.

Evans, G. (1999a) Economics and politics revisited: exploring the decline in Conservative support, 1992–1995. *Political Studies* 47: 139–51.

Evans, G. (1999b) Economics, politics and the pursuit of exogeneity: why Pattie, Johnston and Sanders are wrong. *Political Studies* 47: 933–8.

Evans, G. and Andersen, R. (2004) Do issues decide? Partisan conditioning and perceptions of party issue positions across the electoral cycle. In R. Scully, J. Fisher, P. Webb, and D. Broughton, editors, *British Elections and Parties Review 14*. London: Frank Cass, 18–39.

Evans, G. and Andersen, R. (2006) The political conditioning of economic perceptions. *The Journal of Politics* 68: 194–207.

Evans, G. and Heath, A. (1993) A tactical error in the analysis of tactical voting: a response to Niemi, Whitten and Franklin. *British Journal of Political Science* 23: 131–7.

Evans, G. and Heath, A. (1995) The measurement of left–right and libertarian–authoritarian values: a comparison of balanced and unbalanced scales. *Quality and Quantity* 29: 191–206.

Evans, G., Curtice, J. and Norris, P. (1998) New Labour, new tactical voting? The causes and consequences of tactical voting in the 1997 general election. In D. Denver, J. Fisher, P. Cowley, and C. Pattie, editors, *British Elections and Parties Review 8*. London; Frank Cass, 65–79.

Evans, G., Heath, A. and Lalljee, M. (1996) Measuring left–right and libertarian–authoritarian attitudes in the British electorate. *British Journal of Sociology* 47: 93–112.

Fearon, J. D. (1998) Deliberation as discussion. In J. Elster, editor, *Deliberative Democracy*. Cambridge: Cambridge University Press, 44–68.

Field, W. H. (1997) *Regional Dynamics: The Basis of Electoral Support in Britain.* London: Frank Cass.

Fieldhouse, E. A. (1995) Thatcherism and the changing geography of political attitudes, 1964–87. *Political Geography* 14: 3–30.

Fieldhouse, E. A. and Cutts, D. J. (2005) The Liberal Democrats: Steady Progress or Failure to Seize the Moment? In A. Geddes and J. Tonge, editors, *Britain Decides: The UK General Election 2005.* London: Palgrave Macmillan, 70–88.

Fieldhouse, E. A. and Purdam, K. (2002) *Voter Engagement among Black and Minority Ethnic Communities.* London: The Electoral Commission.

Fieldhouse, E. A. and Russell, A. T. (2001) Latent Liberalism? Sympathy and support for the Liberal Democrats at the 1997 general election. *Party Politics* 7: 711–38.

Finifter, A. (1974) The friendship group as a protective environment for political deviants. *American Political Science Review* 68: 607–25.

Fiorina, M. (1981) *Retrospective Voting In American National Elections.* New Haven, CT: Yale University Press.

Fisher, J. (1999a) Modelling the decision to donate by individual party members: the case of British parties. *Party Politics* 5: 19–38.

Fisher, J. (1999b) Party expenditure and electoral prospects: a national level analysis of Britain. *Electoral Studies* 18: 519–32.

Fisher, J. (2000a) Economic performance or electoral necessity? Evaluating the system of voluntary income to political parties. *British Journal of Politics and International Relations* 2: 179–204.

Fisher, J. (2000b) Small kingdoms and crumbling organizations: examining the variation in constituency part membership and resources. In P. Cowley, D. Denver, A. Russell, and L. Harrison, editors, *British Elections and Parties Review 10.* London: Frank Cass, 133–50.

Fisher, J., Denver, D. and Hands, G. (2006) The relative electoral impact of central party co-ordination and size of party membership at constituency level. *Electoral Studies* 25: in press.

Fisher, J., Denver, D., Fieldhouse, E., Cutts, D. and Russell, A. (2005) Constituency campaigning in the 2005 British General Election. Paper presented at the annual conference of the Political Studies Association Specialist Group on Elections, Public Opinion and Parties, University of Essex, September 2005. Available at http://www.essex.ac.uk/bes/EPOP%202005/index.htm

Fisher, S. (2000) Class contextual effects on the Conservative vote in 1983. *British Journal of Political Science* 30: 347–60.

Fisher, S. (2004) Definition and measurement of tactical voting: the role of rational choice. *British Journal of Political Science* 34: 152–66.

Fisher, S. and Curtice, J. (2005) Tactical unwind. Paper presented at the annual conference of the Political Studies Association Specialist Group on Elections, Public Opinion and Parties, University of Essex, September 2005. Available at http://www.essex.ac.uk/bes/EPOP%202005/index.htm

Fishkin, J. S. (1995) *The Voice of the People: Public Opinion and Democracy.* New Haven, CT: Yale University Press.

Fitton, M. (1973) Neighbourhood and voting: a sociometric explanation. *British Journal of Political Science* 3: 445–72.

Foot, P. (1969) *The Rise of Enoch Powell.* London: Penguin Books.

Forrest, J., Johnston, R. J. and Pattie, C. J. (1999) The effectiveness of constituency campaign spending in Australian state elections during times of electoral volatility: the New South Wales case, 1988–1995. *Environment and Planning A* 31: 1119–28.

Franklin, M. N. (1985) *The Decline of Class Voting in Britain*. Oxford: Oxford University Press.

Franklin, M. N. (1999) Electoral engineering and cross-national turnout differences: what role for compulsory voting? *British Journal of Political Science* 29: 205–24.

Franklin, M. N. (2002) The dynamics of electoral participation. In L. LeDuc, R. G. Niemi and P. Norris, editors, *Comparing Democracies 2: New Challenges in the Study of Elections and Voting*. London: Sage, 148–68.

Franklin, M. N. (2004) *Voter Turnout and the Dynamics of Electoral Competition in Established Democracies since 1945*. Cambridge: Cambridge University Press.

Galbraith, J. K. (1992) *The Culture of Contentment*. London: Sinclair-Stevenson.

Galbraith, J. W. and Rae, N. C. (1989) A test of the importance of tactical voting, Great Britain, 1987. *British Journal of Political Science* 19: 126–36.

Garrett, G. (1994) Popular capitalism: the electoral legacy of Thatcherism. In A. Heath, R. Jowell and J. Curtice, editors, *Labour's Last Chance? The 1992 Election and Beyond*. Aldershot: Dartmouth, 107–24.

Gelman, A. and King, G. (1993) Why are American presidential election campaign polls so variable when votes are so predictable? *British Journal of Political Science* 25: 409–51.

Gentle, C., Dorling, D. and Cornford, J. (1994) Negative equity and British housing in the 1990s: cause and effect. *Urban Studies* 31: 181–99.

Gerber, A. S. (1998) Estimating the effect of campaign spending on Senate election outcomes using instrumental variables. *American Political Science Review* 92: 401–11.

Gerber, A. S. and Green, D. P. (2000) The effects of canvassing, telephone calls and direct mail on voter turnout: a field experiment. *American Political Science Review* 94: 653–63.

Gerber, A. S. and Green, D. P. (2001) Do phone calls increase voter turnout? A field experiment. *Public Opinion Quarterly* 65: 75–85.

Gibson, R. (2001) Elections online: assessing internet voting in light of the Arizona Democratic Primary. *Political Science Quarterly* 116: 561–83.

Giddens, A. (1984) *The Constitution of Society*. Cambridge: Polity Press.

Gimpel, J. G. and Schuknecht, J. E. (2003) Political participation and the accessibility of the ballot box. *Political Geography* 22: 471–88.

Goldstein, K. and Freedman, P. (2000) New evidence for new arguments: money and advertising in the 1996 Senate elections. *The Journal of Politics* 62: 1087–108.

Goldstein, K. M. and Ridout, T. N. (2002) The politics of participation: mobilization and turnout over time. *Political Behavior* 24: 3–29.

Goldthorpe, J. H. (1999) Modelling the pattern of class voting in British elections, 1964–1992. In G. Evans, editor, *The End of Class Politics? Class Voting in Comparative Context*. Oxford: Oxford University Press, 59–82.

Goldthorpe, J., Lockwood, D., Bechhofer, F. and Platt, J. (1968) *The Affluent Worker: Political Attitudes and Behaviour*. Cambridge: Cambridge University Press.

Gomez, B. T. and Wilson, J. M. (2001) Political sophistication and economic voting in the American electorate: a theory of heterogeneous attribution. *American Journal of Political Science* 45: 899–914.

Goodhart, C. A. E. and Bhansali, R. J. (1970) Political economy. *Political Studies* 18: 43–106.

Gordon, I. and Whiteley, P. (1980) Comment: Johnston on campaign expenditure and the efficacy of advertising. *Political Studies* 28: 293–4.

Gould, P. (1998) *The Unfinished Revolution: How the Modernisers Saved the Labour Party*. London: Abacus.

Granovetter, M. S. (1973) The strength of weak ties. *American Journal of Sociology* 78: 1360–80.

Gray, M. and Caul, M. (2000) Declining voter turnout in advanced industrial democracies, 1950 to 1997: the effects of declining group mobilization. *Comparative Political Studies* 33: 1091–122.

Green, D. P. and Gerber, A. S. (2004) *Get Out the Vote! How to Increase Voter Turnout*. Washington, DC: Brookings Institution Press.

Green, D. P. and Krasno, J. S. (1988) Salvation for the spendthrift incumbent: reestimating the effects of campaign spending in House elections. *American Journal of Political Science* 32: 884–907.

Green, D. P. and Krasno, J. S. (1990) Rebuttal to Jacobson's "New evidence for old arguments". *American Journal of Political Science* 34: 363–72.

Green, D. P. and Palmquist, B. (1990) Of artefacts and partisan instability. *American Journal of Political Science* 34: 872–902.

Green, D. P. and Palmquist, B. (1994) How stable is party identification? *Political Behavior* 16: 437–66.

Gudgin, G. and Taylor, P. J. (1979) *Seats, Votes and the Spatial Organisation of Elections*. London: Pion.

Habermas, J. (1984) *The Theory of Communicative Action: Reason and the Rationalization of Society*. London: Heinemann.

Hamnett, C. (1989) The owner-occupied housing market in Britain: a north–south divide? In J. Lewis and A. Townsend, editors, *The North–South Divide: Regional Change in Britain in the 1980s*. London: Paul Chapman Publishing, 97–113.

Hamnett, C. (1993) The spatial impact of the British home ownership market slump, 1989–91. *Area* 25: 217–27.

Hamnett, C. (1999) *Winners and Losers: Home Ownership in Modern Britain*. London: UCL Press.

Hampton, W. A. (1970) *Democracy and Community: A Study of Politics in Sheffield*. Oxford: Oxford University Press.

Harrop, M. (1980) The urban basis of political alignment: a comment. *British Journal of Political Science* 10: 388–98.

Harrop, M. Heath, A. and Openshaw, S. (1992) Does neighbourhood influence voting behaviour—and why? In I. Crewe, P. Norris, D. Denver and D. Broughton, editors, *British Elections and Parties Yearbook 1991*. Hemel Hempstead: Harvester Wheatsheaf, 103–20.

Heath, A. and Taylor, B. (1999) New sources of abstention? In G. Evans and P. Norris, editors, *Critical Elections: British Parties and Voters in Long Term Perspective*, London: Sage Publications, 164–80.

Heath, A., Evans, G. and Martin, J. (1993) The measurement of core beliefs and values: the development of balanced socialist/laissez faire and libertarian/authoritarian scales. *British Journal of Political Science* 24: 115–32.

Heath, A., Jowell, R. and Curtice, J. (1987) Trendless fluctuation: a reply to Crewe. *Political Studies* 35: 256–77.

Heath, A., Jowell, R. and Curtice, J. (2001) *The Rise of New Labour: Party Policies and Voter Choices*. Oxford: Oxford University Press.

Heath, A., Jowell, R., Curtice, J., Evans, G, Field, J. and Witherspoon, S. (1991) *Understanding Political Change: the British Voter 1963–1987*. Oxford: Pergamon Press.

Heath, A., McLean, I., Taylor, B. and Curtice, J. (1999) Between first and second order: a comparison of voting behaviour in European and local elections in Britain. *European Journal of Political Research* 35: 389–414.

Heitshusen, V., Young, G. and Wood, D. M. (2005) Electoral context and MP constituency focus in Australia, Canada, Ireland, New Zealand and the United Kingdom. *American Journal of Political Science* 49: 32–45.

Hibbs, D. and Vasilatos, N. (1981) Macroeconomic performance and mass political support in the United States and Great Britain. In D. Hibbs and H. Fassbender, editors, *Contemporary Political Economy*. Amsterdam: North-Holland, 73–100.

Highton. B. (2000) Residential mobility, community mobility and electoral participation. *Political Behaviour* 22: 109–20.

Hill, D. (1995) The Labour Party's strategy. In I. Crewe and B. Gosschalk, editors, *Political Communications: The General Election Campaign of 1992*. Cambridge: Cambridge University Press, 36–40.

Holbrook, T. M. (1996) *Do Campaigns Matter?* Thousand Oaks, CA: Sage.

Holme, R. and Holmes, A. (1998) Sausages or policemen? The role of the Liberal Democrats in the 1997 General Election Campaign. In I. Crewe, B. Gosschalk, and J. Bartle, editors, *Political Communications: Why Labour Won the General Election of 1997*. London: Frank Cass, 16–27.

Holt, A. T. and Turner, J. E. (1968) *Political Parties in Action*. New York: The Free Press.

Huckfeldt, R. (2001) The social communication of political expertise. *American Journal of Political Science* 45: 425–38.

Huckfeldt, R. and Sprague, J. (1987) Networks in context: the social flow of political information. *American Political Science Review* 81: 1197–216.

Huckfeldt, R. and Sprague, J. (1988) Choice, social structure and political information: the information coercion of minorities. *American Journal of Political Science* 32: 467–82.

Huckfeldt, R. and Sprague, J. (1991) Discussant effects on vote choice: intimacy, structure and interdependence. *The Journal of Politics* 53: 122–58.

Huckfeldt, R. and Sprague, J. (1995) *Citizens, Politics and Social Communication: Information and Influence in an Election Campaign*. Cambridge: Cambridge University Press.

Huckfeldt, R., Ikeda, K. and Pappi, F. U. (2000) Political expertise, interdependent citizens, and the value added problem in democratic politics. *Japanese Journal of Political Science* 1: 171–95.

Huckfeldt, R., Johnson, P. E. and Sprague, J. (2002) Political environments, political dynamics, and the survival of disagreement. *The Journal of Politics* 64: 1–21.

Huckfeldt, R., Johnson, P. E. and Sprague, J. (2004) *Political Disagreement: The Survival of Diverse Opinions within Communication Networks*. Cambridge: Cambridge University Press.

Huckfeldt, R., Sprague, J. and Levine, J. (2000) The dynamics of collective deliberation in the 1996 election: campaign effects on accessibility, certainty and accuracy. *American Political Science Review* 94: 641–51.

Huckfeldt, R., Beck, P. A., Dalton, R. J. and Levine, J. (1995) Political environments, cohesive social groups, and the communication of public opinion. *American Journal of Political Science* 39: 1025–54.

Hudson, R. and Williams, A. M. (1989) *Divided Britain*. London: Belhaven.

Ikeda, K. and Huckfeldt, R. (2001) Political communication and disagreement among citizens in Japan and the United States. *Political Behavior* 23: 23–51.

Jacobson, G. C. (1978) The effects of campaign spending in Congressional elections. *American Political Science Review* 72: 469–91.

Jacobson, G. C. (1990) The effects of campaign spending in House elections: new evidence for old arguments. *American Journal of Political Science* 34: 334–62.

Jamieson, K. H. (1992a) *Dirty Politics: Deception, Distraction and Democracy*. New York: Oxford University Press.

Jamieson, K. H. (1992b) *Packaging the Presidency: A History and Criticism of Presidential Campaign Advertising*. New York: Oxford University Press.

Jencks, C. and Mayer, S. (1990) The social consequences of growing up in a poor neighborhood. In L. Lynn and M. McGeary, editors, *Inner-City Poverty in the United States*. Washington, DC: National Academy Press, 111–86.

Jessop, B. (1974) *Traditionalism, Conservatism and British Political Culture*. London: George Allen & Unwin.

Johnson, R. W. (1972) The nationalisation of English rural politics. *Parliamentary Affairs* 26: 8–55.

Johnston, R. J. (1979a) Campaign expenditure and the efficacy of advertising at the 1974 general election in England. *Political Studies* 27: 114–19.

Johnston, R. J. (1979b) *Political, Electoral and Spatial Systems*. Oxford: The Clarendon Press.

Johnston, R. J. (1981a) Campaign expenditure and the efficacy of advertising: a response. *Political Studies* 29: 113–14.

Johnston, R. J. (1981b) Embourgeoisement, the property-owning democracy, and ecological models of voting in England. *British Journal of Political Science* 11: 499–503.

Johnston, R. J. (1983a) The neighbourhood effect won't go away: observations on the electoral geography of England in the light of Dunleavy's critique. *Geoforum* 14: 161–8.

Johnston, R. J. (1983b) Spatial continuity and individual variability. *Electoral Studies* 2: 53–68.

Johnston, R. J. (1985) *The Geography of English Politics*. London: Croom Helm.

Johnston, R. J. (1986a) A space for place (or a place for space) in British psephology: a review of recent writings with especial reference to the general election of 1983. *Environment and Planning A* 18: 599–618.

Johnston, R. J. (1986b) Putting context into context? *Environment and Planning A* 18: 1537–9.

Johnston, R. J. (1987) *Money and Votes: Constituency Campaign Spending and Election Results*. London: Croom Helm.

Johnston, R. J. and Griffiths, M. J. (1991) What's in a place? An approach to the concept of place as illustrated by the British National Union of Mineworkers Strike 1984–85. *Antipode* 23: 185–213.

Johnston, R. J. and Hay, A. M. (1982) On the parameters of uniform swing in single-member constituency electoral systems. *Environment and Planning A* 14: 61–74.

Johnston, R. J. and Hay, A. M. (1983) Voter transition probability estimates: an entropy-maximizing approach. *European Journal of Political Research* 11: 93–8.

Johnston, R. J. and Pattie, C. J. (1985) The impact of spending on party constituency campaigns in recent British general elections. *Party Politics* 1: 261–73.

Johnston, R. J. and Pattie, C. J. (1987) A dividing nation? An initial exploration of the changing electoral geography of Great Britain, 1979–1987. *Environment and Planning A* 19: 1001–13.

Johnston, R. J. and Pattie, C. J. (1988) Are we really all Alliance nowadays? Discriminating by discriminant analysis. *Electoral Studies* 7: 27–32.

Johnston, R. J. and Pattie, C. J. (1989a) The changing electoral geography of Great Britain. In J. Mohan, editor, *The Political Geography of Contemporary Britain.* Basingstoke: Macmillan, 51–68.

Johnston, R. J. and Pattie, C. J. (1989b) A growing north–south divide in British voting patterns, 1979–1987. *Geoforum* 20: 93–106.

Johnston, R. J. and Pattie, C. J. (1989c) A nation dividing? Economic well-being, voter response and the changing electoral geography of Great Britain. *Parliamentary Affairs* 42: 37–57.

Johnston, R. J. and Pattie, C. J. (1989d) Voting in Britain since 1979: a growing north–south divide? In J. Lewis and A. Townsend, editors, *The North–South Divide: Regional Change in Britain in the 1980s.* London: Paul Chapman, 213–47.

Johnston, R. J. and Pattie, C. J. (1991) Tactical voting in Britain 1983 and 1987: an alternative approach. *British Journal of Political Science* 21: 95–108.

Johnston, R. J. and Pattie, C. J. (1992a) Class dealignment and the regional polarization of voting patterns in Great Britain, 1964–1987. *Political Geography* 11: 73–86.

Johnston, R. J. and Pattie, C. J. (1992b) Is the seesaw tipping back? The end of Thatcherism and changing voting patterns in Great Britain 1979–92. *Environment and Planning A* 24: 1491–1505.

Johnston, R. J. and Pattie, C. J. (1992c) Unemployment, the poll tax and the British general election of 1992. *Environment and Planning C: Government and Policy* 10: 467–83.

Johnston, R. J. and Pattie, C. J. (1996) The strength of party identification among the British electorate. *Electoral Studies* 15: 295–309.

Johnston, R. J. and Pattie, C. J. (1997a) Fluctuating party identification in Great Britain: Patterns revealed by four years of a longitudinal study. *Politics* 17: 67–77.

Johnston, R. J. and Pattie, C. J. (1997b) The region is not dead: long live the region—personal evaluations and voting at the 1992 British General Election. *Space and Polity* 1: 103–13.

Johnston, R. J. and Pattie, C. J. (1997c) Towards an understanding of turnout at general elections: voluntary and involuntary abstentions in 1992. *Parliamentary Affairs* 50: 280–91.

Johnston, R. J. and Pattie, C. J. (1998a) Campaigning and advertising: an evaluation of the components of constituency activism at recent British General Elections. *British Journal of Political Science* 28: 677–85.

Johnston, R. J. and Pattie, C. J. (1998b) Composition and context: region and voting in Britain revisited during Labour's 1990s' revival. *Geoforum* 29: 309–29.

Johnston, R. J. and Pattie, C. J. (1999a) Aspects of the inter-relationships of attitudes and behaviour as illustrated by a longitudinal study of British adults: 2. Predicting voting intention, strength of party identification, and change in both. *Environment and Planning A* 31: 1279–94.

Johnston, R. J. and Pattie, C. J. (1999b) Constituency campaign intensity and split-ticket voting: New Zealand's first election under MMP, 1996. *Political Science* 51: 164–81.

Johnston, R. J. and Pattie, C. J. (1999c) Feeling good and changing one's mind: a longitudinal investigation of voters' economic evaluations and partisan choices. *Party Politics* 5: 39–54.

Johnston, R. J. and Pattie, C. J. (2000) Ecological inference and entropy-maximizing: an alternative estimation procedure for split-ticket voting. *Political Analysis* 8: 333–45.

Johnston, R. J. and Pattie, C. J. (2001a) Dimensions of retrospective voting: economic performance, public service standards and Conservative party support at the 1997 British general election. *Party Politics* 7: 469–90.

Johnston, R. J. and Pattie, C. J. (2001b) 'It's the economy, stupid'—But which economy? Geographical scales, retrospective economic evaluations and voting at the 1997 British General Election. *Regional Studies* 35: 309–19.

Johnston, R. J. and Pattie, C. J. (2001c) Is there a crisis of democracy in Great Britain? Turnout at general elections reconsidered. In K. Dowding, J. Hughes and H. Margetts, editors, *Challenges to Democracy: Ideas, Involvement and Institutions*. London: Palgrave, 61–80.

Johnston, R. J. and Pattie, C. J. (2001d) On geographers and ecological inference. *Annals of the Association of American Geographers* 91: 281–2.

Johnston, R. J. and Pattie, C. J. (2002a) Campaigning and split-ticket voting in new electoral systems: the first MMP elections in New Zealand, Scotland and Wales. *Electoral Studies* 21: 583–600.

Johnston, R. J. and Pattie, C. J. (2002b) Geographical scale, the attribution of credit/blame, local economic circumstances and retrospective economic voting in Great Britain 1997: an extension of the model. *Environment and Planning C: Government and Policy* 20: 421–38.

Johnston, R. J. and Pattie, C. J. (2003a) Evaluating an entropy-maximizing solution to the ecological inference problem: split-ticket voting in New Zealand 1999. *Geographical Analysis* 35: 1–23.

Johnston, R. J. and Pattie, C. J. (2003b) The growing problem of electoral turnout in Britain? Voluntary and involuntary voters in 2001. *Representation* 40: 30–43.

Johnston, R. J. and Pattie, C. J. (2003c) Spatial variations in straight-and split-ticket voting and the role of constituency campaigning at New Zealand's first two MMP elections: individual-level tests. *Australian Journal of Political Science* 38: 535–47.

Johnston, R. J. and Pattie, C. J. (2005) Putting voters in their place: local context and voting in England and Wales, 1997. In A. Zuckerman, editor, *The Social Logic of Politics: Personal Networks as Contexts for Political Behavior*. Philadelphia, PA: Temple University Press, 184–208.

Johnston, R. J., Gschwend, T. and Pattie, C. J. (2005) *On estimates of split-ticket voting: EI and EMax*. Sonderforschungbereich 504 Publication 04–40, Universität Mannheim.

Johnston, R. J., McAllister, I. and Pattie, C. J. (1999) The funding of constituency party general election campaigns in Great Britain. *Environment and Planning C: Government and Policy* 17: 391–409.

Johnston, R. J., Pattie, C. J. and Allsopp, J. G. (1988) *A Nation Dividing? The Electoral Map of Great Britain 1979–1987*. London: Longman.

Johnston, R. J., Pattie, C. J. and Johnston, L. C. (1989) The impact of constituency spending on the result of the 1987 British general election. *Electoral Studies* 8: 143–57.

Johnston, R. J., Pattie, C. J. and Rossiter, D. J. (2005) The election results in the UK regions. In P. Norris and C. Wlezien, editors, *Britain Votes 2005*. Oxford: Oxford University Press, 130–45.

Johnston, R. J., Pattie, C. J. and Russell, A. T. (1993) Dealignment, spatial polarization and economic voting: an exploration of recent trends in British voting behaviour. *European Journal of Political Research* 23: 67–90.

Johnston, R. J., Rossiter, D. J. and Pattie, C. J. (2006) Disproportionality and bias in the results of the 2005 general election in Great Britain: evaluating the electoral system's impact. *Journal of Elections, Public Opinion and Parties* 2: 37–54.

Johnston, R. J., Pattie, C. J., Dorling, D. F. L., Rossiter, D. J., McAllister, I. and Tunstall, H. (1997) Spatial variations in voter choice: modelling tactical voting at the 1997 general election in Great Britain. *Geographical and Environmental Modelling* 1: 153–77.

Johnston, R. J., Pattie, C. J., Dorling, D. F. L., McAllister, I., Tunstall, H. and Rossiter, D. J. (2000a) Local context, retrospective economic evaluations and voting: the 1997 general election in England and Wales. *Political Behavior* 22: 121–43.

Johnston, R. J., Dorling, D., Tunstall, H., Rossiter, D. J., McAllister, I. and Pattie, C. J. (2000b) Locating the altruistic voter: context, egocentric voting and support for the Conservative party at the 1997 general election in England and Wales. *Environment and Planning A* 32: 673–94.

Johnston, R. J., Pattie, C. J., Dorling, D. F. L., McAllister, I., Tunstall, H. and Rossiter, D. J. (2000c) The neighbourhood effect and voting in England and Wales: real or imagined? In P. Cowley, D. Denver, A. Russell and L. Harrison, editors, *British Elections and Parties Review, Volume 10*. London: Frank Cass, 47–63.

Johnston, R. J., Pattie, C. J., Dorling, D. F. L., McAllister, I., Tunstall, H. and Rossiter, D. J. (2001a) Housing tenure, local context, scale and voting in England and Wales, 1997. *Electoral Studies* 20: 195–216.

Johnston, R. J., Pattie, C. J., Dorling, D. F. L. and Rossiter, D. J. (2001b) *From Votes to Seats: The Operation of the UK Electoral System since 1945*. Manchester: Manchester University Press.

Johnston, R. J., Rossiter, D. J., Pattie, C. J. and Dorling, D. F. L. (2002a) Labour electoral landslides and the changing efficiency of voting distributions. *Transactions of the Institute of British Geographers* NS27: 336–61.

Johnston, R. J., Cowley, P. J., Pattie, C. J. and Stuart, M. (2002b) Voting in the House or wooing the voters at home: Labour MPs and the 2001 general election campaign. *Journal of Legislative Studies* 8: 9–22.

Johnston, R. J., Pattie, C. J., Dorling, D. F. L. and Rossiter, D. J. (2003) The Conservative Century? Geography and Conservative electoral success during the twentieth century. In D. Gilbert, D. Matless and B. Short, editors, *Geographies of British Modernity: Space and Society in the Twentieth Century*. Oxford: Blackwell Publishers, 54–79.

Johnston, R. J., Jones, K., Sarker, R., Propper, C., Burgess, S. and Bolster, A. (2004) Party support and the neighbourhood effect: spatial polarisation of the British electorate 1991–2001. *Political Geography* 23: 367–402.

Johnston, R. J., Sarker, R., Jones, K., Bolster, A., Propper, C. and Burgess, S. (2005a) Egocentric economic voting and changes in party choice: Great Britain, 1992–2001. *Journal of Elections, Public Opinions and Parties*. 1: 129–44.

Johnston, R. J., Jones, K., Propper, C., Sarker, R., Burgess, S. and Bolster, A. (2005b) A missing level in the analysis of British voting behaviour: the household as context as shown by analyses of a 1992–1997 longitudinal survey. *Electoral Studies* 24: 201–25.

Johnston, R. J., Propper, C., Sarker, R., Jones, K., Bolster, A. and Burgess, S. (2005c) Neighbourhood social capital and neighbourhood effects. *Environment and Planning A* 37: 1443–59.

Johnston, R. J., Propper, C., Burgess, S., Sarker, R., Bolster, A. and Jones, K. (2005d) Spatial scale and the neighbourhood effect: multinomial models of voting at two recent British general elections. *British Journal of Political Science* 35: 487–514.

Jones, K., Gould, M. and Watt, R. (1998) Multiple contexts as cross-classified models: the Labour vote in the British general election of 1992. *Geographical Analysis* 30: 65–93.

Jones, K., Johnston, R. J. and Pattie, C. J. (1992) People, places and regions: exploring the use of multi-level modelling in the analysis of electoral data. *British Journal of Political Science* 22: 343–80.

Karp, J. and Banducci, S. (2000) Going postal: how all-mail elections influence turnout. *Political Behavior* 22: 223–39.

Katz, E. and Lazarsfeld, P. (1955) *Personal Influence*. Glencoe, IL: The Free Press.

Kavanagh, D. (1970) *Constituency Electioneering in Britain*. London, Longmans.

Kavanagh, D. (1995) *Election Campaigning: The New Marketing of Politics*. Oxford: Blackwell Publishers.

Kendall, M. G. and Stuart, A. (1950) The law of cubic proportions in election results. *British Journal of Sociology* 1: 183–96.

Kenny, C. (1994) The microenvironment of attitude change. *The Journal of Politics* 56: 715–28.

Kenny, C. (1998) The behavioral consequences of political discussion: another look at discussant effects on vote choice. *The Journal of Politics* 60: 231–44.

Kenny, C. and McBurnett, M. (1994) An individual-level multiequation model of expenditure effects in contested House elections. *American Political Science Review* 88: 699–707.

Key, V. O. Jr (1949) *Southern Politics in State and Nation*. New York: Alfred A. Knopf.

Key, V. O. Jr (1964) *Politics, Parties and Pressure Groups,* 5th edn. New York: Crowell.

Key, V. O. Jr (1966) *The Responsible Electorate: Rationality in Presidential Voting, 1936–1960*. Cambridge, MA: Harvard University Press.

Kinder, D. R. and Kiewiet, D. R. (1979) Economic discontent and political behaviour: the role of personal and collective economic judgements in Congressional voting. *American Journal of Political Science* 23: 495–527.

Kinder, D. R. and Kiewiet, D. R. (1981) Sociotropic politics: the American case. *British Journal of Political Science*. 11: 129–61.

King, G. (1996) Why context should not count. *Political Geography* 15: 159–64.

King, G. (1997) *A Solution to the Ecological Inference Problem: Reconstructing Individual Behavior from Aggregate Data*. Princeton, NJ: Princeton University Press.

Kotler-Berkowitz, L. A. (2001) Religion and voting behaviour in Great Britain: a reassessment. *British Journal of Political Science* 31: 523–54.

Kwak, N., Williams, A. E, Wang, X. and Lee, H. (2005) Talking politics and engaging politics: an examination of the interactive relationships between structural features of political talk and discussion engagement. *Communication Research* 32: 87–111.

Lazarsfeld, P., Berelson, B. and Gaudet, H. (1944) *The People's Choice: How the Voter Makes Up His Mind in a Presidential Campaign*. New York: Columbia University Press.

Leighley, J. E. and Nagler, J. (1992) Individual and systemic influences on turnout: who votes? 1984. *The Journal of Politics* 54: 718–40.

Lewis, J. and Townsend, A. editors (1989) *The North–South Divide: Regional Change in Britain in the 1980s*. London: Paul Chapman Publishing.

Lewis-Beck., M. (1985) Pocketbook voting in U. S. national election studies: fact or artefact? *American Journal of Political Science* 29: 348–56.

Lewis-Beck, M. (1986) Comparative economic voting: Britain, France, Germany, Italy. *American Journal of Political Science* 30: 315–46.

Lewis-Beck, M. (1988) *Economics and Elections: The Major Western Democracies*. Ann Arbor, MI: University of Michigan Press.

Lewis-Beck, M. (2005) Election forecasting: principles and practice. *British Journal of Politics and International Relations* 7: 145–64.

Lewis-Beck, M. (2006) Does economics still matter? Econometrics and the vote. *The Journal of Politics* 68: 208–12.

Lipset, S. M. and Rokkan, S. E. (1967) Cleavage structures, party systems and voter alignments. In S. M. Lipset and S. E. Rokkan, editors, *Party Systems and Voter Alignments*. New York: The Free Press, 3–64.

Lupia, A. and McCubbins, M. D. (1998) *The Democratic Dilemma: Can Citizens Learn What They Need to Know?* Cambridge: Cambridge University Press.

Lusoli, W. and Ward, S. (2005) Logging on or switching off?. In S. Coleman and S. Ward, editors, *Spinning the Web: Online Campaigning in the 2005 General Election*. London: Hansard Society, 13–21.

McAllister, I. and Studlar, D. T. (1992) Region and voting in Britain 1979–87: territorial polarization or artifact? *American Journal of Political Science* 36: 168–99.

McAllister, I., Fieldhouse, E. and Russell, A. (2000) Yellow fever? The ;political geography of Liberal voting in Great Britain. *Political Geography* 21: 421–47.

McAllister, I., Johnston, R. J., Pattie, C. J., Tunstall, H., Dorling, D. F. L. and Rossiter, D. J. (2001) Class dealignment and the neighbourhood effect: Miller revisited. *British Journal of Political Science* 31: 41–59.

McCallum, R. B. and Readman, A. (1947) *The British General Election of 1945.* Oxford: Oxford University Press.

MacKuen, M. B., Erikson, R. S. and Stimson, J. A. (1989) Macropartisanship. *American Political Science Review* 83: 1125–42.

MacKuen, M. B., Erikson, R. S. and Stimson, J. A. (1992) Peasants or Bankers? The American electorate and the U. S. economy. *American Political Science Review* 86: 597–611.

McLean, I. (1995) Are Scotland and Wales over-represented in the House of Commons? *The Political Quarterly* 66: 250–68.

McLean, I. and Mortimore, R. (1992) Apportionment and the Boundary Commission for England. *Electoral Studies* 11: 292–308.

McMahon, D., Heath, M., Harrop, M. and Curtice, J. (1992) The electoral consequences of north–south migration. *British Journal of Political Science* 22: 419–43.

Martin, F. M. (1952) Social status and electoral choice in two constituencies. *British Journal of Sociology* 3: 231–41.

Martin, R. L. (1988) The political economy of Britain's north–south divide. *Transactions, Institute of British Geographers* NS 13: 389–418.

Martin, R. L. and Rowthorn, B., editors, (1986) *The Geography of De-industrialisation.* Basingstoke: Macmillan.

Martin, R. L., Sunley, P. J. and Wills, J. (1993) The geography of trade union decline: spatial dispersal or regional resilience? *Transactions, Institute of British Geographers* NS18: 36–62.

Massey, D. and Meegan, R. (1982) *The Anatomy of Job Loss: The How, Why and Where of Employment Decline.* London: Methuen.

Merrill, S. and Grofman, B. (1999) *A Unified Theory of Voting: Directional and Proximity Spatial Models.* Cambridge: Cambridge University Press.

Miller, W. L. (1977) *Electoral Dynamics in Britain since 1918.* London: Macmillan.

Miller, W. L. (1978) Social class and party choice in England: a new analysis. *British Journal of Political Science* 8: 259–84.

Miller, W. L. (1991) *Media and Voters: The Audience, Content and Influence of Press and Television at the 1987 General Election.* Oxford: The Clarendon Press.

Miller, W. L., Raab, G. and Britto, K. (1974) Voting research and the population census 1918–1971: surrogate data for constituency analyses. *Journal of the Royal Statistical Society A*, 137: 384–411.

Milne, R. S. and MacKenzie, H. C. (1954) *Straight Fight.* London: The Hansard Society.

Milne, R. S. and MacKenzie, H. C. (1958) *Marginal Seat.* London: The Hansard Society.

Monmonier, M. S. (2002) *Bushmanders and Bullwinkles: How Politicians Manipulate Electronic Maps and Census Data to Win Elections.* Chicago, IL: University of Chicago Press.

Moon, N. (1999) *Opinion Polls: History, Theory and Practice.* Manchester: Manchester University Press.

Mughan, A. (1986) *Party and Participation in British Elections.* London: Frances Pinter.

Mutz, D. (2002a) The consequences of cross-cutting networks for political participation. *American Journal of Political Science* 46: 838–55.

Mutz, D. (2002b) Cross-cutting social networks: testing democratic theory in practice. *American Political Science Review* 96: 111–26.

Mutz, D. and Mondak, J. (2006) The workplace as a context for cross-cutting political discourse. *The Journal of Politics* 68: 140–55.

Nadeau, R., Niemi, R. G., and Yoshinaka, A. (2002) A cross-national analysis of economic voting: taking account of the political context across time and nations. *Electoral Studies* 21: 403–23.

Newby, H. (1977) *The Deferential Worker*. London: Allen Lane.

Niemi, R. G., Whitten, G. and Franklin, M. N. (1992) Constituency characteristics, individual characteristics and tactical voting at the 1987 British general election. *British Journal of Political Science* 22: 229–40.

Nieuwbeerta, P. and Flap, H. (2000) Crosscutting social circles and political choice: effects of personal network composition on voting behaviour in the Netherlands. *Social Networks* 22: 313–35.

Norpoth, H. (1987) Guns and butter and government popularity in Britain. *American Political Science Review* 81: 949–59.

Norpoth, H. (1992) *Confidence Regained: Economics, Mrs Thatcher and the British Voter*. Ann Arbor, MI: The University of Michigan Press.

Norris, P. (1990) *British By-Elections: the Volatile Electorate*. Oxford: The Clarendon Press.

Norris, P. (2002) *Democratic Phoenix: Political Activism Worldwide*. Cambridge: Cambridge University Press.

Norris, P., Curtice, J., Sanders, D., Scammell, M. and Semetko, H. (1999) *On Message: Communicating the Campaign*. London: Sage Publications.

Olson, M. (1965) *The Logic of Collective Action: Public Goods and the Theory of Groups*. Cambridge, MA: Harvard University Press.

Owens, J. R. and Wade. L. (1988) Economic conditions and constituency voting in Great Britain. *Political Studies* 36: 30–51.

Paldam, M. and Nannestad, P. (2000) What do voters know about the economy? A study of Danish data, 1990–1993. *Electoral Studies* 19: 363–91.

Pappi, F. U. (1996) Personal environments in the process of political intermediation as a topic of the comparative National Election Study. In H. Chikio and E. Scheuch, editors, *Quantitative Social Research in Germany and Japan*. Opladen: Leske und Budrich, 122–40.

Park, A. (2004) Has modern politics disenchanted the young?. In A. Park, J. Curtice, K. Thomson, C. Bromley and Phillips, M., editors, *British Social Attitudes: the 21st Report*. London: Sage Publications, 23–47.

Parry, G., Moyser, G. and Day, N. (1992) *Political Participation and Democracy in Britain*. Cambridge: Cambridge University Press.

Partin, R. W. (2002) Assessing the impact of campaign spending in Governors' races. *Political Research Quarterly* 55: 213–33.

Pattie, C. J. and Johnston, R. J. (1990) One nation or two? The changing geography of unemployment in Great Britain, 1983–1988. *The Professional Geographer* 42: 288–98.

Pattie, C. J. and Johnston, R. J. (1995) It's not like that round here: region, economic evaluations and voting at the 1992 British General Election. *European Journal of Political Research* 28: 1–32.

Pattie, C. J. and Johnston, R. J. (1996) Paying their way: local associations, the constituency quota scheme and Conservative party finance. *Political Studies*. 44: 921–35.

Pattie, C. J. and Johnston, R. J. (1997a) Funding the national party: changing geographies of local fund-raising for the British Conservative party, 1984/85–1993/94. *Political Geography* 16: 387–406.

Pattie, C. J. and Johnston, R. J. (1997b) Local economic contexts and changing party allegiances at the 1992 British General Election. *Party Politics* 3: 79–96.

Pattie, C. J. and Johnston, R. J. (1998a) The role of regional context in voting: evidence from the 1992 British general election. *Regional Studies* 32: 249–63.

Pattie, C. J. and Johnston, R. J. (1998b) Voter turnout at the British general election of 1992: rational choice, social standing or political efficacy? *European Journal of Political Research* 33: 263–83.

Pattie, C. J. and Johnston, R. J. (1998c) Voter turnout and constituency marginality: geography and rational choice. *Area* 10: 38–48.

Pattie, C. J. and Johnston, R. J. (1999) Context, conversation and conviction: social networks and voting at the 1992 British General Election. *Political Studies* 47: 877–89.

Pattie, C. J. and Johnston, R. J. (2000) 'People who talk together vote together': an exploration of contextual effects in Great Britain. *Annals of the Association of American Geographers* 90: 41–66.

Pattie, C. J. and Johnston, R. J. (2001a) Losing the voters' trust: evaluations of the political system and voting at the 1997 British General Election. *British Journal of Politics and International Relations* 3: 191–222.

Pattie, C. J. and Johnston, R. J. (2001b) A low turnout landslide: abstention at the British general election of 1997. *Political Studies* 49: 286–305.

Pattie, C. J. and Johnston, R. J. (2001c) Routes to party choice: ideology, economic evaluations and voting at the 1997 British general election. *European Journal of Political Research* 39: 373–89.

Pattie, C. J. and Johnston, R. J. (2001d) Talk as a political context: conversation and electoral change in British elections, 1992–1997. *Electoral Studies* 20: 17–40.

Pattie, C. J. and Johnston, R. J. (2002a) Assessing the television campaign: the impact of party election broadcasting on voters' opinions in the 1997 British general election. *Political Communication* 19: 333–58.

Pattie, C. J. and Johnston, R. J. (2002b) Political talk and voting: does it matter to whom one talks? *Environment and Planning A* 34: 1113–35.

Pattie, C. J. and Johnston, R. J. (2003a) Hanging on the telephone? Doorstep and telephone canvassing at the British general election of 1997. *British Journal of Political Science*. 33: 303–22.

Pattie, C. J. and Johnston, R. J. (2003b) Local battles in a national landslide: constituency campaigning at the 2001 British general election. *Political Geography* 22: 381–414.

Pattie, C. J. and Johnston, R. J. (2004) Party knowledge and candidate knowledge: constituency campaigning and voting and the 1997 British general election. *Electoral Studies* 23: 795–819.

Pattie, C. J., Dorling, D. and Johnston, R. J. (1995) A debt-owing democracy: the political impact of housing market recession at the British General Election of 1992. *Urban Studies* 32: 1293–315.

Pattie, C. J., Dorling, D. and Johnston, R. J. (1997) The electoral geography of recession: local economic conditions, public perceptions and the economic vote in the 1992 British general election. *Transactions, Institute of British Geographers* NS22: 147–61.

Pattie, C. J., Fieldhouse, E. and Johnston, R. J. (1994) The price of conscience: the electoral correlates and consequences of free votes and rebellions in the British House of Commons, 1987–1992. *British Journal of Political Science* 24: 359–80.

Pattie, C. J., Fieldhouse, E. A. and Johnston, R. J. (1995) Individual vote choice and constituency economic conditions at the 1992 British General Election. *Electoral Studies* 14: 399–415.

Pattie, C. J., Johnston, R. J. and Fieldhouse, E. A. (1994) Gaining on the swings? The changing geography of the flow-of-the-vote and government fortunes in British general elections, 1979–1992. *Regional Studies* 28: 141–54.

Pattie, C. J., Johnston, R. J. and Fieldhouse, E. A. (1995) Winning the local vote: the effectiveness of constituency campaign spending in Great Britain. *American Political Science Review* 89: 969–83.

Pattie, C. J., Johnston, R. J. and Sanders, D. J. (1999) On babies and bathwater: a comment on Evans' 'Economics and politics revisited'. *Political Studies* 47: 918–32.

Pattie, C. J., Johnston, R. J. and Stuart, M. (1998) Voting without party? In P. Cowley, editor, *Conscience and Parliament*. London: Frank Cass, 146–76.

Pattie, C. J., Seyd, P. and Whiteley, P. (2003) Citizenship and civic engagement: attitudes and behaviour in Britain. *Political Studies* 51: 443–68.

Pattie, C. J., Seyd, P. and Whiteley, P. (2004) *Citizenship in Britain: Values, Participation and Democracy*. Cambridge: Cambridge University Press.

Pattie, C. J., Whiteley, P. F., Johnston, R. J. and Seyd, P. (1994) Measuring local campaign effects: Labour party constituency campaigning at the 1987 British General Election. *Political Studies* 42: 469–79.

Pelling, H. (1967) *Social Geography of British Elections 1885–1910*. London: Macmillan.

Popkin, S. L. (1994) *The Reasoning Voter: Communication and Persuasion in Presidential Campaigns*. Chicago, IL: University of Chicago Press.

Powell, G. B. and Whitten, J. D. (1993) A cross-national analysis of economic voting: taking account of the political context. *American Journal of Political Science* 37: 391–414.

Prescott, J. R. V. (1972) *Political Geography*. London: Methuen.

Price, S. and Sanders, D. (1995) Economic expectations and voting intentions in the UK, 1979–87: a pooled cross-section approach. *Political Studies* 43: 451–71.

Price, V., Cappella, J. N. and Nir, L. (2002) Does disagreement contribute to more deliberative opinion? *Political Communication* 19: 95–112.

Przeworski, A. (1974) Contextual models of political behavior. *Political Methodology* 1: 27–61.

Putnam, R. D. (1993) *Making Democracy Work: Civic Traditions in Modern Italy*. Princeton, NJ: Princeton University Press.

Putnam, R. D. (2000) *Bowling Alone: The Collapse and Revival of American Community*. New York: Simon and Schuster.

Rallings, C. and Thrasher, M. (1997) *Local Elections in Britain*. London: Routledge.

Rasmussen, J. (1973) The impact of constituency structural characteristics upon political preferences in Great Britain. *Comparative Politics* 5: 123–45.

Reif, K. (1984) National electoral cycles and European Elections 1979 and 1984. *Electoral Studies* 3: 244–55.

Reif, K. (1997) European elections as member state second-order elections revisited. *European Journal of Political Research* 31: 115–24.

Reif, K. and Schmitt, H. (1980) Nine second-order national elections: a conceptual framework for the analysis of European election results. *European Journal of Political Research* 8: 3–44.

Rennard, C. (2002) Liberal democrat strategy. In J. Bartle, R. Mortimore, and S. Atkinson, editors, *Political Communications: The General Election Campaign of 2001*. London: Frank Cass, 75–83.

Reynolds, D. R. (1969a) A 'friends-and-neighbors' voting model as a spatial inter-actional model for electoral geography. In K. R. Cox and R. G. Golledge, editors, *Behavioral Problems in Geography*. Evanston, IL: Northwestern University, North-western Studies in Geography, 81–100.

Reynolds, D. R. (1969b) A spatial model for analysing voting behavior. *Acta Sociologica* 12: 122–30.

Riddell, P. (2005) *The Unfulfilled Prime Minister: Tony Blair's Quest for a Legacy*. London: Politico's.

Ridley, F. F. and Doig, A., editors (1995) *Sleaze: Politicians, Private Interests and Public Reaction*. Oxford: Oxford University Press.

Roberts, M. C. and Rumage, K. W. (1965) The spatial variations in urban left-wing voting in England and Wales in 1951. *Annals of the Association of American Geographers* 55: 161–78.

Robinson, W. (1950) Ecological correlation and the behaviour of individuals. *American Sociological Review* 15: 351–57.

Romero, D. W. and Stambough, S. J. (1996) Personal economic well-being and the individual vote for Congress: a pooled analysis, 1980–1990. *Political Research Quarterly* 49: 607–16.

Rose, D. and Pevalin, D. J. editors (2003) *A Researcher's Guide to the National Statistics Socio-Economic Classification*. London: Sage Publications.

Rose, R. and McAllister, I. (1986) *Voters Begin to Choose: From Closed-Class to Open Elections in Britain*. London: Sage Publications.

Rose, R. and McAllister, I. (1990) *The Loyalties of Voters: A Lifetime Learning Model*. London: Sage Publications.

Rosenbaum, N. (1997) *From Soapbox to Soundbite: Party Political Campaigning in Britain Since 1945*. Basingstoke: Macmillan.

Rossiter, D. J. and Johnston, R. J. (1981) Program GROUP: the identification of all possible solutions to a constituency-delimitation problem. *Environment and Planning A* 13: 231–38.

Rossiter, D. J., Johnston, R. J., and Pattie, C. J. (1998) The partisan impacts of non-partisan redistricting: Northern Ireland 1993–1995. *Transactions, Institute of British Geographers* NS23: 455–80.

Rossiter, D. J., Johnston, R. J. and Pattie, C. J. (1999a) *The Boundary Commissions: Redrawing the UK's Map of Parliamentary Constituencies*. Manchester: Manchester University Press.

Rossiter, D. J., Johnston, R. J. and Pattie, C. J. (1999b) Integrating and decomposing the sources of partisan bias: Brookes' method and the impact of redistricting in

Great Britain. *Electoral Studies* 18: 367–78. (Addendum: *Electoral Studies*, 19, 2000, 649–50.)

Russell, A. T. (1997) A question of interaction: using logistic regression to examine geographic effects on British voting behaviour. In C Pattie, D. Denver, J. Fisher, and S. Ludlam, editors, *British Elections and Parties Review 7*. London: Frank Cass, 91–109.

Russell, A. T. (2005) The Liberal Democrat campaign. In P. Norris and C. Wlezien, editors, *Britain Votes 2005*. Oxford: Oxford University Press, 87–100.

Russell, A. T. and Fieldhouse, E. A. (2005) *Neither Left nor Right: The Liberal Democrats and the Electorate*. Manchester: Manchester University Press.

Russell, A. T., Fieldhouse, E. A., and McAllister, I. (2002) The anatomy of Liberal support in Britain, 1974–1997. *British Journal of Politics and International Relations* 4: 49–74.

Saggar, S. (2000) *Race and Representation: Electoral Politics and Ethnic Pluralism in Britain*. Manchester: Manchester University Press.

Sanders, D. (1991) Government popularity and the next General Election. *Political Quarterly* 62: 235–61.

Sanders, D. (1994) Economic influences on the vote: modelling electoral decisions. In I. Budge and D. McKay, editors, *Developing Democracy*. London: Sage Publications, 79–97.

Sanders, D. (1996) Economic performance, management competence and the outcome of the next general election. *Political Studies* 44: 203–31.

Sanders, D. (1998) The new electoral battleground. In A. King, editor, *New Labour Triumphs: Britain at the Polls*. Chatham, NJ: Chatham House, 209–48.

Sanders, D. (1999) Conservative incompetence, Labour responsibility and the feel-good factor: why the economy failed to save the Conservatives in 1997. *Electoral Studies* 18: 251–70.

Sanders, D. (2000) The real economy and the perceived economy in popularity functions: how much do voters need to know? A study of British data, 1974–97. *Electoral Studies* 19: 275–94.

Sanders, D. (2003) Party identification, economic perceptions and voting in British general elections, 1974–1997. *Electoral Studies* 22: 239–63.

Sanders, D. (2004) Vote functions and popularity functions in British politics. *Electoral Studies* 23: 307–13.

Sanders, D. (2005a) The political economy of UK party support, 1997–2004: forecasts for the 2005 election. *Journal of Elections, Public Opinion and Parties* 1: 47–71.

Sanders, D. (2005b) Popularity function forecasts for the 2005 UK General Election. *British Journal of Politics and International Relations* 7: 174–90.

Sanders, D., Ward, H. and Marsh, D. (1987) Government popularity and the Falklands War: a reassessment. *British Journal of Political Science* 17: 281–313.

Sanders, D., Ward, H. and Marsh, D. (1992) Macro-economics, the Falklands War and the popularity of the Thatcher government: a contrary view. In H. Norpoth, J.-D. Lefay, and M. Lewis-Beck, editors, *Economics and Politics: The Calculus of Support*. Ann Arbor, MI: University of Michigan Press.

Särlvik, B. and Crewe, I. (1983) *Decade of Dealignment: the Conservative Victory if 1970 and Electoral Trends in the 1970s*. Cambridge: Cambridge University Press.

Savage, M. (1997) Space, networks and class formation. In N. Kirk, editor, *Social Class and Marxism: Defences and Challenges*. London: Scolar Press, 58–86.

Scammell, M. (1995) *Designer Politics: How Elections are Won*. Basingstoke: Macmillan.

Scarbrough, E. (1984) *Political Ideology and Voting*. Oxford: The Clarendon Press.

Scarbrough, E. (2000) The British Election Study and electoral research. *Political Studies* 48: 391–414.

Schmitt, H. (2005) The European Parliament elections of June 2004: still second order? *West European Politics* 28: 650–79.

Searing, D. A. (1985) The role of the good constituency member and the practice of representation in Great Britain. *The Journal of Politics* 47: 348–81.

Seyd, P. (1998) In praise of party. *Parliamentary Affairs* 51: 198–208.

Seyd, P. and Whiteley, P. (1992) *Labour's Grassroots: The Politics of Party Membership*. Oxford: The Clarendon Press.

Seyd, P. and Whiteley, P. (2002) *New Labour's Grassroots: The Transformation of the Labour Party Membership*. London: Palgrave Macmillan.

Shaw, E. (1994) *The Labour Party Since 1979: Crisis and Transformation*. London: Routledge.

Shickler, E. and Green, D. (1997) The stability of party identification in western democracies: results from eight panel surveys. *Comparative Political Studies* 30: 450–83.

Smith, M. J. (2005) It's not the economy, stupid! The disappearance of the economy from the 2005 campaign. In A. Geddes and J. Tonge, editors, *Britain Decides: The UK General Election 2005*. Basingstoke: Palgrave Macmillan, 225–39.

Sniderman, P. M., Brody, R. A. and Tetlock, P. E. (1991) *Reasoning and Choice: Explorations in Political Psychology*. Cambridge: Cambridge University Press.

Sobolewska, M. (2005) Ethnic agenda: relevance of political attitudes to party choice. *Journal of Elections, Public Opinion and Parties* 1: 197–214.

Solop, F. I. (2001) Digital democracy comes of age: internet voting and the 2000 Arizona Democratic Primary election. *PS—Political Science and Politics* 34: 289–93.

Sprague, J. (1982) Is there a micro-theory consistent with contextual analysis? In E. Ostrom, editor, *Strategies of Political Inquiry*. Beverly Hills, CA: Sage, 99–121.

Stoker, L. and Jennings, K. M. (2005) Political similarity and influence between husbands and wives. In A. S. Zuckerman, editor, *The Social Logic of Politics: Personal Networks as Contexts for Political Behavior*. Philadelphia, PA: Temple University Press, 51–74.

Stokes, D. (1963) Spatial models of party competition. *American Political Science Review* 57: 368–77.

Stratmann, T. (2005) Some talk: money in politics. A (partial) review of the literature. *Public Choice* 124: 135–56.

Swaddle, K. and Heath, A. (1989) Official and reported turnout in the British general election of 1987. *British Journal of Political Science* 19: 537–51.

Taylor, A. (1973) Journey time, perceived distance and electoral turnout—Victoria Ward, Swansea. *Area* 5: 59–63.

Thielemann, G. S. (1993) Local advantage in campaign financing: friends, neighbours and their money in Texas Supreme Court elections. *The Journal of Politics* 55: 472–8.

Thrift, N. J. (1983) On the determination of social action in space and time. *Environment and Planning D: Society and Space* 1: 23–57.

Tingsten, H. (1937) *Political Behaviour*. London: P. S. King.

Toynbee, P. and Walker, D. (2001) *Did Things Get Better? An Audit of Labour's Successes and Failures*. London: Penguin.

Tufte, E. R. (1973) The relationship between seats and votes in two-party systems. *American Political Science Review* 67: 540–54.

Upton, G. J. G. (1991) The impact of by-elections on general elections: England 1950–1987. *British Journal of Political Science* 21: 108–19.

Verba, S., Schlozman, K. L. and Brady, H. E. (1995) *Voice and Equality: Civic Voluntarism in American Politics*. Cambridge, MA: Harvard University Press.

Walks, R. A. (2004a) Place of residence, party preferences and political attitudes in Canadian cities and suburbs. *Journal of Urban Affairs* 26: 269–95.

Walks, R. A. (2004b) Suburbanization, the vote and changes in federal and provincial political representation and influence between inner cities and suburbs in large Canadian urban regions, 1945–1999. *Urban Affairs Review* 39: 411–40.

Walks, R. A. (2005) City–suburban electoral polarization in Great Britain, 1950–2001. *Transactions of the Institute of British Geographers* NS30: 500–17.

Waller, R. J. (1983) *The Dukeries Transformed*. Oxford: The Clarendon Press.

Ward, S. and Gibson, R. (1998) The first internet election? UK political parties and campaigning in cyberspace. In I. Crewe, B. Gosschalk, and J. Bartle, editors, *Political Communications: Why Labour Won the General Election of 1997*. London: Frank Cass, 93–112.

Ward, S., Gibson, R. and Lusoli, W. (2003) On-line participation and mobilisation in Britain: hype, hope and reality. *Parliamentary Affairs* 56: 652–68.

Watt, B. (2005) *UK Election Law: A critical Examination*. London: Glasshouse Press.

Wattenberg, M. P. (2002) *Where Have All the Voters Gone?* Cambridge MA: Harvard University Press.

Weatherford, S. (1982) Interpersonal networks and political behavior. *American Journal of Political Science* 26: 117–43.

Webber, M. M. (1963) Order diversity: community without propinquity. In L. Wingo, editor, *Cities and Space*. Baltimore, MD: Johns Hopkins University Press, 23–56.

Webber, M. M. (1964) Culture, territoriality and the elastic mile. *Papers of the Regional Science Association* 13: 59–70.

Whiteley, P. (1984) Inflation, unemployment and government popularity: dynamic models for the United States, Britain and West Germany. *Electoral Studies* 3: 3–24.

Whiteley, P. (1986) Macroeconomic performance and government popularity in Britain: the short run dynamics. *European Journal of Political Research* 14: 45–61.

Whiteley, P. and Seyd, P. (1994) Local party campaigning and electoral mobilization in Britain. *The Journal of Politics* 56: 242–52.

Whiteley, P. and Seyd, P. (2002) *High Intensity Participation: The Dynamics of Party Activism in Britain*. Ann Arbor, MI: Michigan University Press.

Whiteley, P. and Seyd, P. (2003a) How to win a landslide by really trying: the effects of local campaigning on voting in the 1997 British General Election. *Electoral Studies* 22: 301–24.

Whiteley, P. and Seyd, P. (2003b) Party election campaigning and electoral mobilization in Britain. *Party Politics* 56: 242–52.

Whiteley, P., Seyd, P. and Richardson, J. J. (1994) *True Blues: The Politics of Conservative Party Membership*. Oxford: Oxford University Press.

Whiteley, P., Clarke, H., Sanders, D. and Stewart, M. (2001) Turnout. In P. Norris, editor, *Britain Votes 2001*. Oxford: Oxford University Press, 211–24.

Whiteley, P., Stewart, M. C., Sanders, D. and Clarke, H. D. (2005) The issue agenda and voting in 2005. *Parliamentary Affairs* 58: 802–17.

Whitten, G. D. and Palma, H. D. (1999) Cross-national analyses of economic voting. *Electoral Studies* 18: 49–67.

Wolfinger, R. E. and Rosenstone, S. J. (1980) *Who Votes?* New Haven, CT: Yale University Press.

Wood, P. and Norton, P. (1992) Do candidates matter? Constituency-specific vote changes for incumbent MPs, 1983–1987. *Political Studies* 40: 227–38.

Wright, T. (2005) The candidate: Tony Wright. In A. Geddes and J. Tonge, editors, *Britain Decides: The UK General Election 2005*. Basingstoke: Palgrave Macmillan, 91–7.

Zuckerman, A. S. (2005) Returning to the social logic of politics. In A. S. Zuckerman, editor, *The Social Logic of Politics: Personal Networks as Contexts for Political Behavior*. Philadelphia, PA: Temple University Press, 3–20.

Zuckerman, A. S. and Kotler-Berkowitz, L. A. (1998) Politics and society: political diversity and uniformity in households as a theoretical puzzle. *Comparative Political Studies* 31: 464–97.

Zuckerman, A. S, Fitzgerald, J. and Dasović, J. (2005) Do couples support the same political parties? Sometimes: evidence from British and German household panel surveys. In A. S. Zuckerman, editor, *The Social Logic of Politics: Personal Networks as Contexts for Political Behavior*. Philadelphia, PA: Temple University Press, 75–94.

Zuckerman, A. S., Valentino, N. A. and Zuckerman, E. W. (1994) A structural theory of vote choice: social and political networks and electoral flows in Britain and the United States. *The Journal of Politics* 56: 1008–33.

INDEX

Lightning Source UK Ltd.
Milton Keynes UK
UKOW06f1138050715

254614UK00002B/26/P